BUSINESS
Ethics

BUSINESS
Ethics
The **BIG** Picture

edited by

MARK C. VOPAT
& ALAN TOMHAVE

broadview press

BROADVIEW PRESS – www.broadviewpress.com
Peterborough, Ontario, Canada

Founded in 1985, Broadview Press remains a wholly independent publishing house. Broadview's focus is on academic publishing; our titles are accessible to university and college students as well as scholars and general readers. With over 600 titles in print, Broadview has become a leading international publisher in the humanities, with world-wide distribution. Broadview is committed to environmentally responsible publishing and fair business practices.

This book is made of paper from well-managed FSC® -certified forests, recycled materials, and other controlled sources.

Library and Archives Canada Cataloguing in Publication

Business ethics (2018)
   Business ethics : the big picture / edited by Mark C. Vopat and Alan Tomhave.

Includes bibliographical references.
ISBN 978-1-55481-430-5 (softcover)

   1. Business ethics. 2. Business ethics—Philosophy. 3. Business—Philosophy. I. Vopat, Mark C., 1971–, editor II. Tomhave, Alan, editor III. Title.

HF5387.B8692 2018   174'.4   C2018-903308-8

Broadview Press handles its own distribution in North America:
PO Box 1243, Peterborough, Ontario K9J 7H5, Canada
555 Riverwalk Parkway, Tonawanda, NY 14150, USA
Tel: (705) 743-8990; Fax: (705) 743-8353
email: customerservice@broadviewpress.com

Distribution is handled by Eurospan Group in the UK, Europe, Central Asia, Middle East, Africa, India, Southeast Asia, Central America, South America, and the Caribbean. Distribution is handled by Footprint Books in Australia and New Zealand.

Canada

Broadview Press acknowledges the financial support of the Government of Canada through the Canada Book Fund for our publishing activities.

Copy-edited by Michel Pharand
Book design by Michel Vrana

PRINTED IN CANADA

CONTENTS

Introduction   1

I. FOUNDATIONS

II. THE NATURE OF BUSINESS

III. THE CONDUCT OF BUSINESS

IV. BUSINESS, THE INDIVIDUAL, AND SOCIETY

V. CASE STUDIES

INTRODUCTION

Suppose that you work for a company that must decide how to dispose of some waste which is the by-product of some industrial process. Suppose further that proper disposal of the waste will cost more money than simply finding some place to dump it, whether that dumping place is a field or storm drain, or even a river or lake. It is your decision in the company to decide what to do to rid the company of this waste. What should your decision be? What should you do?

You might first hit on the idea that what matters most is the financial costs and savings to the company. Assume that dumping the waste is in fact illegal, but that the cost of the fines is far lower than the cost of properly disposing of the waste. If financial costs are all that matters, then (from an economic standpoint) the dumping of the waste in an improper manner is the best course. It would save the company the most money.

Suppose that you ask a further question though. Suppose that your interest is in deciding what the moral thing to do is? There are several ways to think about this question. The first thing to keep in mind is that, in morality, there is a difference between right and wrong. Wrong actions are, of course, the things that we are not supposed to do; they are *impermissible.* Right actions are trickier. It turns out that there are a couple of options here. Some right actions are *obligatory*, whereas others are merely *permissible.* Obligatory actions are the ones that we have to do; it would be wrong not to do them. Permissible actions are those that we may choose to either do or not do. The question for our example then is: What category does the dumping of the waste fall into? Is it wrong, obligatory, or permissible?

You might hit on the idea that the dumping of the waste is illegal. You are not supposed to take illegal actions, and so should dispose of the waste properly. However, there is an additional distinction that is important to keep in mind when looking at the morality of a situation, namely, the distinction between morality and legality. Morality and legality differ in important ways. Most relevant to keep in mind, without worrying about the philosophical discussions regarding the two, are simply examples that show that the two are separate. Take a moment to consider some actions that are legal but that might be immoral, and others that might be illegal but moral. Think about slavery as it was once practiced in the United States. It was legal to own another person against his or her will. Should we jump from the claim that because it was legal to own people against their will, that it was moral to do so? Consider that in England, motorists drive on the left side of the road. Yet doing this is illegal in the United States. Should we jump to the conclusion that driving on the left is immoral? This leaves open a number of possibilities. That which is legal may be moral, immoral, or amoral. That which is illegal may also be moral, immoral, or amoral. For the purposes of this book, the focus is on the moral question, not the legal one.

To deal with this legality question in the dumping scenario, let us suppose that industry in this case has outpaced regulations. The waste that needs to be disposed of has no regulations guiding it, and so there can be no claim that the company would be acting illegally by dumping the waste. Now, there is no legal downside to dumping the waste: there will be no fine if you are caught dumping it. But there are economic upsides to dumping the waste. It seems like the answer is clear. However, the company knows that the waste is dangerous. The conflict is between the economic gains versus the ethics of dumping the waste.

While the question above regarding the wrongness, obligatoriness, or permissibility of dumping the waste seems to define the issue to the level of specificity required, a moment's reflection should lead to a further question, one that is not easily answered. After breaking actions down into the three broad categories of wrong, obligatory, and permissible, the next question to ask is this: What is it that makes certain actions fall into some categories and not others? For example, murder is typically taken to fall into the category of being wrong. But what is it that makes murder wrong? What is its wrong-making property? And for that matter, what is the permissible-making property of eating pizza (or the obligatory-making property of eating ice cream)?

Suppose that you attempt to decide what to do by making a list of pros and cons. You reason that this will help you figure out which decision will lead to the best outcome and that, surely, the action which leads to the best outcome must be the way to go! On the side of dumping the waste is the cost savings, which may allow the company to do other things with the money that will be very beneficial to the company and its employees. These benefits might also extend to the community in which the company is located. On the other side of the column is the environmental damage that might be done by dumping the waste. Further, there are potential health costs to the community and a risk that the community might discover the dumping of the waste. If the community were to find out, this could lead to the company getting into a lot of trouble, not just from being hit with governmental fines, but also from community anger. This anger could result in boycotts of the company and even lead other businesses to cease doing business with your company. This could lead to the closing of the company altogether.

After deliberating the pros and cons of the issue for a short time, you come to the realization that you might be violating the chief rule according to which your parents raised you: the Golden Rule. You are supposed to *do unto others as you would have them do unto you.* This is the case even if that doing unto others does not lead to the best overall outcome—maybe focusing only on the consequences of the action is not the best way after all! Maybe there is some set of rules that you should be following. Consider that we have these rights which are supposed to be inalienable. Maybe in deciding to dump the waste, it would be a violation of someone's rights? Maybe it would be using others and the community in some way. It is, in a way, imposing business costs on the community.

Another way you may think about this case is from the perspective of a professional, such as a doctor or lawyer. These individuals have something called a "fiduciary duty" which requires them to act in the best interests of clients and patients. Maybe you have a fiduciary duty to the business to look out for its interests. You have, after all, entered into a kind of contract with the business. You promise to act in the best interests of your employer, while they promise to pay you and provide certain benefits. It is certainly the case that a promise to act in a certain way must put certain actions in the category of obligatory. However, there is also the possibility that the business might have some kind of contract with the community in which the business operates. Your promise to the business is easy, but what kind of promise might the business have made to the community? Whatever it was, it probably included a promise to refrain from harming it, and in return the community promises certain municipal services (e.g., police, fire service, etc.). Further, the fiduciary duties of lawyers and doctors end where there is a harm to the client/patient or others (which would include the community).

An additional way to consider the case at hand is to ask whether one should be the kind of person that would engage in the activity that produces the waste. This may not be helpful in deciding the current case, but it is something that students should keep in mind when choosing an employer or career. For example, being a contract killer might be a lucrative career. However, a lucrative career is not the only consideration. Do you want to be the kind of person that makes money from the deaths of other people? This way of thinking about ethics is usually referred to as "virtue ethics." In this book, we will only touch on virtue ethics, though as we explore questions of right and wrong action, it will be up to you to use what you have learned to guide your own decision-making.

Finally, we may want to ask if there are those to whom we have a special relationship or duty of care, which would make the act of dumping the waste wrong. The idea here is that the impersonal approaches that we have previously discussed fail to capture the real nature of our relationship to others. In many instances, we don't do the morally right thing because we have some duty, or believe it will maximize overall happiness; rather, we do it because we care about the people in our lives. We are concerned about the well-being of family, friends, and even the broader community. This approach is referred to as care ethics, and is often found (though not exclusively) in the works of feminist ethicists.

There are then at least five different answers for how we might categorize different actions. First, we have the possibility that the action to take is the one that leads to the best outcome. Second, we have the option that there is some rule or set of rules that we should follow. Third, we have the option that there is some kind of agreement that dictates what we may and may not do. Fourth, we have the option to ask which decisions would exemplify a person of good character or virtue. Fifth, we have the option to ask which action would best satisfy a duty of care we owe to other people? Finally, we may want to ask, Which option is correct?

In the first few chapters of this book, we will take a more in-depth look at each of the above five answers. We will do this by reading sections from a major work in each category. Following this introduction to ethics, we will turn to specific issues of importance to business and business ethics. The considerations raised above will resurface in these readings.

I.
FOUNDATIONS

1.

FOUNDATIONS

1.
UTILITARIANISM
FROM *UTILITARIANISM* (1871)

JOHN STUART MILL

About This Reading

Consequentialism

The consequentialist perspective is often tied to a philosophical movement called utilitarianism, which flourished in Britain in the nineteenth century but continues to be very influential even today. The consequentialist holds that the effects of action determine the moral quality of action and that our moral duties and rights are traceable to the desire to maximize good consequences for the most people. While there are many definitions of the word "good," the utilitarians tended to view goodness in terms of either human pleasure or human happiness. Pleasure was viewed as the satisfaction of physical desire while happiness was viewed as the satisfaction of intellectual or artistic desire. The key to this approach to ethics is that actions are said to be right to the degree that they maximize pleasure or happiness. In effect, we grant rights and impose duties in order to secure maximal pleasure or happiness. Ethics is about producing the best possible outcomes.

Types of Consequentialism

Let us begin with a more careful consideration of consequentialism. Consequentialists argue that actions are classified as right on the basis of their effects or consequences. The consequences of actions, however, are usually a mixture of good and bad, and in order to determine the moral worth of an act, one must weigh these consequences. For example, watching TV may be enjoyable and relaxing (pleasurable) but it also tends to increase weight and boredom and decrease health (pain). Consequentialists are powerfully influenced by the work of John Stuart Mill, whose book *Utilitarianism* (1871) advances his "Greatest Happiness Principle" as a universal decision principle within ethics. The precept states that actions are right if "they tend to promote happiness, wrong as they tend to produce the reverse of happiness." This principle of utility contains Mill's answer to two fundamental questions, namely "what things are good" and "what actions are right?" Philosophers often distinguish between two kinds of good, extrinsic and intrinsic. Extrinsic goods are things that we desire because they produce something else. TV can produce both boredom (pain) and relaxation (pleasure). TV is like your coat. Both are extrinsically good and extrinsically bad in the sense that in certain conditions they can both produce a mixture of pain and pleasure. You want your TV or your coat not for their own sake but because they provide relaxation or keep you warm. An intrinsic good is something that we desire for its own sake. One wants an intrinsic good even if it does not lead to other goods. Utilitarians maintain that pleasure and happiness are the only intrinsic goods. Other objects are extrinsically good or valuable because they advance happiness and pleasure, or retard pain and unhappiness. We will see that what we take to be extrinsically good is very diverse, and it is because of this diversity that the question of freedom becomes so vital for the utilitarians.

What is crucial to notice, however, is that all actions produce both happiness and pain. Rightness is therefore a property of actions or kinds of actions insofar as they maximize pleasure over pain. Furthermore, for utilitarians, right actions are those that produce maximal happiness for the greatest number of people. Finally, the rightness of an action is something that one "calculates" on the basis of the amounts of pleasure and pain produced by an act or a rule of action. Right actions are those that produce the most happiness over pain. Wrong actions are those that produce more pain than happiness. Let us now turn to two versions of utilitarianism that are critical to understanding the theory as a whole.

Act Utilitarianism

The first version of utilitarianism which we will discuss is often called act utilitarianism. It begins with the idea that the principle of utility or general happiness is somewhat ambiguous because it does not explicitly state whether one should apply the greatest happiness principle to specific acts or to general rules of behavior. Act utilitarian ethical theory resolves this ambiguity by stating that the greatest happiness principle applies to specific actions. For example, if a patient is near death and competently directs his doctor to kill him, then killing may be justified if the killing maximizes benefits over harms in this particular situation. Defenders of active euthanasia (or mercy killing) often argue that in specific cases it may be best to allow voluntary killing because this eliminates a great deal of useless suffering. People who support voluntary active killing of terminally ill patients often argue that there are legitimate exceptions to the "do not kill" rule. The act utilitarian admits that while there is a social rule against killing and that this rule is generally legitimate, this rule should be violated in specific cases. In these limited cases, obedience to the "do not kill" rule produces more harm than good. For act utilitarians, we ought to apply the principle of utility directly to actions and ethically select particular actions only if the particular act will produce more benefits than alternative actions. For the act utilitarian, social rules of conduct such as the "do not kill" rule have exceptions, and we should identify the exceptions by applying the greatest happiness rule to particular acts.

Rule Utilitarianism

The second version of utilitarianism has a very different conception of social rules. This version argues that we should not in general apply this principle of utility to specific acts but rather to general rules of action. For the rule utilitarian, what produces maximal happiness is obedience to socially useful rules. Granting people the right to selectively "pick and choose" which rules to obey in specific situations threatens the very practice of "setting down" rules to govern human behavior. We can see this idea if we look at legislatures. The Congress of the United States does not pass laws and allow citizens to decide for themselves whether to obey these laws. Laws apply universally. Indeed, the rule utilitarian argues that following the act utilitarian suggestion may produce chaos, because all persons would be able to decide for themselves whether a rule was binding in a given situation. This freedom to disobey laws may harm society. For example, if doctors could decide for themselves to kill patients who were suffering from a terrible disease, then patients might avoid seeking medical treatment.

Another example of how act utilitarianism might be unethical involves hatred. Assume that millions of people hate Smith, who is innocent of breaking a law but is also someone who is obnoxious. This hatred may motivate Jones to kill Smith. Furthermore, Jones might be able to do a "calculation" which "establishes" that killing Smith will produce more good than harm. The millions who hate Smith would be happier if Smith were dead and no one would really be unhappy over the death of this obnoxious person. Does this justify killing Smith?

The rule utilitarian says No! If there are rules of conduct then we cannot pick and choose to obey them or not.

Furthermore, according to the rule utilitarian, rules should not be broken on a "case-by-case basis" because this would tend to blur the distinction between what is right and what is convenient. To return to our illustration involving Jones and Smith, it may be convenient to kill Smith because it would make millions happier, but it is surely questionable whether it is morally right to kill an individual merely because doing so would produce happiness for millions. Rule utilitarians argue that these difficulties can be avoided if we apply the greatest happiness principle to rules rather than to particular acts. Furthermore, once a rule is judged to maximize social welfare, everyone is obliged to follow that rule. This is true even in particular cases where obedience to the rule may produce more harm than good. Rule utilitarians admit that following a rule in some circumstances can produce more harm than good. However, the rule utilitarian claims that rules bind the individual because obedience to these rules produces more good than harm, in general. The "do not kill" rule may currently prevent us from helping a terminally ill patient who wishes to die, and this may prevent us from maximizing the greatest good in this case. However, obedience to this rule may produce more social welfare than its alternatives.

The rule utilitarian, however, accepts the idea that rules can change. Social rules are not absolute. Our society currently has rules against the direct killing of terminally ill patients who voluntarily wish to have their lives ended. Do these rules produce more good than harm by preventing unjustified killings? The rule utilitarian would argue that it is permissible for a society to change these rules if society can demonstrate that alternative rules would advance social happiness without producing more harm. We already have three exceptions to the "do not kill" rule (selfdefense, capital punishment, and just war). It may be that we can develop a rule covering a fourth exception, namely, "killing for mercy." The rule utilitarians will demand proof that new rules will not violate the "greatest happiness principle."

We can see how the rule utilitarian principle has affected the ethics of business decision-making. For many, business decisions and the very structure of a free market system are justified by appealing to the overall good that is generated. While we may not like it when businesses lay off employees, an efficient economic system is best for the general welfare (or so the argument goes). Whether or not this is true will depend on how we measure well-being. Is it in terms of average income, GDP, unemployment, quality of life, or some combination of these and other factors?

On the present occasion, I shall, without further discussion of the other theories, attempt to contribute something towards the understanding and appreciation of the Utilitarian or Happiness theory, and towards such proof as it is susceptible of. It is evident that this cannot be proof in the ordinary and popular meaning of the term. Questions of ultimate ends are not amenable to direct proof. Whatever can be proved to be good, must be so by being shown to be a means to something admitted to be good without proof. The medical art is proved to be good, by its conducing to health; but how is it possible to prove that health is good? The art of music is good, for the reason, among others, that it produces pleasure; but what proof is it possible to give that pleasure is good? If, then, it is asserted that there is a comprehensive formula, including all things which are in themselves good, and that whatever else is good, is not so as an end, but as a mean, the formula may be accepted or rejected, but is not a subject of what is commonly understood by proof. We are not, however, to infer that its acceptance or rejection must depend on blind impulse, or arbitrary choice. There is a larger meaning of the word proof, in which this question is as amenable to it as any other of the disputed questions of philosophy. The subject is within the cognizance of the rational faculty; and neither does that faculty deal with it solely in the way of intuition. Considerations may be presented capable of determining the intellect either to give or withhold its assent to the doctrine; and this is equivalent to proof.

We shall examine presently of what nature are these considerations; in what manner they apply to the case, and what rational grounds, therefore, can be given for accepting or rejecting the utilitarian formula. But it is a preliminary condition of rational acceptance or rejection, that the formula should be correctly understood. I believe that the very imperfect notion ordinarily formed of its meaning, is the chief obstacle which impedes its reception; and that could it be cleared, even from only the grosser misconceptions, the question would be greatly simplified, and a large proportion of its difficulties removed. Before, therefore, I attempt to enter into the philosophical grounds which can be given for assenting to the utilitarian standard, I shall offer some illustrations of the doctrine itself; with the view of showing more clearly what it is, distinguishing it from what it is not, and disposing of such of the practical objections to it as either originate in, or are closely connected with, mistaken interpretations of its meaning. Having thus prepared the ground, I shall afterwards endeavour to throw such light as I can upon the question, considered as one of philosophical theory.

* * *

A passing remark is all that needs be given to the ignorant blunder of supposing that those who stand up for utility as the test of right and wrong, use the term in that restricted and merely colloquial sense in which utility is opposed to pleasure. An apology is due to the philosophical opponents of utilitarianism, for even the momentary appearance of confounding them with any one capable of so absurd a misconception; which is the more extraordinary, inasmuch as the contrary accusation, of referring everything to pleasure, and that too in its grossest form, is another of the common charges against utilitarianism: and, as has been pointedly remarked by an able writer, the same sort of persons, and often the very same persons, denounce the theory "as impracticably dry when the word utility precedes the word pleasure, and as too practicably voluptuous when the word pleasure precedes the word utility." Those who know anything about the matter are aware that every writer, from Epicurus to Bentham, who maintained the theory of utility, meant by it, not something to be contradistinguished from pleasure, but pleasure itself, together with exemption from pain; and instead of opposing the useful to the agreeable or the ornamental, have always declared that the useful means these, among other things. Yet the common herd, including the herd of writers, not only in newspapers and periodicals, but in books of weight and pretension, are perpetually falling into this shallow mistake. Having caught up the word utilitarian, while knowing nothing whatever about it but its sound, they habitually express by it the rejection, or the neglect, of pleasure in some of its forms; of beauty, of ornament, or of amusement. Nor is the term thus ignorantly misapplied solely in disparagement, but occasionally in compliment; as though it implied superiority to frivolity and the mere pleasures of the moment. And this perverted use is the only one in which the word is popularly known, and the one from which the new generation are acquiring their sole notion of its meaning. Those who introduced the word, but who had for many years discontinued it as a distinctive appellation, may well feel themselves called upon to resume it, if by doing so they can hope to contribute anything towards rescuing it from this utter degradation.

The creed which accepts as the foundation of morals, Utility, or the Greatest Happiness Principle, holds that actions are right in proportion as they tend to promote happiness, wrong as they tend to produce the reverse of happiness. By happiness is intended pleasure, and the absence of pain; by unhappiness, pain, and the privation of pleasure. To give a clear view of the moral standard set up by the theory, much more requires to be said; in particular, what things it includes in the ideas of pain and pleasure; and to what extent this is left an open question. But these supplementary explanations do not affect the theory of life on which this theory of morality is grounded—namely, that pleasure, and freedom from pain, are the only things desirable as ends; and that all desirable things (which are as numerous in the utilitarian as in any other scheme) are desirable either for the pleasure inherent in themselves, or as means to the promotion of pleasure and the prevention of pain.

Now, such a theory of life excites in many minds, and among them in some of the most estimable in feeling and purpose, inveterate dislike. To suppose that life has (as they express it) no higher end than pleasure—no better and nobler object of desire and pursuit—they designate as utterly mean and grovelling; as a doctrine worthy only of swine, to whom the followers of Epicurus were, at a very early period, contemptuously likened; and modern holders of the doctrine are occasionally made the subject of equally polite comparisons by its German, French, and English assailants.

When thus attacked, the Epicureans have always answered, that it is not they, but their accusers, who represent human nature in a degrading light; since the accusation supposes human beings to be capable of no pleasures except those of which swine are capable. If this supposition were true, the charge could not be gainsaid, but would then be no longer an imputation; for if the sources of pleasure were precisely the same to human beings and to swine, the rule of life which is good enough for the one would be good enough for the other. The comparison of the Epicurean life to that of beasts is felt as degrading, precisely because a beast's pleasures do not satisfy a human being's conceptions of happiness. Human beings have faculties more elevated than the animal appetites, and when once made conscious of them, do not regard anything as happiness which does not include their gratification. I do not, indeed, consider the Epicureans to have been by any means faultless in drawing out their scheme of consequences from the utilitarian principle. To do this in any sufficient manner, many Stoic, as well as Christian elements require to be included. But there is no known Epicurean theory of life which does not assign to the pleasures of the intellect; of the feelings and imagination, and of the moral sentiments, a much higher value as pleasures than to those of mere sensation. It must be admitted, however, that utilitarian writers in general have placed the superiority of mental over bodily pleasures chiefly in the greater permanency, safety, uncostliness, &c., of the former—that is, in their circumstantial advantages rather than in their intrinsic nature. And on all these points utilitarians have fully proved their case; but they might have taken the other, and, as it may be called, higher ground, with entire consistency. It is quite compatible with the principle of utility to recognise the fact, that some *kinds* of pleasure are more desirable and more valuable than others. It would be absurd that while, in estimating all other things, quality is considered as well as quantity, the estimation of pleasures should be supposed to depend on quantity alone.

If I am asked, what I mean by difference of quality in pleasures, or what makes one pleasure more valuable than another, merely as a pleasure, except its being greater in amount, there is but one possible answer. Of two pleasures, if there be one to which all or almost all who have experience of both give a decided preference, irrespective of any feeling of moral obligation to prefer it, that is the more desirable pleasure. If one of the two is, by those who are competently acquainted with both, placed so far above the other that they prefer it, even though knowing it to be attended with a greater amount of discontent, and would not resign it for any quantity of the other pleasure which their nature is capable of, we are justified in ascribing to the preferred enjoyment a superiority in quality, so far outweighing quantity as to render it, in comparison, of small account.

Now it is an unquestionable fact that those who are equally acquainted with, and equally capable of appreciating and enjoying, both, do give a most marked preference to the manner of existence which employs their higher faculties. Few human creatures would consent to be changed into any of the lower animals, for a promise of the fullest allowance of a beast's pleasures; no intelligent human being would consent to be a fool, no instructed person would be an ignoramus, no person of feeling and conscience would be selfish and base, even though they should be persuaded that the fool, the dunce, or the rascal is better satisfied with his lot than they are with theirs. They would not resign what they possess more than he, for the most complete satisfaction of all the desires which they have in common with him. If they ever fancy they would, it is only in cases of unhappiness so extreme, that to escape from it they would exchange their lot for almost any other, however undesirable in their own eyes. A being of higher faculties requires more to make him happy, is capable probably of more acute suffering, and is certainly accessible to it at more points, than one of an inferior type; but in spite of these liabilities, he can never really wish to sink into what he feels to be a lower grade of existence. We may give what explanation we please of this unwillingness; we may attribute it to pride, a name which is given indiscriminately to some of the most and to some of the least estimable feelings of which man kind are capable; we may refer it to the love of liberty and personal independence, an appeal to which was with the Stoics one of the most effective means for the inculcation of it; to the love of power, or to the love of excitement, both of which do really enter into and contribute to it: but its most appropriate appellation is a sense of dignity, which all human beings possess in one form or other, and in some, though by no means in exact, proportion to their higher faculties, and which is so essential a part of the happiness of those in whom it is strong, that nothing which conflicts with it could be, otherwise than momentarily, an object of desire to them. Whoever supposes that this preference takes place at a sacrifice of happiness—that the superior being, in anything like equal circumstances, is not happier than the inferior—confounds the two very different ideas, of happiness, and content. It is indisputable that the being whose capacities of enjoyment are low, has the greatest chance of having them fully satisfied; and a highly-endowed being will always feel that any happiness which he can look for, as the world is constituted, is imperfect. But he can learn to bear its imperfections, if they are at all bearable; and they will not make him envy the being who is indeed unconscious of the imperfections, but only because he feels not at all the good which those imperfections qualify. It is better to be a human being dissatisfied than a pig satisfied; better to be Socrates dissatisfied than a fool satisfied. And if the fool, or the pig, is of a different opinion, it is because they only know their own side of the question. The other party to the comparison knows both sides.

It may be objected, that many who are capable of the higher pleasures, occasionally, under the influence of temptation, postpone them to the lower. But this is quite compatible with a full appreciation of the intrinsic superiority of the higher. Men often, from infirmity of character, make their election for the nearer good, though they know it to be the less valuable; and this no less when the choice is between two bodily pleasures, than when it is between bodily and mental. They pursue sensual indulgences to the injury of health, though perfectly aware that health is the greater good. It may be further objected, that many who begin with youthful enthusiasm for everything noble, as they advance in years sink into indolence and selfishness. But I do not believe that those who undergo this very common change, voluntarily choose the lower description of pleasures in preference to the higher. I believe that before they devote themselves exclusively to the one, they have already become incapable of the other. Capacity for the nobler feelings is in most natures a very tender plant, easily killed, not only by hostile influences, but by mere want of sustenance; and in the majority of young persons it speedily dies away if the occupations to which their position in life has devoted them, and the society into which it has thrown them, are not favourable to keeping that higher capacity in exercise. Men lose their high aspirations as they lose their intellectual tastes, because they have not time or opportunity for indulging them; and they addict themselves to inferior pleasures, not because they deliberately prefer them, but because they are either the only ones to which they have access, or the only ones which they are any longer capable of enjoying. It may be questioned whether any one who has remained equally susceptible to both classes of pleasures, ever knowingly and calmly preferred the lower; though many, in all ages, have broken down in an ineffectual attempt to combine both.

From this verdict of the only competent judges, I apprehend there can be no appeal. On a question which is the best worth having of two pleasures, or which of two modes of existence is the most grateful to the feelings, apart from its moral attributes and from its consequences, the judgment of those who are qualified by knowledge of both, or, if they differ, that of the majority among them, must be admitted as final. And there needs be the less hesitation to accept this judgment respecting the quality of pleasures, since there is no other tribunal to be referred to even on the question of quantity. What means are there of determining which is the acutest of two pains, or the intensest of two pleasurable sensations, except the general suffrage of those who are familiar with both? Neither pains nor pleasures are homogeneous, and pain is always heterogeneous with pleasure. What is there to decide whether a particular pleasure is worth purchasing at the cost of a particular pain, except the feelings and judgment of the experienced? When, therefore, those feelings and judgment declare the pleasures derived from the higher faculties to be preferable *in kind*, apart from the question of intensity, to those of which the animal nature, disjoined from the higher faculties, is susceptible, they are entitled on this subject to the same regard.

I have dwelt on this point, as being a necessary part of a perfectly just conception of Utility or Happiness, considered as the directive rule of human conduct. But it is by no means an indispensable condition to the acceptance of the utilitarian standard; for that standard is not the agent's own greatest happiness, but the greatest amount of happiness altogether; and if it may possibly be doubted whether a noble character is always the happier for its nobleness, there can be no doubt that it makes other people happier, and that the world in general is immensely a gainer by it. Utilitarianism, therefore, could only attain its end by the general cultivation of nobleness of character, even if each individual were only benefited by the nobleness of others, and his own, so far as happiness is concerned, were a sheer deduction from the benefit. But the bare enunciation of such an absurdity as this last, renders refutation superfluous.

According to the Greatest Happiness Principle, as above explained, the ultimate end, with reference to and for the sake of which all other things are desirable (whether we are considering our own good or that of other people), is an existence exempt as far as possible from pain, and as rich as possible in enjoyments, both in point of quantity and quality; the test of quality, and the rule for measuring it against quantity, being the preference felt by those who, in their opportunities of experience, to which must be added their habits of self-consciousness and self-observation, are best furnished with the means of comparison. This, being, according to the utilitarian opinion, the end of human action, is necessarily also the standard of morality; which may accordingly be defined, the rules and precepts for human conduct, by the observance of which an existence such as has been described might be, to the greatest extent possible, secured to all mankind; and not to them only, but, so far as the nature of things admits, to the whole sentient creation.

Questions

1. Explain how some seeming trivial action (e.g., brushing one's teeth) could, according to utilitarianism, be considered a moral act.

2. One difficulty with utilitarian calculations is deciding between long-term and short-term utility. Give an example of a business decision in which there is a conflict between the long-term and short-term interests of the business.

3. Company X is attempting to decide whether or not to offshore its production facilities to China. If they were using good utilitarian reasoning, whose utilities (happiness) should be included in their calculations? Explain.

4. In 2008 the United States Government bailed out the auto and banking industry in the amount of $426 billion. Although the government made an overall profit of $15

billion on these loans, the auto rescue portion lost $9.5 billion—mainly to GM, which paid back $39 billion of the $49.5 billion it borrowed.[1] How would a utilitarian view the bailout of these industries? Should the government have bailed out one, both, or neither? Explain your answer.

Further Reading

Cavanaugh, Gerald F., Dennis J. Moberg, and Manuel Velasquez. "Making Business Ethics Practical." *Business Ethics Quarterly*, vol. 5, no. 3, July 1995, pp. 399–418.

Gustafson, Andrew. "In Defense of a Utilitarian Business Ethic." *Business and Society Review*, vol. 118, issue 3, Fall 2013, pp. 325–60.

Mill, J.S. *Utilitarianism*. 2nd ed. Indianapolis: Hackett Publishing Company, 2002.

Smart, J.J.C., and Bernard Williams. *Utilitarianism: For and Against.* Cambridge: Cambridge University Press, 1973.

---

1   Weisman, Jonathan. "U.S. Declares Bank and Auto Bailouts Over, and Profitable." *The New York Times*, 19 Dec. 2014.

2.
DEONTOLOGY
FROM *GROUNDWORK FOR THE*
METAPHYSICS OF MORALS (1785)

IMMANUEL KANT

About This Reading

There are many forms of deontology, or duty-based ethics, but all of them emphasize that there are traits of action other than consequences that determine whether an action is morally right. Deontologists often speak of offering a "*rights-based approach to ethics*" rather than a consequences-based approach because they argue that individuals have rights that in some sense can ethically override what is best for society as a whole. For deontologists, individual rights in many cases morally override social welfare considerations.

Perhaps the most famous deontological theory is associated with the eighteenth-century philosopher Immanuel Kant, who maintained that it was not the effects of actions that determined their moral worth but the causes. The causes of human action were motives or intentions. Morally right actions were those that flowed from good intentions or motives. Wrong actions flowed from bad intentions. For Kant, the cause of an action and not its effects is what makes an action morally correct. Morality is based on good intentions, not good results.

Kant defended his theory by noticing that great harms could flow from accidental actions and that these accidents were morally neutral. For example, Hurricane Katrina produced enormous harm but none of us would say that this hurricane was immoral. Accidental actions are neither moral nor immoral actions. For example, a guest at your house may fall and accidentally damage your favorite chair. The act causes you harm, but is the action immoral? For Kant, this last question can only be answered by examining the cause of the act. If the fall was a genuine accident, then the fall was neither moral nor immoral. It was an accident. It was like Hurricane Katrina. However, if you discover that your guest intentionally slipped in order to break your favorite chair, and that your guest did this because of envy, then we have an action which may be immoral. Intentions are what make the difference between moral and nonmoral actions.

Attorneys know this idea very well. You might be accused of a murder and in fact you may have killed someone, but that does not mean that it was a murder. You might have done it by accident and the attorney may be called upon to prove that position to a jury of your peers. If you had no evil motive, and if your attorney can establish that fact, there is a good chance that you will not be sent to jail. We see this same effect in business contexts as well. A company that accidentally sells a defective product, for which it quickly takes steps to correct when the defect is discovered, will be treated much differently from a company that knowingly sells a product that is defective—or even dangerous to customers—and that drags its feet when the problem is discovered by those outside the company.

What then makes a motive moral or immoral? Kant answers this question by distinguishing hypothetical from categorical imperatives. Imperatives are commands such as "Close the door!" Most imperatives are hypothetical in the sense that the commands apply only if they are goal-directed. For example, the imperative "Study that philosophy book!" applies to someone only if that person cares to obtain a degree or become competent at philosophy. A hypothetical imperative is one that applies only if certain other conditions are satisfied. If someone does not wish to acquire knowledge of philosophy or obtain a degree or other goals related to reading the book, then the imperative to "study that philosophy book" does not apply to him or her. Kant claims that nearly all imperatives are hypothetical in the sense that they are goal- or condition-directed. However, for Kant, there is one imperative that is categorical in the sense that it universally applies to everyone under all conditions whatever their goals in life. Furthermore, for Kant, if one obeys this imperative, then one has good intentions. If one violates this imperative, then one has bad intentions.

Kant calls this imperative "the categorical imperative" because he claims that this rule applies under all circumstances. The imperative sounds very much like the golden rule, which states that we should treat others as we would wish to be treated. Kant has several formulations of this imperative, but the one that is most famous requires us to "act only on the basis of maxims that we could will to become universal laws." Another formulation of the imperative commands us to always treat others as ends, never as means. For Kant, both of these formulations assert the same categorical rule, which he believes is derived not from our desire to maximize our happiness but from reason itself. This single categorical rule is the source of all morality for Kant. For, even if it were beneficial for society as a whole to keep slaves, it would still be wrong because keeping slaves violates the categorical imperative to avoid using others as means. Reason would allow us to keep slaves only if we could find a trait that distinguished slaves from persons. But for Kant, there is no such trait and therefore reason requires that we prohibit slavery. In effect, because we are rational, we could not will to be slaves ourselves. Therefore, we cannot rationally will that other persons be slaves even if this would produce more general happiness. The imperative to produce general happiness is hypothetical and conditional. Therefore, no consequence-based theory could be the basis of our moral life.

Multi-Ruled Deontology

What is critical to note about Kant's theory is that it is a single-rule deontology. All of our moral duties and rights are presented as coming from the one categorical rule. However, many deontologists have argued that we cannot account for the great variety of our duties and rights by an appeal to a single rule of morality. W.D. Ross's "many ruled" deontological theory pictures our moral life as resting on several rules. For Ross, utilitarianism and Kantianism both suffer from a common error. Both try to derive our complex moral convictions and intuitions from a single rule. However, according to Ross, neither the "greatest happiness principle" nor the categorical imperative can account for the great variety of moral rules that bind us. No single moral rule is more important than the rest. We can illustrate this point by looking at two such rules. "Keep your promises" and "assist the injured" are widely accepted as duties that bind us on many occasions throughout our lives. Both these rules are vital within our moral life, but on occasion they can come into conflict with each other. Suppose Jones faces the following conflict. He needs to break a promise to meet you this evening because he believes that he must stop and bring aid to an injured motorist. Jones is in a state of conflict, which is derived from being obligated by two different moral rules. Our moral life is complex. For Ross, we are bound by many rules, and frequently individuals and societies must choose between fundamentally opposing values. Should Jones keep his promise or assist the injured motorist? Ross asserts that rules such as "keep your promises" or "assist the injured" are "prima facie obligatory." This means that at first glance, if we have made a promise, then we are bound to keep it. However, the situation demands that we either break our promise or avoid aiding the injured person. If we assume that we cannot do both, then we must decide what rule actually obligates us in this situation. "Many ruled theories" admit that there may be no precise mechanism or algorithm for determining that one rule actually obligates us. Ross asserts that humans "intuit" which rule actually obligates them in given situations and thus it is possible that disagreement in ethics will continue.

The business context allows for a clear contrast between consequentialist and deontological views of ethics. Often, we take individuals to be in possession of rights that protect them from interference by larger groups, e.g., a right to privacy. However, when an individual is an employee, this right may come into conflict with the drive by the employee's company to make (or maximize) profits. The company may wish to keep an eye on what the employee does when not at work, e.g., by monitoring the employee's online activities. This conflict, a conflict between the rights of individuals and what is best for the group, helps illustrate why the ethical foundation adopted is of great importance. If the consequentialist position is the correct one, then there is no conflict, the individual has no rights, so there is no conflict. The same can be said if the deontological position is the correct one. If the employee has a right to privacy, then it does not matter that it would be better for the company to violate that right, as it simply may not be done.

Of course, this brief description of the conflict between rights and consequences is not the end of the story. It also helps to illustrate the difficulty of ethical reasoning. It might lead to the best outcome for all involved if the company actually respects some level of privacy on the part of the employee. Thus, the consequentialist picture is not simply a matter of what the company actually desires, but what the actual outcomes of actions are. Would it be the case that having a "no privacy" policy would lead to a lower quality of employee? If so, then it might be better to grant employees privacy, even if they had no right to it. Further, supposing that the employee does have a right to privacy, we need to ask if there are rights held by the company that are in possible conflict with the rights of the employee. Thus, settling on either a consequentialist or deontological view does not settle all the issues. And, of course, these are not the only two options, as we will see as we continue.

Nothing can possibly be conceived in the world, or even out of it, which can be called good, without qualification, except a good will. Intelligence, wit, judgement, and the other talents of the mind, however they may be named, or courage, resolution, perseverance, as qualities of temperament, are undoubtedly good and desirable in many respects; but these gifts of nature may also become extremely bad and mischievous if the will which is to make use of them, and which, therefore, constitutes what is called character, is not good. It is the same with the gifts of fortune. Power, riches, honour, even health, and the general well-being and contentment with one's condition which is called happiness, inspire pride, and often presumption, if there is not a good will to correct the influence of these on the mind, and with this also to rectify the whole principle of acting and adapt it to its end. The sight of a being who is not adorned with a single feature of a pure and good will, enjoying unbroken prosperity, can never give pleasure to an impartial rational spectator. Thus a good will appears to constitute the indispensable condition even of being worthy of happiness.

* * *

A good will is good not because of what it performs or effects, not by its aptness for the attainment of some proposed end, but simply by virtue of the volition; that is, it is good in itself, and considered by itself is to be esteemed much higher than all that can be brought about by it in favour of any inclination, nay even of the sum total of all inclinations. Even if it should happen that, owing to special disfavour of fortune, or the niggardly provision of a step-motherly nature, this will should wholly lack power to accomplish its purpose, if with its greatest efforts it should yet achieve nothing, and there should remain only the good will (not, to be sure, a mere wish, but the summoning of all means in our power), then, like a jewel, it would still shine by its own light, as a thing which has its whole value in itself. Its usefulness or fruitlessness can neither add nor take away anything from this value. It would be, as it were, only the setting to enable us to handle it the more conveniently in common commerce, or to attract to it the attention of those who are not yet connoisseurs, but not to recommend it to true connoisseurs, or to determine its value.

There is, however, something so strange in this idea of the absolute value of the mere will, in which no account is taken of its utility, that notwithstanding the thorough assent of even common reason to the idea, yet a suspicion must arise that it may perhaps really be the product of mere high-flown fancy, and that we may have misunderstood the purpose of nature in assigning reason as the governor of our will. Therefore we will examine this idea from this point of view.

* * *

[O]ur existence has a different and far nobler end, for which, and not for happiness, reason is properly intended, and which must, therefore, be regarded as the supreme condition to which the private ends of man must, for the most part, be postponed.

* * *

I omit here all actions which are already recognized as inconsistent with duty, although they may be useful for this or that purpose, for with these the question whether they are done from duty cannot arise at all, since they even conflict with it. I also set aside those actions which really conform to duty, but to which men have no direct inclination, performing them because they are impelled thereto by some other inclination. For in this case we can readily distinguish whether the action which agrees with duty is done from duty, or from a selfish view. It is much harder to make this distinction when the action accords with duty and the subject has besides a direct inclination to it. For example, it is always a matter of duty that a dealer should not over charge an inexperienced purchaser; and wherever there is much commerce the prudent tradesman does not overcharge, but keeps a fixed price for everyone, so that a child buys of him as well as any other. Men are thus honestly served; but this is not enough to make us believe that the tradesman has so acted from duty and from principles of honesty: his own advantage required it; it is out of the question in this case to suppose that he might besides have a direct inclination in favour of the buyers, so that, as it were, from love he should give no advantage to one over another. Accordingly the action was done neither from duty nor from direct inclination, but merely with a selfish view.

On the other hand, it is a duty to maintain one's life; and, in addition, everyone has also a direct inclination to do so. But on this account the often anxious care which most men take for it has no intrinsic worth, and their maxim has no moral import. They preserve their life as duty requires, no doubt, but not because duty requires. On the other hand, if adversity and hopeless sorrow have completely taken away the relish for life; if the unfortunate one, strong in mind, indignant at his fate rather than desponding or dejected, wishes for death, and yet preserves his life without loving it—not from inclination or fear, but from duty—then his maxim has a moral worth.

To be beneficent when we can is a duty; and besides this, there are many minds so sympathetically constituted that, without any other motive of vanity or self-interest, they find a pleasure in spreading joy around them and can take delight in the satisfaction of others so far as it is their own work. But I maintain that in such a case an action of this kind, however proper, however amiable it may be, has nevertheless no true moral worth, but is on a level with other inclinations, e.g., the inclination to honour, which, if it is happily directed to that which is in fact of public utility and

accordant with duty and consequently honourable, deserves praise and encouragement, but not esteem. For the maxim lacks the moral import, namely, that such
actions be done from duty, not from inclination. Put the case that the mind of that
philanthropist were clouded by sorrow of his own, extinguishing all sympathy with
the lot of others, and that, while he still has the power to benefit others in distress,
he is not touched by their trouble because he is absorbed with his own; and now
suppose that he tears himself out of this dead insensibility, and performs the action
without any inclination to it, but simply from duty, then first has his action its genuine
moral worth. Further still; if nature has put little sympathy in the heart of this or that
man; if he, supposed to be an upright man, is by temperament cold and indifferent
to the sufferings of others, perhaps because in respect of his own he is provided
with the special gift of patience and fortitude and supposes, or even requires, that
others should have the same—and such a man would certainly not be the meanest
product of nature—but if nature had not specially framed him for a philanthropist,
would he not still find in himself a source from whence to give himself a far higher
worth than that of a good-natured temperament could be? Unquestionably. It is just
in this that the moral worth of the character is brought out which is incomparably
the highest of all, namely, that he is beneficent, not from inclination, but from duty.

To secure one's own happiness is a duty, at least indirectly; for discontent with
one's condition, under a pressure of many anxieties and amidst unsatisfied wants,
might easily become a great temptation to transgression of duty. But here again, without looking to duty, all men have already the strongest and most intimate inclination
to happiness, because it is just in this idea that all inclinations are combined in one
total. But the precept of happiness is often of such a sort that it greatly interferes with
some inclinations, and yet a man cannot form any definite and certain conception of
the sum of satisfaction of all of them which is called happiness. It is not then to be
wondered at that a single inclination, definite both as to what it promises and as to
the time within which it can be gratified, is often able to overcome such a fluctuating
idea, and that a gouty patient, for instance, can choose to enjoy what he likes, and
to suffer what he may, since, according to his calculation, on this occasion at least,
he has not sacrificed the enjoyment of the present moment to a possibly mistaken
expectation of a happiness which is supposed to be found in health. But even in this
case, if the general desire for happiness did not influence his will, and supposing that
in his particular case health was not a necessary element in this calculation, there
yet remains in this, as in all other cases, this law, namely, that he should promote
his happiness not from inclination but from duty, and by this would his conduct
first acquire true moral worth.

It is in this manner, undoubtedly, that we are to understand those passages of
Scripture also in which we are commanded to love our neighbour, even our enemy.
For love, as an affection, cannot be commanded, but beneficence for duty's sake may;

even though we are not impelled to it by any inclination—nay, are even repelled by a natural and unconquerable aversion. This is practical love and not pathological—a love which is seated in the will, and not in the propensions of sense—in principles of action and not of tender sympathy; and it is this love alone which can be commanded.

The second proposition is: That an action done from duty derives its moral worth, not from the purpose which is to be attained by it, but from the maxim by which it is determined, and therefore does not depend on the realization of the object of the action, but merely on the principle of volition by which the action has taken place, without regard to any object of desire. It is clear from what precedes that the purposes which we may have in view in our actions, or their effects regarded as ends and springs of the will, cannot give to actions any unconditional or moral worth. In what, then, can their worth lie, if it is not to consist in the will and in reference to its expected effect? It cannot lie anywhere but in the principle of the will without regard to the ends which can be attained by the action. For the will stands between its a priori principle, which is formal, and its a posteriori spring, which is material, as between two roads, and as it must be determined by something, it follows that it must be determined by the formal principle of volition when an action is done from duty, in which case every material principle has been withdrawn from it.

The third proposition, which is a consequence of the two preceding, I would express thus: Duty is the necessity of acting from respect for the law. I may have inclination for an object as the effect of my proposed action, but I cannot have respect for it, just for this reason, that it is an effect and not an energy of will. Similarly I cannot have respect for inclination, whether my own or another's; I can at most, if my own, approve it; if another's, sometimes even love it; i.e., look on it as favourable to my own interest. It is only what is connected with my will as a principle, by no means as an effect—what does not subserve my inclination, but overpowers it, or at least in case of choice excludes it from its calculation—in other words, simply the law of itself, which can be an object of respect, and hence a command. Now an action done from duty must wholly exclude the influence of inclination and with it every object of the will, *so* that nothing remains which can determine the will except objectively the law, and subjectively pure respect for this practical law, and consequently the maxim[1] that I should follow this law even to the thwarting of all my inclinations.

Thus the moral worth of an action does not lie in the effect expected from it, nor in any principle of action which requires to borrow its motive from this expected effect. For all these effects—agreeableness of one's condition and even the promotion of the happiness of others—could have been also brought about by other causes, so

---

1   A maxim is the subjective principle of volition. The objective principle (i.e., that which would also serve subjectively as a practical principle to all rational beings if reason had *full* power over the faculty of desire) is the practical law.

that for this there would have been no need of the will of a rational being; whereas it is in this alone that the supreme and unconditional good can be found. The pre-eminent good which we call moral can therefore consist in nothing else than the conception of law in itself, which certainly is only possible in a rational being, in so far as this conception, and not the expected effect, determines the will. This is a good which is already present in the person who acts accordingly, and we have not to wait for it to appear first in the result.

But what sort of law can that be, the conception of which must determine the will, even without paying any regard to the effect expected from it, in order that this will may be called good absolutely and without qualification? As I have deprived the will of every impulse which could arise to it from obedience to any law, there remains nothing but the universal conformity of its actions to law in general, which alone is to serve the will as a principle, i.e., I am never to act otherwise than so that I could also will that my maxim should become a universal law. Here, now, it is the simple conformity to law in general, without assuming any particular law applicable to certain actions, that serves the will as its principle and must so serve it, if duty is not to be a vain delusion and a chimerical notion. The common reason of men in its practical judgements perfectly coincides with this and always has in view the principle here suggested. Let the question be, for example: May I when in distress make a promise with the intention not to keep it? I readily distinguish here between the two significations which the question may have: Whether it is prudent, or whether it is right, to make a false promise? The former may undoubtedly often be the case. I see clearly indeed that it is not enough to extricate myself from a present difficulty by means of this subterfuge, but it must be well considered whether there may not hereafter spring from this lie much greater inconvenience than that from which I now free myself, and as, with all my supposed cunning, the consequences cannot be so easily foreseen but that credit once lost may be much more injurious to me than any mischief which I seek to avoid at present, it should be considered whether it would not be more prudent to act herein according to a universal maxim and to make it a habit to promise nothing except with the intention of keeping it. But it is soon clear to me that such a maxim will still only be based on the fear of consequences. Now it is a wholly different thing to be truthful from duty and to be *so* from apprehension of injurious consequences. In the first case, the very notion of the action already implies a law for me; in the second case, I must first look about elsewhere to see what results may be combined with it which would affect myself. For to deviate from the principle of duty is beyond all doubt wicked; but to be unfaithful to my maxim of prudence may often be very advantageous to me, although to abide by it is certainly safer. The shortest way, however, and an unerring one, to discover the answer to this question whether a lying promise is consistent with duty, is to ask myself, "Should

I be content that my maxim (to extricate myself from difficulty by a false promise) should hold good as a universal law, for myself as well as for others?" and should I be able to say to myself, "Every one may make a deceitful promise when he finds himself in a difficulty from which he cannot otherwise extricate himself?" Then I presently become aware that while I can will the lie, I can by no means will that lying should be a universal law. For with such a law there would be no promises at all, since it would be in vain to allege my intention in regard to my future actions to those who would not believe this allegation, or if they over hastily did so would pay me back in my own coin. Hence my maxim, as soon as it should be made a universal law, would necessarily destroy itself.

I do not, therefore, need any far-reaching penetration to discern what I have to do in order that my will may be morally good. Inexperienced in the course of the world, incapable of being prepared for all its contingencies, I only ask myself: Canst thou also will that thy maxim should be a universal law? If not, then it must be rejected, and that not because of a disadvantage accruing from it to myself or even to others, but because it cannot enter as a principle into a possible universal legislation, and reason extorts from me immediate respect for such legislation. I do not indeed as yet discern on what this respect is based (this the philosopher may inquire), but at least I understand this, that it is an estimation of the worth which far outweighs all worth of what is recommended by inclination, and that the necessity of acting from pure respect for the practical law is what constitutes duty, to which every other motive must give place, because it is the condition of a will being good in itself, and the worth of such a will is above everything.

Thus, then, without quitting the moral knowledge of common human reason, we have arrived at its principle. And although, no doubt, common men do not conceive it in such an abstract and universal form, yet they always have it really before their eyes and use it as the standard of their decision. Here it would be easy to show how, with this compass in hand, men are well able to distinguish, in every case that occurs, what is good, what bad, conformably to duty or inconsistent with it, if, without in the least teaching them anything new, we only, like Socrates, direct their attention to the principle they themselves employ; and that, therefore, we do not need science and philosophy to know what we should do to be honest and good, yea, even wise and virtuous. Indeed we might well have conjectured beforehand that the knowledge of what every man is bound to do, and therefore also to know, would be within the reach of every man, even the commonest. Here we cannot forbear admiration when we see how great an advantage the practical judgement has over the theoretical in the common understanding of men. In the latter, if common reason ventures to depart from the laws of experience and from the perceptions of the senses, it falls into mere inconceivabilities and self-contradictions, at least into a chaos of uncertainty, obscurity, and instability. But in the practical sphere it is just when the common understanding excludes all sensible springs from practical laws that its power of judgement begins to show itself to advantage. It then becomes even subtle, whether it be that it chicanes with its own conscience or with other claims respecting what is to be called right, or whether it desires for its own instruction to determine honestly the worth of actions; and, in the latter case, it may even have as good a hope of hitting the mark as any philosopher whatever can promise himself. Nay, it is almost more sure of doing so, because the philosopher cannot have any other principle, while he may easily perplex his judgement by a multitude of considerations foreign to the matter, and so turn aside from the right way. Would it not therefore be wiser in moral concerns to acquiesce in the judgement of common reason, or at most only to call in philosophy for the purpose of rendering the system of morals more complete and intelligible, and its rules more convenient for use (especially for disputation), but not so as to draw off the common understanding from its happy simplicity, or to bring it by means of philosophy into a new path of inquiry and instruction?

***

Now all imperatives command either hypothetically or categorically. The former represent the practical necessity of a possible action as means to something else that is willed (or at least which one might possibly will). The categorical imperative would be that which represented an action as necessary of itself without reference to another end, i.e., as objectively necessary.

Since every practical law represents a possible action as good and, on this account, for a subject who is practically determinable by reason, necessary, all imperatives are formulae determining an action which is necessary according to the principle of a will good in some respects. If now the action is good only as a means to something else, then the imperative is hypothetical; if it is conceived as good in itself and consequently as being necessarily the principle of a will which of itself conforms to reason, then it is categorical.

Thus the imperative declares what action possible by me would be good and presents the practical rule in relation to a will which does not forthwith perform an action simply because it is good, whether because the subject does not always know that it is good, or because, even if it know this, yet its maxims might be opposed to the objective principles of practical reason.

Accordingly the hypothetical imperative only says that the action is good for some purpose, possible or actual. In the first case it is a problematical, in the second an assertorial practical principle. The categorical imperative which declares an action to be objectively necessary in itself without reference to any purpose, i.e., without any other end, is valid as an apodeictic (practical) principle.

* * *

Finally, there is an imperative which commands a certain conduct immediately, without having as its condition any other purpose to be attained by it. This imperative is categorical. It concerns not the matter of the action, or its intended result, but its form and the principle of which it is itself a result; and what is essentially good in it consists in the mental disposition, let the consequence be what it may. This imperative may be called that of morality.

There is a marked distinction also between the volitions on these three sorts of principles in the dissimilarity of the obligation of the will. In order to mark this difference more clearly, I think they would be most suitably named in their order if we said they are either rules of skill, or counsels of prudence, or commands (laws) of morality. For it is law only that involves the conception of an unconditional and objective necessity, which is consequently universally valid; and commands are laws which must be obeyed, that is, must be followed, even in opposition to inclination. Counsels, indeed, involve necessity, but one which can only hold under a contingent subjective condition, viz., they depend on whether this or that man reckons this or that as part of his happiness; the categorical imperative, on the contrary, is not limited by any condition, and as being absolutely, although practically, necessary, may be quite properly called a command. We might also call the first kind of imperatives technical (belonging to art), the second pragmatic (to welfare), the third moral (belonging to free conduct generally, that is, to morals).

* * *

There is therefore but one categorical imperative, namely, this: Act only on that maxim whereby thou canst at the same time will that it should become a universal law.

Now if all imperatives of duty can be deduced from this one imperative as from their principle, then, although it should remain undecided what is called duty is not merely a vain notion, yet at least we shall be able to show what we understand by it and what this notion means.

Since the universality of the law according to which effects are produced constitutes what is properly called nature in the most general sense (as to form), that is the existence of things so far as it is determined by general laws, the imperative of duty may be expressed thus: Act as if the maxim of thy action were to become by thy will a universal law of nature.

We will now enumerate a few duties, adopting the usual division of them into duties to ourselves and ourselves and to others, and into perfect and imperfect duties.

* * *

1. A man reduced to despair by a series of misfortunes feels wearied of life, but is still so far in possession of his reason that he can ask himself whether it would not be contrary to his duty to himself to take his own life. Now he inquires whether the maxim of his action could become a universal law of nature. His maxim is: "From self-love I adopt it as a principle to shorten my life when its longer duration is likely to bring more evil than satisfaction." It is asked then simply whether this principle founded on self-love can become a universal law of nature. Now we see at once that a system of nature of which it should be a law to destroy life by means of the very feeling whose special nature it is to impel to the improvement of life would contradict itself and, therefore, could not exist as a system of nature; hence that maxim cannot possibly exist as a universal law of nature and, consequently, would be wholly inconsistent with the supreme principle of all duty.

2. Another finds himself forced by necessity to borrow money. He knows that he will not be able to repay it, but sees also that nothing will be lent to him unless he promises stoutly to repay it in a definite time. He desires to make this promise, but he has still so much conscience as to ask himself: "Is it not unlawful and inconsistent with duty to get out of a difficulty in this way?" Suppose however that he resolves to do so: then the maxim of his action would be expressed thus: "When I think myself in want of money, I will borrow money and promise to repay it, although I know that I never can do so." Now this principle of self-love or of one's own advantage may perhaps be consistent with my whole future welfare; but the question now is, "Is it right?" I change then the suggestion of self-love into a universal law, and state the question thus: "How would it be if my maxim were a universal law?" Then I see at once that it could never hold as a universal law of nature, but would necessarily contradict itself. For supposing it to be a universal law that everyone when he thinks himself in a difficulty should be able to promise whatever he pleases, with the purpose of not keeping his promise, the promise itself would become impossible, as well as the end that one might have in view in it, since no one would consider that anything was promised to him, but would ridicule all such statements as vain pretences.

3. A third finds in himself a talent which with the help of some culture might make him a useful man in many respects. But he finds himself in comfortable circumstances and prefers to indulge in pleasure rather than to take pains in enlarging and improving his happy natural capacities. He asks, however, whether his maxim of neglect of his natural gifts, besides agreeing with his inclination to indulgence, agrees also with what is called duty. He sees then that a system of nature could indeed subsist with such a universal law although men (like the South Sea islanders) should let their talents rest and resolve to devote their lives merely to idleness, amusement, and propagation of their species—in a word, to enjoyment; but he cannot possibly will that this should be a universal law of nature, or be implanted in us as such by a natural instinct. For, as a rational being, he necessarily wills that his faculties be developed, since they serve him and have been given him, for all kinds of possible purposes.

4. A fourth, who is in prosperity, while he sees that others have to contend with great wretchedness and that he could help them, thinks: "What concern is it of mine? Let everyone be as happy as Heaven pleases, or as he can make himself; I will take nothing from him nor even envy him, only I do not wish to contribute anything to his welfare or to his assistance in distress!" Now no doubt if such a mode of thinking were a universal law, the human race might very well subsist and doubtless even better than in a state in which everyone talks of sympathy and good-will, or even takes care occasionally to put it into practice, but, on the other side, also cheats when he can, betrays the rights of men, or otherwise violates them. But although it is possible that a universal law of nature might exist in accordance with that maxim, it is impossible to will that such a principle should have the universal validity of a law of nature. For a will which resolved this would contradict itself, inasmuch as many cases might occur in which one would have need of the love and sympathy of others, and in which, by such a law of nature, sprung from his own will, he would deprive himself of all hope of the aid he desires.

These are a few of the many actual duties, or at least what we regard as such, which obviously fall into two classes on the one principle that we have laid down. We must be able to will that a maxim of our action should be a universal law. This is the canon of the moral appreciation of the action generally. Some actions are of such a character that their maxim cannot without contradiction be even conceived as a universal law of nature, far from it being possible that we should will that it should be so. In others this intrinsic impossibility is not found, but still it is impossible to will that their maxim should be raised to the universality of a law of nature, since such a will would contradict itself. It is easily seen that the former violate strict or rigorous (inflexible) duty; the latter only laxer (meritorious) duty. Thus it has been completely shown how all duties depend as regards the nature of the obligation (not the object of the action) on the same principle.

* * *

Now I say: man and generally any rational being exists as an end in himself, not merely as a means to be arbitrarily used by this or that will, but in all his actions, whether they concern himself or other rational beings, must be always regarded at the same time as an end. All objects of the inclinations have only a conditional worth, for if the inclinations and the wants founded on them did not exist, then their object would be without value. But the inclinations, themselves being sources of want, are so far from having an absolute worth for which they should be desired that on the contrary it must be the universal wish of every rational being to be wholly free from them. Thus the worth of any object which is to be acquired by our action is always conditional. Beings whose existence depends not on our will but on nature's, have nevertheless, if they are irrational beings, only a relative value as means, and are therefore called things; rational beings, on the contrary, are called persons, because their very nature points them out as ends in themselves, that is as something which must not be used merely as means, and so far therefore restricts freedom of action (and is an object of respect). These, therefore, are not merely subjective ends whose existence has a worth for us as an effect of our action, but objective ends, that is, things whose existence is an end in itself; an end moreover for which no other can be substituted, which they should subserve merely as means, for otherwise nothing whatever would possess absolute worth; but if all worth were conditioned and therefore contingent, then there would be no supreme practical principle of reason whatever.

If then there is a supreme practical principle or, in respect of the human will, a categorical imperative, it must be one which, being drawn from the conception of that which is necessarily an end for everyone because it is an end in itself, constitutes an objective principle of will, and can therefore serve as a universal practical law. The foundation of this principle is: rational nature exists as an end in itself. Man necessarily conceives his own existence as being so; so far then this is a subjective principle of human actions. But every other rational being regards its existence similarly, just on the same rational principle that holds for me:[2] so that it is at the same time an objective principle, from which as a supreme practical law all laws of the will must be capable of being deduced. Accordingly the practical imperative will be as follows: So act as to treat humanity, whether in thine own person or in that of any other, in every case as an end withal, never as means only. We will now inquire whether this can be practically carried out.

To abide by the previous examples:

Firstly, under the head of necessary duty to oneself: He who contemplates suicide should ask himself whether his action can be consistent with the idea of humanity as an end in itself. If he destroys himself in order to escape from painful circumstances, he uses a person merely as a means to maintain a tolerable condition up to the end of life. But a man is not a thing, that is to say, something which can be used merely as means, but must in all his actions be always considered as an end in himself. I cannot, therefore, dispose in any way of a man in my own person so as to mutilate him, to damage or kill him. (It belongs to ethics proper to define this principle more precisely, so as to avoid all misunderstanding, e.g., as to the amputation of the limbs in order to preserve myself, as to exposing my life to danger with a view to preserve it, etc. This question is therefore omitted here.)

---

2   This proposition is here stated as a postulate. The ground of it will be found in the concluding section.

Secondly, as regards necessary duties, or those of strict obligation, towards others: He who is thinking of making a lying promise to others will see at once that he would be using another man merely as a means, without the latter containing at the same time the end in himself. For he whom I propose by such a promise to use for my own purposes cannot possibly assent to my mode of acting towards him and, therefore, cannot himself contain the end of this action. This violation of the principle of humanity in other men is more obvious if we take in examples of attacks on the freedom and property of others. For then it is clear that he who transgresses the rights of men intends to use the person of others merely as a means, without considering that as rational beings they ought always to be esteemed also as ends, that is, as beings who must be capable of containing in themselves the end of the very same action.[3]

Thirdly, as regards contingent (meritorious) duties to oneself: It is not enough that the action does not violate humanity in our own person as an end in itself, it must also harmonize with it. Now there are in humanity capacities of greater perfection, which belong to the end that nature has in view in regard to humanity in ourselves as the subject: to neglect these might perhaps be consistent with the maintenance of humanity as an end in itself, but not with the advancement of this end.

Fourthly, as regards meritorious duties towards others: The natural end which all men have is their own happiness. Now humanity might indeed subsist, although no one should contribute anything to the happiness of others, provided he did not intentionally withdraw anything from it; but after all this would only harmonize negatively not positively with humanity as an end in itself, if every one does not also endeavour, as far as in him lies, to forward the ends of others. For the ends of any subject which is an end in himself ought as far as possible to be my ends also, if that conception is to have its full effect with me.

This principle, that humanity and generally every rational nature is an end in itself (which is the supreme limiting condition of every man's freedom of action), is not borrowed from experience, firstly, because it is universal, applying as it does to all rational beings whatever, and experience is not capable of determining anything about them; secondly, because it does not present humanity as an end to men (subjectively), that is as an object which men do of themselves actually adopt as an end; but as an objective end, which must as a law constitute the supreme limiting condition of all our subjective ends, let them be what we will; it must therefore spring from pure reason. In fact the objective principle of all practical legislation lies (according

---

3   Let it not be thought that the common "quod tibi non visfieri, etc." could serve here as the rule or principle. For it is only a deduction from the former, though with several limitations; it cannot be a universal law, for it does not contain the principle of duties to oneself, nor of the duties of benevolence to others (for many a one would gladly consent that others should not benefit him, provided only that he might be excused from showing benevolence to them), nor finally that of duties of strict obligation to one another, for on this principle the criminal might argue against the judge who punishes him, and so on.

to the first principle) in the rule and its form of universality which makes it capable of being a law (say, e.g., a law of nature); but the subjective principle is in the end; now by the second principle the subject of all ends is each rational being, inasmuch as it is an end in itself. Hence follows the third practical principle of the will, which is the ultimate condition of its harmony with universal practical reason, viz.: the idea of the will of every rational being as a universally legislative will.

On this principle all maxims are rejected which are inconsistent with the will being itself universal legislator. Thus the will is not subject simply to the law, but so subject that it must be regarded as itself giving the law and, on this ground only, subject to the law (of which it can regard itself as the author).

Questions

1. Kant believes that all moral rules or laws are absolute. Can you think of an example where two absolute moral rules might conflict? How would Kant determine what one's moral duty is in such situations?

2. Kant's third formulation of the Categorical Imperative holds that one should "Act in such a way that you treat humanity, whether in your own person or in the person of any other, never merely as a means to an end, but always at the same time as an end." Since businesses operate on a profit (as opposed to non-profit) model, even if workers are compensated for their work, is the fact that they are not paid the full value of their labor (since profit is what a business has after it pays its employees) a violation of the third formulation? Are workers being treated as a means to an end? Why or why not?

3. Kant's theory is based on the idea that only rational agents are worthy of moral respect. Similarly, only rational agents can be said to have moral obligations. Is a Kantian approach to ethics compatible with the idea of "corporate personhood"?

Further Reading

Altman, Matthew C. "The Decomposition of the Corporate Body: What Kant Cannot Contribute to Business Ethics." *Journal of Business Ethics*, vol. 74, issue 3, Sept. 2007, pp. 253–66.

Bowie, Norman E. *Business Ethics: A Kantian Perspective.* New York: Cambridge University Press, 1999.

Kant, Immanuel. *Kant: Groundwork of the Metaphysics of Morals* (Cambridge Texts in the History of Philosophy). 2nd ed. Trans. Mary Gregor and Jens Timmermann. Intro. Christine M. Korsgaard. New York: Cambridge University Press, 2012.

L'Etang, Jacquie. "A Kantian Approach to Codes of Ethics." *Journal of Business Ethics,* vol. 11, issue 10, Oct. 1992, pp. 737–44.

3.

CONTRACTARIANISM

FROM *LEVIATHAN* (1651)

THOMAS HOBBES

About This Reading

In many ways, contractual approaches to ethics combine aspects of both consequentialist and deontological thinking. Contractarians hold that morality should be viewed as if it were the result of a contract between individuals. For some contractarians, these agreements are and should be actual agreements between individuals. For others, the contract is hypothetical, that is, it is used to help us imagine what contracting parties would agree to if they were perfectly rational, or if they were placed in some idealized negotiating position. Here, we will look at representatives from each of these approaches.

Mutual Self-Interest

One of the most famous contractarian approaches can be found in Thomas Hobbes's *Leviathan*. In *Leviathan* (1651), Hobbes asks us to imagine what it was like before people had established governments, laws, or morality. He refers to this condition as the "state of nature." In the state of nature, all people are free to do whatever they want without any constraints—moral or otherwise. According to Hobbes, this is (or was) the natural state of people before the establishment of civil society.

To some, the state of nature may not seem to be a bad thing. After all, it might be nice not to be constrained by government. No laws or taxes; no zoning boards or planning commissions; and from a business perspective, the freedom to contract and exchange with others without interference. But for Hobbes, the state of nature was anything but idyllic. Rather than living in harmony with one another, the state of nature is characterized as a perpetual state of war of

---

all against all. This conflict is caused by our competition for scarce resources, distrust of others, and our desire for glory. This constant state of war makes the benefits of social cooperation impossible. According to Hobbes, the state of nature is described as lacking "culture, navigation, commodious building, arts, letters, [and living with a] constant fear of violent death." In short, says Hobbes, the state of nature is "solitary, poor, nasty, brutish, and short."

It is the very nastiness of the state of nature that leads people to leave the state of nature. No one wants to live in fear of constant death, and so the same psychological forces that drive us to compete with one another also compel us to seek peace. Our desire to preserve our life, along with a desire for comfort, motivates us to enter into mutually beneficial agreements with others. But mere agreement with others is not enough. Since I cannot be certain that you will keep your agreements, and you cannot be sure I will keep mine, we require an overarching authority to enforce our agreements. Although Hobbes advocated the establishment of an absolute sovereign, contemporary theorists have argued that the contract could also justify the establishment of a democratic state.

Hobbes's social contract was based on the explicit agreement of those that would be bound by its terms. Contemporary social contract theorists who follow the Hobbesian tradition do not rely on the agreement of actual people; rather they argue that a social contract is justified if it *would* be agreed to by people that were perfectly rational and motivated by self-interest. This of course raises the question of what is meant by "rational." The traditional notion of rationality is generally tied to maximizing self-interest. The rational course of action is the one that leads me to be better off. This differs from the utilitarian approach in that it does not require that one take into account the well-being of others. I may take others into account, but generally I do so because it benefits me to do so. For example, I may agree not to harm you—not because I care about your well-being, or think you have a right not to be harmed gratuitously—but because that is the only way you will agree not to harm me. In other words, it is in my self-interest to make such an agreement.

In many respects, this form of the social contract resonates with business. For economists such as Milton Friedman (who will be discussed later in this book), business really is about self-interested agreements. The pursuit of profit (the "interest" of business) is best served by the minimal regulation of business by society. But, there is good reason to question whether self-interested agreements, either in business or society in general, can provide an adequate foundation for morality.

Non-Self-Interested Accounts

While the Hobbesian contract approach relies on self-interested agreements (whether actual or ideal), other contractarians have focused more on the contract as a kind of procedure for determining what rule or principles people ought to adopt. One of the most prominent of these approaches is that of John Rawls in *A Theory of Justice*.

The Rawlsian approach was originally intended as a way of deriving principles of distributive justice, that is, as a way of deciding how things such as rights, duties, and economic goods should be distributed by society. Like Hobbesian contractarians, Rawls's approach begins by asking what morality people would choose were they setting up society from a state of nature or "original position" (to use Rawls's term). Unlike Hobbesian approaches, Rawls does not characterize his original position as made up of people like you and I. People can be radically different in their talents, abilities, and social starting points. Placing very different people around a bargaining table would likely lead to unfair agreements. Some people would likely be better bargainers than others, while others who come to the table with more goods might be less likely to agree to give up any of what they have.

To correct what he sees as the problem with actual agreements, Rawls asks us to think of the original position as a hypothetical situation consisting of people who have limited information about themselves. This "veil of ignorance" includes a lack of knowledge about things such as the individual's position or social status, intelligence, strength, religious convictions, or conception of the good. Rawls then asks us to imagine what kinds of principles of justice such people would create. For example, suppose our hypothetical contractors are trying to determine how wages should be distributed. One of the contractors offers the following: "Men should be paid more than women for the same work." Would the contracting parties agree to this? Obviously, they would not, since none of them would know whether they were male or female. In other words, given their ignorance of their particular characteristics, the people in the original position would want to make sure that once the veil of ignorance was lifted (which would happen once they were done formulating the principles) they would not end up too badly off. In other words, they would want to maximize what they would get, even if they ended up in the worst off position in the society. Rawls refers to this type of reasoning as *maximin* reasoning.

Rawls's contract theory attempts to remove our individual biases from moral reasoning. In this respect, the original position along with the veil of ignorance is a helpful way of thinking about moral issues. On the other hand, critics of Rawls's approach have argued that as a means of justification, the decisions that idealized hypothetical individuals make carry little weight for real people.

Part I: Of Man

Chapter XIII: Of the Natural Condition of Mankind as Concerning Their Felicity and Misery

1. Nature hath made men so equal in the faculties of body and mind, as that, though there be found one man sometimes manifestly stronger in body or of quicker mind than another, yet when all is reckoned together, the difference between man and man is not so considerable as that one man can thereupon claim to himself any benefit to which another may not pretend as well as he. For as to the strength of body, the weakest has strength enough to kill the strongest, either by secret machination or by confederacy with others that are in the same danger with himself.

2. And as to the faculties of the mind, setting aside the arts grounded upon words, and especially that skill of proceeding upon general and infallible rules, called science, which very few have and but in few things, as being not a native faculty born with us, nor attained, as prudence, while we look after somewhat else, I find yet a greater equality amongst men than that of strength. For prudence is but experience, which equal time equally bestows on all men in those things they equally apply themselves unto. That which may perhaps make such equality incredible is but a vain conceit of one's own wisdom, which almost all men think they have in a greater degree than the vulgar, that is, than all men but themselves and a few others, whom by fame or for concurring with themselves, they approve. For such is the nature of men that howsoever they may acknowledge many others to be more witty or more eloquent or more learned, they will hardly believe there be many so wise as themselves; for they see their own wit at hand and other men's at a distance. But this proveth rather that men are in that point equal, than unequal. For there is not ordinarily a greater sign of the equal distribution of anything than that every man is contented with his share.

3. From this equality of ability ariseth equality of hope in the attaining of our ends. And therefore if any two men desire the same thing, which nevertheless they cannot both enjoy, they become enemies; and in the way to their end (which is principally their own conservation, and sometimes their delectation only) endeavour to destroy or subdue one another. And from hence it comes to pass that where an invader hath no more to fear than another man's single power, if one plant, sow, build, or possess a convenient seat, others may probably be expected to come prepared with forces united to dispossess and deprive him, not only of the fruit of his labour, but also of his life or liberty. And the invader again is in the like danger of another.

4. And from this diffidence of one another, there is no way for any man to secure himself so reasonable as [by] anticipation, that is, by force or wiles to master the persons of all men he can so long till he see no other power great enough to endanger him; and this is no more than his own conservation requireth, and is generally allowed. Also, because there be some that, taking pleasure in contemplating their own power in the acts of conquest, which they pursue farther than their security requires; if others that otherwise would be glad to be at ease within modest bounds should not by invasion increase their power, [then] they would not be able, long time, by standing only on their defence, to subsist. And by consequence, such augmentation of dominion over men being necessary to a man's conservation, it ought to be allowed him.

5. Again, men have no pleasure (but on the contrary a great deal of grief) in keeping company where there is no power able to overawe them all. For every man looketh that his companion should value him at the same rate he sets upon himself, and upon all signs of contempt or undervaluing naturally endeavours, as far as he dares (which amongst them that have no common power to keep them in quiet is far enough to make them destroy each other), to extort a greater value from his contemners, by damage; and from others, by the example.

6. So that in the nature of man, we find three principal causes of quarrel. First, competition; secondly, diffidence; thirdly, glory.

7. The first maketh men invade for gain; the second, for safety; and the third, for reputation. The first use violence to make themselves masters of other men's persons, wives, children, and cattle; the second, to defend them; the third, for trifles, as a word, a smile, a different opinion, and any other sign of undervalue, either direct in their persons or by reflection in their kindred, their friends, their nation, their profession, or their name.

8. Hereby it is manifest that during the time men live without a common power to keep them all in awe, they are in that condition which is called war; and such a war as is of every man against every man. For war consisteth not in battle only, or the act of fighting, but in a tract of time, wherein the will to contend by battle is sufficiently known; and therefore the notion of *time* is to be considered in the nature of war, as it is in the nature of weather. For as the nature of foul weather lieth not in a shower or two of rain, but in an inclination thereto of many days together, so the nature of war consisteth not in actual fighting, but in the known disposition thereto during all the time there is no assurance to the contrary. All other time is peace.

9. Whatsoever therefore is consequent to a time of war, where every man is enemy to every man, the same is consequent to the time wherein men live without other security than what their own strength and their own invention shall furnish them withal. In such condition there is no place for industry, because the fruit thereof is uncertain; and consequently no culture of the earth; no navigation, nor use of the commodities that may be imported by sea; no commodious building; no instruments of moving and removing such things as require much force; no knowledge of the face of the earth; no account of time; no arts; no letters; no society; and which is worst of all, continual fear, and danger of violent death; and the life of man, solitary, poor, nasty, brutish, and short.

10. It may seem strange to some man that has not well weighed these things that nature should thus dissociate and render men apt to invade and destroy one another; and he may therefore, not trusting to this inference, made from the passions, desire perhaps to have the same confirmed by experience. Let him therefore consider with himself; when taking a journey, he arms himself and seeks to go well accompanied; when going to sleep, he locks his doors; when even in his house he locks his chests; and this when he knows there be laws and public officers, armed to revenge all injuries shall be done him; what opinion he has of his fellow subjects, when he rides armed; of his fellow citizens, when he locks his doors; and of his children, and servants, when he locks his chests. Does he not there as much accuse mankind by his actions as I do by my words? But neither of us accuse man's nature in it. The desires and other passions of man are in themselves no sin. No more are the actions that proceed from those passions till they know a law that forbids them; which, till laws be made, they cannot know; nor can any law be made till they have agreed upon the person that shall make it.

11. It may peradventure be thought there was never such a time nor condition of war as this; and I believe it was never generally so, over all the world; but there are many places where they live so now. For the savage people in many places of America, except the government of small families, the concord whereof dependeth on natural lust, have no government at all, and live at this day in that brutish manner, as I said before. Howsoever, it may be perceived what manner of life there would be, where there were no common power to fear, by the manner of life which men that have formerly lived under a peaceful government use to degenerate into in a civil war.

12. But though there had never been any time wherein particular men were in a condition of war one against another; yet in all times kings and persons of sovereign authority, because of their independency, are in continual jealousies, and in the state and posture of gladiators, having their weapons pointing and their eyes fixed on one another, that is, their forts, garrisons, and guns upon the frontiers of their kingdoms, and continual spies upon their neighbours, which is a posture of war. But because they uphold thereby the industry of their subjects, there does not follow from it that misery which accompanies the liberty of particular men.

13. To this war of every man against every man, this also is consequent; that nothing can be unjust. The notions of right and wrong, justice and injustice, have there no place. Where there is no common power, there is no law; where no law, no injustice. Force and fraud are in war the two cardinal virtues. Justice and injustice are none of the faculties neither of the body nor mind. If they were, they might be in a man that were alone in the world, as well as his senses and passions. They are qualities that relate to men in society, not in solitude. It is consequent also to the same condition that there be no propriety, no dominion, no *mine* and *thine* distinct; but only that to be every man's that he can get, and for so long as he can keep it. And thus much for the ill condition which man by mere nature is actually placed in; though with a possibility to come out of it, consisting partly in the passions, partly in his reason.

14. The passions that incline men to peace are fear of death, desire of such things as are necessary to commodious living, and a hope by their industry to obtain them. And reason suggesteth convenient articles of peace upon which men may be drawn to agreement. These articles are they which otherwise are called the laws of nature, whereof I shall speak more particularly in the two following chapters.

Chapter XIV: Of the First and Second Natural Laws, and of Contracts

1. The right of nature, which writers commonly call *jus naturale*, is the liberty each man hath to use his own power as he will himself for the preservation of his own nature; that is to say, of his own life; and consequently, of doing anything which, in his own judgement and reason, he shall conceive to be the aptest means thereunto.

2. By liberty is understood, according to the proper signification of the word, the absence of external impediments; which impediments may oft take away part of a man's power to do what he would, but cannot hinder him from using the power left him according as his judgement and reason shall dictate to him.

3. A Law of Nature (*lex naturalis*) is a precept or general rule, found out by reason, by which a man is forbidden to do that which is destructive of his life, or taketh away the means of preserving the same, and to omit that by which he thinketh it may be best preserved. For though they that speak of this subject use to confound *jus* and *lex*, *right* and *law*; yet they ought to be distinguished, because right consisteth in liberty to do or to forbear; whereas law determineth and bindeth to one of them; so that law and right differ as much as obligation and liberty, which in one and the same matter are inconsistent.

4. And because the condition of man (as hath been declared in the precedent chapter) is a condition of war of every one against every one, in which case every one is governed by his own reason, and there is nothing he can make use of that may not be a help unto him in preserving his life against his enemies; it followeth that in such a condition every man has a right to every thing, even to one another's body. And therefore, as long as this natural right of every man to every thing endureth, there can be no security to any man, how strong or wise soever he be, of living out the time which nature ordinarily alloweth men to live. And consequently it is a precept, or general rule of reason *that every man ought to endeavour peace, as far as he has hope of obtaining it; and when he cannot obtain it, that he may seek and use all helps and advantages of war.* The first branch of which rule containeth the first and fundamental law of nature, which is *to seek peace and follow it.* The second, the sum of the right of nature, which is *by all means we can to defend ourselves.*

5. From this fundamental law of nature, by which men are commanded to endeavour peace, is derived this second law: *that a man be willing, when others are so too, as far forth as for peace and defence of himself he shall think it necessary, to lay down this right to all things; and be contented with so much liberty against other men as he would allow other men against himself.* For as long as every man holdeth this right of doing anything he liketh, so long are all men in the condition of war. But if other men will not lay down their right, as well as he, then there is no reason for anyone to divest himself of his, for that were to expose himself to prey, which no man is bound to, rather than to dispose himself to peace. This is that law of the gospel: *Whatsoever you require that others should do to you, that do ye to them.* And that law of all men, *quod tibi fieri non vis, alteri ne feceris* [What you do not want done to you, do not do to another].

6. To *lay down* a man's *right* to anything is to *divest* himself of the *liberty* of hindering another of the benefit of his own right to the same. For he that renounceth or passeth away his right giveth not to any other man a right which he had not before, because there is nothing to which every man had not right by nature, but only standeth out of his way that he may enjoy his own original right without hindrance from him, not without hindrance from another. So that the effect which redoundeth to one man by another man's defect of right is but so much diminution of impediments to the use of his own right original.

7. Right is laid aside either by simply renouncing it or by transferring it to another. By *simply* renouncing, when he cares not to whom the benefit thereof redoundeth. By transferring, when he intendeth the benefit thereof to some certain person or persons. And when a man hath in either manner abandoned or granted away his right, then is he said to be obliged or bound, not to hinder those to whom such right is granted, or abandoned, from the benefit of it; and that he *ought*, and it is duty, not to make void that voluntary act of his own; and that such hindrance is injustice and injury, as being *sine jure* [without right]; the right being before renounced or transferred. So that *injury* or *injustice*, in the controversies of the world, is somewhat like to that which in the disputations of scholars is called *absurdity*. For as it is there called an absurdity to contradict what one maintained in the beginning, so in the world it is called injustice and injury voluntarily to undo that which from the beginning he had voluntarily done. The way by which a man either simply renounceth or transferreth his right is a declaration or signification by some voluntary and sufficient sign or signs that he doth so renounce or transfer or hath so renounced or transferred the same to him that accepteth it. And these signs are either words only, or actions only; or, as it happeneth most often, both words and actions. And the same are the bonds, by which men are bound and obliged, bonds that have their strength, not from their own nature (for nothing is more easily broken than a man's word), but from fear of some evil consequence upon the rupture.

8. Whensoever a man transferreth his right, or renounceth it, it is either in consideration of some right reciprocally transferred to himself, or for some other good he hopeth for thereby. For it is a voluntary act; and of the voluntary acts of every man, the object is some *good to himself*. And therefore there be some rights which no man can be understood by any words, or other signs, to have abandoned or transferred. As first a man cannot lay down the right of resisting them that assault him by force to take away his life, because he cannot be understood to aim thereby at any good to himself. The same may be said of wounds, and chains, and imprisonment, both because there is no benefit consequent to such patience as there is to the patience of suffering another to be wounded or imprisoned, as also because a man cannot tell when he seeth men proceed against him by violence whether they intend his death or not. And lastly the motive and end for which this renouncing and transferring of right is introduced is nothing else but the security of a man's person in his life, and in the means of so preserving life as not to be weary of it. And therefore if a man by words, or other signs, seem to despoil himself of the end for which those signs were intended, he is not to be understood as if he meant it, or that it was his will, but that he was ignorant of how such words and actions were to be interpreted.

9. The mutual transferring of right is that which men call contract.

10. There is difference between transferring of right to the thing, and transferring or tradition, that is, delivery of the thing itself. For the thing may be delivered together with the translation of the right, as in buying and selling with ready money, or exchange of goods or lands; and it may be delivered some time after.

11. Again, one of the contractors may deliver the thing contracted for on his part, and leave the other to perform his part at some determinate time after, and in the meantime be trusted; and then the contract on his part is called pact or covenant; or both parts may contract now to perform hereafter, in which cases he that is to perform in time to come, being trusted, his performance is called *keeping of promise,* or faith, and the failing of performance, if it be voluntary, *violation of faith.*

12. When the transferring of right is not mutual, but one of the parties transferreth in hope to gain thereby friendship or service from another or from his friends; or in hope to gain the reputation of charity or magnanimity; or to deliver his mind from the pain of compassion; or in hope of reward in heaven; this is not contract, but gift, free gift, grace; which words signify one and the same thing.

13. Signs of contract are either *express* or *by inference.* Express are words spoken with understanding of what they signify; and such words are either of the time *present* or *past,* as, *I give, I grant, I have given, I have granted, I will that this be yours*; or of the future, as, *I will give, I will grant,* which words of the future are called promise.

14. Signs by inference are sometimes the consequence of words, sometimes the consequence of silence, sometimes the consequence of actions, sometimes the consequence of forbearing an action; and generally a sign by inference, of any contract, is whatsoever sufficiently argues the will of the contractor.

15. Words alone, if they be of the time to come, and contain a bare promise, are an insufficient sign of a free gift and therefore not obligatory. For if they be of the time to come, as, *tomorrow I will give,* they are a sign I have not given yet, and consequently that my right is not transferred, but remaineth till I transfer it by some other act. But if the words be of the time present or past, as, *I have given,* or *do give to be delivered tomorrow,* then is my tomorrow's right given away today; and that by the virtue of the words, though there were no other argument of my will. And there is a great difference in the signification of these words, *volo hoc tuum esse cras*, and *cras dabo*; that is, between *I will that this be thine tomorrow*, and, *I will give it thee tomorrow*, for the word *I will*, in the former manner of speech, signifies an act of the will present; but in the latter, it signifies a promise of an act of the will to come; and therefore the former words, being of the present, transfer a future right; the latter, that be of the future, transfer nothing. But if there be other signs of the will to transfer a right besides words, then, though the gift be free, yet may the right be understood to pass by words of the future, as [for example] if a man propound a prize to him that comes first to the end of a race, the gift is free; and though the words be of the future, yet the right passeth, for if he would not have his words so be understood, he should not have let them run.

16. In contracts the right passeth, not only where the words are of the time present or past, but also where they are of the future, because all contract is mutual translation or change of right; and therefore he that promiseth only, because he hath already received the benefit for which he promiseth, is to be understood as if he intended the right should pass; for unless he had been content to have his words so understood, the other would not have performed his part first. And for that cause, in buying and selling, and other acts of contract, a promise is equivalent to a covenant, and therefore obligatory.

17. He that performeth first in the case of a contract is said to merit that which he is to receive by the performance of the other, and he hath it as *due*. Also when a prize is propounded to many, which is to be given to him only that winneth, or money is thrown amongst many to be enjoyed by them that catch it, though this be a free gift; yet so to win or so to catch is to *merit*, and to have it as due. For the right is transferred in the propounding of the prize and in throwing down the money, though it be not determined to whom, but by the event of the contention. But there is between these two sorts of merit this difference, that in contract I merit by virtue of my own power and the contractor's need, but in this case of free gift I am enabled to merit only by the benignity [kindness] of the giver; in contract I merit at the contractor's hand that he should depart with [relinquish] his right; in this case of gift, I merit not that the giver should part with his right, but that when he has parted with it, it should be mine rather than another's. And this I think to be the meaning of that distinction of the Schools between *meritum congrui* and *meritum condigni*. For God Almighty, having promised paradise to those men (hoodwinked with carnal desires) that can walk through this world according to the precepts and limits prescribed by him, they say he that shall so walk shall merit paradise *ex congruo* [from its appropriateness]. But because no man can demand a right to it by his own righteousness, or any other power in himself, but by the free grace of God only, they say no man can merit paradise *ex* *condigno* [from being deserved]. This, I say, I think is the meaning of that distinction; but because disputers do not agree upon the signification of their own terms of art longer than it serves their turn, I will not affirm anything of their meaning; only this I say; when a gift is given indefinitely, as a prize to be contended for, he that winneth meriteth, and may claim the prize as due.

18. If a covenant be made wherein neither of the parties perform presently but trust one another, in the condition of mere nature (which is a condition of war of every man against every man), [then] upon any reasonable suspicion, it is void; but if there be a common power set over them both, with right and force sufficient to compel performance, it is not void. For he that performeth first has no assurance the other will perform after, because the bonds of words are too weak to bridle men's ambition, avarice, anger, and other passions, without the fear of some coercive power; which in the condition of mere nature [the state of nature], where all men are equal, and judges of the justness of their own fears, cannot possibly be supposed. And therefore he which performeth first does but betray himself to his enemy, contrary to the right he can never abandon of defending his life and means of living.

19. But in a civil estate, where there is a power set up to constrain those that would otherwise violate their faith, that fear is no more reasonable; and for that cause, he which by the covenant is to perform first is obliged so to do.

20. The cause of fear, which maketh such a covenant invalid, must be always something arising after the covenant made, as some new fact or other sign of the will not to perform, else it cannot make the covenant void. For that which could not hinder a man from promising ought not to be admitted as a hindrance of performing.

Questions

1. Are people really motivated by self-interest?

2. Although many modern-day economists also assume that people act in accordance with their rational self-interest, others such as behavioral economists believe our actions as less rationally motivated than we imagine. What impact would the latter view have on Hobbes's theory?

3. Is acting out of self-interest the same thing as acting morally?

4. Unlike Hobbes, John Locke believes that people in the state of nature would not be in a state of constant war. According to Locke, people would generally get along, and

would engage in social and business interactions. This alternate state of nature would only be abandoned in order to rectify certain "inconveniences," such as the lack of adequate and fair enforcement and punishment for transgressions (e.g., theft, harm, murder, etc.). Whose view of human relations is more realistic?

Further Reading

Hampton, Jean. *Hobbes and the Social Contract Tradition*. Cambridge: Cambridge University Press, 1988.

Hobbes, Thomas. *Hobbes: Leviathan*. Revised Student Edition (Cambridge Texts in the History of Political Thought). 2nd rev. ed. Cambridge: Cambridge University Press, 1996.

Gauthier, David. *Morals by Agreement*. Oxford: Oxford University Press, 1987.

Rawls, John. *Justice as Fairness: A Restatement*. Cambridge: The Belknap Press of Harvard University Press, 2001.

4.
VIRTUE ETHICS
FROM *NICOMACHEAN ETHICS* (340 BCE)

ARISTOTLE

About This Reading

Unlike other approaches to ethics that focus on what a person ought to do in a particular situation, utilitarians concern themselves with the consequences of actions, while deontologists concern themselves with the right rule to follow. On the other hand, virtue ethicists ask a different question: "How ought a person to be?" In other words, virtue ethics is concerned with the moral character of an individual. It is through the development of one's character that the virtue ethicists believe we can achieve eudaemonia. Eudaemonia is a Greek term that roughly translates as "happiness," "flourishing," or "well-being." It is through the cultivation of virtuous characteristics that we can achieve this type of life. One of the questions Aristotle attempts to answer in the *Nicomachean Ethics* (340 BCE) is how to determine which actions are virtuous. For Aristotle the virtuous act is the one that is the mean between extremes. For example, the virtue of bravery can be viewed as lying between the extremes of foolhardiness and cowardice.

Book I

1 [Ends and Goods]

Every craft and every line of inquiry, and likewise every action and decision, seems to seek some good; that is why some people were right to describe the good as what everything seeks....

7 [An Account of the Human Good]

But let us return once again to the good we are looking for, and consider just what it could be. For it is apparently one thing in one action or craft, and another thing in another; for it is one thing in medicine, another in generalship, and so on for the rest. What, then, is the good of each action or craft? Surely it is that for the sake of which the other things are done; in medicine this is health, in generalship victory, in house-building a house, in another case something else, but in every action and decision it is the end, since it is for the sake of the end that everyone does the other actions. And so, if there is some end of everything achievable in action, the good achievable in action will be this end; if there are more ends than one, [the good achievable in action] will be these ends.

Our argument, then, has followed a different route to reach the same conclusion. But we must try to make this still more perspicuous. Since there are apparently many ends, and we choose some of them (for instance, wealth, flutes, and, in general, instruments) because of something else, it is clear that not all ends are complete. But the best good is apparently something complete. And so, if only one end is complete, the good we are looking for will be this end; if more ends than one are complete, it will be the most complete end of these.

We say that an end pursued in its own right is more complete than an end pursued because of something else, and that an end that is never choiceworthy because of something else is more complete than ends that are choiceworthy both in their own right and because of this end. Hence an end that is always choiceworthy in its own right, never because of something else, is complete without qualification.

Now happiness, more than anything else, seems complete without qualification. For we always choose it because of itself, never because of something else. Honor, pleasure, understanding, and every virtue we certainly choose because of themselves, since we would choose each of them even if it had no further result; but we also choose them for the sake of happiness, supposing that through them we shall be happy. Happiness, by contrast, no one ever chooses for their sake, or for the sake of anything else at all.

The same conclusion [that happiness is complete] also appears to follow from self-sufficiency. For the complete good seems to be self-sufficient. What we count as self-sufficient is not what suffices for a solitary person by himself, living an isolated life, but what suffices also for parents, children, wife, and, in general, for friends and fellow citizens, since a human being is a naturally political [animal]. Here, however, we must impose some limit; for if we extend the good to parents' parents and children's children and to friends of friends, we shall go on without limit; but we must examine this another time.

Anyhow, we regard something as self-sufficient when all by itself it makes a life choiceworthy and lacking nothing; and that is what we think happiness does. Moreover, we think happiness is most choiceworthy of all goods, [since] it is not counted as one good among many. [If it were] counted as one among many, then, clearly, we think it would be more choiceworthy if the smallest of goods were added; for the good that is added becomes an extra quantity of goods, and the larger of two goods is always more choiceworthy.

Happiness, then, is apparently something complete and self-sufficient, since it is the end of the things achievable in action.

But presumably the remark that the best good is happiness is apparently something [generally] agreed, and we still need a clearer statement of what the best good is. Perhaps, then, we shall find this if we first grasp the function of a human being. For just as the good, i.e., [doing] well, for a flautist, a sculptor, and every craftsman, and, in general, for whatever has a function and [characteristic] action, seems to depend on its function, the same seems to be true for a human being, if a human being has some function.

Then do the carpenter and the leather worker have their functions and actions, but has a human being no function? Is he by nature idle, without any function? Or, just as eye, hand, foot, and, in general, every [bodily] part apparently has its function, may we likewise ascribe to a human being some function apart from all of these?

What, then, could this be? For living is apparently shared with plants, but what we are looking for is the special function of a human being; hence we should set aside the life of nutrition and growth. The life next in order is some sort of life of sense perception; but this too is apparently shared with horse, ox, and every animal. The remaining possibility, then, is some sort of life of action of the [part of the soul] that has reason. One [part] of it has reason as obeying reason; the other has it as itself having reason and thinking. Moreover, life is also spoken of in two ways [as capacity and as activity], and we must take [a human being's special function to be] life as activity, since this seems to be called life more fully. We have found, then, that the human function is activity of the soul in accord with reason or requiring reason.

Now we say that the function of a [kind of thing]—of a harpist, for instance—is the same in kind as the function of an excellent individual of the kind—of an excellent harpist, for instance. And the same is true without qualification in every case, if we add to the function the superior achievement in accord with the virtue; for the function of a harpist is to play the harp, and the function of a good harpist is to play it well. Moreover, we take the human function to be a certain kind of life, and take this life to be activity and actions of the soul that involve reason; hence the function of the excellent man is to do this well and finely.

Now each function is completed well by being completed in accord with the virtue proper [to that kind of thing]. And so the human good proves to be activity of the soul in accord with virtue, and indeed with the best and most complete virtue, if there are more virtues than one. Moreover, in a complete life. For one swallow does not make a spring, nor does one day; nor, similarly, does one day or a short time make us blessed and happy....

13 *[Introduction to the Virtues]*

Since happiness is a certain sort of activity of the soul in accord with complete virtue, we must examine virtue; for that will perhaps also be a way to study happiness better. Moreover, the true politician seems to have put more effort into virtue than into anything else, since he wants to make the citizens good and law-abiding. We find an example of this in the Spartan and Cretan legislators and in any others who share their concerns. Since, then, the examination of virtue is proper for political science, the inquiry clearly suits our decision at the beginning.

It is clear that the virtue we must examine is human virtue, since we are also seeking the human good and human happiness. By human virtue we mean virtue of the soul, not of the body, since we also say that happiness is an activity of the soul. If this is so, it is clear that the politician must in some way know about the soul, just as someone setting out to heal the eyes must know about the whole body as well. This is all the more true to the extent that political science is better and more honorable than medicine; even among doctors, the cultivated ones devote a lot of effort to finding out about the body. Hence the politician as well [as the student of nature] must study the soul. But he must study it for his specific purpose, far enough for his inquiry [into virtue]; for a more exact treatment would presumably take more effort than his purpose requires.

[We] have discussed the soul sufficiently [for our purposes] in [our] popular works as well [as our less popular], and we should use this discussion. We have said, for instance, that one [part] of the soul is nonrational, while one has reason. Are these distinguished as parts of a body and everything divisible into parts are? Or are they two [only] in definition, and inseparable by nature, as the convex and the concave are in a surface? It does not matter for present purposes.

Consider the nonrational [part]. One [part] of it, i.e., the cause of nutrition and growth, would seem to be plantlike and shared [with all living things]; for we can ascribe this capacity of the soul to everything that is nourished, including embryos, and the same capacity to full-grown living things, since this is more reasonable than to ascribe another capacity to them.

Hence the virtue of this capacity is apparently shared, not [specifically] human. For this part and this capacity more than others seem to be active in sleep, and here the good and the bad person are least distinct; hence happy people are said to be no better off than miserable people for half their lives. This lack of distinction is not surprising, since sleep is inactivity of the soul insofar as it is called excellent or base, unless to some small extent some movements penetrate [to our awareness], and in this way the decent person comes to have better images [in dreams] than just any random person has. Enough about this, however, and let us leave aside the nutritive part, since by nature it has no share in human virtue.

Another nature in the soul would also seem to be nonrational, though in a way it shares in reason. For in the continent and the incontinent person we praise their reason, that is to say, the [part] of the soul that has reason, because it exhorts them correctly and toward what is best; but they evidently also have in them some other [part] that is by nature something apart from reason, clashing and struggling with reason. For just as paralyzed parts of a body, when we decide to move them to the right, do the contrary and move off to the left, the same is true of the soul; for incontinent people have impulses in contrary directions. In bodies, admittedly, we see the part go astray, whereas we do not see it in the soul; nonetheless, presumably, we should suppose that the soul also has something apart from reason, countering and opposing reason. The [precise] way it is different does not matter.

However, this [part] as well [as the rational part] appears, as we said, to share in reason. At any rate, in the continent person it obeys reason; and in the temperate and the brave person it presumably listens still better to reason, since there it agrees with reason in everything.

The nonrational [part], then, as well [as the whole soul] apparently has two parts. For while the plantlike [part] shares in reason not at all, the [part] with appetites and in general desires shares in reason in a way, insofar as it both listens to reason and obeys it. This is the way in which we are said to "listen to reason" from father or friends, as opposed to the way in which [we "give the reason"] in mathematics. The nonrational part also [obeys and] is persuaded in some way by reason, as is shown by correction, and by every sort of reproof and exhortation.

If, then, we ought to say that this [part] also has reason, then the [part] that has reason, as well [as the nonrational part], will have two parts. One will have reason fully, by having it within itself; the other will have reason by listening to reason as to a father.

The division between virtues accords with this difference. For some virtues are called virtues of thought, others virtues of character; wisdom, comprehension, and prudence are called virtues of thought, generosity and temperance virtues of character. For when we speak of someone's character we do not say that he is wise or has good comprehension, but that he is gentle or temperate. And yet, we also praise the wise person for his state, and the states that are praiseworthy are the ones we call virtues.

Book II

1 [How a Virtue of Character Is Acquired]

Virtue, then, is of two sorts, virtue of thought and virtue of character. Virtue of thought arises and grows mostly from teaching; that is why it needs experience and time. Virtue of character [i.e., of *ethos*] results from habit [*ethos*]; hence its name "ethical," slightly varied from "ethos."

Hence it is also clear that none of the virtues of character arises in us naturally. For if something is by nature in one condition, habituation cannot bring it into another condition. A stone, for instance, by nature moves downwards, and habituation could not make it move upwards, not even if you threw it up ten thousand times to habituate it; nor could habituation make fire move downwards, or bring anything that is by nature in one condition into another condition. And so the virtues arise in us neither by nature nor against nature. Rather, we are by nature able to acquire them, and we are completed through habit.

Further, if something arises in us by nature, we first have the capacity for it, and later perform the activity. This is clear in the case of the senses; for we did not acquire them by frequent seeing or hearing, but we already had them when we exercised them, and *did* not get them by exercising them. Virtues, by contrast, we acquire, just as we acquire crafts, by having first activated them. For we learn a craft by producing the same product that we must produce when we have learned it; we become builders, for instance, by building, and we become harpists by playing the harp. Similarly, then, we become just by doing just actions, temperate by doing temperate actions, brave by doing brave actions.

What goes on in cities is also evidence for this. For the legislator makes the citizens good by habituating them, and this is the wish of every legislator; if he fails to do it well he misses his goal. Correct habituation distinguishes a good political system from a bad one.

Further, the sources and means that develop each virtue also ruin it, just as they do in a craft. For playing the harp makes both good and bad harpists, and it is analogous in the case of builders and all the rest; for building well makes good builders, and building badly makes bad ones. Otherwise no teacher would be needed, but everyone would be born a good or a bad craftsman.

It is the same, then, with the virtues. For what we do in our dealings with other people makes some of us just, some unjust; what we do in terrifying situations, and the habits of fear or confidence that we acquire, make some of us brave and others cowardly. The same is true of situations involving appetites and anger; for one or another sort of conduct in these situations makes some temperate and mild, others intemperate and irascible. To sum it up in a single account: a state [of character] results from [the repetition of] similar activities.

That is why we must perform the right activities, since differences in these imply corresponding differences in the states. It is not unimportant, then, to acquire one sort of habit or another, right from our youth. On the contrary, it is very important, indeed all-important.

2 [Habituation]

Our present discussion does not aim, as our others do, at study; for the purpose of our examination is not to know what virtue is, but to become good, since otherwise the inquiry would be of no benefit to us. And so we must examine the right ways of acting; for, as we have said, the actions also control the sorts of states we acquire.

First, then, actions should accord with the correct reason. That is a common [belief], and let us assume it. We shall discuss it later, and say what the correct reason is and how it is related to the other virtues.

But let us take it as agreed in advance that every account of the actions we must do has to be stated in outline, not exactly. As we also said at the beginning, the type of accounts we demand should accord with the subject matter; and questions about actions and expediency, like questions about health, have no fixed answers.

While this is the character of our general account, the account of particular cases is still more inexact. For these fall under no craft or profession; the agents themselves must consider in each case what the opportune action is, as doctors and navigators do. The account we offer, then, in our present inquiry is of this inexact sort; still, we must try to offer help.

First, then, we should observe that these sorts of states naturally tend to be ruined by excess and deficiency. We see this happen with strength and health—for we must use evident cases [such as these] as witnesses to things that are not evident. For both excessive and deficient exercise ruin bodily strength, and, similarly, too much or too little eating or drinking ruins health, whereas the proportionate amount produces, increases, and preserves it.

The same is true, then, of temperance, bravery, and the other virtues. For if, for instance, someone avoids and is afraid of everything, standing firm against nothing, he becomes cowardly; if he is afraid of nothing at all and goes to face everything, he becomes rash. Similarly, if he gratifies himself with every pleasure and abstains from none, he becomes intemperate; if he avoids them all, as boors do, he becomes some sort of insensible person. Temperance and bravery, then, are ruined by excess and deficiency, but preserved by the mean.

But these actions are not only the sources and causes both of the emergence and growth of virtues and of their ruin; the activities of the virtues [once we have acquired them] also consist in these same actions. For this is also true of more evident cases; strength, for instance, arises from eating a lot and from withstanding much hard labor, and it is the strong person who is most capable of these very actions. It is the same with the virtues. For abstaining from pleasures makes us become temperate, and once we have become temperate we are most capable of abstaining from pleasures. It is similar with bravery; habituation in disdain for frightening situations and in standing firm against them makes us become brave, and once we have become brave we shall be most capable of standing firm.

3 [The Importance of Pleasure and Pain]

But we must take someone's pleasure or pain following on his actions to be a sign of his state. For if someone who abstains from bodily pleasures enjoys the abstinence itself, he is temperate; if he is grieved by it, he is intemperate. Again, if he stands firm against terrifying situations and enjoys it, or at least does not find it painful, he is brave; if he finds it painful, he is cowardly. For virtue of character is about pleasures and pains.

For pleasure causes us to do base actions, and pain causes us to abstain from fine ones. That is why we need to have had the appropriate upbringing—right from early youth, as Plato says—to make us find enjoyment or pain in the right things; for this is the correct education.

Further, virtues are concerned with actions and feelings; but every feeling and every action implies pleasure or pain; hence, for this reason too, virtue is about pleasures and pains. Corrective treatments also indicate this, since they use pleasures and pains; for correction is a form of medical treatment, and medical treatment naturally operates through contraries.

Further, as we said earlier, every state of soul is naturally related to and about whatever naturally makes it better or worse; and pleasures and pains make people base, from pursuing and avoiding the wrong ones, at the wrong time, in the wrong ways, or whatever other distinctions of that sort are needed in an account. These [bad effects of pleasure and pain] are the reason why people actually define the virtues as ways of being unaffected and undisturbed [by pleasures and pains]. They are wrong, however, because they speak of being unaffected without qualification, not of being unaffected in the right or wrong way, at the right or wrong time, and the added qualifications.

We assume, then, that virtue is the sort of state that does the best actions concerning pleasures and pains, and that vice is the contrary state.

The following will also make it evident that virtue and vice are about the same things. For there are three objects of choice—fine, expedient, and pleasant—and three objects of avoidance—their contraries, shameful, harmful, and painful. About all these, then, the good person is correct and the bad person is in error, and especially about pleasure. For pleasure is shared with animals, and implied by every object of choice, since what is fine and what is expedient appear pleasant as well.

Further, pleasure grows up with all of us from infancy on. That is why it is hard to rub out this feeling that is dyed into our lives. We also estimate actions [as well as feelings]—some of us more, some less—by pleasure and pain. For this reason, our whole discussion must be about these; for good or bad enjoyment or pain is very important for our actions.

Further, it is more difficult to fight pleasure than to fight spirit—and Heracleitus tells us [how difficult it is to fight spirit]. Now both craft and virtue are in every case about what is more difficult, since a good result is even better when it is more difficult. Hence, for this reason also, the whole discussion, for virtue and political science alike, must consider pleasures and pains; for if we use these well, we shall be good, and if badly, bad.

To sum up: Virtue is about pleasures and pains; the actions that are its sources also increase it or, if they are done badly, ruin it; and its activity is about the same actions as those that are its sources.

4 [Virtuous Actions versus Virtuous Character]

Someone might be puzzled, however, about what we mean by saying that we become just by doing just actions and become temperate by doing temperate actions. For [one might suppose that] if we do grammatical or musical actions, we are grammarians or musicians, and, similarly, if we do just or temperate actions, we are thereby just or temperate.

But surely actions are not enough, even in the case of crafts; for it is possible to produce a grammatical result by chance, or by following someone else's instructions. To be grammarians, then, we must both produce a grammatical result and produce it grammatically—that is to say, produce it in accord with the grammatical knowledge in us.

Moreover, in any case, what is true of crafts is not true of virtues. For the products of a craft determine by their own qualities whether they have been produced well; and so it suffices that they have the right qualities when they have been produced. But for actions in accord with the virtues to be done temperately or justly it does not suffice that they themselves have the right qualities. Rather, the agent must also be in the right state when he does them. First, he must know [that he is doing virtuous actions]; second, he must decide on them, and decide on them for themselves; and, third, he must also do them from a firm and unchanging state.

As conditions for having a craft, these three do not count, except for the bare knowing. As a condition for having a virtue, however, the knowing counts for nothing, or [rather] for only a little, whereas the other two conditions are very important, indeed all-important. And we achieve these other two conditions by the frequent doing of just and temperate actions.

Hence actions are called just or temperate when they are the sort that a just or temperate person would do. But the just and temperate person is not the one who [merely] does these actions, but the one who also does them in the way in which just or temperate people do them.

It is right, then, to say that a person comes to be just from doing just actions and temperate from doing temperate actions; for no one has the least prospect of becoming good from failing to do them.

The many, however, do not do these actions. They take refuge in arguments, thinking that they are doing philosophy, and that this is the way to become excellent people. They are like a sick person who listens attentively to the doctor, but acts on none of his instructions. Such a course of treatment will not improve the state of the sick person's body; nor will the many improve the state of their souls by this attitude to philosophy.

5 [Virtue of Character: Its Genus]

Next we must examine what virtue is. Since there are three conditions arising in the soul—feelings, capacities, and states—virtue must be one of these.

By feelings I mean appetite, anger, fear, confidence, envy, joy, love, hate, longing, jealousy, pity, and in general whatever implies pleasure or pain. By capacities I mean what we have when we are said to be capable of these feelings—capable of being angry, for instance, or of being afraid or of feeling pity. By states I mean what we have when we are well or badly off in relation to feelings. If, for instance, our feeling is too intense or slack, we are badly off in relation to anger, but if it is intermediate, we are well off; the same is true in the other cases.

First, then, neither virtues nor vices are feelings. For we are called excellent or base insofar as we have virtues or vices, not insofar as we have feelings. Further, we are neither praised nor blamed insofar as we have feelings; for we do not praise the angry or the frightened person, and do not blame the person who is simply angry, but only the person who is angry in a particular way. We are praised or blamed, however, insofar as we have virtues or vices. Further, we are angry and afraid without decision; but the virtues are decisions of some kind, or [rather] require decision. Besides, insofar as we have feelings, we are said to be moved; but insofar as we have virtues or vices, we are said to be in some condition rather than moved.

For these reasons the virtues are not capacities either; for we are neither called good nor called bad, nor are we praised or blamed, insofar as we are simply capable of feelings. Further, while we have capacities by nature, we do not become good or bad by nature; we have discussed this before.

If, then, the virtues are neither feelings nor capacities, the remaining possibility is that they are states. And so we have said what the genus of virtue is.

6 [Virtue of Character: Its Differentia]

But we must say not only, as we already have, that it is a state, but also what sort of state it is.

It should be said, then, that every virtue causes its possessors to be in a good state and to perform their functions well. The virtue of eyes, for instance, makes the eyes and their functioning excellent, because it makes us see well; and similarly, the virtue of a horse makes the horse excellent, and thereby good at galloping, at carrying its rider, and at standing steady in the face of the enemy. If this is true in every case, the virtue of a human being will likewise be the state that makes a human being good and makes him perform his function well.

We have already said how this will be true, and it will also be evident from our next remarks, if we consider the sort of nature that virtue has.

In everything continuous and divisible we can take more, less, and equal, and each of them either in the object itself or relative to us; and the equal is some intermediate between excess and deficiency. By the intermediate in the object I mean what is equidistant from each extremity; this is one and the same for all. But relative to us the intermediate is what is neither superfluous nor deficient; this is not one, and is not the same for all.

If, for instance, ten are many and two are few, we take six as intermediate in the object, since it exceeds [two] and is exceeded [by ten] by an equal amount, [four]. This is what is intermediate by numerical proportion. But that is not how we must take the intermediate that is relative to us. For if ten pounds [of food], for instance, are a lot for someone to eat, and two pounds a little, it does not follow that the trainer will prescribe six, since this might also be either a little or a lot for the person who is to take it—for Milo [the athlete] a little, but for the beginner in gymnastics a lot; and the same is true for running and wrestling. In this way every scientific expert avoids excess and deficiency and seeks and chooses what is intermediate—but intermediate relative to us, not in the object.

This, then, is how each science produces its product well, by focusing on what is intermediate and making the product conform to that. This, indeed, is why people regularly comment on well-made products that nothing could be added or subtracted;

they assume that excess or deficiency ruins a good [result], whereas the mean preserves it. Good craftsmen also, we say, focus on what is intermediate when they produce their product. And since virtue, like nature, is better and more exact than any craft, it will also aim at what is intermediate.

By virtue I mean virtue of character; for this is about feelings and actions, and these admit of excess, deficiency, and an intermediate condition. We can be afraid, for instance, or be confident, or have appetites, or get angry, or feel pity, and in general have pleasure or pain, both too much and too little, and in both ways not well. But having these feelings at the right times, about the right things, toward the right people, for the right end, and in the right way, is the intermediate and best condition, and this is proper to virtue. Similarly, actions also admit of excess, deficiency, and an intermediate condition.

Now virtue is about feelings and actions, in which excess and deficiency are in error and incur blame, whereas the intermediate condition is correct and wins praise, which are both proper to virtue. Virtue, then, is a mean, insofar as it aims at what is intermediate.

Moreover, there are many ways to be in error—for badness is proper to the indeterminate, as the Pythagoreans pictured it, and good to the determinate. But there is only one way to be correct. That is why error is easy and correctness is difficult, since it is easy to miss the target and difficult to hit it. And so for this reason also excess and deficiency are proper to vice, the mean to virtue; "for we are noble in only one way, but bad in all sorts of ways."

Virtue, then, is a state that decides, consisting in a mean, the mean relative to us, which is defined by reference to reason, that is to say, to the reason by reference to which the prudent person would define it. It is a mean between two vices, one of excess and one of deficiency.

It is a mean for this reason also: Some vices miss what is right because they are deficient, others because they are excessive, in feelings or in actions, whereas virtue finds and chooses what is intermediate.

That is why virtue, as far as its essence and the account stating what it is are concerned, is a mean, but, as far as the best [condition] and the good [result] are concerned, it is an extremity.

Now not every action or feeling admits of the mean. For the names of some automatically include baseness—for instance, spite, shamelessness, envy [among feelings], and adultery, theft, murder, among actions. For all of these and similar things are called by these names because they themselves, not their excesses or deficiencies, are base. Hence in doing these things we can never be correct, but must invariably be in error. We cannot do them well or not well—by committing adultery, for instance, with the right woman at the right time in the right way. On the contrary, it is true without qualification that to do any of them is to be in error.

[To think these admit of a mean], therefore, is like thinking that unjust or cowardly or intemperate action also admits of a mean, an excess and a deficiency. If it did, there would be a mean of excess, a mean of deficiency, an excess of excess and a deficiency of deficiency. On the contrary, just as there is no excess or deficiency of temperance or of bravery (since the intermediate is a sort of extreme), so also there is no mean of these vicious actions either, but whatever way anyone does them, he is in error. For in general there is no mean of excess or of deficiency, and no excess or deficiency of a mean.

7 [The Particular Virtues of Character]

However, we must not only state this general account but also apply it to the particular cases. For among accounts concerning actions, though the general ones are common to more cases, the specific ones are truer, since actions are about particular cases, and our account must accord with these. [...]

First, then, in feelings of fear and confidence the mean is bravery. The excessively fearless person is nameless (indeed many cases are nameless), and the one who is excessively confident is rash. The one who is excessive in fear and deficient in confidence is cowardly.

In pleasures and pains—though not in all types, and in pains less than in pleasures—the mean is temperance and the excess intemperance. People deficient in pleasure are not often found, which is why they also lack even a name; let us call them insensible.

In giving and taking money the mean is generosity, the excess wastefulness and the deficiency ungenerosity. Here the vicious people have contrary excesses and defects; for the wasteful person is excessive in spending and deficient in taking, whereas the ungenerous person is excessive in taking and deficient in spending. At the moment we are speaking in outline and summary, and that is enough; later we shall define these things more exactly.

In questions of money there are also other conditions. Another mean is magnificence; for the magnificent person differs from the generous by being concerned with large matters, while the generous person is concerned with small. The excess is ostentation and vulgarity, and the deficiency is stinginess. These differ from the vices related to generosity in ways we shall describe later.

In honor and dishonor the mean is magnanimity, the excess something called a sort of vanity, and the deficiency pusillanimity. And just as we said that generosity differs from magnificence in its concern with small matters, similarly there is a virtue concerned with small honors, differing in the same way from magnanimity, which is concerned with great honors. For honor can be desired either in the right way or more or less than is right. If someone desires it to excess, he is called an honor-lover, and if his desire is deficient he is called indifferent to honor, but if he is intermediate he has no name. The corresponding conditions have no name either, except the condition of the honor-lover, which is called honor-loving.

This is why people at the extremes lay claim to the intermediate area. Moreover, we also sometimes call the intermediate person an honor-lover, and sometimes call him indifferent to honor; and sometimes we praise the honor-lover, sometimes the person indifferent to honor. We will mention later the reason we do this; for the moment, let us speak of the other cases in the way we have laid down.

Anger also admits of an excess, deficiency, and mean. These are all practically nameless; but since we call the intermediate person mild, let us call the mean mildness. Among the extreme people, let the excessive person be irascible, and his vice irascibility, and let the deficient person be a sort of inirascible person, and his deficiency inirascibility.

There are also three other means, somewhat similar to one another, but different. For they are all concerned with common dealings in conversations and actions, but differ insofar as one is concerned with truth telling in these areas, the other two with sources of pleasure, some of which are found in amusement, and the others in daily life in general. Hence we should also discuss these states, so that we can better observe that in every case the mean is praiseworthy, whereas the extremes are neither praiseworthy nor correct, but blameworthy. Most of these cases are also nameless, and we must try, as in the other cases also, to supply names ourselves, to make things clear and easy to follow.

In truth-telling, then, let us call the intermediate person truthful, and the mean truthfulness; pretense that overstates will be boastfulness, and the person who has it boastful; pretense that understates will be self-deprecation, and the person who has it self-deprecating.

In sources of pleasure in amusements let us call the intermediate person witty, and the condition wit; the excess buffoonery and the person who has it a buffoon; and the deficient person a sort of boor and the state boorishness.

In the other sources of pleasure, those in daily life, let us call the person who is pleasant in the right way friendly, and the mean state friendliness. If someone goes to excess with no [ulterior] aim, he will be ingratiating; if he does it for his own advantage, a flatterer. The deficient person, unpleasant in everything, will be a sort of quarrelsome and ill-tempered person.

There are also means in feelings and about feelings. Shame, for instance, is not a virtue, but the person prone to shame as well as [the virtuous people we have described] receives praise. For here also one person is called intermediate, and another—the person excessively prone to shame, who is ashamed about everything—is called excessive; the person who is deficient in shame or never feels shame at all is said to have no sense of disgrace; and the intermediate one is called prone to shame.

Proper indignation is the mean between envy and spite; these conditions are concerned with pleasure and pain at what happens to our neighbors. For the properly indignant person feels pain when someone does well undeservedly; the envious person exceeds him by feeling pain when anyone does well, while the spiteful person is so deficient in feeling pain that he actually enjoys other people's misfortunes.

There will also be an opportunity elsewhere to speak of these. We must consider justice after these. Since it is spoken of in more than one way, we shall distinguish its two types and say how each of them is a mean. Similarly, we must also consider the virtues that belong to reason.

8 [Relations between Mean and Extreme States]

Among these three conditions, then, two are vices—one of excess, one of deficiency—and one, the mean, is virtue. In a way, each of them is opposed to each of the others, since each extreme is contrary both to the intermediate condition and to the other extreme, while the intermediate is contrary to the extremes.

For, just as the equal is greater in comparison to the smaller, and smaller in comparison to the greater, so also the intermediate states are excessive in comparison to the deficiencies and deficient in comparison to the excesses—both in feelings and in actions. For the brave person, for instance, appears rash in comparison to the coward, and cowardly in comparison to the rash person; the temperate person appears intemperate in comparison to the insensible person, and insensible in comparison with the intemperate person; and the generous person appears wasteful in comparison to the ungenerous, and ungenerous in comparison to the wasteful person. That is why each of the extreme people tries to push the intermediate person to the other extreme, so that the coward, for instance, calls the brave person rash, and the rash person calls him a coward, and similarly in the other cases.

Since these conditions of soul are opposed to each other in these ways, the extremes are more contrary to each other than to the intermediate. For they are further from each other than from the intermediate, just as the large is further from the small, and the small from the large, than either is from the equal.

Further, sometimes one extreme—rashness or wastefulness, for instance—appears somewhat like the intermediate state, bravery or generosity. But the extremes are most unlike one another; and the things that are furthest apart from each other are defined as contraries. And so the things that are further apart are more contrary.

In some cases the deficiency, in others the excess, is more opposed to the intermediate condition. For instance, cowardice, the deficiency, not rashness, the excess, is more opposed to bravery, whereas intemperance, the excess, not insensibility, the deficiency, is more opposed to temperance.

This happens for two reasons: One reason is derived from the object itself. Since sometimes one extreme is closer and more similar to the intermediate condition, we oppose the contrary extreme, more than this closer one, to the intermediate condition. Since rashness, for instance, seems to be closer and more similar to bravery, and cowardice less similar, we oppose cowardice, more than rashness, to bravery; for what is further from the intermediate condition seems to be more contrary to it. This, then, is one reason, derived from the object itself.

The other reason is derived from ourselves. For when we ourselves have some natural tendency to one extreme more than to the other, this extreme appears more opposed to the intermediate condition. Since, for instance, we have more of a natural tendency to pleasure, we drift more easily toward intemperance than toward orderliness. Hence we say that an extreme is more contrary if we naturally develop more in that direction; and this is why intemperance is more contrary to temperance, since it is the excess [of pleasure].

9 [How Can We Reach the Mean?]

We have said enough, then, to show that virtue of character is a mean and what sort of mean it is; that it is a mean between two vices, one of excess and one of deficiency; and that it is a mean because it aims at the intermediate condition in feelings and actions.

That is why it is also hard work to be excellent. For in each case it is hard work to find the intermediate; for instance, not everyone, but only one who knows, finds the midpoint in a circle. So also getting angry, or giving and spending money, is easy and everyone can do it; but doing it to the right person, in the right amount, at the right time, for the right end, and in the right way is no longer easy, nor can everyone do it. Hence doing these things well is rare, praiseworthy, and fine.

That is why anyone who aims at the intermediate condition must first of all steer clear of the more contrary extreme, following the advice that Calypso also gives: "Hold the ship outside the spray and surge." For one extreme is more in error, the other less. Since, therefore, it is hard to hit the intermediate extremely accurately, the second-best tack, as they say, is to take the lesser of the *evils*. We shall succeed best in this by the method we describe.

We must also examine what we ourselves drift into easily. For different people have different natural tendencies toward different goals, and we shall come to know our own tendencies from the pleasure or pain that arises in us. We must drag ourselves off in the contrary direction; for if we pull far away from error, as they do in straightening bent wood, we shall reach the intermediate condition.

And in everything we must beware above all of pleasure and its sources; for we are already biased in its favor when we come to judge it. Hence we must react to it as the elders reacted to Helen, and on each occasion repeat what they said; for if we do this, and send it off, we shall be less in error.

In summary, then, if we do these things we shall best be able to reach the intermediate condition. But presumably this is difficult, especially in particular cases, since it is not easy to define the way we should be angry, with whom, about what, for how long. For sometimes, indeed, we ourselves praise deficient people and call them mild, and sometimes praise quarrelsome people and call them manly.

Still, we are not blamed if we deviate a little in excess or deficiency from doing well, but only if we deviate a long way, since then we are easily noticed. But how great and how serious a deviation receives blame is not easy to define in an account; for nothing else perceptible is easily defined either. Such things are among particulars, and the judgment depends on perception.

This is enough, then, to make it clear that in every case the intermediate state is praised, but we must sometimes incline toward the excess, sometimes toward the deficiency; for that is the easiest way to hit the intermediate and good condition.

Questions

1. What is the "end" that Aristotle believes we all aim at?

2. What is the "Golden Mean"?

3. How might the concept of *eudaemonia* apply in a business context?

4. According to Aristotle, are the virtues the same for each person?

5. How would a virtuous CEO or manager differ in his or her approach to a business decision from one who applied utilitarian or deontological reasoning?

Further Reading

Adler, M.I. *Aristotle for Everybody: Difficult Thought Made Easy*. New York: Touchstone, 1997.

Aristotle. *Nicomachean Ethics*. Edited and translated by Roger Crisp. Cambridge: Cambridge Texts in the History of Philosophy, 2014.

Crisp, Roger, and Michael A. Slote, eds. *Virtue Ethics*. Vol. 10. Oxford Readings in Philosophy. Oxford: Oxford University Press, 1997.

Kraut, R., ed. *The Blackwell Guide to Aristotle's Nicomachean Ethics*. Malden: Blackwell Publishing, 2006.

Whetstone, J. Thomas. "How Virtue Fits within Business Ethics." *Journal of Business Ethics*, vol. 33, no. 2, 2001, pp. 101–14.

5.

"ON THE HARMONY OF FEMINIST ETHICS AND BUSINESS ETHICS"

JANET BORGERSON[1]

About This Reading

In the same way that virtue ethics presents an alternative way of approaching ethics, feminist ethics also asks us to think differently about the way we approach moral questions. As Janet Borgerson notes in her essay, feminist ethics provides us with a heightened awareness of how relationships, responsibility, and experience need to play a role in ethical decision-making. She also wants to clarify what she views as a commonly confused view of what feminist ethics consists by distinguishing between feminist, feminine, and care ethics. These three approaches to ethics are often mistakenly viewed as interchangeable.

In addition to providing the reader with a basic presentation of feminist ethical theory, Borgerson also has a more ambitious goal, namely, to show the relevance feminist ethical theory can have for business. In particular she focuses on how feminist ethics can reframe the aforementioned issues of responsibility, relationships, and experiences in business contexts. She does so by presenting three examples of feminist approaches that use these concepts to bring to light moral issues that would otherwise go unnoticed by more traditional approaches.

---

1   Janet L. Borgerson is Reader (Associate Professor) in Philosophy and Management in the School of Business and Economics, University of Exeter, UK.

If business requires ethical solutions that are viable in the liminal landscape between concepts and corporate office, then business ethics and corporate social responsibility should offer tools that can survive the trek, that flourish in this well-traveled, but often unarticulated environment. Feminist ethics has preceded business ethics and corporate social responsibility into crucial domains that these fields now seek to engage. Indeed, feminist ethics has developed theoretical and conceptual resources for mapping, investigating, and comprehending these complex, often undefined, realms and, moreover, greeting and communicating with the diverse human beings who make their lives there. Nevertheless, feminist ethics has been consistently overlooked, misunderstood, and improperly applied within business ethics and corporate social responsibility. This article provides conceptual clarification, illustrative examples, and furthermore develops a framework for future research.

This article demonstrates that the common and consistent failure in the business ethics context to make basic differentiations between *feminist* and *feminine* ethics, as well as conflating feminist ethics with care ethics has resulted in misapprehension, theoretical misunderstanding, and, most importantly, missed opportunities to benefit from feminist ethics' extensive and flexible assets. "Feminist ethics," "feminine ethics," and "care ethics" each designates potentially fertile, yet at times wholly discrete, realms of philosophical insight. Crucial and fundamental discord exists among them.

I argue that feminist ethics has yet to live up to its potential in business ethics and corporate social responsibility in part because many researchers in these fields have failed to recognize four key points:

1. Feminist ethics and feminine ethics are different;

2. All versions of care ethics are *not* founded upon feminine traits and characteristics;

3. Care ethics and feminist ethics are different; and

4. Feminist ethics is not merely a version of "postmodern ethics."

Whereas confusion remains around these four basic points in the business ethics literature, a scholarly search can reveal numerous publications over the decades that have clearly differentiated, distinguished, and mobilized the discrete potentials of the diverse positions (e.g., Borgerson 2001; 2005b; Derry 2002; McNay 2000; Noddings 1984; Nunner-Winkler 1993; Tong 1997; Tronto 1993; Whitbeck 1983). Whereas aspects of care ethics and feminine ethics arguably have potential contributions to make in business ethics research (White 1998), the focus of this essay will remain on *feminist* ethics to elucidate potential resources for business ethics. Throughout the course of this article, I address each misunderstanding in turn in hopes of providing a more accurate and useful rendering of feminist ethics.

After presenting the philosophical background of feminist ethics and feminist ethical theory, I illustrate the four misunderstandings, including a textbook case of the misrepresentation and underestimation of feminist ethics within the domain of business ethics. Then, to begin expressing the harmony of feminist and business ethics, I discuss crucial intersections of interest emerging around concepts of *relationships*, *responsibility*, and *experience*. A research example demonstrates how feminist ethical awareness intervenes in business ethics research, countering the tendency to employ "gender differences" in the study of "ethical sensitivity"—defined as "an ability to recognize that a particular situation poses an ethical dilemma," and exemplifies intolerance toward unethical behaviors, and a proneness to do the right thing (Collins 2000: 6). In conclusion, I provide examples of three feminist ethicists "in action" whose investigations into (1) the "grey zones" of harms; (2) identity and representational conventions; and (3) the enlarging potential of "asymmetrical reciprocity" provide insight into feminist ethics' analytic power. First, however, I ask "Why feminist ethics?" and provide an orientation regarding this article's theoretical sympathies.

Why Feminist Ethics?

Feminist ethics calls attention to relationships, responsibility, and experience and their cultural, historical, and psychological contexts. Strikingly, whereas compelling business ethics scenarios often call for experience in the organization of and engagement with the context at hand, traditional ethical considerations that aim at versions of principle-based objectivity and universality often judge such experience and attention "inappropriately subjective" or "unworthy of consideration" in solving problems and coming to terms with conflicts of interest. In other words, a gulf sometimes emerges between business ethics discussions and the way dilemmas are actually resolved.

Moreover, in much ethical discourse, notions of responsibility typically function in reference to fulfilling—usually abstract—duties and obligations provoking scarce investigation into the implied relations. The importance of relationships, or sociality, lies at the core of business organization and practices. Nevertheless, responsibility's more comprehensive and insightful modes—as a context for agency based in relationships, developed and borne out intersubjectively or in conjunction with others—have little hope of emerging within traditional discussions of business ethics and corporate social responsibility, yet become apparent readily in feminist ethics.

The field of feminist ethics simultaneously draws upon and develops theoretical foundations that question and pose alternatives to traditional ontological and epistemological assumptions. Fundamental reflection unveils productive possibilities. To put this another way, feminist ethics engages broad concerns of interest, motivating powerful and novel ways of thinking and, furthermore, providing diverse approaches to central issues in business ethics and corporate social responsibility (e.g., Calás and Smircich 1997; Derry 2002). In extending the context for feminist ethical interventions in the areas of business ethics and corporate social responsibility, this essay animates key concepts derived from feminist ethics, and reveals that—far from being limited to discussions based in gender differences—feminist ethics provides pathways for recognizing, evaluating, and addressing ethical problems generally.

Orienting Theoretical Sympathies

Echoing Rosemarie Tong's concerns for bioethics, if business ethics does not want to become "just a subfield of law—another rule, regulation and policy generating enterprise," if it wants to encourage and support investigation of and interventions in difficult ethical questions and conflicts, then "it must make some changes" (Tong 1996: 89). This article is informed by analytic philosophy, including analytic philosophers' work in feminist ethics, but also in some respects by philosophical work in existential phenomenology. As this term may appear unfamiliar to some, let us define it. *Phenomenology*, as the study of the movement of consciousness through time—including *the way things appear to us*—becomes *existential* with an emphasis upon understanding diversities of human experience in the world, including notions of lived experiences' contingency and uncertainty. Moreover, the body and particular conditions of embodiment become lenses for comprehending intersubjectivity, engagement, and relations with others. In short, this article explores the harmony of feminist ethics and business ethics, mobilizing an existential–phenomenological perspective, broadly conceived.

A number of prejudices and habits of thinking may lurk in business ethics' philosophical background—militating against opportunities for Tong's called-for "changes"—and influential Oxford philosopher G.J. Warnock provides a relevant example. In his entertaining commentary on what he undoubtedly views as unfortunate Hegelian influences on late 19th-century English philosophy, Warnock (1969) insists that most people are not wracked with existential concerns, such as how to live. He writes, "to practice philosophy in the manner of [G.E.] Moore, it is not necessary to have (as most of us doubtless have not) nor pretend to have (as some at least would be unwilling to do) large-scale metaphysical anxieties. It is necessary only to want to get things clear" (Warnock 1969: 42). Clarity, seemingly, is not what Warnock found in Hegel—an influential theorist in existential phenomenology's background; apparently "large-scale metaphysical anxieties" are not only rare, but also decidedly pretentious distractions in "real" philosophy.

Animating a prominent philosophical brand as Warnock does here calls attention to the delineation of philosophical questions, including the kinds of questions philosophy—and as a result, philosophically informed business ethics—has the potential, or inclination, to raise. This is not to say that analytic philosophy will take business ethics and corporate social responsibility down a dead-end road. However, the particular resources displayed thus far arguably have been unsuccessful in wresting business ethics and corporate social responsibility away from those who would indeed turn them into a "rule, regulation, and policy generating exercise." Perhaps if these fields are to flourish and philosophy is to play a part, then turning to alternative perspectives such as feminist ethics and, moreover, remaining open to the potential of an existential phenomenological perspective, offer a productive opportunity as the impact of global business and corporate social responsibility continues to grow.

Feminist Ethics: Accessing the Field

Feminist ethics places the tendency to value connection—and demonstrate alternatives to traditional notions of autonomy—outside conventional visions of a natural or an essential female-gender-based way of being in the world. Feminist ethics turns instead to concrete and particular, yet theoretically elaborated, cultural and historical understandings of diverse marginal or subordinated groups' experience.

Furthermore, tendency to critical inquiry, especially regarding the frequently forgone "givens" of particular situations marks feminist ethics *not* as a list of essential sex-based ethically relevant traits or a set of predetermined gender-based applicable principles, but rather as an intervention that calls for active engagement in dilemmas. The following sections elaborate on important aspects of feminist ethics, including a brief discussion of the distinction between sex (female) and gender (feminine).

Feminist Interventions and Investigations

Feminist ethics states a motive for investigating the ethics of an ethos itself. The word ethic, derived from the Greek *ethos*, refers to the disposition, character, or fundamental value peculiar to a specific person, people, culture, or movement, and usually is conceived of as a set of principles of right conduct or a theory or system of moral values. Feminist ethicists have insisted that "The process by which a community arrives at its standards or moral norms is itself open to moral scrutiny" (Brennan 1999: 864), forcing attention upon the context and structure of moral reflection and judgment and attending to signs of oppression. Such an understanding clearly evokes an array of questions: How does an ethos make itself known? How is the ethos experienced in day-to-day life? Or in law? Why do some people or groups have one ethos rather than another? Claudia Card, articulating the work of feminist ethics, writes, "oppressive sexual politics sets the stage for ethical inquiries into character, interpersonal relationships, emotional response, and choice in persistently stressful, damaging contexts" (Card 1991: 5). In other words, the systematically subordinated positions in which women have found themselves—throughout global history—provoke a range of ethical investigations.

In addition, the concerns of feminist ethics exceed women's oppression and engage the welfare of other groups as well. Feminist ethics often operates against the backdrop of traditional ethical theories' marginalization of females generally. However, feminist ethics articulates, theorizes, and works to understand modes of exclusion, subordination, and oppression—and the damage inflicted by these processes and practices. And, clearly, females have not been the only segment, nor the private domestic sphere the only arena, marginalized or excluded from the traditional vision of moral theory (Tong 1993: 224). Indeed, as Alison Jaggar argues, the concepts of traditional moral theory were often "ill-suited to the contexts under discussion," failing to account for the experience of many within those contexts (Brennan 1999: 861). Moreover, writes Susan Sherwin, "feminist ethics proposes that when we engage in moral deliberation, it is not sufficient just to calculate utilities or to follow a set of moral principles. We must also ask whose happiness is increased, or how the principles in question affect those who are now oppressed in the circumstances at hand" (Sherwin 1996: 52). In short, feminist ethics pays attention to who tends to benefit from a particular way of viewing, evaluating, and philosophizing about the world, and who tends to bear the burden.

Recognizing the Sex/Gender Distinction

A fundamental theoretical issue must be recognized in this discussion, that is, the distinction between sex and gender. By marking the sex/gender distinction, it becomes clear in what ways a "female" perspective differs from a "feminist" perspective. Moreover, a proponent of "care" ethics may distinguish some aspects of care from stereotypically articulated "feminine," self-sacrificing caring behaviors, yet nevertheless not take on board a feminist perspective. "Gender" is "used as an analytic category to draw a line of demarcation between biological sex differences and the way these are used to inform behaviors or competencies, which are then assigned as either 'masculine' or 'feminine'" (Pilcher and Whelehan 2004: 56). To put this another way, behaviors and traits associated with females are often termed "feminine"; in turn, males' characteristics and behaviors are often termed "masculine." Yet it is clear that masculine and feminine traits are not necessarily connected to males or females.

Stereotypically masculine traits can be prominent in females, and stereotypically feminine traits can describe certain gestures in males. Indeed, many traits and behaviors said to be masculine or feminine have no "natural" or essential connection to either sexed body. Rather, it could be said that male and female human beings learn and adopt these gendered traits, behaviors, and roles depending on the social and cultural requirements of their families, communities, and cultures at particular points in history. Moreover, whereas a color such as blue can be "gendered" masculine, this is not a claim that blue is a naturally "male" color.

The distinction between sex and gender allows researchers to separate biological sex difference from traits and characteristics that are often stereotypically gendered. Thus, feminist ethics claims that self-sacrificing caring traits are not naturally occurring female traits, but rather that females in certain places and at certain times for various reasons have had self-sacrificing caring traits forced upon them as appropriate to their sex. As these traits and concomitant roles are enforced and modeled in female lives, the traits and roles are said to be "natural," an essential part of being female. The concerns with naturalizing traits and roles that damage human lives and the connection of this with feminist ethics will be explored in depth below.

Differentiating Feminist Ethics and Care Ethics

Let us explore more specifically the way in which care ethics and the feminine-trait-based ethical positions that followed (e.g., Noddings 1984; Ruddick 1989) diverge from feminist ethics. Tong succinctly articulates the distinction that has emerged between feminist ethics and versions of care ethics: "any approach to ethics so naïve as to celebrate the value of caring without caring who cares for whom is not feminist" (Tong 1996: 72). Given the common erroneous sense that feminist ethics is care ethics, and given the goal of this essay, it will be useful to explicitly differentiate the positions here.

Psychologist Carol Gilligan, routinely recognized as a forerunner in feminist ethics, remains a relevant, though troubled starting point (e.g., White 1998: 11). Focused upon moral development—as exhibited in decision-making around ethical dilemmas—Gilligan's research challenged attributions of moral superiority usually granted to those research subjects who solved the ethical dilemmas by referring to abstract values derived from universal principles (Gilligan 1982). Her work responded to psychologist Lawrence Kohlberg's influential hierarchical scale of moral maturity, based in dominant Kantian notions of rational morality. Gilligan's early studies—of her subjects' ethical deliberations—revealed "different" approaches, perspectives, or voices, including a voice of "care," that defied abstract, universal positioning. Kohlberg's scale would judge them inferior, yet Gilligan argued that these voices deserved recognition for mature moral reasoning: a care perspective was different, yet equally capable of morally mature judgment.

These alternative ethical considerations—centered around values of care and heard most often in Gilligan's female subjects' voices—have been misapprehended as expressing an essentially female ethos, or women's natural way of being. In fact, Gilligan never identified the caring voice with the voices of all, and only, women. Whereas sexual dualism—the opposing and hierarchical ordering of male and female—and female gender roles increase the likelihood that a female "voice" expresses care, great variation persists in who voices care and why.

In later research, Gilligan (1995) made a crucial distinction between a feminine ethic and a feminist ethic. Conceptions of femininity—understood theoretically as the subordinated element in the gender dualism masculinity/femininity—carry meanings derived from often-associated essentialized female traits, such as passivity, irrationality, and desire to nurture even at the expense of self. A *feminine* ethic in a patriarchal social order is an ethic of "special obligations and interpersonal relationships." Gilligan writes, "Selflessness or self-sacrifice is built into the very definition of care when caring is premised on an opposition between relationships and self-development" (Gilligan 1995: 122). To put this another way, a relationship informed by so-called feminine traits emerges as fundamentally unequal—a one-sided concern with the well-being and development of others that demands prior assumption of female sacrifice made unproblematic by essentialist claims. In other words, combining traditional modes of femininity with notions of responsibility and caring puts into play a particularly debilitating permutation of ethical agency, where agency is understood as action that "transcends its material context" (McNay 2000: 22). In short, the ability to act suffers under a feminine ethos, or a feminized way of being.

Alternatively, by remaining reflective upon potential sites of oppression and subordination, feminist ethical theory informs care ethics' focus on relation differently. A *feminist* ethic "begins with connection, theorized as primary and seen as fundamental in human life" (Gilligan 1995: 122). In this context, "disconnection" and expectations of autonomy appear as problems. Such a perspective shares certain conceptual points with Emmanuel Levinas's model of responsibility; but as I argue later, adaptations of Levinas's ethical model often underestimate feminist ethics' fundamental contribution. Feminist ethics bears witness to intersubjectivity—or the interrelatedness of subject positions—yet maintains or develops "the capacity to manage actively the often discontinuous, overlapping or conflicting relations of power" (McNay 2000: 16–17).

Whereas some versions of care ethics take up this feminist perspective, others do not. Sherwin (1996) writes, "some feminists have argued that if we are to recommend a place for caring in ethics, we do so only in conjunction with a political evaluation of the role of caring in our moral deliberations, and others have rejected caring outright as the central element of feminist ethics" (p. 51). She continues, "I do not believe it is appropriate to characterize the ethics of care as specifically feminist. It does not capture the dimensions that I regard as distinctively feminist" (p. 51). Many, if not most, researchers in feminist ethics concur with Sherwin, and considerable work has been done to explicate precisely why this is so. Hence, care ethics and feminist ethics are different, though at times certain articulations of care ethics may express feminist concerns.

In attempting to bring together insights manifested in light of such perspectives, focus and reflection on embodied experience of marginalized existence often produce observations on—and new understandings of—living with, enduring, and attempting to resist forms of exclusion, subordination, and oppression; and furthermore may generate instances of previously unrecognized diversity and variation, frequently evoking, demonstrating, and elaborating alternative ontological and epistemological mappings that provoke rethinking of typical mainstream understandings of meaning, being interaction and theorizing itself. By motivating an investigation of feminist ethics' theoretical foundations, a stronger and expanded contribution from feminist ethics will be forthcoming.

Feminist Ethical Theory

Generally, feminist ethical theories are those that aim "to achieve a theoretical understanding of women's oppression with the purpose of providing a route to ending women's oppression [and] to develop an account of morality which is based on women's moral experience" in the sense that, previously, women's experience has been excluded (Brennan 1999: 860). However, this attempt to gather and comprehend varieties of experience in particular contexts—that formerly remained beyond philosophical ethics' consideration—is not a claim about how women naturally, and hence necessarily, experience the world. Indeed, what we want to be cautious of in the present endeavor is that "in our efforts to explain various realities that are saturated with the weight of the interests that created them, we often present 'neat' versions of reality to suit our agendas" (Gordon 1995: 133).

Tong has condensed the most important feminist ethical contributions into what she calls "challenges to the assumptions of traditional ontology and epistemology" (Tong 1993: 49–77). Ontologically, the dualism of self versus other, or individual versus community—in which the discrete existence of each element is linked to conceptions of autonomy—becomes a question of relationships between self and other and responsibilities of self to the other, and vice versa, in particular contexts. That is, feminist ethical theory attempts to account for intersubjectivity, or interrelations between moral agents even as the boundaries between these become blurred. These interactions include situations of inequality and power rather than contracts among assumedly equal partners. In addition, traditional oppositions in epistemology such as abstract versus concrete knowledge, universal versus particular standpoints, impartial judgment versus partiality, and reason versus emotion also fall under scrutiny.

The epistemological shifts in feminist ethical theory require a sensibility that maintains a closer contact with practice and the particular and, hence, remains receptive of concrete experience's details and insights. Investigations undertaken from a feminist ethical perspective are less likely to accept elements and structures of a dilemma as given. To put this another way, feminist ethical theories often spur expansion of the contexts in which problems are to be understood, allowing a broader range of problem recognition, possible solutions, and, moreover, preemptive work (see Dienhart 2000: 263; Weston 1992). So, for example, whereas research in business ethics has explored the phenomenon of "ethical sensitivity" (e.g., Collins 2000: 11) as a gender difference issue that expresses aspects of apparently natural female, or sex-based, virtues, feminist ethics refuses to essentialize, or treat as naturally occurring, so-called women's experience, thus provoking productively alternative inquiries into "ethical sensitivity." As Card argues, feminist ethics calls upon us to interrogate the very occurrence and manifestation of such "sensitivity."

Misunderstanding Feminist Ethics: A Textbook Case

The following discussion—focused on one main textual example—illustrates the impetus to collapse the field of feminist ethics into a "theory" that reduces to a common ontological trope of essentialized female traits and characteristics assumedly drawn upon in ethical "consideration." *Business Ethics* (Crane and Matten 2004; 2007), an influential business ethics textbook published by the prestigious Oxford University Press, provides an obvious yet not inconsequential site of analysis for relevant confusions regarding feminist ethics. Interestingly, Fisher and Lovell's textbook (2003) places a brief, uncritical, yet reasonable discussion of care ethics under a broader section on virtue ethics—pairing care with "wisdom" (pp. 74–75). Velasquez (2002) provides a superior discussion of care ethics in his well-established textbook. Although he does not elaborate on feminist ethics at all, he nevertheless provides an informed and useful articulation of care ethics, which avoids conflating feminist ethics and care ethics.

Although presenting the familiar ethical perspectives arguably relevant for business ethics—utilitarianism and deontology—Crane and Matten also include short sections on "virtue," "feminist," "discourse," and "postmodern" ethics. Business ethics desperately needs this augmentation. Nevertheless, the text inaccurately reduces feminist ethics to "care ethics," mistakenly grounds care ethics in a "feminine approach," and moreover states that a feminist ethical perspective solves ethical problems by "intuition" and "personal, subjective assessment" (Crane and Matten 2007: 112). Such a set of misunderstandings and conceptual confusions explains much about the remarkable underestimation of feminist ethics in business ethics.

Feminist ethics, a field of philosophical research in itself, appears somewhat misleadingly within both the first and second editions of *Business Ethics* under the heading of "Contemporary Ethical Theories" (Crane and Matten 2004: 95; 2007:

110)—defined as those theories that include "consideration of decision-makers, their context, and their relations with others as opposed to just abstract universal principles" (2004: 95). In short, such a theory would offer consideration for ethics emerging from concrete positions and particular situations rather than prescribe preordained principles or duties in choosing or judging the good or right thing to do. Thus, traditional ethical theories, and more recent versions derived from them (e.g., Rawls 1971), are set against contemporary ethical theories. Indeed, contemporary ethical theories often retain aspirations for seeing the bigger picture, yet at the same time seriously consider details that traditional ethics' approaches have been known to disdain and disregard. Nevertheless, various contradictions arise in attempting to generalize "effects" of a certain ethic, or ethos, on all others and in all situations.

Moreover, this understanding obscures the provocative and fundamental tenuousness that feminist ethics locates in notions of essentialism, necessity, and universality. In the wake of feminist ethics' ontological and epistemological shifts, the impact of such essentialist assumptions would emerge as a site for critical analysis. In the short "Feminist Ethics" section (Crane & Matten 2004: 97–98; 2007: 111–13), "male approaches" are directly contrasted with "feminist perspectives." This ill-conceived opposition suggests a lack of understanding around the distinction between sex and gender basic to thinking in feminist theory and feminist ethics. Employing coherent concepts in the explication of feminist ethics as a contemporary ethical theory would require marking masculinity's distinction from the male and femininity's distinction from the female. Indeed, given that essentialist notions of "being" male or female are rejected in feminist ethics, it is a theoretical error to speak of a universally recognizable male or female mode of ethical reflection, response, or action as the text does.

As discussed earlier, the "feminist" term in "feminist ethics" designates a theoretical position distinct from both a "female" or a "feminine" perspective. Indeed, a more accurate introduction to feminist ethics would interrogate why aspects of stereotypical femininity such as being passive, emotional, other-focused, or "sensitive"—often expected of, imposed upon, and developed in female bodies in certain groups, times, and places, including in contemporary Western society—are more likely to coordinate with and express a "care ethic," than are corresponding "masculine" aspects. This likelihood of embodied females taking on, exhibiting, and acting out—often subordinating—feminine traits in a sexist context is recognized as a problem with which feminist ethics has been particularly concerned.

In addition, notions of female "intuition"—presented by the textbook as a source of feminist ethics' ethical response—reduce "feminist ethics" to an informal process of applying feminized female common sense. For example, "Feminism rather proposes a particular attitude toward ethical conflicts that is more within the framework of what women would allegedly do by intuition anyway" (Crane and Matten 2007: 112). Of course, "feminism" does not concern only women. Furthermore, this glaring gaffe marks a fundamental misunderstanding and reiterates dualist notions of men as rational and women as "intuitive." As Jean Grimshaw puts it, "the view that women do not act on principle, that they are intuitive and more influenced by 'personal' considerations, has so often been used in contexts where women have been seen as deficient that it is well to be suspicious of any distinction between women and men which seems to depend on this difference" (Grimshaw 1993: 43). This diminutive characterization exacerbates the underestimation of feminist ethics. Moreover, as these misunderstandings have been reproduced in the new edition of the textbook, the impact on students and others who turn to this source will be witnessed for years to come.

Not All Caring Relationships Are Feminist: Facing Levinasian Ethics

The debate over which characteristics are crucial for ethical agency, including appropriate approaches to responsibility, has been around for some time; yet the attempt to privilege so-called feminine virtues, for example certain forms of "caring," without careful consideration of their context defies the wisdom of centuries of antisexist work (Wollstonecraft 1975/1790; Young 1990: 73–91). Feminist criticisms of feminine trait-based ethics have raised crucial questions about damaging relationships, desirable boundaries, and ethical agency under oppressive conditions (e.g., Borgerson 2001).

In Western patriarchal culture and in other cultures as well, *being* has traditionally been divided into two. This binary mode has given rise to well-recognized, hierarchically ordered dualisms of meaning and being: the self/other, white/black, heaven/earth, civilized/primitive, rational/irrational, finite/infinite dichotomies that Val Plumwood finds implicated in the "logic of colonialism" (1993: 51–55). The field of feminist ethics recognizes that processes of ontological "othering" have perpetuated and reinforced historically evident privileging of the male, the white, and the rational (Goldberg 1993).

Traditionally, philosophers have granted ethical superiority to traits and behaviors arising from a stereotypically masculine way of being. Kant, for example, in his *Observations on the Feeling of the Beautiful and the Sublime*, insists upon maintaining the "charming distinction that nature has chosen to make between the two sorts of human beings" (Kant 1960: 77). In this context, males exemplify capacities for depth, abstract speculation, reason, universal rules, and principles. Females are said to be modest, sympathetic, sensitive, and capable of particular judgments, but not principles. In Kant's philosophical universe, this "charming distinction" leaves women unilaterally unable to attain full ethical agency. Feminist ethics has attempted to confront the impact of such sexist dualisms.

However, given this traditional underestimation, should not feminist ethics welcome the opportunity to award female contributions and feminine characteristics their long-overdue recognition of moral or ethical worth? After all, the reevaluation of ghettoized caring traits has opened up discussions of the role of care-taking and relationships with others within ethics generally, including a much-heralded challenge to notions of disembodied, contextless, autonomous agents. Moreover, women's experience of relationships seems to suggest the permeable nature of boundaries between individual beings, self, and other, pointing out possibilities for communication between persons, rather than contracts (Held 1993: 28).

Nevertheless, designations of "typical" feminine or masculine habits of deliberation, no matter how apparently virtuous, maintain a troublesome and damaging sexist dualism not extinguished even as the value of traits shift. Socialized female and stereotypical feminine traits have long been valued by philosophers as "charming distinctions" appropriate to women's ways of being, yet this valuing has not changed the overall judgments of female ontological and epistemological potential (see e.g., Card 1996: 49–71; Sherwin 1996: 49–54). Thus, in the field of ethics and western philosophy generally the legacy of hierarchical dualism dominates, even in the work of those who in other contexts seem extraordinarily concerned with power, subordination, and marginality.

For example, Levinas-inspired ethicists elaborating responsibility for and response to the Other—in ways that echo a feminine version of caring—have not listened to the feminist call for full consideration of histories of subordination both in theory and lived experience. In *Closeness: An Ethics* (Jodalen and Vetlesen 1997), philosophers working in the "ethics of proximity" reassert a kind of essential human responsiveness in the face of the Other, but disconnect the apparently related human traits from sexist and racist dualisms.

Caring—in particular, feminine trait-based caring—often opposes concern for self with concern for other (Card 1996), evident when a self-forgetting caring response is held in contrast to alternative modes of being. The ethics of closeness, or proximity, emerges from a phenomenological conceptual lineage, especially from the apparent move beyond phenomenology by Levinas. From this perspective, human beings express their freedom in their response to the Other, not in a cognitive process, of willing or "taking" responsibility, not as a matter of contract or reciprocity, but as a precondition to being human (Jodalen and Vetlesen 1997: 1–19). They write, "Responsibility means to respond, to respond to the call for responsibility issued wordlessly from the Other and received pre-voluntarily by the subject" (1997: 9). This formulation, an example of "having" responsibility, raises an interesting paradox. The manner of response that a Levinas-inspired intimate ethic lauds is precisely the kind of response demanded of subordinate being, evoking a traditional feminine caring or mothering model (see e.g., Gilligan 1982; Noddings 1984).

Yet, Levinasian responsibility is proposed as simply human (cf. Borgerson 2001: 82–84; Nietzsche 1998: 36–37). The lack of reflection upon such essential "responsibility" and, moreover, the failure to acknowledge the shared oppressions of subordinated peoples leave crucial domains of ethics untouched by the "bare givenness of intersubjectivity," or a Levinas-inspired vision of human relation (Jodalen and Vetlesen 1997: 7). To put this another way, the one who must answer *the call* becomes uncritically *feminine*, invoking the interrelations of oppressions that share position and characterization in semiotically and existentially relevant dualistic hierarchies.

Indeed, work in feminist theory and philosophy of race suggests that other-centeredness will be recognized most readily in semiotically associated oppressed groups (Gordon, 1997; Stack 1993). In ignoring the critical discourse from, specifically, the field of feminist ethics, proponents of ethical closeness have steered clear of acknowledging the relation between the mode of being they celebrate and the actual circumstances of those who have modeled and still model—willingly or not—those behaviors, regardless of whether there is anything essentially ethical about them (Bell 1993: 17–48). In other words, the "proximity ethics" interpretation of Levinas—and arguably Levinas himself—fails to incorporate insights from feminist ethics into the notion of responsibility based in uncompromising intersubjectivity, ignoring the ethical implications of being a particular human being, or kind of agent, in contexts of marginalization, subordination, and oppression.

Feminist Ethics Is Not Merely a Version of Postmodern Ethics

Many of the insights credited to "postmodern ethics," as discussed in Crane and Matten (2004; 2007: 115–118), could be derived from work in feminist ethical theory—as will be discussed later—and indeed often emerged earlier within feminist thought. In equally relevant exclusions, critical race theory (e.g., Gordon 1997) and disability studies (e.g., Shildrick 2005) raise crucial, complex issues of identity, intersubjectivity, and agency, and—this should be obvious—not only as a result of specific engagement and ideological agreement with poststructural theory or thinkers. Insights that have emerged from the experiences, innovations, and theorizations of marginalized groups—such as women, racial minorities, and the disabled—often ascribed solely to what is known as postmodern theory and poststructural theorists. Such careless attribution both reveals and breeds ignorance (and worse) and serves to reintroduce the marginalization such theory often seeks to acknowledge.

Whereas feminist ethical theory does share some fundamental assumptions with poststructural theory—a ground for the so-called postmodern ethics—this emerges not because all feminist theory, and therefore feminist ethics, is derivative. Rather, many feminist philosophers and theorists, as well as their critical race theory and disability studies colleagues, have trained in similar intellectual traditions—philosophical phenomenology, epistemology, and semiotics—as, for example, have Foucault,

Deleuze, and Derrida (Borgerson 2005a). Sharing, therefore, academic heritage and disciplinary genealogies, feminist ethical theory has, in some instances, exploited derived tools to develop conceptual and practice-based contributions often along the lines of gender, theoretically understood (Alcoff 1988; Diprose 1994; Walker 1998). Such work includes attention to the intersecting meanings, instantiations, and functionings of hierarchical dualisms in lived human experience, and thus has implications beyond gender difference (Borgerson 2001).

Considerable development in various disciplinary territories has been culti-vated with insights derived from theorizing multiple and particular experiences of living in divergent societies, places, times, and bodies. Yet, recognition of such fundamental data tends to vanish in attempts to maintain the status of an abstract and authoritative voice. Given this observation, it is not surprising that a certain kind of discourse intimately connected to, and privileged by, this "tradition" contin-ues processes of exclusion and marginalization. Focusing upon feminist ethics as a feminine trait-based ethic of care concerned with "harmonious and healthy social relationships" and relying upon "personal, subjective reasoning" (Crane and Matten 2004: 98) underestimates and undermines the critical power of feminist ethics' ana-lytical examinations and philosophical arguments around unequal power relations, agency and identity formation, and systemic subordination. We turn, now, to three key concepts that emerge from feminist ethics.

Insights from Feminist Ethics

Recognizing, of course, that conceptual foundations and debates are as diverse in feminist ethics as in other fields of philosophy, for present purposes three theoretical signposts will be indicated as fundamental to feminist ethical terrain. These include attention to responsibility in conjunction with the recognition of the primacy of relation—including aspects of co-creative intersubjective agency—and a focus upon particular experience in context. Whereas alternative aspects of feminist ethics' rich genealogical conceptual heritage could also inspire us here, feminist ethical theories' reframing of responsibility, relationships, and experience adequately exemplifies new possibilities for the impact, complexity, and potential of business ethics.

Robin Derry, in particular, has argued that feminist ethical theory, and related research methods, "could significantly extend the scope of issues addressed and the depth of learning from research in the field of business ethics" (Derry 2002, 81). As a brief example, consider elements of an "ethical decision-making process" offered for business decision-making (e.g., Hartman 2001: 6). First, "identify the dilemma." Second, "obtain unbiased facts." Next, identify a variety of choices; identify stake-holders; then "identify the impact of each alternative on each stakeholder and the stakeholders' resulting impacts on you and your firm" (Hartman 2001: 6); and so on.

At each of these steps, rich understandings from feminist ethics—of relationships, responsibility, and experience, as explicated in the following sections—could provide resources for spurring crucial inquiry in these ethical investigations. Readers are encouraged to reflect upon the way in which aspects of relationships, responsibility, and experience would expand and in some cases rearticulate responses to each step of such an ethical decision-making process checklist (cf. Weston 1992: 12–36).

Relationships

Traditionally, relationships might be hypothesized as between autonomous individuals (agents); or between agents who themselves are the products of relations and therefore represent some modified version of autonomy. Arguments have been made in business ethics stating that autonomy must be the basis for ethical action and reflection—with a focus on recognizing the sight of agency, decision-making, and, of course, blame tending to minimize incidences of multiple influence, manipulation, and chance. However, reflection on relationships and intersubjectivity's interference with autonomy models has provoked alternative articulations of autonomy (Lippke 1995). For example,

> The idea is not that we should involve others in our deliberations because they will help us come to the right decision. Rather, because the question is always what to do in light of the various relationships we have to others, there is no way of specifying the right decision independent of others' input. And since the relevant relationships are often reciprocal, appropriate deliberation must often be collective. (Darwall 1998: 224)

Stephen Darwall points to the distinction between acknowledging the fundamental role of relationships and accepting a more vulgar understanding of an almost democratically compromised autonomy.

In a theoretical model of co-creation and development, these relationships could be understood as formed between the self, or subject, and some other, in and across a hypothesized gap that separates these agents and protects their status as independent, responsibility-bearing decision-makers. The interactions and exchanges form the basis of subject- and self-formation and the development of relationships over time. Feminist ethical notions of self/other relations—as Tong's notion of ontological shifts suggests—are largely intersubjective and interdependent in just this way: that is, self and other are conceived of as developing in relation with each other.

Indeed, calling attention to intersubjectivity and interdependence raises varying degrees of doubt about the very nature of the distance that supposedly separates self and other, and this provides a critical context for interrogating autonomy. In ethical theory, relationships have often appeared threatening to autonomy and moral integrity because of the role strict boundaries in individual rational decision-making and choice have played in making one's decisions one's own (see Card 1996: 21–48). Feminist ethical theory faces this threat to the perceived site of agency, examining and observing revealed contradictions and emergent insights, yet acknowledging that relationships—actual or imagined, lived or theoretically conceptualized—form the foundation for notions of responsibility.

Paying greater attention to the fundamental role of relationships in human existence invokes notions of responsibility to and for others beyond traditional moral contract-based and principle-justified duties and obligations. Furthermore, human agents may be conceived of as "having" or "taking" responsibility. Manifestations of this discussion are wide-ranging and complex, and will be developed later in the next section.

Responsibility

As Darwall notes above, human embeddedness in relationships, our intersubjectivity, cannot be disregarded in discussions and elaborations of responsibility. Card writes:

> The challenge is to show how the importance and point of responsibility can survive the realization that the quality of our character and our deeds is not entirely up to us as individuals. (Card 1996: 22)

Responsibility is often understood to describe an ability to respond to a situation—whether this involves another person, a group, or simply a scenario in which one acts to accomplish an action—and may take the form of recognizing or refusing ties, duties, or obligations that we have in relation to this world around us. Such a notion may also be expanded to include possibilities of responsibility to self.

Alternatively, Levinas turns to being-in-relation's inescapable sociality, a scenario in which the challenge is to recognize and accept, as human beings, responsibility for the other in a preexisting relation (Levinas 1985). This is a case of what Card would call "having" rather than "taking" responsibility (Card 1996). For Levinas, this response scenario is demanded by ethics, the foundational mode of intersubjectivity, a "face to face" relation of responsibility for the Other that Levinas calls the "curvature of intersubjective space" (Levinas 1969: 290–91, cited in Oliver 2001: 204). In this sense, each must choose to recognize their responsibility, yet there is no choice about entering into the relationship itself as this has emerged in "the bare givenness of intersubjectivity." Ethics, the condition of the always already-existing intersubjectivity, sets the stage for appropriate modes of responsibility. Whereas Levinas offers a complex vision of responsibility, its lack of feminist reflections embeds a troubling lack of boundaries, as discussed earlier. For now, Card's notion of "taking" responsibility shall be the focus.

Card (1996) argues that whereas someone or something may *have* responsibility for a set of situations or actions, *taking* responsibility requires a center of agency, a choosing to act or follow through in a certain way. This has implications in a feminist ethical context in that females and other subordinated groups may be perceived as having less agency if they have not chosen their responsibilities. In other words, being unable to choose one's responsibilities, having them thrust upon one, may have ontological implications. In short, over time, certain groups may be perceived as unable to "take" responsibility. Diverse scenarios exist: "We may be given responsibility, assigned it, inherit it, and then accept or refuse it" (Card 1996: 29). Card continues, "Agents are more responsible when they take responsibility in a sense that shows more initiative than when they do not" (29). As Larry May has argued, tracing "initiatives" and hence responsibility in groups requires understandings of realms in which shared actions take place and attitudes and values are transformed (May 1992).

Card designates four different senses of taking responsibility each with its own related accomplishments (Card 1996: 28):

1. *Administrative* or *managerial*—estimation and organization of possibilities, deciding which should be realized and how

2. *Accountability*—being answerable or accountable, either through specific agreement or "finding" oneself such, for something and following through

3. *Care-taking*—a commitment of support or backing of something or someone, and holding to the commitment

4. *Credit*—taking the credit or blame for something that did or did not happen, "owning up"

Administrative or managerial responsibility clearly involves decision-making, setting out boundaries, and suggesting the form that various organizational processes will take. Being responsible in the sense of being "accountable" reflects the position to which others will turn when decisions have been made, outcomes are under scrutiny, or results are in. Care-taking here invokes a commitment, perhaps a promise, to put resources or support behind a person or project and seeing this through to an end. In other words, one does not withdraw support from a person or project that is expecting such, even if perceived outcomes have changed. Taking responsibility in the sense of credit or blame may evoke not the decision-making process or following or supporting something through to an end; rather credit or blame may fall to one outside the general workings of organizational or institutional processes.

For Card, "having" responsibility cannot generate the same sense of agency as "taking" it, perhaps undermining the very means by which responsible actions are produced. In this way, contexts that encourage "having" rather than "taking" responsibility, may provide support for unethical behaviors and attitudes. Taking responsibility requires an active willingness: and what kind of agent manifests such willingness becomes an issue for investigation. Of course, some people, or agents, may not be willing to "take" responsibility in these ways if as a result they incur more burdens or blame than they would have had otherwise. There is, then, a potential flight from responsibility—or bad faith—that remains troubling. Levinas, for example, engages this concern, attempting to place ethics and relations of responsibility beyond human choice. Feminist ethics, instead, tends to elaborate on being a certain kind of agent, and, thus, having particular kinds of experiences.

Experience

Knowledge gained through experience in situations not generally regarded as morally relevant nevertheless generates ways of functioning and modes of decision-making that have broad ethical import. Feminist ethics has taken a special interest in the understandings acquired by particular, often marginalized, groups and individuals. Ethical investigations that include such perspectives require listening to others' voices and emphasizing a broader acknowledgement of human interaction and attention to the lives people lead.

As Iris Marion Young has noted, descriptions of experience express "a subject's doing and undergoing from the point of view of the subject" (Young 1990: 13). Therefore, "talk about experience expresses subjectivity, describes the feelings, motives, and reactions of subjects as they affect and are affected by the context in which they are situated" (Young: 13). Vikki Bell discusses experience in conjunction with the notion of embodiment (Bell 1999: 113–38). In the sense that in the past, notions of embodiment were understood as invoking an essentialist stance, Bell argues that "being 'anti-essentialist' need not be a reason not to consider the phenomena and import of embodiment" (Bell 1999: 132). She suggests theorizing "the body in a way that captures the import of the proximity of the body, the debt of identity to the body" (Bell 1999: 132). Echoing this recognition of the impact of particular histories and position on a subject's perspective, Grimshaw writes, "Ethical concerns and priorities arise from different forms of social life" (Grimshaw 1993: 42). Experience emerges through and with diverse and nonsubstitutable modes of embodiment.

Feminist ethical theory may push us to critically reflect on a phenomenon rather than simply assume its merits, and hence interrogate the emergence and effects, for example, of "ethical sensitivity." May has argued that sensitivity to the lives of others and their particular experiences can serve as an opening to acting ethically in relation (May 1992). Whereas sensitivity to others has often been understood as feminine gender's domain, May does not find such an essentialized limitation necessary, rather regarding sensitivity a basic human capacity that can be cultivated.

Recalling Hobbes's statement in *Leviathan*, May points out that the opportunity to learn and develop from experience is one of the fundamental equalities that exists in the state of nature (May 1992: 130). Clearly, such an opportunity is altered by prevailing experiential circumstances: and ultimately, some people seem to learn more than others from the lessons of their lives and even succeed in applying these to solve future dilemmas. Moreover, there is no guarantee that the lessons learned point toward "ethical" behavior and actions, sensitive or otherwise, as life is not an ethically reliable teacher.

Focus on acknowledgment of lived experience and learning invites a distinction between the "natural" and "unnatural" conditions under which people make choices, including recognition of how histories of oppression circumscribe the contexts in which relationships and responsibility emerge. Card writes, "It is not enough to confront the inequities of the 'natural lottery' from which we may inherit various physical and psychological assets and liabilities. It is important also to reflect on the unnatural lottery created by networks of unjust institutions and histories that bequeath to us further inequities in our starting positions and that violate principles that would have addressed, if not redressed, inequities of nature" (Card 1996: 20). Being born into a situation may be a "natural fact," but how the nation or race into which one is born has been treated historically and how various effects emerging from these historical variables will place a newborn are not natural facts. Contingent—though not necessarily accidental—historical circumstances, shaped and held in place by systems of power and status, may be ascribed to the just and unjust functioning of "institutions": Such institutions may be as intimately related to an individual as her family relations, her skin color, and her gender. The following section explicates the impact these insights from feminist ethics could have on research in business ethics.

Shared Research Concerns: Revisiting "Ethical Sensitivity"

To explore further feminist ethics' potential to impact research being done in the field of business ethics, I turn to the example of "ethical sensitivity." The *Journal of Business Ethics* has given witness to the role that ethical sensitivity plays in ethical dilemmas in business contexts (Collins 2000). As suggested in the introduction to this essay, feminist ethical theory opens understanding around the issue of "ethical sensitivity," offering insight into, and tools to address, the concern that "many gender studies lack a theoretical framework that predicts when and why women are more ethically sensitive than men" (Collins 2000: 11). The emphasis upon relationships, responsibility, and lived experience found in feminist ethics provides penetration into the realm of business that traditional moral theories may fail to accomplish.

Ethical sensitivity has often been examined in terms of gender differences, in particular, an interest in whether women's so-called feminine characteristics, including caring traits, form the foundation for greater ethical sensitivity. As Collins has noted, the results and conclusions have been mixed (see, e.g., Shultz and Brender-Ilan 2004: 305–06). However, conceptual innovations and analysis motivated by feminist ethics suggest that ethical sensitivity could be studied as a matter of attention to certain details, more obvious, compelling, and relevant to some ethical agents than to others.

Recall that feminist ethical conceptualizations support the conclusion that context matters. To put this another way, feminist ethical theory encourages us to explore why it is that agents with experience of certain kinds—for example, a lived awareness of intersubjectivity and particularity arising in daily life practices and culturally socialized ways of being still regularly expected of and manifested in women in contemporary Western cultures—are more likely to be ethically sensitive. (What such agents ultimately do, of course, is a different question.)

The contributions of feminist ethics push us beyond an essentialist view of gender difference—which bases female predilection for ethical sensitivity in an unfathomable natural, "intuitive," or even cognitive, difference—to conceive, perceive, and construct alternative and supplementary understandings that can be mobilized, theorized, and applied in future scenarios. Thus, the phenomenon of ethical sensitivity emerges as an outcome of specific epistemological and ontological assumptions and cultural preconceptions that play out in lived experience of being female, or conversely male, at a historically specific time and place. In short, ethical sensitivity derives from experience generally and, further, out of experience in relationships of responsibility with others. Such critical reflection gives us a depth of perspective regarding ethical tendencies and traits. The next section investigates three feminist ethicists in action.

Feminist Ethics in Action: Three Examples

As suggested above, feminist ethics in many ways preceded business ethics into areas now recognized as of concern to business ethics and corporate social responsibility, such as complex relations of power between unequal parties. Feminist ethicists drew upon theoretical insights derived from bringing to bear notions of responsibility, relationships and experience informed by the challenging, shifting, and reformulating of basic ontological and epistemological assumptions. Examples from the work of three prominent feminist ethicists, Claudia Card, Margaret Urban Walker, and Iris Marion Young are offered to demonstrate the way feminist ethical insights inform analysis, articulation, and intervention in the world—past, present, and future.

The context and depth of these philosophers' theoretical work is far greater than can be expressed in brief here. Readers are encouraged to seek out the writings of these and other feminist ethicists on their own. Moreover, insofar as bioethics engages critical contours of business and organizational practices, the works of feminist bioethicists such as Tong, Sherwin, and Wolf are indispensable (e.g., Sherwin 1996; Tong 1997; Wolf 1996).

Claudia Card: Harm and "Grey Zones"

Card, a student of John Rawls, demonstrates in *The Atrocity Paradigm* (2002) philosophical strengths gleaned from charting and developing the concepts, dimensions, and ultimately the field of feminist ethics. She defines "evil" most basically as "foreseeable intolerable harms produced by culpable wrongdoing" (Card 2002: 3). She writes, "One reason that many evils go unrecognized is that the source of harm is an institution, not just the intentions or choices of individuals (many of whom may not share the goals of the institution, even when their conduct is governed by its norms). Another is that the harm is the product of many acts, some of which might have been individually harmless in other contexts. Victims are more likely than perpetrators to appreciate the harm. But when the source is an institution, even victims can be hard-pressed to know whom to hold accountable" (Card 2002: 24–25). Particularly in situations in which privilege meets disadvantage, wealth meets poverty, or power meets constraint—constantly emerging for example in globalized labor, or international health research practices (Borgerson 2005b)—decision-making processes to avoid real harms in the face of apparent benefits become ever more opaque.

"Feminists," writes Card, "have long struggled with the question of how ethically responsible agency is possible under oppression, given that oppressive practices are coercive" (Card 2002: 234). In her discussion of "the grey zone," Card elaborates on "the complex and difficult predicaments of some who are simultaneously victims and perpetrators." Such a situation might be seen arising in a rural community adjusting, for example, to the presence of new out-sourced factory work in which some people come to hold the means of survival for others, perhaps suddenly, perhaps with nearly impossible demands from those further up the supply chain. What Card argues is that, "evils may be prevented from perpetuating themselves in a potentially unending chain as long as victims who face grim alternatives continue to distinguish between bad and worse and refuse, insofar as possible, to abdicate responsibility for one another" (Card 2002: 26). Some of her analysis specifically addresses social institutions; nevertheless discussions of "institutions" might as well suggest the organization or corporation. Card argues that institutions that create "grey zones," sometimes intentionally, are particularly culpable.

Margaret Urban Walker: Moral Understandings and Representational Practices

Walker contends that the assumption that people are a kind or type is propagated and created by representational practices, which "are among those that construct socially salient identities for people" (Walker 1998: 178). She argues that if practices of representation "affect some people's morally significant perceptions of and interactions with other people, and if they can contribute to those perceptions or interactions going seriously wrong, these activities have bearing on fundamental ethical questions" (p. 179). That is, a person influenced by such images may treat members of the represented group as less than human or undeserving of moral recognition.

Drawing upon and developing such insights allow marketing communications scholars to articulate the way in which representations are part of lived experience. Representations from advertising images, film, and the Internet inform and co-create notions of reality. Mobilizing an "ethics of representation" can sensitize international marketing campaigns to their interactions with, and impact upon cultural difference, global race relations, and the constitution of the consuming subjects (Ahmed 2000; Borgerson and Schroeder 2002, 2005; Chouliaraki 2006; Schroeder and Borgerson 2005).

Philosophers concerned with ethical norms and behavior have traditionally proceeded as though all problematic situations of moral recognition could be countered in three ways: through constructive definitions of personhood, through formal requirements of universality or universalizability, and through substantial demands for impartial or equal consideration (Walker 1998). From Walker's feminist ethical perspective, these three formulations lack sufficient conceptual strength to handle representations that characteristically manipulate and damage the identity of subordinate groups. Moreover, these prescriptions fail to provide sufficiently complex considerations to deal with problems of representation and, worse, damaging representations often fail to even qualify as ethical or moral problems.

Not surprisingly, then, we find in Robert Solomon's chapter on business ethics a discussion of "consumer intelligence and responsibility," including issues of advertising. The use of "sex"—apparently referring to displayed sexuality—to lend appeal to products and "the offensive portrayals of women and minorities" become a "lack of taste": but, asks Solomon, is it "an ethical issue?" What Solomon utterly misses here is advertising's role beyond appeal, information, and persuasion, its perpetual representation of an entire vision of life and the world around us, often provoking responses and consequences equivalent to and as "serious" as "outright lying in advertising" (Solomon 1993: 362; cf. Borgerson and Schroeder 2002; Schroeder and Borgerson 2005; Vaver 2008; Schroeder 2008).

Iris Marion Young: Asymmetrical Reciprocity

Young addresses the issue of attempting to understand "the point of view of others before drawing conclusions about what is right or just," for example in encouraging a more privileged group to fairly consider the importance of some benefit to a less privileged group. Believing in the potential for dialogue between people that happens "across difference without reversing perspectives and identifying with each other," Young finds the common sense thought experiment of "putting yourself in the place of the other" not only misleading and politically suspect, but reinforcing "subjective understanding of issues," disregarding the "nonsubstitutable relation of moral subjects" and disrupting opportunities for what she calls enlarged thought (Young 1997: 39).

This response to work on theories of communicative ethics invokes "asymmetrical reciprocity" based on a subject's unique temporality and position, and moreover recognition of asymmetry of power, opportunities, and understandings. Young writes, "with regard to the Hegelian ontology of self and other, each social position is structured by the configuration of relationships among positions. Persons may flow and shift among structured social positions, and the positions themselves may flow and shift, but the positions cannot be plucked from their contextualized relations and substituted for one another" (Young 1997: 52). Work in business ethics and corporate social responsibility that requires "efforts to express experience and values from different perspectives"—as discussions between corporations and countries do—may take note of the dangers of collapsing diverse perspectives and experiences into "shared" expectations. Furthermore, recognition of inequalities, and the opportunities they offer, may help build understandings, for example, of the way trust works, or does not, in corporate and organizational environments (e.g., Gustafsson 2005).

This article has sought to clarify what business ethics can learn from feminist ethics—understood in a robust way that makes an educated exploration of resources beyond care ethics and uncritical notions of femininity. The introduction of three feminist ethicists in action attempts to bring to light notions that business ethics and corporate social responsibility might find useful. Nevertheless, this is only a brief sketch, and the true benefits of engaging with feminist ethics, as with most areas of philosophy, may only emerge with further reading and reflection.

Conclusion

As has been suggested here, feminist ethics in many ways preceded business ethics into areas of concern that business ethics and corporate social responsibility now seek to engage in. This includes the work of feminist ethics in developing theoretical and conceptual resources for charting courses through these complex, often unarticulated, realms.

Feminist ethics does more than displace traditional ethical voices, only to assert a "different" voice with alternative concerns. As illustrated in the preceding discussions, simply asserting the primacy of relationships, recognizing the existence of permeable boundaries between the self and the other, and questioning the site of agency may fail to attend to the existential-phenomenological realities of intersubjectivity and responsibility—including issues of power—that shed light on business ethics and organizational environments. This requires noting both in theorizing, and in day-to-day life experience, that lack of boundaries between self and other—as evoked in the case of Levinas's ethics, but also often in some care ethics and feminine ethics—may have dangerous effects and, moreover, forms the typical situation of oppressed groups.

Furthermore, an insistence on residing closer to understandings of lived experience may have a particular attraction challenging—yet making sense to—those who work in business contexts, and who can be expected to invoke on-site experience-based insights that traditionally trained business ethicists may lack. The underestimation of feminist ethics in business ethics could be viewed as in unfortunate continuity with modes of privileged, traditional philosophical discourse that have ignored, excluded, and subordinated marginalized alternative views of identity, society, and the world for centuries. However, business ethics, a field with its own shadowed subordinations and feminized margins, may well defy the underestimation of feminist ethics, recognizing powerful philosophical opportunities and conceptual innovations in the potentially harmonious landscape of feminist ethics and business ethics.

Acknowledgments

I want to thank David Bevan, Laura Hartmann, Campbell Jones, Jonathan Schroeder, and the anonymous reviewers for support on this project.

References

Ahmed, S. 2000. *Strange Encounters: Embodied Others in Post-Coloniality.* London: Routledge.
Alcoff, L. 1988. "Cultural feminism versus post-structuralism: The identity crisis in feminist theory." *Signs* 13(3): 405–36.

Bell, L. 1993. *Rethinking Ethics in the Midst of Violence: A Feminist Approach to Freedom.* Lanham, MD: Rowman and Littlefield.

Bell, V. 1999. *Feminist Imagination.* London: Sage.

Borgerson, J.L. 2001. "Feminist ethical ontology: Contesting the 'bare givenness of intersubjectivity'." *Feminist Theory* 2 (2): 173–89.

Borgerson, J.L. 2005a. "Judith Butler: On organizing subjectivities." *Sociological Review* 53 (October): 63–79.

Borgerson, J.L. 2005b. "Addressing the global basic structure in the ethics of international biomedical research involving human subjects." *Journal of Philosophical Research* special supplement: 235–49.

Borgerson, J.L., and Schroeder, J.E. 2002. "Ethical issues in global marketing: Avoiding bad faith in visual representation." *European Journal of Marketing* 36 (5/6): 570–94.

Borgerson, J.L., and Schroeder, J.E. 2005. "Identity in marketing communications: An ethics of visual representation." In A.J. Kimmel, ed., *Marketing Communication: New Approaches, Technologies, and Styles*, pp. 256–77. Oxford: Oxford University Press.

Brennan, S. 1999. "Recent work in feminist ethics." *Ethics* 109 (July): 858–93.

Calás, M.B., and Smircich, L. (eds.) 1997. "Predicando la moral en calzoncillos. Feminist Inquiries into business ethics." In A. Larson, and R.E. Freeman, eds., *Business Ethics and Women's Studies.* Oxford: Oxford University Press.

Card, C. 1991. *Feminist Ethics.* Lawrence: University Press of Kansas.

Card, C. 1996. *The Unnatural Lottery: Character and Moral Luck.* Philadelphia: Temple University Press.

Card, C. 2002. *The Atrocity Paradigm: A Theory of Evil.* Oxford: Oxford University Press.

Chouliaraki, L. 2006. "The aestheticization of suffering on television." *Visual Communication* 5 (3): 261–85.

Collins, D. 2000. "The quest to improve the human condition: The first 1,500 articles published in Journal of Business Ethics." *Journal of Business Ethics* 26: 1–73.

Crane, A., and Matten, D. 2004. *Business Ethics: A European Perspective.* Oxford: Oxford University Press.

Crane, A., and Matten, D. 2007. *Business Ethics: Managing Corporate Citizenship and Sustainability in the Age of Globalization*, 2nd ed. Oxford: Oxford University Press.

Darwall, S. 1998. *Philosophical Ethics.* Boulder, CO: Westview.

Derry, R. 2002. "Feminist theory and business ethics." In R. Fredrick, ed., *A Companion to Business Ethics*, pp. 81–87. Oxford: Blackwell.

Dienhart, J. 2000. "Just caring, caring justice." *Business and Society Review* 105 (2): 247–67.

Diprose, R. 1994. *The Bodies of Women: Ethics, Embodiment and Sexual Difference.* London: Routledge.

Fisher, C., and Lovell, A. 2003. *Business Ethics and Values.* Harlow: Prentice-Hall.

Gilligan, C. 1982. *In a Different Voice: Psychological Theory and Women's Development.* Cambridge, MA: Harvard University Press.

Gilligan, C. 1995. "Hearing the difference: Theorizing connection." *Hypatia* 10 (2): 120–27.

Goldberg, D. 1993. *Racist Culture: Philosophy and the Politics of Meaning.* Oxford: Blackwell.

Gordon, L. 1995. "Rethinking ethics in the midst of violence: A feminist approach to freedom." *Sartre Studies International* 1 (1&2): 133–50.

Gordon, L. 1997. *Her Majesty's Other Children: Sketches of Racism from a Neocolonial Age.* Lanham, MD: Rowman and Littlefield.

Grimshaw, J. 1993. "The idea of a female ethic." In P. Singer, ed., *A Companion to Ethics*, pp. 491–99. Oxford: Blackwell.

Gustafsson, C. 2005. "Trust as an example of asymmetrical reciprocity: An ethics perspective on corporate brand management." *Business Ethics—A European Review* 14 (2): 143–50.

Hartman, L. 2001. "Technology and ethics: Privacy in the workplace." *Business and Society Review* 106 (1): 1–27.

Held, V. 1993. *Feminist Morality: Transforming Culture, Society, and Politics.* Chicago: University of Chicago Press.

Jodalen, H., and Vetlesen, A. (eds.) 1997. *Closeness: An Ethics.* Oslo: Scandinavian University Press.

Kant, I. 1960. *Observations on the Feeling of the Beautiful and the Sublime*, trans. J.T. Goldthwait. Berkeley: University of California Press.

Levinas, E. 1969. *Totality and Infinity*, trans. A. Lingis. Pittsburgh: Duquesne University Press.

Levinas, E. 1985. *Ethics and Infinity*, trans. R. Cohen. Pittsburgh: Duquesne University Press.

Lippke, R. 1995. *Radical Business Ethics.* Lanham, MD: Rowman and Littlefield.

May, L. 1992. *Sharing Responsibility.* Chicago: University of Chicago Press.

McNay, L. 2000. *Gender and Agency: Reconfiguring the Subject in Feminist and Social Theory.* Cambridge: Polity.

Nietzsche, F. 1998. *On the Genealogy of Morality*, trans. M. Clark, and A. Swensen. Indianapolis: Hackett.

Noddings, N. 1984. *Caring: A Feminine Approach to Ethics and Moral Education.* Berkeley: University of California Press.

Nunner-Winkler, G. 1993. "Two moralities: A critical discussion of an ethics of care and responsibility versus an ethic of rights and justice." In M.J. Larrabee, ed., *An Ethic of Care*. New York: Routledge.

Oliver, K. 2001. *Witnessing: Beyond Recognition.* Minneapolis: University of Minnesota Press.

Pilcher, J., and Whelehan, I. (eds.) 2004. *50 Key Concepts in Gender Studies.* London: Sage.

Plumwood, V. 1993. *Feminism and the Mastery of Nature.* London: Routledge.

Rawls, J. 1971. *A Theory of Justice.* Cambridge, MA: Harvard University Press.

Ruddick, S. 1989. *Maternal Thinking: Toward a Politics of Peace.* Boston: Beacon Press.

Schroeder, J.E. 2008. "Brand culture: Trade marks, marketing and consumption." In L. Bently, J. Davis, and J.C. Ginsberg, eds., *Trade Marks and Brands: An Interdisciplinary Critique.* Cambridge: Cambridge University Press, in press.

Schroeder, J.E., and Borgerson, J.L. 2005. "An ethics of representation for international marketing." *International Marketing Review* 22: 578–600.

Sherwin, S. 1996. "Feminism and bioethics." In S.M. Wolf, ed., *Feminism and Bioethics: Beyond Reproduction*, pp. 47–66. Oxford: Oxford University Press.

Shildrick, M. 2007. "Dangerous Discourses: Anxiety, Desire and Disability." *Studies in Gender and Sexuality* 8 (3): 221–44.

Shultz, T., and Brender-Ilan, Y. 2004. "Beyond justice: Introducing personal moral philosophies to ethical evaluations of human resource practices." *Business Ethics: A European Review* 13 (4): 302–16.

Solomon, R. 1993. "Business ethics." In P. Singer, ed., *A Companion to Ethics*, pp. 354–65. Oxford: Blackwell.

Stack, C.B. 1993. "The culture of gender. Women and men of color." In M.J. Larrabee, ed., *An Ethic of Care: Feminist and Interdisciplinary Perspectives*. New York: Routledge.

Tong, R. 1993. *Feminine and Feminist Ethics*. Belmont, CA: Wadsworth.

Tong, R. 1996. "Feminist Approaches to Bioethics." In S. Wolf, ed., *Feminism and Bioethics: Beyond Reproduction*, pp. 67–94. Oxford: Oxford University Press.

Tong, R. 1997. *Feminist Approaches to Bioethics: Theoretical Reflections and Practical Applications*. Boulder, CO: Westview.

Tronto, J. 1993. *Moral Boundaries: A Political Argument for an Ethic of Care*. New York: Routledge.

Vaver, D. 2008. "Images in brand culture: Responding legally to Professor Schroeder's paper." In L. Bently, J. Davis, and J.C. Ginsberg, eds., *Trade Marks and Brands: An Interdisciplinary Critique*. Cambridge: Cambridge University Press.

Velasquez, M.G. 2002. *Business Ethics: Concepts and Cases*, 5th ed. Upper Saddle River, NJ: Prentice-Hall.

Walker, M. 1998. *Moral Understandings: A Feminist Study in Ethics*. New York: Routledge.

Warnock, J.G. 1969. *Contemporary Moral Philosophy*. New York: St. Martin's Press.

Weston, A. 1992. *Toward Better Problems*. Philadelphia: Temple University Press.

Whitbeck, C. 1983. "A different reality: Feminist ontology." In C.C. Gould, ed., *Beyond Domination*. Totowa, NJ: Rowman & Allenheld.

White, T. 1998. "Sexual harassment: Trust and the ethics of care." *Business and Society Review* 100/101: 9–20.

Wolf, S. (ed.) 1996. *Feminism and Bioethics: Beyond Reproduction*. Oxford: Oxford University Press.

Wollstonecraft, M. 1975. *A Vindication of the Rights of Woman* [1790]. London: Penguin.

Young, I.M. 1990. *Throwing Like a Girl and Other Essays in Feminist Philosophy and Social Theory*. Bloomington: Indiana University Press.

Young, I.M. 1997. *Intersecting Voices: Dilemmas of Gender, Political Philosophy, and Policy*. Princeton, NJ: Princeton University Press.

Questions

1. What are some of the problems with traditional approaches to ethics?

2. What is the difference between a feminist, feminine, and care approach to ethics?

3. Why does Borgerson hold that care ethics is not necessarily feminist ethics?

4. What insights can feminist approaches to ethics bring to issues in business ethics?

5. What are some of the examples Borgerson provides to demonstrate the relevance of feminist ethics to business ethics?

Further Reading

Brennan, Samantha. "Recent Work in Feminist Ethics." *Ethics: An International Journal of Social, Political, and Legal Philosophy*, vol. 109, no. 4, 1 July 1999, pp. 858–93.

Derry, Robbin. "Feminist Theory and Business Ethics." In *A Companion to Business Ethics*, Cambridge: Blackwell, 2002.

Machold, Silke, Pervaiz K. Ahmed, and Stuart S. Farquhar. "Corporate Governance and Ethics: A Feminist Perspective." *Journal of Business Ethics*, vol. 81, no. 3, 2008, pp. 665–78.

Rabouin, Michelle. "Lyin' T(*)gers, and 'Cares,' Oh My: The Case for Feminist Integration of Business Ethics." *Journal of Business Ethics*, vol. 16, no. 3, 1 Feb. 1997, pp. 247–61.

6.

"ON THE DISCONNECT BETWEEN BUSINESS AND PROFESSIONAL ETHICS"

ALAN TOMHAVE AND MARK C. VOPAT

There are many different ways we commonly use the word *professional*. When we say someone is a professional, we sometimes simply mean that the person is paid for the work he or she does. A professional athlete is someone who is paid to play a sport. A professional artist is someone who makes a living producing and selling his or her art. Oftentimes we think of a professional as someone who brings a certain approach or attitude to a *job*. We may also think of a professional as someone who has extensive train- ing or experience in an area—a view that may overlap with the concept of *expertise*. Unlike these everyday notions of *professional*, many philosophers define a professional in a much narrower sense. Professions are occupations that carry with them special rights or responsibilities. They have their own moral code. The classic example is found in law. A lawyer is allowed to "lie" to the court, as when she says "not guilty," even though she may know that her client committed the crime.

There are those who believe businesspersons also operate according to a different moral code. It is the view that people in business—as businessper- sons—cannot be held to the same moral standards or be required to follow the same moral principles as everyone else. In this article, Tomhave and Vopat argue against the idea that businesspersons are professionals (in the more technical sense) and hold that they should be held to the same moral standards as everyone else.

Introduction

We begin our paper with a hypothetical question: Is there a distinction to be made between Professional Ethics and Business Ethics?[1] This is a conceptual question, but one with pedagogical import. The answer hinges on both the nature of "professional" and the further question of whether business is subsumed under this understanding. For the purposes of this paper, we shall adopt the admittedly controversial position that for an occupation to be a profession, it must be governed by moral rules, principles, privileges, and responsibilities that differ from our everyday morality. To act in a professional manner is thus to act according to a moral code that would be considered morally wrong if applied outside of a professional context. If a businessperson is a professional by this definition, then clearly an understanding of the complexities of navigating between a professional code of conduct and one's everyday moral responsibilities is best achieved by a course in professional ethics. On the other hand, if a businessperson is not a professional, then what requires emphasis is the way in which moral rules and principles ought to be applied within a business context.

In this paper we shall argue that businesspersons are not professionals in the technical sense presented above, and consequently business students are best served not by a course in professional ethics, but by a course in business ethics. In making this case we shall argue: 1) that the nature of the professional entails a special morality, one that may allow for actions normally seen as unethical to be ethical, while business ethics concerns no such special morality, and 2) that unlike the concerns that are well-studied in professional ethics, business has numerous fundamental assumptions that are taken for granted by most business students, and hence go unquestioned (e.g., the nature of capitalism and markets, the profit motive, and the nature of business itself). An approach that treats business ethics as distinct from professional ethics—and hence leads to a separate business ethics course—allows for an examination of these fundamental assumptions.

What Is a Profession?

There is an ongoing debate as to what exactly constitutes a profession. Since professions may carry with them special moral responsibilities, it will be necessary to distinguish a profession from non-professions. Unfortunately, our common use of the word "professional" is often fraught with ambiguity. We often refer to "professional athletes" and "professional sportscasters," while holding that doctors and lawyers are also professionals.

---

1   An earlier version of this chapter was presented at the Thirteenth International Conference on Ethics Across the Curriculum, Saint Louis, Missouri, 4 November 2011.

Non-moral Sense of Professional

The term "professional" is often applied to a wide variety of disparate activities. In everyday non moral usage, the term is often applied in three ways. First, we often attribute the status of "professional" to anyone who receives financial compensation for his or her activity. This sense allows anyone engaged in an activity for pay to be termed a "professional." Secondly, the term "professional" is often associated with someone who has attained a certain level of expertise. So, when people in business talk about being a professional, what they are really pointing to is a certain level of expertise; for example, the distinctions between a carpenter and a master carpenter, and other occupations as well. Consequently, one initial distinction that we may want to make is between an occupation and a profession. For our purposes, an occupation is anything that one does as a job. On the other hand, a profession is an occupation that carries with it some special features that other occupations lack.[2] For example, most people would agree that lawyers are professionals and that fast-food workers are not. An objection to this last point suggests a third common usage of "professional" that must also be rejected. "Professional" is often also used as a way to denote a specific type of attitude when engaging in work. Thus, there may be "professional" fast-food workers and non-professional fast-food workers. The professional is the one who takes work seriously and brings a good attitude to the workplace (hard worker, proper dress code, etc.). However, this is simply a different way of distinguishing between good employees and bad ones, or those who take their job seriously and those who do not. This same distinction exists in those who we will argue are truly professionals. There are lawyers who take their job seriously and those who do not. This misses the point when considering the question at hand. The question is what characteristics does the practice of law have that distinguishes it in some significant way from the food preparer at a fast food enterprise. What we are seeking then are the necessary or sufficient conditions for distinguishing between occupations and professions.

Bayles and Barber

In the attempt to specify the salient features of professions, philosophers such as Michael Bayles (Bayles, 1981, pp. 7–11) and Bernard Barber have each offered either necessary or sufficient conditions for distinguishing professions from occupations (Barber, 1963, pp. 669–88). It should be noted from the outset that these criteria are not somehow set in stone. The fact that Bayles or Barber believes these criteria

---

2   The implication of this definition is of course that all professions are occupations, while not all occupations are professions.

adequately describe professions does not settle the issue, but acts as a starting point for our thinking about the nature of professions.

According to Bayles (1981), there are three necessary conditions that define a profession. Remove any one of these conditions and the occupation fails to qualify as a profession. First, all professions require some sort of extensive training. Second, this extensive training must have an intellectual component. Third, the occupation must provide a valuable or essential service to society. Taken individually, it seems that almost any occupation could be considered a profession. It is only when we note that all three conditions must be met, that it becomes apparent how restrictive Bayles's criteria actually are in practice. Take for example the idea of a "professional athlete." While it is true that a professional athlete undergoes extensive training, this training does not include an intellectual component. Furthermore, it is fairly easy to argue that professional athletes don't provide an essential or important service to society. On the other hand, it is easy to see how physicians would qualify as professionals, since they meet each of the three criteria. There is extensive training involved in becoming a physician. That training includes both a physical component and a substantial intellectual component (an undergraduate degree, three years of medical school and additional training as a resident). Unlike the professional athlete, physicians do provide an essential and important service to society, since I can easily choose not to watch an athletic event, but cannot avoid going to the hospital when I am extremely ill.[3]

While Bayles's approach is fairly straightforward, not everyone agrees with his characterization of the nature of professions. In particular, some have argued that not all occupations fit neatly into the professional or non-professional category. There are some occupations that seem to have some of the aspects of professions, but lack others. Rather than viewing the definition of a profession as an either-or, some view professions on a continuum with non-profession at one end and profession at the other. Thus, occupations may admit of gradations of professionalism—and one such approach is endorsed by Bernard Barber.

According to Barber (1963), the idea of a profession is one of degree. Barber argues that there are a number of sufficient conditions for an occupation to be a profession. First, a profession is something that has a high degree of systematic knowledge. Second, the primary orientation of the professional is toward community interests rather than individual interests. Third, professionals require a high degree of self-control of behavior based on internalized codes of ethics derived from voluntary

---

3   Assuming of course I desire to be in good health. I may avoid going to the hospital because I have made a decision not to seek help for a particular (perhaps terminal) condition. Nevertheless, most of us do not view healthcare as something that is merely one optional activity among many. If all professional sport were to disappear tomorrow, our way of life would not be fundamentally altered. On the other hand, if the medical practice ceased to exist tomorrow, our lives would be affected in a fundamental way.

associations with others in the profession. Finally, professions are associated with a system of rewards that are primarily symbolic of work achievement, and are thus ends in themselves, rather than a means to some end of individual self-interest.

Since Barber's criteria are not necessary conditions, some things that would not be considered professions by Bayles would be classified as such by Barber. For example, journalism is considered by many to be a profession. While it is true that many journalists have college degrees and even master's degrees, it is also true that no degree (college or otherwise) is necessary to obtain a job in journalism. Nevertheless, we still might want to say that journalists are professionals. They do have community-oriented interest (journalism as the "fourth estate"); a code of ethics that internally regulates their behavior; and a system of awards (Polk, Peabody, Pulitzer) that are primarily symbolic. So, on Barber's account, there may be a sufficient number of criteria to make the determination that journalism is a profession.

While Bayles and Barber differ as to whether the criteria that define a profession are necessary or sufficient, they do generally agree on a couple of key features. Both hold that professions require some sort of intellectual training, namely, a college degree. They also agree that the primary focus of a profession is on community interest. How we define that interest is beyond the scope of this paper, but we do have an intuitive sense of what is meant by a community interest, namely, something without which our lives would be fundamentally altered for the worse. For example, if law, medicine and architecture ceased to exist, our lives would be without a doubt the worse for their absence.

Moral Aspects of a Profession

While different theorists have different particular notions about what constitutes a profession, all agree that once something has the title of a profession it implicitly carries with it special obligations. These obligations are normally thought to follow from the unique position professionals occupy within society. In other words, to assume a professional role entails that one has special obligations or special privileges to certain other specific individuals. These obligations derive from the relevant special circumstances surrounding those individuals, and presumably the relationship or circumstances are unique in that they don't include everyone (which would thus make the obligation general). This view that certain roles carry with them a separate morality is what has been termed the "separatist thesis."[4]

---

4   See, for example, Alan Gewirth, (1986). "Professional ethics: The separatist thesis," *Ethics*, 96, pp. 282–300. Alternatively, Alan Goldman (1980) refers to these roles as "strongly differentiated." Goldman, describing strongly differentiated roles, writes that, "For the stronger concept of role differentiation to apply, it must be the case that the occupant of the position be permitted or required to ignore or weigh less heavily what would otherwise be morally overriding considerations in the relations into which he enters as a professional.

The separatist thesis holds that professional morality may at times contradict ordinary morality, but that the follower of the professional ethic is not acting unjustly, but is in fact abiding by a different moral code altogether. Individuals engaging in the practice of law, medicine, nursing, social science research, etc., may do things that might be considered immoral if done outside of a professional context. For example, we expect lawyers to "lie" about the guilt of his or her client. When a judge asks the defense attorney how his or her client pleads, it is understood that the attorney may respond "not guilty," though what he or she means is not legally guilty, and may later imply not factually guilty during closing arguments. While a similar dishonesty would be morally problematic if it occurred between friends, the need to maintain an adversarial system that (hopefully) punishes the guilty and exonerates the innocent justifies granting lawyers certain privileges.

When we combine the idea of what is a professional with the idea of role-differentiated behavior, we gain a clearer picture of what constitutes a profession in a moral sense. As Bayles and Barber have suggested, a profession provides a valuable social service, among other things. Consequently, we would suggest that a valuable service is one that protects what Rawls would term a primary good. Rights, freedoms, bodily integrity, opportunity, income, wealth, and the social bases of self-respect are all types of things that constitute a primary good. Professionals are those individuals who contribute to the protection or realization of these fundamentally important goods. Doctors provide the requisite medical care that leads to the health needed to take advantage of opportunities. Educators provide the tools necessary to perform the jobs that provide the income needed to survive, as well as for preparing individuals to exercise citizenship responsibly.

But, there is an additional aspect of a professional that sets him or her apart from other occupations. Not only does a professional provide a valuable service, but the nature of the service necessitates a different set of moral standards in order to perform the service. While doctors assist in our well-being, they also need to be able to act in emergency situations to circumvent things such as consent, e.g., when a patient is unconscious. Since they also deal with extremely intimate aspects of a person's life, and candor is required to provide proper patient care, confidentiality is nearly absolute. Similarly, lawyers not only have an obligation to be a zealous advocate for their clients, but they are also required to maintain confidentiality in order to provide an adequate defense. Here, too, the role of the professional is to protect the rights of the individual and contribute to the broader goal of a just legal system. The nature of the work of the professional requires a different moral code in order to effectively perform his or her job.

Professional duty must systematically outweigh these considerations, as it would not if each such relation were evaluated individually from the point of view of general moral theory" (Goldman, 1980, p. 3).

This view of what defines a professional in the moral sense entails that a fairly narrow range of occupations qualifies as professions. While there is considerable debate as to which occupations should make the list, for the purposes of this paper, we focus on what should not make the list, namely, business.

Business Is Not a Profession

We begin by admitting that businesspersons are professionals in the non-moral senses described at the outset. Businesspersons are paid for their work, they often have a great deal of expertise in their area of business, and they frequently take their jobs seriously and work with a good attitude. However, as should be clear by now, we are not interested in these non-moral senses of "professional," but in the moral sense described above.

We would also like to be very clear on one point: we accept that the list of occupations counting as professions may be ever-expanding. This discussion is not to be taken as excluding engineers, for example, from the list of professions. Our discussion here may be limited to businesspersons generically speaking.

The crux of our definition of profession is found in the fact that for a professional to do her job correctly, it is necessary that she be able to engage in actions that would normally be considered unethical (performing medical procedures on one's body without consent, helping to free murderers from punishment, etc.). Thus, the question is this: is it necessary for businesspersons to engage in behaviors that would normally be considered unethical in order for them to do their jobs? The answer is clearly, no. However, some further discussion is warranted.

The types of activities in which businesspersons engage are things like sales, manufacturing, and various decisions related to those activities (hiring and firing, design, plant management, advertising, accounting, etc.). There is nothing in these activities that necessitates a typically unethical action be taken. In fact, businesses are frequently criticized specifically because they engage in actions like deception or failure to satisfy social obligations. No exceptions are made for businesses, as is the case for professionals in the moral sense described above.

At this point, there is an objection that could come from the likes of Milton Friedman. Friedman is well known for defending a view of business that holds that it has no responsibilities beyond increasing its profits.[5] While it may be true that businesspersons have a right to increase profits, there are limits. Moreover, there is nothing special about those engaged in business with regard to earning profits.

---

5   Friedman's (1970) view is actually more nuanced than this, and we could be accused of making the same category mistake that he criticizes, that is, "business" is not the sort of thing that can have responsibilities at all.

Everyone has that right. Moreover, even Friedman admits that the actions of businesspersons should be limited by ethical considerations (along with legal restrictions).

A special case that is common in business ethics classes may help further illustrate our point. Whistleblowing is a common topic of discussion in business ethics. It must be admitted that businesses have an expectation of privacy and the ability to protect proprietary processes and products and innovations. This expectation would include the expectation that employees not expose business knowledge integral to the functioning of the specific business that may be harmful to that business. However, this protection does not necessarily extend to employees remaining silent when a business makes a decision to engage in some action that may be harmful to the community or individual customers (a la Boeing's DC10, Ford's Pinto, Enron's profits, etc.). In cases where the business is engaged in actions that are actually harmful to others, then there can be little complaint when an employee informs the public of the behavior.[6]

The Subject of Business Ethics

Given the distinction between professions and businesspersons generally, we would now like to argue that this leads to the conclusion that business ethics should be taught in a stand-alone class, distinct from a course is professional ethics. There are two basic reasons that we will offer. First, a business ethics class allows for an examination of assumptions in business that go unexamined by many business students. Second, a business ethics class allows for an examination of how to apply moral principles in a business context. We will examine both of these reasons in turn.

The first reason for teaching business in a stand-alone course is that it allows one to examine assumptions in business that go unchallenged by most students. This is particularly important for business students. In professional courses of study the issue of ethics is common and commonly studied. In business this is not the case. Many students think of business as described by Milton Friedman or Albert Carr.[7] Both of these views are problematic. Friedman (1970) is problematic because he argues that there are no responsibilities for those in business roles beyond increasing profits. Carr (1968) is problematic because he argues that business should be treated like a game, where ethics do not really apply. Carr's position contributes well to the

---

6   This final point is made with full acknowledgement of the difficulty of specifying harms that may be permissible for business to cause and those that may not be. For example, a business may harm the community in which it is located by making certain permissible business decisions (e.g., to relocate a manufacturing plant). Such decisions may be harmful, yet permissible for the business in question.

7   In Friedman's "The Social Responsibility Is to Increase Profits" (1970) and Carr's "Is Business Bluffing Ethical?" (1968).

view that when treating someone poorly in business, we are justified in thinking, "it is not personal, it is just business."

It may be the case business only has a responsibility to increase profits, and that there are clear and definite distinctions to be made between business and personal life. However, these are important issues worthy of examination, even if they are true. If these positions cannot be justified, then they should be rejected. We will not know either way, unless we examine these assumptions.

In "The Why's of Business Revisited," Ronald Duska (1997) examines the dominant view that the purpose of business is simply profits. This idea is closely related to claims like those mentioned above, that a certain action by a business professional could be excused with the claim that it is "just business." In thinking that business is only concerned with profits (as opposed to the production of goods and services for Duska), and allowing this view to go unexamined by business students, we limit their ability to engage critically with this claim, because the very language needed to conceptualize a criticism is lacking. Duska writes:

> This dominant view, though, is not neutral. No view of purpose is. Such a view legitimates the institutional practices of business, and in this case does so to such an extent that even if we are opposed to the practices we do not have the language to critique them. So we are faced with an anomaly—even those who would claim that the purpose of business is to provide goods and services slip into talk about business which legitimizes some of the behavior they would not approve of in theory. (Duska, 1997, p. 1402)

It is a failing of educators to simply allow students that will engage in business generally to enter the workforce without the language and concepts necessary to examine fundamental assumptions about their choice of employment. For students entering into the professions where a role-differentiated behavior is a part of the profession, then a professional ethics class is useful, specifically because these fundamental questions are asked and discussed (the nature of confidentiality, zealous representation, competency, the nature of the professional client relationship, etc.). To not provide the same service to our business students is to allow them to enter the workforce unprepared to address real issues they will encounter and is once again to fail those students. Moreover, not asking such questions allows a culture of business to continue that may be detrimental to all aspects of the lives of our students, other third parties, the companies they will work for, and ourselves. Consider a further comment by Duska:

> … to the extent that "maximizing profits" becomes a legitimation of greedy practices we have an erosion of the ethical climate of the business

environment. To the extent that we allow phrases such as "that's business" to legitimate cut-throat competition we have an unethical climate. One of the most insidious mistakes made in discussing business ethics is that made in viewing the only responsibility of business to be maximizing profits. (Duska, 1997, p. 1407)

Thus, to allow this most fundamental and widely held view to go unchallenged by students is to perpetuate an unethical climate.

If the question about the purpose of business and whether or not there are options beyond profit maximization were the only important one to address in business ethics, then it might be that we could simply incorporate this question into a professional ethics course. After all, it is not only business students that take this view of business, and many would benefit by an examination of the question. However, there are also questions about the nature of markets. For example, should everything that can be dealt with in the marketplace be put in the marketplace? Is it true that everything we can do to make money is an endeavor that we can permissibly engage in? For example, is it moral for a business to make money by denying a sick individual access to healthcare? Alternatively, are there other mechanisms better suited to dealing with some circumstances (medical care, roads, etc.)? Even the very nature of capitalism needs to be examined, not simply from the position of trying to figure out how it works, which presumably is explained in standard business curriculums, but also a fundamental examination of capitalism with a critical eye to what it entails and whether or not it is a good practice, morally speaking.

All of these questions are those that business students should consider, yet this is clearly too much to include in a professional ethics course, where the focus would be on questions of role-differentiated moral considerations. The solution to this problem, where these fundamental assumptions go unexamined, is to have a separate business ethics course for business students (preferably required, not optional).

The second reason we advance for having a stand-alone business ethics course is that it allows for the application of moral principles specifically to business settings. This has two distinct advantages. First, students are more engaged if the examples are interesting and relevant to their course of study. Presumably business students would be very interested in business examples. Second, it helps form views about how business should be conducted, while using as examples the very types of scenarios that students may one day face. This allows for a clearer understanding of how moral principles apply to business settings.

Both of these reasons lead to a distinct pedagogical advantage to teaching a stand-alone business ethics course rather than a professional ethics course that also applies to business students. The advantage comes from the reasons just explained and from the fact that a professional ethics course is already difficult enough to teach and ensure proper coverage of topics in professional ethics, even without the most important topics in business ethics. To include both topics in a single course is to do a disservice to students in business and those with a professional trajectory.

An Objection

At this point we would like to entertain an objection that could be raised to the view outlined above. This objection is not conceptual so much as pedagogical. It stems from the claim that it is good for business students to have an ethics course that specifically uses business examples. If this is the case, then why not argue for stand-alone courses in every area of ethics and the various occupations that should include an ethics course in the curriculum? For example, we should also be arguing for a stand-alone course in engineering ethics, journalism ethics, ethics in teaching, etc. Thus, the above argument seems to lead to an explosion of ethics courses. To some extent, our response to this objection is to agree. Students in those disciplines may very well benefit from such focused courses. Moreover, some disciplines have issues that seem to require such a stand-alone course (journalism, for example). However, many of the issues that would come up in these other courses also arise in business ethics (whistleblowing, for example). Thus, while it may be beneficial to allow for such an explosion of ethics courses to occur, the benefits for on-professional-trajectory students will largely be met in a business ethics course. However, we would advocate for such an explosion if there were sufficient faculty in a department to teach all these courses and sufficient students to justify teaching such courses.

In Conclusion

The separability thesis and the argument against businesspersons as professionals have implications beyond the pedagogical. The recent financial crisis demonstrates just how dangerous it can be to view business as adhering to a different set of moral standards. The risk undertaken by financial institutions, the loans granted without proper collateral, and the insuring of mortgage-backed securities all represent—in part—a moral failing on the part of businesspersons. They exposed investors, including pensioners, to undue risk and eventual harm. While these practices and their associated risks may be viewed as business as usual, for many they clearly represent a failure to reflect on the moral implications of unbridled profit maximization. More than ever, students need to learn how not to conflate legally acceptable actions with morally acceptable ones.

References

Barber, B. (1963). "Some problems in the sociology of the professions." *Daedalus, 92,* 669–88.

Bayles, M. (1981). *Professional Ethics.* Belmont, California: Wadsworth Publishing Company.

Carr, A. (1968). "Is business bluffing ethical?" *Harvard Business Review, 46,* 143–53.

Duska, R. (1997). "The why's of business revisited." *Journal of Business Ethics, 16,* 1401–09.

Friedman, M. (1970). "The social responsibility of business is to increase its profits." *The New York Times Magazine, 13.*

Gewirth, A. (1986). "Professional ethics: The separatist thesis." *Ethics, 96,* 282–300.

Goldman, A. (1980). *The Moral Foundations of Professional Ethics.* Totowa, New Jersey: Rowman and Littlefield.

Questions

1. What is the difference between moral and non-moral senses of professions?

2. In what ways are the moral obligations of a doctor or lawyer different from those of someone working in business?

3. What are the necessary and/or sufficient conditions for some occupations to be considered professions?

4. How does viewing profit maximization as the purpose of business lead to an unethical climate?

5. What would a special code of ethics for business professionals look like?

Further Reading

Barber, Bernard. "Some Problems in the Sociology of the Professions." *Daedalus,* vol. 92, 1963, pp. 669–88.

Bayles, Michael. *Professional Ethics.* Belmont: Wadsworth, 1981.

Gewirth, Alan. "Professional Ethics: The Separatist Thesis." *Ethics,* vol. 96, 1986, pp. 282–300.

Goldman, Alvin. *The Moral Foundations of Professional Ethics.* Totowa, NJ: Rowman and Littlefield, 1980.

II.
THE NATURE OF BUSINESS

7.

FROM
THE WEALTH OF NATIONS (1776)

ADAM SMITH

About This Reading

An Inquiry into the Nature and Causes of the Wealth of Nations was published by Adam Smith in 1776, at the beginning of the Industrial Revolution, and is the first economic treatise to look at the rise of wealth. One of its main topics is the development of and motivations for the division of labor, discussed in these excerpts. Additionally, he discusses a potential problem with the division of labor, claiming that too much focus on small repetitive tasks can make a worker become "as stupid and ignorant as it is possible for a human creature to become." Thus, while the division of labor may bring with it many benefits, it is not without cost.

Book I. Of the Causes of Improvement ...

Chapter I. Of the Division of Labour

The greatest improvements in the productive powers of labour, and the greater part of the skill, dexterity, and judgment, with which it is anywhere directed, or applied, seem to have been the effects of the division of labour. The effects of the division of labour, in the general business of society, will be more easily understood, by considering in what manner it operates in some particular manufactures. It is commonly supposed to be carried furthest in some very trifling ones; not perhaps that it really is carried further in them than in others of more importance: but in those trifling manufactures which are destined to supply the small wants of but a small number of people, the whole number of workmen must necessarily be small; and those employed in every different branch of the work can often be collected into the same workhouse, and placed at once under the view of the spectator.

In those great manufactures, on the contrary, which are destined to supply the great wants of the great body of the people, every different branch of the work employs so great a number of workmen, that it is impossible to collect them all into the same workhouse. We can seldom see more, at one time, than those employed in one single branch. Though in such manufactures, therefore, the work may really be divided into a much greater number of parts, than in those of a more trifling nature, the division is not near so obvious, and has accordingly been much less observed.

To take an example, therefore, from a very trifling manufacture, but one in which the division of labour has been very often taken notice of, the trade of a pin-maker: a workman not educated to this business (which the division of labour has rendered a distinct trade), nor acquainted with the use of the machinery employed in it (to the invention of which the same division of labour has probably given occasion), could scarce, perhaps, with his utmost industry, make one pin in a day, and certainly could not make twenty. But in the way in which this business is now carried on, not only the whole work is a peculiar trade, but it is divided into a number of branches, of which the greater part are likewise peculiar trades. One man draws out the wire; another straights it; a third cuts it; a fourth points it; a fifth grinds it at the top for receiving the head; to make the head requires two or three distinct operations; to put it on is a peculiar business; to whiten the pins is another; it is even a trade by itself to put them into the paper; and the important business of making a pin is, in this manner, divided into about eighteen distinct operations, which, in some manufactories, are all performed by distinct hands, though in others the same man will sometimes perform two or three of them. I have seen a small manufactory of this kind, where ten men only were employed, and where some of them consequently performed two or three distinct operations. But though they were very poor, and therefore but indifferently accommodated with the necessary machinery, they could, when they exerted themselves, make among them about twelve pounds of pins in a day. There are in a pound upwards of four thousand pins of a middling size. Those ten persons, therefore, could make among them upwards of forty-eight thousand pins in a day. Each person, therefore, making a tenth part of forty-eight thousand pins, might be considered as making four thousand eight hundred pins in a day. But if they had all wrought separately and independently, and without any of them having been educated to this peculiar business, they certainly could not each of them have made twenty, perhaps not one pin in a day; that is, certainly, not the two hundred and fortieth, perhaps not the four thousand eight hundredth, part of what they are at present capable of performing, in consequence of a proper division and combination of their different operations.

In every other art and manufacture, the effects of the division of labour are similar to what they are in this very trifling one, though, in many of them, the labour can neither be so much subdivided, nor reduced to so great a simplicity of operation. The division of labour, however, so far as it can be introduced, occasions, in every art, a proportionable increase of the productive powers of labour. The separation of different trades and employments from one another, seems to have taken place in consequence of this advantage. This separation, too, is generally carried furthest in those countries which enjoy the highest degree of industry and improvement; what is the work of one man, in a rude state of society, being generally that of several in an improved one. In every improved society, the farmer is generally nothing but a farmer; the manufacturer, nothing but a manufacturer. The labour, too, which is necessary to produce any one complete manufacture, is almost always divided among a great number of hands. How many different trades are employed in each branch of the linen and woollen manufactures, from the growers of the flax and the wool, to the bleachers and smoothers of the linen, or to the dyers and dressers of the cloth! The nature of agriculture, indeed, does not admit of so many subdivisions of labour, nor of so complete a separation of one business from another, as manufactures. It is impossible to separate so entirely the business of the grazier from that of the corn-farmer, as the trade of the carpenter is commonly separated from that of the smith. The spinner is almost always a distinct person from the weaver; but the ploughman, the harrower, the sower of the seed, and the reaper of the corn, are often the same. The occasions for those different sorts of labour returning with the different seasons of the year, it is impossible that one man should be constantly employed in any one of them. This impossibility of making so complete and entire a separation of all the different branches of labour employed in agriculture, is perhaps the reason why the improvement of the productive powers of labour, in this art, does not always keep pace with their improvement in manufactures. The most opulent nations, indeed, generally excel all their neighbours in agriculture as well as in manufactures; but they are commonly more distinguished by their superiority in the latter than in the former. Their lands are in general better cultivated, and having more labour and expense bestowed upon them, produce more in proportion to the extent and natural fertility of the ground. But this superiority of produce is seldom much more than in proportion to the superiority of labour and expense. In agriculture, the labour of the rich country is not always much more productive than that of the poor; or, at least, it is never so much more productive, as it commonly is in manufactures. The corn of the rich country, therefore, will not always, in the same degree of goodness, come cheaper to market than that of the poor. The corn of Poland, in the same degree of goodness, is as cheap as that of France, notwithstanding the superior opulence and improvement of the latter country. The corn of

France is, in the corn-provinces, fully as good, and in most years nearly about the same price with the corn of England, though, in opulence and improvement, France is perhaps inferior to England. The corn-lands of England, however, are better cultivated than those of France, and the corn-lands of France are said to be much better cultivated than those of Poland. But though the poor country, notwithstanding the inferiority of its cultivation, can, in some measure, rival the rich in the cheapness and goodness of its corn, it can pretend to no such competition in its manufactures, at least if those manufactures suit the soil, climate, and situation, of the rich country. The silks of France are better and cheaper than those of England, because the silk manufacture, at least under the present high duties upon the importation of raw silk, does not so well suit the climate of England as that of France. But the hardware and the coarse woollens of England are beyond all comparison superior to those of France, and much cheaper, too, in the same degree of goodness. In Poland there are said to be scarce any manufactures of any kind, a few of those coarser household manufactures excepted, without which no country can well subsist.

This great increase in the quantity of work, which, in consequence of the division of labour, the same number of people are capable of performing, is owing to three different circumstances; first, to the increase of dexterity in every particular workman; secondly, to the saving of the time which is commonly lost in passing from one species of work to another; and, lastly, to the invention of a great number of machines which facilitate and abridge labour, and enable one man to do the work of many.

First, the improvement of the dexterity of the workmen, necessarily increases the quantity of the work he can perform; and the division of labour, by reducing every man's business to some one simple operation, and by making this operation the sole employment of his life, necessarily increases very much the dexterity of the workman. A common smith, who, though accustomed to handle the hammer, has never been used to make nails, if, upon some particular occasion, he is obliged to attempt it, will scarce, I am assured, be able to make above two or three hundred nails in a day, and those, too, very bad ones. A smith who has been accustomed to make nails, but whose sole or principal business has not been that of a nailer, can seldom, with his utmost diligence, make more than eight hundred or a thousand nails in a day. I have seen several boys, under twenty years of age, who had never exercised any other trade but that of making nails, and who, when they exerted themselves, could make, each of them, upwards of two thousand three hundred nails in a day. The making of a nail, however, is by no means one of the simplest operations. The same person blows the bellows, stirs or mends the fire as there is occasion, heats the iron, and forges every part of the nail: in forging the head, too, he is obliged to change his tools. The different operations into which the making of a pin, or of a metal button, is subdivided, are all of them much more simple, and the dexterity of the person, of whose life it has been the sole business to perform them, is usually much greater. The rapidity with which some of the operations of those manufactures are performed, exceeds what the human hand could, by those who had never seen them, be supposed capable of acquiring.

Secondly, the advantage which is gained by saving the time commonly lost in passing from one sort of work to another, is much greater than we should at first view be apt to imagine it. It is impossible to pass very quickly from one kind of work to another, that is carried on in a different place, and with quite different tools. A country weaver, who cultivates a small farm, must loose a good deal of time in passing from his loom to the field, and from the field to his loom. When the two trades can be carried on in the same workhouse, the loss of time is, no doubt, much less. It is, even in this case, however, very considerable. A man commonly saunters a little in turning his hand from one sort of employment to another. When he first begins the new work, he is seldom very keen and hearty; his mind, as they say, does not go to it, and for some time he rather trifles than applies to good purpose. The habit of sauntering, and of indolent careless application, which is naturally, or rather necessarily, acquired by every country workman who is obliged to change his work and his tools every half hour, and to apply his hand in twenty different ways almost every day of his life, renders him almost always slothful and lazy, and incapable of any vigorous application, even on the most pressing occasions. Independent, therefore, of his deficiency in point of dexterity, this cause alone must always reduce considerably the quantity of work which he is capable of performing.

Thirdly, and lastly, everybody must be sensible how much labour is facilitated and abridged by the application of proper machinery. It is unnecessary to give any example. I shall only observe, therefore, that the invention of all those machines by which labour is so much facilitated and abridged, seems to have been originally owing to the division of labour. Men are much more likely to discover easier and readier methods of attaining any object, when the whole attention of their minds is directed towards that single object, than when it is dissipated among a great variety of things. But, in consequence of the division of labour, the whole of every man's attention comes naturally to be directed towards some one very simple object. It is naturally to be expected, therefore, that some one or other of those who are employed in each particular branch of labour should soon find out easier and readier methods of performing their own particular work, whenever the nature of it admits of such improvement. A great part of the machines made use of in those manufactures in which labour is most subdivided, were originally the invention of common workmen, who, being each of them employed in some very simple operation, naturally turned their thoughts towards finding out easier and readier methods of performing it. Whoever has been much accustomed to visit such manufactures, must frequently have been shewn very pretty machines, which were the inventions of such workmen, in order to facilitate and quicken their own particular part of the work. In the first fire engines [this was the current designation for steam engines], a boy was constantly employed to open and shut alternately the communication between the boiler and the cylinder, according as the piston either ascended or descended. One of those boys, who loved to play with his companions, observed that, by tying a string from the handle of the valve which opened this communication to another part of the machine, the valve would open and shut without his assistance, and leave him at liberty to divert himself with his play-fellows. One of the greatest improvements that has been made upon this machine, since it was first invented, was in this manner the discovery of a boy who wanted to save his own labour.

All the improvements in machinery, however, have by no means been the inventions of those who had occasion to use the machines. Many improvements have been made by the ingenuity of the makers of the machines, when to make them became the business of a peculiar trade; and some by that of those who are called philosophers, or men of speculation, whose trade it is not to do any thing, but to observe every thing, and who, upon that account, are often capable of combining together the powers of the most distant and dissimilar objects in the progress of society, philosophy or speculation becomes, like every other employment, the principal or sole trade and occupation of a particular class of citizens. Like every other employment, too, it is subdivided into a great number of different branches, each of which affords occupation to a peculiar tribe or class of philosophers; and this subdivision of employment in philosophy, as well as in every other business, improve dexterity, and saves time. Each individual becomes more expert in his own peculiar branch, more work is done upon the whole, and the quantity of science is considerably increased by it.

It is the great multiplication of the productions of all the different arts, in consequence of the division of labour, which occasions, in a well-governed society, that universal opulence which extends itself to the lowest ranks of the people. Every workman has a great quantity of his own work to dispose of beyond what he himself has occasion for; and every other workman being exactly in the same situation, he is enabled to exchange a great quantity of his own goods for a great quantity or, what comes to the same thing, for the price of a great quantity of theirs. He supplies them abundantly with what they have occasion for, and they accommodate him as amply with what he has occasion for, and a general plenty diffuses itself through all the different ranks of the society.

Observe the accommodation of the most common artificer or day-labourer in a civilized and thriving country, and you will perceive that the number of people, of whose industry a part, though but a small part, has been employed in procuring him this accommodation, exceeds all computation. The woollen coat, for example, which covers the day-labourer, as coarse and rough as it may appear, is the produce of the joint labour of a great multitude of workmen. The shepherd, the sorter of the wool, the wool-comber or carder, the dyer, the scribbler, the spinner, the weaver, the fuller, the dresser, with many others, must all join their different arts in order to complete even this homely production. How many merchants and carriers, besides, must have been employed in transporting the materials from some of those workmen to others who often live in a very distant part of the country? How much commerce and navigation in particular, how many ship-builders, sailors, sail-makers, rope-makers, must have been employed in order to bring together the different drugs made use of by the dyer, which often come from the remotest corners of the world? What a variety of labour, too, is necessary in order to produce the tools of the meanest of those workmen! To say nothing of such complicated machines as the ship of the sailor, the mill of the fuller, or even the loom of the weaver, let us consider only what a variety of labour is requisite in order to form that very simple machine, the shears with which the shepherd clips the wool. The miner, the builder of the furnace for smelting the ore, the feller of the timber, the burner of the charcoal to be made use of in the smelting-house, the brickmaker, the bricklayer, the workmen who attend the furnace, the millwright, the forger, the smith, must all of them join their different arts in order to produce them. Were we to examine, in the same manner, all the different parts of his dress and household furniture, the coarse linen shirt which he wears next his skin, the shoes which cover his feet, the bed which he lies on, and all the different parts which compose it, the kitchen-grate at which he prepares his victuals, the coals which he makes use of for that purpose, dug from the bowels of the earth, and brought to him, perhaps, by a long sea and a long land-carriage, all the other utensils of his kitchen, all the furniture of his table, the knives and forks, the earthen or pewter plates upon which he serves up and divides his victuals, the different hands employed in preparing his bread and his beer, the glass window which lets in the heat and the light, and keeps out the wind and the rain, with all the knowledge and art requisite for preparing that beautiful and happy invention, without which these northern parts of the world could scarce have afforded a very comfortable habitation, together with the tools of all the different workmen employed in producing those different conveniencies; if we examine, I say, all these things, and consider what a variety of labour is employed about each of them, we shall be sensible that, without the assistance and co-operation of many thousands, the very meanest person in a civilized country could not be provided, even according to, what we very falsely imagine, the easy and simple manner in which he is commonly accommodated. Compared, indeed, with the more extravagant luxury of the great, his accommodation must no doubt appear extremely simple and easy; and yet it may be true, perhaps, that the accommodation of an European prince does not always so much exceed that of an industrious and frugal peasant, as the accommodation of the latter exceeds that of many an African king, the absolute masters of the lives and liberties of ten thousand naked savages.

Chapter II. Of the Principle Which Gives Occasion to the Division of Labour

This division of labour, from which so many advantages are derived, is not originally the effect of any human wisdom, which foresees and intends that general opulence to which it gives occasion. It is the necessary, though very slow and gradual, consequence of a certain propensity in human nature, which has in view no such extensive utility; the propensity to truck, barter, and exchange one thing for another.

Whether this propensity be one of those original principles in human nature, of which no further account can be given, or whether, as seems more probable, it be the necessary consequence of the faculties of reason and speech, it belongs not to our present subject to inquire. It is common to all men, and to be found in no other race of animals, which seem to know neither this nor any other species of contracts. Two grey-hounds, in running down the same hare, have sometimes the appearance of acting in some sort of concert. Each turns her towards his companion, or endeavours to intercept her when his companion turns her towards himself. This, however, is not the effect of any contract, but of the accidental concurrence of their passions in the same object at that particular time. Nobody ever saw a dog make a fair and deliberate exchange of one bone for another with another dog. Nobody ever saw one animal, by its gestures and natural cries signify to another, this is mine, that yours; I am willing to give this for that. When an animal wants to obtain something either of a man, or of another animal, it has no other means of persuasion, but to gain the favour of those whose service it requires. A puppy fawns upon its dam, and a spaniel endeavours, by a thousand attractions, to engage the attention of its master who is at dinner, when it wants to be fed by him. Man sometimes uses the same arts with his brethren, and when he has no other means of engaging them to act according to his inclinations, endeavours by every servile and fawning attention to obtain their good will. He has not time, however, to do this upon every occasion. In civilized society he stands at all times in need of the co-operation and assistance of great multitudes, while his whole life is scarce sufficient to gain the friendship of a few persons. In almost every other race of animals, each individual, when it is grown up to maturity, is entirely independent, and in its natural state has occasion for the assistance of no other living creature. But man has almost constant occasion for the help of his brethren, and it is in vain for him to expect it from their benevolence only. He will be more likely to prevail if he can interest their self-love in his favour, and shew them that it is for their own advantage to do for him what he requires of them. Whoever offers to another a bargain of any kind, proposes to do this. Give me that which I want, and you shall have this which you want, is the meaning of every such offer; and it is in this manner that we obtain from one another the far greater part of those good offices which we stand in need of. It is not from the benevolence of the butcher, the brewer, or the baker that we expect our dinner, but from their regard to their own interest. We address ourselves, not to their humanity, but to their self-love, and never talk to them of our own necessities, but of their advantages. Nobody but a beggar chooses to depend chiefly upon the benevolence of his fellow-citizens. Even a beggar does not depend upon it entirely. The charity of well-disposed people, indeed, supplies him with the whole fund of his subsistence. But though this principle ultimately provides him with all the necessaries of life which he has occasion for, it neither does nor can provide him with them as he has occasion for them. The greater part of his occasional wants are supplied in the same manner as those of other people, by treaty, by barter, and by purchase. With the money which one man gives him he purchases food. The old clothes which another bestows upon him he exchanges for other clothes which suit him better, or for lodging, or for food, or for money, with which he can buy either food, clothes, or lodging, as he has occasion.

As it is by treaty, by barter, and by purchase, that we obtain from one another the greater part of those mutual good offices which we stand in need of, so it is this same trucking disposition which originally gives occasion to the division of labour. In a tribe of hunters or shepherds, a particular person makes bows and arrows, for example, with more readiness and dexterity than any other. He frequently exchanges them for cattle or for venison, with his companions; and he finds at last that he can, in this manner, get more cattle and venison, than if he himself went to the field to catch them. From a regard to his own interest, therefore, the making of bows and arrows grows to be his chief business, and he becomes a sort of armourer. Another excels in making the frames and covers of their little huts or moveable houses. He is accustomed to be of use in this way to his neighbours, who reward him in the same manner with cattle and with venison, till at last he finds it his interest to dedicate himself entirely to this employment, and to become a sort of house-carpenter. In the same manner a third becomes a smith or a brazier; a fourth, a tanner or dresser of hides or skins, the principal part of the clothing of savages. And thus the certainty of being able to exchange all that surplus part of the produce of his own labour, which is over and above his own consumption, for such parts of the produce of other men's labour as he may have occasion for, encourages every man to apply himself to a particular occupation, and to cultivate and bring to perfection whatever talent of genius he may possess for that particular species of business.

The difference of natural talents in different men, is, in reality, much less than we are aware of; and the very different genius which appears to distinguish men of different professions, when grown up to maturity, is not upon many occasions so much the cause, as the effect of the division of labour. The difference between the most dissimilar characters, between a philosopher and a common street porter, for example, seems to arise not so much from nature, as from habit, custom, and education. When they came in to the world, and for the first six or eight years of their existence, they were, perhaps, very much alike, and neither their parents nor play-fellows could perceive any remarkable difference. About that age, or soon after, they come to be employed in very different occupations. The difference of talents comes then to be taken notice of, and widens by degrees, till at last the vanity of the philosopher is willing to acknowledge scarce any resemblance. But without the disposition to truck, barter, and exchange, every man must have procured to himself every necessary and conveniency of life which he wanted. All must have had the same duties to perform, and the same work to do, and there could have been no such difference of employment as could alone give occasion to any great difference of talents.

As it is this disposition which forms that difference of talents, so remarkable among men of different professions, so it is this same disposition which renders that difference useful. Many tribes of animals, acknowledged to be all of the same species, derive from nature a much more remarkable distinction of genius, than what, antecedent to custom and education, appears to take place among men. By nature a philosopher is not in genius and disposition half so different from a street porter, as a mastiff is from a grey-hound, or a grey-hound from a spaniel, or this last from a shepherd's dog. Those different tribes of animals, however, though all of the same species are of scarce any use to one another. The strength of the mastiff is not in the least supported either by the swiftness of the grey-hound, or by the sagacity of the spaniel, or by the docility of the shepherd's dog. The effects of those different geniuses and talents, for want of the power or disposition to barter and exchange, cannot be brought into a common stock, and do not in the least contribute to the better accommodation and conveniency of the species. Each animal is still obliged to support and defend itself, separately and independently, and derives no sort of advantage from that variety of talents with which nature has distinguished its fellows. Among men, on the contrary, the most dissimilar geniuses are of use to one another; the different produces of their respective talents, by the general disposition to truck, barter, and exchange, being brought, as it were, into a common stock, where every man may purchase whatever part of the produce of other men's talents he has occasion for.

Book V. Of the Revenue of the Sovereign or Commonwealth

Chapter I. Of the Expenses of the Sovereign or Commonwealth

PART III. OF THE EXPENSE OF PUBLIC WORKS AND PUBLIC INSTITUTIONS

... Were there no public institutions for education, no system, no science, would be taught, for which there was not some demand, or which the circumstances of the times did not render it either necessary or convenient, or at least fashionable to learn. A private teacher could never find his account in teaching either an exploded and antiquated system of a science acknowledged to be useful, or a science universally believed to be a mere useless and pedantic heap of sophistry and nonsense. Such systems, such sciences, can subsist nowhere but in those incorporated societies for education, whose prosperity and revenue are in a great measure independent of their industry. Were there no public institutions for education, a gentleman, after going through, with application and abilities, the most complete course of education which the circumstances of the times were supposed to afford, could not come into the world completely ignorant of everything which is the common subject of conversation among gentlemen and men of the world.

There are no public institutions for the education of women, and there is accordingly nothing useless, absurd, or fantastical, in the common course of their education. They are taught what their parents or guardians judge it necessary or useful for them to learn, and they are taught nothing else. Every part of their education tends evidently to some useful purpose; either to improve the natural attractions of their person, or to form their mind to reserve, to modesty, to chastity, and to economy; to render them both likely to became the mistresses of a family, and to behave properly when they have become such. In every part of her life, a woman feels some conveniency or advantage from every part of her education. It seldom happens that a man, in any part of his life, derives any conveniency or advantage from some of the most laborious and troublesome parts of his education.

Ought the public, therefore, to give no attention, it may be asked, to the education of the people? Or, if it ought to give any, what are the different parts of education which it ought to attend to in the different orders of the people? and in what manner ought it to attend to them?

In some cases, the state of society necessarily places the greater part of individuals in such situations as naturally form in them, without any attention of government, almost all the abilities and virtues which that state requires, or perhaps can admit of. In other cases, the state of the society does not place the greater part of individuals in such situations; and some attention of government is necessary, in order to prevent the almost entire corruption and degeneracy of the great body of the people.

In the progress of the division of labour, the employment of the far greater part of those who live by labour, that is, of the great body of the people, comes to be confined to a few very simple operations; frequently to one or two. But the understandings of the greater part of men are necessarily formed by their ordinary employments. The man whose whole life is spent in performing a few simple operations, of which the effects, too, are perhaps always the same, or very nearly the same, has no occasion to exert his understanding, or to exercise his invention, in finding out expedients for removing difficulties which never occur. He naturally loses, therefore, the habit of such exertion, and generally becomes as stupid and ignorant as it is possible for a human creature to become. The torpor of his mind renders him not only incapable of relishing or bearing a part in any rational conversation, but of conceiving any

generous, noble, or tender sentiment, and consequently of forming any just judgment concerning many even of the ordinary duties of private life. Of the great and
extensive interests of his country he is altogether incapable of judging; and unless
very particular pains have been taken to render him otherwise, he is equally incapable of defending his country in war. The uniformity of his stationary life naturally
corrupts the courage of his mind, and makes him regard, with abhorrence, the
irregular, uncertain, and adventurous life of a soldier. It corrupts even the activity
of his body, and renders him incapable of exerting his strength with vigour and
perseverance in any other employment, than that to which he has been bred. His
dexterity at his own particular trade seems, in this manner, to be acquired at the
expense of his intellectual, social, and martial virtues. But in every improved and
civilized society, this is the state into which the labouring poor, that is, the great body
of the people, must necessarily fall, unless government takes some pains to prevent it.

It is otherwise in the barbarous societies, as they are commonly called, of hunters, of shepherds, and even of husbandmen in that rude state of husbandry which
precedes the improvement of manufactures, and the extension of foreign commerce.
In such societies, the varied occupations of every man oblige every man to exert his
capacity, and to invent expedients for removing difficulties which are continually
occurring. Invention is kept alive, and the mind is not suffered to fall into that drowsy
stupidity, which, in a civilized society, seems to benumb the understanding of almost
all the inferior ranks of people. In those barbarous societies, as they are called, every
man, it has already been observed, is a warrior. Every man, too, is in some measure a
statesman, and can form a tolerable judgment concerning the interest of the society,
and the conduct of those who govern it. How far their chiefs are good judges in peace,
or good leaders in war, is obvious to the observation of almost every single man
among them. In such a society, indeed, no man can well acquire that improved and
refined understanding which a few men sometimes possess in a more civilized state.
Though in a rude society there is a good deal of variety in the occupations of every
individual, there is not a great deal in those of the whole society. Every man does, or
is capable of doing, almost every thing which any other man does, or is capable of
being. Every man has a considerable degree of knowledge, ingenuity, and invention
but scarce any man has a great degree. The degree, however, which is commonly pos-
sessed, is generally sufficient for conducting the whole simple business of the society.
In a civilized state, on the contrary, though there is little variety in the occupations
of the greater part of individuals, there is an almost infinite variety in those of the
whole society. These varied occupations present an almost infinite variety of objects
to the contemplation of those few, who, being attached to no particular occupation
themselves, have leisure and inclination to examine the occupations of other people.
The contemplation of so great a variety of objects necessarily exercises their minds
in endless comparisons and combinations, and renders their understandings, in an

extraordinary degree, both acute and comprehensive. Unless those few, however, happen to be placed in some very particular situations, their great abilities, though honourable to themselves, may contribute very little to the good government or happiness of their society. Notwithstanding the great abilities of those few, all the nobler parts of the human character may be, in a great measure, obliterated and extinguished in the great body of the people.

The education of the common people requires, perhaps, in a civilized and commercial society, the attention of the public, more than that of people of some rank and fortune. People of some rank and fortune are generally eighteen or nineteen years of age before they enter upon that particular business, profession, or trade, by which they propose to distinguish themselves in the world. They have, before that, full time to acquire, or at least to fit themselves for afterwards acquiring, every accomplishment which can recommend them to the public esteem, or render them worthy of it. Their parents or guardians are generally sufficiently anxious that they should be so accomplished, and are in most cases, willing enough to lay out the expense which is necessary for that purpose. If they are not always properly educated, it is seldom from the want of expense laid out upon their education, but from the improper application of that expense. It is seldom from the want of masters, but from the negligence and incapacity of the masters who are to be had, and from the difficulty, or rather from the impossibility, which there is, in the present state of things, of finding any better. The employments, too, in which people of some rank or fortune spend the greater part of their lives, are not, like those of the common people, simple and uniform. They are almost all of them extremely complicated, and such as exercise the head more than the hands. The understandings of those who are engaged in such employments, can seldom grow torpid for want of exercise. The employments of people of some rank and fortune, besides, are seldom such as harass them from morning to night. They generally have a good deal of leisure, during which they may perfect themselves in every branch, either of useful or ornamental knowledge, of which they may have laid the foundation, or for which they may have acquired some taste in the earlier part of life.

It is otherwise with the common people. They have little time to spare for education. Their parents can scarce afford to maintain them, even in infancy. As soon as they are able to work, they must apply to some trade, by which they can earn their subsistence. That trade, too, is generally so simple and uniform, as to give little exercise to the understanding; while, at the same time, their labour is both so constant and so severe, that it leaves them little leisure and less inclination to apply to, or even to think of any thing else.

But though the common people cannot, in any civilized society, be so well instructed as people of some rank and fortune; the most essential parts of education, however, to read, write, and account, can be acquired at so early a period of life, that the greater part, even of those who are to be bred to the lowest occupations, have time to acquire them before they can be employed in those occupations. For a very small expense, the public can facilitate, can encourage and can even impose upon almost the whole body of the people, the necessity of acquiring those most essential parts of education.

The public can facilitate this acquisition, by establishing in every parish or district a little school, where children may be taught for a reward so moderate, that even a common labourer may afford it; the master being partly, but not wholly, paid by the public; because, if he was wholly, or even principally, paid by it, he would soon learn to neglect his business. In Scotland, the establishment of such parish schools has taught almost the whole common people to read, and a very great proportion of them to write and account. In England, the establishment of charity schools has had an effect of the same kind, though not so universally, because the establishment is not so universal. If, in those little schools, the books by which the children are taught to read, were a little more instructive than they commonly are; and if, instead of a little smattering in Latin, which the children of the common people are sometimes taught there, and which can scarce ever be of any use to them, they were instructed in the elementary parts of geometry and mechanics; the literary education of this rank of people would, perhaps, be as complete as can be. There is scarce a common trade, which does not afford some opportunities of applying to it the principles of geometry and mechanics, and which would not, therefore, gradually exercise and improve the common people in those principles, the necessary introduction to the most sublime, as well as to the most useful sciences.

The public can encourage the acquisition of those most essential parts of education, by giving small premiums, and little badges of distinction, to the children of the common people who excel in them.

The public can impose upon almost the whole body of the people the necessity of acquiring the most essential parts of education, by obliging every man to undergo an examination or probation in them, before he can obtain the freedom in any corporation, or be allowed to set up any trade, either in a village or town corporate....

Questions

1. What is the benefit of the division of labor?

2. What drives the division of labor?

3. What is the importance of cooperation in the division of labor?

4. What is "self-love" and what role does it play?

5. What is the potential problem with the division of labor?

6. What is a potential solution to the problems stemming from the division of labor?

Further Reading

The Stanford Encyclopedia of Ethics (online) lists a number of excellent resources on the connection between Smith's moral and economic theories. Below is a sampling of those resources:

Baugh, Daniel A. "Poverty, Protestantism and Political Economy: English Attitudes toward the Poor, 1660–1800." *England's Rise to Greatness*, edited by S. Baxter. Berkeley: University of California Press, 1983, pp. 63–107.

Fleischacker, Samuel. *On Adam Smith's Wealth of Nations: A Philosophical Companion.* Princeton: Princeton University Press, 2004.

Rasmussen, Dennis. *The Problems and Promise of Commercial Society: Adam Smith's Response to Rousseau.* University Park: Penn State University Press, 2009.

Rothschild, Emma. *Economic Sentiments.* Cambridge, MA: Harvard University Press, 2001.

Solomon, Robert C. "Beyond Selfishness: Adam Smith and the Limits of the Market." *Business Ethics Quarterly*, vol. 3, no. 4, 1993, pp. 453–60.

8.
THE COMMUNIST MANIFESTO
(1848)

KARL MARX AND FREDERICK ENGELS

About This Reading

It might seem strange to include *The Communist Manifesto* (1848) in a book on business ethics. After all, Karl Marx did call for a worker revolution to topple the capitalist system. Yet, in Marx we find an interesting critique of the capitalist system. Although written in 1847, Marx's analysis of the relationship between workers (the proletariat) and those who control the means of production (the bourgeoisie) sounds uncannily familiar. The mechanization of manufacturing, overproduction, the need to exploit new markets, the demise of the middle class, and the ever-present pressure to reduce wages and increase efficiency are all present in Marx's analysis of capitalism. We do not have to agree with Marx's solution to these issues in order to appreciate his insights. And although Marx's historical predictions never came to be, one could argue that it was only the formation of unions and the enactment of worker protection laws that kept Communism from taking hold in the United States.

A spectre is haunting Europe—the spectre of communism. All the powers of old Europe have entered into a holy alliance to exorcise this spectre: Pope and Tsar, Metternich and Guizot, French Radicals and German police-spies.

Where is the party in opposition that has not been decried as communistic by its opponents in power? Where is the opposition that has not hurled back the branding reproach of communism against the more advanced opposition parties, as well as against its reactionary adversaries?

Two things result from this fact:

I. Communism is already acknowledged by all European powers to be itself a power.

II. It is high time that Communists should openly, in the face of the whole world, publish their views, their aims, their tendencies, and meet this nursery tale of the Spectre of Communism with a manifesto of the party itself.

To this end, Communists of various nationalities have assembled in London and sketched the following manifesto, to be published in the English, French, German, Italian, Flemish and Danish languages.

I. Bourgeois and Proletarians[1]

The history of all hitherto existing society[2] is the history of class struggles.

Freeman and slave, patrician and plebeian, lord and serf, guild-master[3] and journeyman, in a word, oppressor and oppressed, stood in constant opposition to one another, carried on an uninterrupted, now hidden, now open fight, a fight that each time ended, either in a revolutionary reconstitution of society at large, or in the common ruin of the contending classes.

In the earlier epochs of history, we find almost everywhere a complicated arrangement of society into various orders, a manifold gradation of social rank. In ancient Rome we have patricians, knights, plebeians, slaves; in the Middle Ages, feudal lords, vassals, guild-masters, journeymen, apprentices, serfs; in almost all of these classes, again, subordinate gradations.

---

1   By bourgeoisie is meant the class of modern capitalists, owners of the means of social production and employers of wage labour. By proletariat, the class of modern wage labourers who, having no means of production of their own, are reduced to selling their labour power in order to live. [Engels, 1888 English edition]

2   That is, all written history. In 1847, the pre-history of society, the social organisation existing previous to recorded history, all but unknown. Since then, August von Haxthausen (1792–1866) discovered common ownership of land in Russia, Georg Ludwig von Maurer proved it to be the social foundation from which all Teutonic races started in history, and, by and by, village communities were found to be, or to have been, the primitive form of society everywhere from India to Ireland. The inner organisation of this primitive communistic society was laid bare, in its typical form, by Lewis Henry Morgan's (1818–1861) crowning discovery of the true nature of the gens and its relation to the tribe. With the dissolution of the primeval communities, society begins to be differentiated into separate and finally antagonistic classes. I have attempted to retrace this dissolution in The Origin of the Family, Private Property, and the State, second edition, Stuttgart, 1886. [Engels, 1888 English Edition and 1890 German Edition (with the last sentence omitted)]

3   Guild-master, that is, a full member of a guild, a master within, not a head of a guild. [Engels, 1888 English Edition]

The modern bourgeois society that has sprouted from the ruins of feudal society has not done away with class antagonisms. It has but established new classes, new conditions of oppression, new forms of struggle in place of the old ones.

Our epoch, the epoch of the bourgeoisie, possesses, however, this distinct feature: it has simplified class antagonisms. Society as a whole is more and more splitting up into two great hostile camps, into two great classes directly facing each other— Bourgeoisie and Proletariat.

From the serfs of the Middle Ages sprang the chartered burghers of the earliest towns. From these burgesses the first elements of the bourgeoisie were developed.

The discovery of America, the rounding of the Cape, opened up fresh ground for the rising bourgeoisie. The East-Indian and Chinese markets, the colonisation of America, trade with the colonies, the increase in the means of exchange and in commodities generally, gave to commerce, to navigation, to industry, an impulse never before known, and thereby, to the revolutionary element in the tottering feudal society, a rapid development.

The feudal system of industry, in which industrial production was monopolised by closed guilds, now no longer sufficed for the growing wants of the new markets. The manufacturing system took its place. The guild-masters were pushed on one side by the manufacturing middle class; division of labour between the different corporate guilds vanished in the face of division of labour in each single workshop.

Meantime the markets kept ever growing, the demand ever rising. Even manufacturer no longer sufficed. Thereupon, steam and machinery revolutionised industrial production. The place of manufacture was taken by the giant, Modern Industry; the place of the industrial middle class by industrial millionaires, the leaders of the whole industrial armies, the modern bourgeois.

Modern industry has established the world market, for which the discovery of America paved the way. This market has given an immense development to commerce, to navigation, to communication by land. This development has, in its turn, reacted on the extension of industry; and in proportion as industry, commerce, navigation, railways extended, in the same proportion the bourgeoisie developed, increased its capital, and pushed into the background every class handed down from the Middle Ages.

We see, therefore, how the modern bourgeoisie is itself the product of a long course of development, of a series of revolutions in the modes of production and of exchange.

Each step in the development of the bourgeoisie was accompanied by a corresponding political advance of that class. An oppressed class under the sway of the feudal nobility, an armed and self-governing association in the medieval commune:[4]

---

4 This was the name given their urban communities by the townsmen of Italy and France, after they had purchased or conquered their initial rights of self-government from their feudal lords. [Engels, 1890 German edition] "Commune" was the name taken in France by the nascent towns even before they had conquered

here independent urban republic (as in Italy and Germany); there taxable "third estate" of the monarchy (as in France); afterwards, in the period of manufacturing proper, serving either the semi-feudal or the absolute monarchy as a counterpoise against the nobility, and, in fact, cornerstone of the great monarchies in general, the bourgeoisie has at last, since the establishment of Modern Industry and of the world market, conquered for itself, in the modern representative State, exclusive political sway. The executive of the modern state is but a committee for managing the common affairs of the whole bourgeoisie.

The bourgeoisie, historically, has played a most revolutionary part.

The bourgeoisie, wherever it has got the upper hand, has put an end to all feudal, patriarchal, idyllic relations. It has pitilessly torn asunder the motley feudal ties that bound man to his "natural superiors," and has left remaining no other nexus between man and man than naked self-interest, than callous "cash payment." It has drowned the most heavenly ecstasies of religious fervour, of chivalrous enthusiasm, of philistine sentimentalism, in the icy water of egotistical calculation. It has resolved personal worth into exchange value, and in place of the numberless indefeasible chartered freedoms, has set up that single, unconscionable freedom—Free Trade. In one word, for exploitation, veiled by religious and political illusions, it has substituted naked, shameless, direct, brutal exploitation.

The bourgeoisie has stripped of its halo every occupation hitherto honoured and looked up to with reverent awe. It has converted the physician, the lawyer, the priest, the poet, the man of science, into its paid wage labourers.

The bourgeoisie has torn away from the family its sentimental veil, and has reduced the family relation to a mere money relation.

The bourgeoisie has disclosed how it came to pass that the brutal display of vigour in the Middle Ages, which reactionaries so much admire, found its fitting complement in the most slothful indolence. It has been the first to show what man's activity can bring about. It has accomplished wonders far surpassing Egyptian pyramids, Roman aqueducts, and Gothic cathedrals; it has conducted expeditions that put in the shade all former Exoduses of nations and crusades.

The bourgeoisie cannot exist without constantly revolutionising the instruments of production, and thereby the relations of production, and with them the whole relations of society. Conservation of the old modes of production in unaltered form, was, on the contrary, the first condition of existence for all earlier industrial classes. Constant revolutionising of production, uninterrupted disturbance of all social conditions, everlasting uncertainty and agitation distinguish the bourgeois epoch from all

---

from their feudal lords and masters local self-government and political rights as the "Third Estate." Generally speaking, for the economical development of the bourgeoisie, England is here taken as the typical country, for its political development, France. [Engels, 1888 English Edition] earlier ones. All fixed, fast-frozen relations, with their train of ancient and venerable prejudices and opinions, are swept away, all new-formed ones become antiquated before they can ossify. All that is solid melts into air, all that is holy is profaned, and man is at last compelled to face with sober senses his, real conditions of life, and his relations with his kind.

The need of a constantly expanding market for its products chases the bourgeoisie over the entire surface of the globe. It must nestle everywhere, settle everywhere, establish connexions everywhere.

The bourgeoisie has through its exploitation of the world market given a cosmopolitan character to production and consumption in every country. To the great chagrin of Reactionists, it has drawn from under the feet of industry the national ground on which it stood. All old-established national industries have been destroyed or are daily being destroyed. They are dislodged by new industries, whose introduction becomes a life and death question for all civilised nations, by industries that no longer work up indigenous raw material, but raw material drawn from the remotest zones; industries whose products are consumed, not only at home, but in every quarter of the globe. In place of the old wants, satisfied by the production of the country, we find new wants, requiring for their satisfaction the products of distant lands and climes. In place of the old local and national seclusion and self-sufficiency, we have intercourse in every direction, universal inter-dependence of nations. And as in material, so also in intellectual production. The intellectual creations of individual nations become common property. National one-sidedness and narrow-mindedness become more and more impossible, and from the numerous national and local literatures, there arises a world literature.

The bourgeoisie, by the rapid improvement of all instruments of production, by the immensely facilitated means of communication, draws all, even the most barbarian, nations into civilisation. The cheap prices of commodities are the heavy artillery with which it batters down all Chinese walls, with which it forces the barbarians' intensely obstinate hatred of foreigners to capitulate. It compels all nations, on pain of extinction, to adopt the bourgeois mode of production; it compels them to introduce what it calls civilisation into their midst, i.e., to become bourgeois themselves. In one word, it creates a world after its own image.

The bourgeoisie has subjected the country to the rule of the towns. It has created enormous cities, has greatly increased the urban population as compared with the rural, and has thus rescued a considerable part of the population from the idiocy of rural life. Just as it has made the country dependent on the towns, so it has made barbarian and semi-barbarian countries dependent on the civilised ones, nations of peasants on nations of bourgeois, the East on the West.

The bourgeoisie keeps more and more doing away with the scattered state of the population, of the means of production, and of property. It has agglomerated population, centralised the means of production, and has concentrated property in a few hands. The necessary consequence of this was political centralisation. Independent, or but loosely connected provinces, with separate interests, laws, governments, and systems of taxation, became lumped together into one nation, with one government, one code of laws, one national class-interest, one frontier, and one customs-tariff.

The bourgeoisie, during its rule of scarce one hundred years, has created more massive and more colossal productive forces than have all preceding generations together. Subjection of Nature's forces to man, machinery, application of chemistry to industry and agriculture, steam-navigation, railways, electric telegraphs, clearing of whole continents for cultivation, canalisation or rivers, whole populations conjured out of the ground—what earlier century had even a presentiment that such productive forces slumbered in the lap of social labour?

We see then: the means of production and of exchange, on whose foundation the bourgeoisie built itself up, were generated in feudal society. At a certain stage in the development of these means of production and of exchange, the conditions under which feudal society produced and exchanged, the feudal organisation of agriculture and manufacturing industry, in one word, the feudal relations of property became no longer compatible with the already developed productive forces; they became so many fetters. They had to be burst asunder; they were burst asunder.

Into their place stepped free competition, accompanied by a social and political constitution adapted in it, and the economic and political sway of the bourgeois class.

A similar movement is going on before our own eyes. Modern bourgeois society, with its relations of production, of exchange and of property, a society that has conjured up such gigantic means of production and of exchange, is like the sorcerer who is no longer able to control the powers of the nether world whom he has called up by his spells. For many a decade past the history of industry and commerce is but the history of the revolt of modern productive forces against modern conditions of production, against the property relations that are the conditions for the existence of the bourgeois and of its rule. It is enough to mention the commercial crises that by their periodical return put the existence of the entire bourgeois society on its trial, each time more threateningly. In these crises, a great part not only of the existing products, but also of the previously created productive forces, are periodically destroyed. In these crises, there breaks out an epidemic that, in all earlier epochs, would have seemed an absurdity—the epidemic of overproduction. Society suddenly finds itself put back into a state of momentary barbarism; it appears as if a famine, a universal war of devastation, had cut off the supply of every means of subsistence; industry and commerce seem to be destroyed; and why? Because there is too much civilisation, too much means of subsistence, too much industry, too much commerce. The productive forces at the disposal of society no longer tend to further the development of the conditions of bourgeois property; on the contrary, they have become too powerful for these conditions, by which they are fettered, and so soon as they overcome these fetters, they bring disorder into the whole of bourgeois society, endanger the existence of bourgeois property. The conditions of bourgeois society are too narrow to comprise the wealth created by them. And how does the bourgeoisie get over these crises? On the one hand by enforced destruction of a mass of productive forces; on the other, by the conquest of new markets, and by the more thorough exploitation of the old ones. That is by paving the way for more extensive and more destructive crises, and by diminishing the means whereby crises are prevented.

The weapons with which the bourgeoisie felled feudalism to the ground are now turned against the bourgeoisie itself.

But not only has the bourgeoisie forged the weapons that bring death to itself; it has also called into existence the men who are to wield those weapons—the modern working class—the proletarians.

In proportion as the bourgeoisie, i.e., capital, is developed, in the same proportion is the proletariat, the modern working class, developed—a class of labourers, who live only so long as they find work, and who find work only so long as their labour increases capital. These labourers, who must sell themselves piecemeal, are a commodity, like every other article of commerce, and are consequently exposed to all the vicissitudes of competition, to all the fluctuations of the market.

Owing to the extensive use of machinery, and to the division of labour, the work of the proletarians has lost all individual character, and, consequently, all charm for the workman. He becomes an appendage of the machine, and it is only the most simple, most monotonous, and most easily acquired knack, that is required of him. Hence, the cost of production of a workman is restricted, almost entirely, to the means of subsistence that he requires for maintenance, and for the propagation of his race. But the price of a commodity, and therefore also of labour, is equal to its cost of production. In proportion, therefore, as the repulsiveness of the work increases, the wage decreases. Nay more, in proportion as the use of machinery and division of labour increases, in the same proportion the burden of toil also increases, whether by prolongation of the working hours, by the increase of the work exacted in a given time or by increased speed of machinery, etc.

Modern Industry has converted the little workshop of the patriarchal master into the great factory of the industrial capitalist. Masses of labourers, crowded into the factory, are organised like soldiers. As privates of the industrial army they are placed under the command of a perfect hierarchy of officers and sergeants. Not only are they slaves of the bourgeois class, and of the bourgeois State; they are daily and hourly enslaved by the machine, by the overlooker, and, above all, by the individual bourgeois manufacturer himself. The more openly this despotism proclaims gain to be its end and aim, the more petty, the more hateful and the more embittering it is.

The less the skill and exertion of strength implied in manual labour, in other words, the more modern industry becomes developed, the more is the labour of men superseded by that of women. Differences of age and sex have no longer any distinctive social validity for the working class. All are instruments of labour, more or less expensive to use, according to their age and sex.

No sooner is the exploitation of the labourer by the manufacturer, so far, at an end, that he receives his wages in cash, than he is set upon by the other portions of the bourgeoisie, the landlord, the shopkeeper, the pawnbroker, etc.

The lower strata of the middle class—the small tradespeople, shopkeepers, and retired tradesmen generally, the handicraftsmen and peasants—all these sink gradually into the proletariat, partly because their diminutive capital does not suffice for the scale on which Modern Industry is carried on, and is swamped in the competition with the large capitalists, partly because their specialised skill is rendered worthless by new methods of production. Thus the proletariat is recruited from all classes of the population.

The proletariat goes through various stages of development. With its birth begins its struggle with the bourgeoisie. At first the contest is carried on by individual labourers, then by the workpeople of a factory, then by the operative of one trade, in one locality, against the individual bourgeois who directly exploits them. They direct their attacks not against the bourgeois conditions of production, but against the instruments of production themselves; they destroy imported wares that compete with their labour, they smash to pieces machinery, they set factories ablaze, they seek to restore by force the vanished status of the workman of the Middle Ages.

At this stage, the labourers still form an incoherent mass scattered over the whole country, and broken up by their mutual competition. If anywhere they unite to form more compact bodies, this is not yet the consequence of their own active union, but of the union of the bourgeoisie, which class, in order to attain its own political ends, is compelled to set the whole proletariat in motion, and is moreover yet, for a time, able to do so. At this stage, therefore, the proletarians do not fight their enemies, but the enemies of their enemies, the remnants of absolute monarchy, the landowners, the non-industrial bourgeois, the petty bourgeois. Thus, the whole historical movement is concentrated in the hands of the bourgeoisie; every victory so obtained is a victory for the bourgeoisie.

But with the development of industry, the proletariat not only increases in number; it becomes concentrated in greater masses, its strength grows, and it feels that strength more. The various interests and conditions of life within the ranks of the proletariat are more and more equalised, in proportion as machinery obliterates all distinctions of labour, and nearly everywhere reduces wages to the same low level. The growing competition among the bourgeois, and the resulting commercial crises, make the wages of the workers ever more fluctuating. The increasing improvement of machinery, ever more rapidly developing, makes their livelihood more and more precarious; the collisions between individual workmen and individual bourgeois take more and more the character of collisions between two classes. Thereupon, the workers begin to form combinations (Trades' Unions) against the bourgeois; they club together in order to keep up the rate of wages; they found permanent associations in order to make provision beforehand for these occasional revolts. Here and there, the contest breaks out into riots.

Now and then the workers are victorious, but only for a time. The real fruit of their battles lies, not in the immediate result, but in the ever-expanding union of the workers. This union is helped on by the improved means of communication that are created by modern industry, and that place the workers of different localities in contact with one another. It was just this contact that was needed to centralise the numerous local struggles, all of the same character, into one national struggle between classes. But every class struggle is a political struggle. And that union, to attain which the burghers of the Middle Ages, with their miserable highways, required centuries, the modern proletarian, thanks to railways, achieve in a few years.

This organisation of the proletarians into a class, and, consequently into a political party, is continually being upset again by the competition between the workers themselves. But it ever rises again, stronger, firmer, mightier. It compels legislative recognition of particular interests of the workers, by taking advantage of the divisions among the bourgeoisie itself. Thus, the ten-hours' bill in England was carried.

Altogether collisions between the classes of the old society further, in many ways, the course of development of the proletariat. The bourgeoisie finds itself involved in a constant battle. At first with the aristocracy; later on, with those portions of the bourgeoisie itself, whose interests have become antagonistic to the progress of industry; at all time with the bourgeoisie of foreign countries. In all these battles, it sees itself compelled to appeal to the proletariat, to ask for help, and thus, to drag it into the political arena. The bourgeoisie itself, therefore, supplies the proletariat with its own elements of political and general education, in other words, it furnishes the proletariat with weapons for fighting the bourgeoisie.

Further, as we have already seen, entire sections of the ruling class are, by the advance of industry, precipitated into the proletariat, or are at least threatened in their conditions of existence. These also supply the proletariat with fresh elements of enlightenment and progress.

Finally, in times when the class struggle nears the decisive hour, the progress of dissolution going on within the ruling class, in fact within the whole range of old society, assumes such a violent, glaring character, that a small section of the ruling class cuts itself adrift, and joins the revolutionary class, the class that holds the future in its hands. Just as, therefore, at an earlier period, a section of the nobility went over to the bourgeoisie, so now a portion of the bourgeoisie goes over to the proletariat, and in particular, a portion of the bourgeois ideologists, who have raised themselves to the level of comprehending theoretically the historical movement as a whole.

Of all the classes that stand face to face with the bourgeoisie today, the proletariat alone is a really revolutionary class. The other classes decay and finally disappear in the face of Modern Industry; the proletariat is its special and essential product.

The lower middle class, the small manufacturer, the shopkeeper, the artisan, the peasant, all these fight against the bourgeoisie, to save from extinction their existence as fractions of the middle class. They are therefore not revolutionary, but conservative. Nay more, they are reactionary, for they try to roll back the wheel of history. If by chance, they are revolutionary, they are only so in view of their impending transfer into the proletariat; they thus defend not their present, but their future interests, they desert their own standpoint to place themselves at that of the proletariat.

The "dangerous class," [*lumpenproletariat*] the social scum, that passively rotting mass thrown off by the lowest layers of the old society, may, here and there, be swept into the movement by a proletarian revolution; its conditions of life, however, prepare it far more for the part of a bribed tool of reactionary intrigue.

In the condition of the proletariat, those of old society at large are already virtually swamped. The proletarian is without property; his relation to his wife and children has no longer anything in common with the bourgeois family relations; modern industry labour, modern subjection to capital, the same in England as in France, in America as in Germany, has stripped him of every trace of national character. Law, morality, religion, are to him so many bourgeois prejudices, behind which lurk in ambush just as many bourgeois interests.

All the preceding classes that got the upper hand sought to fortify their already acquired status by subjecting society at large to their conditions of appropriation. The proletarians cannot become masters of the productive forces of society, except by abolishing their own previous mode of appropriation, and thereby also every other previous mode of appropriation. They have nothing of their own to secure and to fortify; their mission is to destroy all previous securities for, and insurances of, individual property.

All previous historical movements were movements of minorities, or in the interest of minorities. The proletarian movement is the self-conscious, independent movement of the immense majority, in the interest of the immense majority. The proletariat, the lowest stratum of our present society, cannot stir, cannot raise itself up, without the whole superincumbent strata of official society being sprung into the air.

Though not in substance, yet in form, the struggle of the proletariat with the bourgeoisie is at first a national struggle. The proletariat of each country must, of course, first of all settle matters with its own bourgeoisie.

In depicting the most general phases of the development of the proletariat, we traced the more or less veiled civil war, raging within existing society, up to the point where that war breaks out into open revolution, and where the violent overthrow of the bourgeoisie lays the foundation for the sway of the proletariat.

Hitherto, every form of society has been based, as we have already seen, on the antagonism of oppressing and oppressed classes. But in order to oppress a class, certain conditions must be assured to it under which it can, at least, continue its slavish existence. The serf, in the period of serfdom, raised himself to membership in the commune, just as the petty bourgeois, under the yoke of the feudal absolutism, managed to develop into a bourgeois. The modern labourer, on the contrary, instead of rising with the process of industry, sinks deeper and deeper below the conditions of existence of his own class. He becomes a pauper, and pauperism develops more rapidly than population and wealth. And here it becomes evident, that the bourgeoisie is unfit any longer to be the ruling class in society, and to impose its conditions of existence upon society as an overriding law. It is unfit to rule because it is incompetent to assure an existence to its slave within his slavery, because it cannot help letting him sink into such a state, that it has to feed him, instead of being fed by him. Society can no longer live under this bourgeoisie, in other words, its existence is no longer compatible with society.

The essential conditions for the existence and for the sway of the bourgeois class is the formation and augmentation of capital; the condition for capital is wage-labour. Wage-labour rests exclusively on competition between the labourers. The advance of industry, whose involuntary promoter is the bourgeoisie, replaces the isolation of the labourers, due to competition, by the revolutionary combination, due to association. The development of Modern Industry, therefore, cuts from under its feet the very foundation on which the bourgeoisie produces and appropriates products. What the bourgeoisie therefore produces, above all, are its own grave-diggers. Its fall and the victory of the proletariat are equally inevitable.

II. Proletarians and Communists

In what relation do the Communists stand to the proletarians as a whole? The Communists do not form a separate party opposed to the other working-class parties.

They have no interests separate and apart from those of the proletariat as a whole.

They do not set up any sectarian principles of their own, by which to shape and mould the proletarian movement.

The Communists are distinguished from the other working-class parties by this only:

1. In the national struggles of the proletarians of the different countries, they point out and bring to the front the common interests of the entire proletariat, independently of all nationality.

2. In the various stages of development which the struggle of the working class against the bourgeoisie has to pass through, they always and everywhere represent the interests of the movement as a whole.

The Communists, therefore, are on the one hand, practically, the most advanced and resolute section of the working-class parties of every country, that section which pushes forward all others; on the other hand, theoretically, they have over the great mass of the proletariat the advantage of clearly understanding the lines of march, the conditions, and the ultimate general results of the proletarian movement.

The immediate aim of the Communists is the same as that of all other proletarian parties: formation of the proletariat into a class, overthrow of the bourgeois supremacy, conquest of political power by the proletariat.

The theoretical conclusions of the Communists are in no way based on ideas or principles that have been invented, or discovered, by this or that would-be universal reformer.

They merely express, in general terms, actual relations springing from an existing class struggle, from a historical movement going on under our very eyes. The abolition of existing property relations is not at all a distinctive feature of communism.

All property relations in the past have continually been subject to historical change consequent upon the change in historical conditions.

The French Revolution, for example, abolished feudal property in favour of bourgeois property.

The distinguishing feature of Communism is not the abolition of property generally, but the abolition of bourgeois property. But modern bourgeois private property is the final and most complete expression of the system of producing and appropriating products, that is based on class antagonisms, on the exploitation of the many by the few.

In this sense, the theory of the Communists may be summed up in the single sentence: Abolition of private property.

We Communists have been reproached with the desire of abolishing the right of personally acquiring property as the fruit of a man's own labour, which property is alleged to be the groundwork of all personal freedom, activity and independence.

Hard-won, self-acquired, self-earned property! Do you mean the property of petty artisan and of the small peasant, a form of property that preceded the bourgeois form? There is no need to abolish that; the development of industry has to a great extent already destroyed it, and is still destroying it daily.

Or do you mean the modern bourgeois private property?

But does wage-labour create any property for the labourer? Not a bit. It creates capital, i.e., that kind of property which exploits wage-labour, and which cannot increase except upon condition of begetting a new supply of wage-labour for fresh exploitation. Property, in its present form, is based on the antagonism of capital and wage labour. Let us examine both sides of this antagonism.

To be a capitalist, is to have not only a purely personal, but a social status in production. Capital is a collective product, and only by the united action of many members, nay, in the last resort, only by the united action of all members of society, can it be set in motion.

Capital is therefore not only personal; it is a social power.

When, therefore, capital is converted into common property, into the property of all members of society, personal property is not thereby transformed into social property. It is only the social character of the property that is changed. It loses its class character.

Let us now take wage-labour.

The average price of wage-labour is the minimum wage, i.e., that quantum of the means of subsistence which is absolutely requisite to keep the labourer in bare existence as a labourer. What, therefore, the wage-labourer appropriates by means of his labour, merely suffices to prolong and reproduce a bare existence. We by no means intend to abolish this personal appropriation of the products of labour, an appropriation that is made for the maintenance and reproduction of human life, and that leaves no surplus wherewith to command the labour of others. All that we want to do away with is the miserable character of this appropriation, under which the labourer lives merely to increase capital, and is allowed to live only in so far as the interest of the ruling class requires it.

In bourgeois society, living labour is but a means to increase accumulated labour. In Communist society, accumulated labour is but a means to widen, to enrich, to promote the existence of the labourer.

In bourgeois society, therefore, the past dominates the present; in Communist society, the present dominates the past. In bourgeois society capital is independent and has individuality, while the living person is dependent and has no individuality.

And the abolition of this state of things is called by the bourgeois, abolition of individuality and freedom! And rightly so. The abolition of bourgeois individuality, bourgeois independence, bourgeois freedom is undoubtedly aimed at.

By freedom is meant, under the present bourgeois conditions of production, free trade, free selling and buying.

But if selling and buying disappears, free selling and buying disappears also. This talk about free selling and buying, and all the other "brave words" of our bourgeois about freedom in general, have a meaning, if any, only in contrast with restricted selling and buying, with the fettered traders of the Middle Ages, but have no meaning when opposed to the Communistic abolition of buying and selling, of the bourgeois conditions of production, and of the bourgeoisie itself.

You are horrified at our intending to do away with private property. But in your existing society, private property is already done away with for nine-tenths of the population; its existence for the few is solely due to its non-existence in the hands of those nine-tenths. You reproach us, therefore, with intending to do away with a form of property, the necessary condition for whose existence is the non-existence of any property for the immense majority of society.

In one word, you reproach us with intending to do away with your property. Precisely so; that is just what we intend.

From the moment when labour can no longer be converted into capital, money, or rent, into a social power capable of being monopolised, i.e., from the moment when individual property can no longer be transformed into bourgeois property, into capital, from that moment, you say, individuality vanishes.

You must, therefore, confess that by "individual" you mean no other person than the bourgeois, than the middle-class owner of property. This person must, indeed, be swept out of the way, and made impossible.

Communism deprives no man of the power to appropriate the products of society; all that it does is to deprive him of the power to subjugate the labour of others by means of such appropriations.

It has been objected that upon the abolition of private property, all work will cease, and universal laziness will overtake us.

According to this, bourgeois society ought long ago to have gone to the dogs through sheer idleness; for those of its members who work, acquire nothing, and those who acquire anything do not work. The whole of this objection is but another expression of the tautology: that there can no longer be any wage-labour when there is no longer any capital.

All objections urged against the Communistic mode of producing and appropriating material products, have, in the same way, been urged against the Communistic mode of producing and appropriating intellectual products. Just as, to the bourgeois, the disappearance of class property is the disappearance of production itself, so the disappearance of class culture is to him identical with the disappearance of all culture.

That culture, the loss of which he laments, is, for the enormous majority, a mere training to act as a machine.

But don't wrangle with us so long as you apply, to our intended abolition of bourgeois property, the standard of your bourgeois notions of freedom, culture, law, &c. Your very ideas are but the outgrowth of the conditions of your bourgeois production and bourgeois property, just as your jurisprudence is but the will of your class made into a law for all, a will whose essential character and direction are determined by the economical conditions of existence of your class.

The selfish misconception that induces you to transform into eternal laws of nature and of reason, the social forms springing from your present mode of production and form of property—historical relations that rise and disappear in the progress of production—this misconception you share with every ruling class that has preceded you. What you see clearly in the case of ancient property, what you admit in the case of feudal property, you are of course forbidden to admit in the case of your own bourgeois form of property.

Abolition [*Aufhebung*] of the family! Even the most radical flare up at this infamous proposal of the Communists.

On what foundation is the present family, the bourgeois family, based? On capital, on private gain. In its completely developed form, this family exists only among the bourgeoisie. But this state of things finds its complement in the practical absence of the family among the proletarians, and in public prostitution.

The bourgeois family will vanish as a matter of course when its complement vanishes, and both will vanish with the vanishing of capital.

Do you charge us with wanting to stop the exploitation of children by their parents? To this crime we plead guilty. But, you say, we destroy the most hallowed of relations, when we replace home education by social.

And your education! Is not that also social, and determined by the social conditions under which you educate, by the intervention direct or indirect, of society, by means of schools, &c.? The Communists have not invented the intervention of society in education; they do but seek to alter the character of that intervention, and to rescue education from the influence of the ruling class.

The bourgeois clap-trap about the family and education, about the hallowed co-relation of parents and child, becomes all the more disgusting, the more, by the action of Modern Industry, all the family ties among the proletarians are torn asunder, and their children transformed into simple articles of commerce and instruments of labour.

But you Communists would introduce community of women, screams the bourgeoisie in chorus.

The bourgeois sees his wife a mere instrument of production. He hears that the instruments of production are to be exploited in common, and, naturally, can come to no other conclusion that the lot of being common to all will likewise fall to the women.

He has not even a suspicion that the real point aimed at is to do away with the status of women as mere instruments of production.

For the rest, nothing is more ridiculous than the virtuous indignation of our bourgeois at the community of women which, they pretend, is to be openly and officially established by the Communists. The Communists have no need to introduce community of women; it has existed almost from time immemorial.

Our bourgeois, not content with having wives and daughters of their proletarians at their disposal, not to speak of common prostitutes, take the greatest pleasure in seducing each other's wives.

Bourgeois marriage is, in reality, a system of wives in common and thus, at the most, what the Communists might possibly be reproached with is that they desire to introduce, in substitution for a hypocritically concealed, an openly legalised community of women. For the rest, it is self-evident that the abolition of the present system of production must bring with it the abolition of the community of women springing from that system, i.e., of prostitution both public and private.

The Communists are further reproached with desiring to abolish countries and nationality.

The working men have no country. We cannot take from them what they have not got. Since the proletariat must first of all acquire political supremacy, must rise to be the leading class of the nation, must constitute itself the nation, it is so far, itself national, though not in the bourgeois sense of the word.

National differences and antagonism between peoples are daily more and more vanishing, owing to the development of the bourgeoisie, to freedom of commerce, to the world market, to uniformity in the mode of production and in the conditions of life corresponding thereto.

The supremacy of the proletariat will cause them to vanish still faster. United action, of the leading civilised countries at least, is one of the first conditions for the emancipation of the proletariat.

In proportion as the exploitation of one individual by another will also be put an end to, the exploitation of one nation by another will also be put an end to. In proportion as the antagonism between classes within the nation vanishes, the hostility of one nation to another will come to an end.

The charges against Communism made from a religious, a philosophical and, generally, from an ideological standpoint, are not deserving of serious examination.

Does it require deep intuition to comprehend that man's ideas, views, and conception, in one word, man's consciousness, changes with every change in the conditions of his material existence, in his social relations and in his social life?

What else does the history of ideas prove, than that intellectual production changes its character in proportion as material production is changed? The ruling ideas of each age have ever been the ideas of its ruling class.

When people speak of the ideas that revolutionise society, they do but express that fact that within the old society the elements of a new one have been created, and that the dissolution of the old ideas keeps even pace with the dissolution of the old conditions of existence.

When the ancient world was in its last throes, the ancient religions were overcome by Christianity. When Christian ideas succumbed in the 18th century to rationalist ideas, feudal society fought its death battle with the then revolutionary bourgeoisie. The ideas of religious liberty and freedom of conscience merely gave expression to the sway of free competition within the domain of knowledge.

"Undoubtedly," it will be said, "religious, moral, philosophical, and juridical ideas have been modified in the course of historical development. But religion, morality, philosophy, political science, and law, constantly survived this change."

"There are, besides, eternal truths, such as Freedom, Justice, etc., that are common to all states of society. But Communism abolishes eternal truths, it abolishes all religion, and all morality, instead of constituting them on a new basis; it therefore acts in contradiction to all past historical experience."

What does this accusation reduce itself to? The history of all past society has consisted in the development of class antagonisms, antagonisms that assumed different forms at different epochs.

But whatever form they may have taken, one fact is common to all past ages, viz., the exploitation of one part of society by the other. No wonder, then, that the social consciousness of past ages, despite all the multiplicity and variety it displays, moves within certain common forms, or general ideas, which cannot completely vanish except with the total disappearance of class antagonisms.

The Communist revolution is the most radical rupture with traditional relations; no wonder that its development involved the most radical rupture with traditional ideas.

But let us have done with the bourgeois objections to Communism.

We have seen above, that the first step in the revolution by the working class is to raise the proletariat to the position of ruling class to win the battle of democracy.

The proletariat will use its political supremacy to wrest, by degree, all capital from the bourgeoisie, to centralise all instruments of production in the hands of the State, i.e., of the proletariat organised as the ruling class; and to increase the total productive forces as rapidly as possible.

Of course, in the beginning, this cannot be effected except by means of despotic inroads on the rights of property, and on the conditions of bourgeois production; by means of measures, therefore, which appear economically insufficient and untenable, but which, in the course of the movement, outstrip themselves, necessitate further inroads upon the old social order, and are unavoidable as a means of entirely revolutionising the mode of production.

These measures will, of course, be different in different countries.

Nevertheless, in most advanced countries, the following will be pretty generally applicable:

1. Abolition of property in land and application of all rents of land to public purposes.

2. A heavy progressive or graduated income tax.

3. Abolition of all rights of inheritance.

4. Confiscation of the property of all emigrants and rebels.

5. Centralisation of credit in the banks of the state, by means of a national bank with State capital and an exclusive monopoly.

6. Centralisation of the means of communication and transport in the hands of the State.

7. Extension of factories and instruments of production owned by the State; the bringing into cultivation of waste-lands, and the improvement of the soil generally in accordance with a common plan.

8. Equal liability of all to work. Establishment of industrial armies, especially for agriculture.

9. Combination of agriculture with manufacturing industries; gradual abolition of all the distinction between town and country by a more equable distribution of the populace over the country.

10. Free education for all children in public schools. Abolition of children's factory labour in its present form. Combination of education with industrial production, &c, &c.

When, in the course of development, class distinctions have disappeared, and all production has been concentrated in the hands of a vast association of the whole nation, the public power will lose its political character. Political power, properly so called, is merely the organised power of one class for oppressing another. If the proletariat during its contest with the bourgeoisie is compelled, by the force of circumstances, to organise itself as a class, if, by means of a revolution, it makes itself the ruling class, and, as such, sweeps away by force the old conditions of production, then it will, along with these conditions, have swept away the conditions for the existence of class antagonisms and of classes generally, and will thereby have abolished its own supremacy as a class.

In place of the old bourgeois society, with its classes and class antagonisms, we shall have an association, in which the free development of each is the condition for the free development of all.

III. Socialist and Communist Literature

1. Reactionary Socialism

A. FEUDAL SOCIALISM Owing to their historical position, it became the vocation of the aristocracies of France and England to write pamphlets against modern bourgeois society. In the French Revolution of July 1830, and in the English reform agitation,[5] these aristocracies again succumbed to the hateful upstart. Thenceforth, a serious political struggle was altogether out of the question. A literary battle alone remained possible. But even in the domain of literature the old cries of the restoration period had become impossible.[6]

In order to arouse sympathy, the aristocracy was obliged to lose sight, apparently, of its own interests, and to formulate their indictment against the bourgeoisie in the interest of the exploited working class alone. Thus, the aristocracy took their revenge by singing lampoons on their new masters and whispering in his ears sinister prophesies of coming catastrophe.

In this way arose feudal Socialism: half lamentation, half lampoon; half an echo of the past, half menace of the future; at times, by its bitter, witty and incisive criticism, striking the bourgeoisie to the very heart's core; but always ludicrous in its effect, through total incapacity to comprehend the march of modern history.

The aristocracy, in order to rally the people to them, waved the proletarian alms-bag in front for a banner. But the people, so often as it joined them, saw on their hindquarters the old feudal coats of arms, and deserted with loud and irreverent laughter.

One section of the French Legitimists and "Young England" exhibited this spectacle.

In pointing out that their mode of exploitation was different to that of the bourgeoisie, the feudalists forget that they exploited under circumstances and conditions that were quite different and that are now antiquated. In showing that, under their rule, the modern proletariat never existed, they forget that the modern bourgeoisie is the necessary offspring of their own form of society.

For the rest, so little do they conceal the reactionary character of their criticism that their chief accusation against the bourgeois amounts to this, that under the

---

5   A reference to the movement for a reform of the electoral law which, under the pressure of the working class, was passed by the British House of Commons in 1831 and finally endorsed by the House of Lords in June, 1832. The reform was directed against monopoly rule of the landed and finance aristocracy and opened the way to Parliament for the representatives of the industrial bourgeoisie. Neither workers nor the petty-bourgeois were allowed electoral rights, despite assurances they would be. [Editor's note]
6   Not the English Restoration (1660–1689), but the French Restoration (1814–1830). [Engels, 1888 German edition]

bourgeois regime a class is being developed which is destined to cut up root and branch the old order of society.

What they upbraid the bourgeoisie with is not so much that it creates a proletariat as that it creates a revolutionary proletariat.

In political practice, therefore, they join in all coercive measures against the working class; and in ordinary life, despite their high-falutin phrases, they stoop to pick up the golden apples dropped from the tree of industry, and to barter truth, love, and honour, for traffic in wool, beetroot-sugar, and potato spirits.[7]

As the parson has ever gone hand in hand with the landlord, so has Clerical Socialism with Feudal Socialism.

Nothing is easier than to give Christian asceticism a Socialist tinge. Has not Christianity declaimed against private property, against marriage, against the State? Has it not preached in the place of these, charity and poverty, celibacy and mortification of the flesh, monastic life and Mother Church? Christian Socialism is but the holy water with which the priest consecrates the heart-burnings of the aristocrat.

B. PETTY-BOURGEOIS SOCIALISM The feudal aristocracy was not the only class that was ruined by the bourgeoisie, not the only class whose conditions of existence pined and perished in the atmosphere of modern bourgeois society. The medieval burgesses and the small peasant proprietors were the precursors of the modern bourgeoisie. In those countries which are but little developed, industrially and commercially, these two classes still vegetate side by side with the rising bourgeoisie.

In countries where modern civilisation has become fully developed, a new class of petty bourgeois has been formed, fluctuating between proletariat and bourgeoisie, and ever renewing itself as a supplementary part of bourgeois society. The individual members of this class, however, are being constantly hurled down into the proletariat by the action of competition, and, as modern industry develops, they even see the moment approaching when they will completely disappear as an independent section of modern society, to be replaced in manufactures, agriculture and commerce, by overlookers, bailiffs and shopmen.

In countries like France, where the peasants constitute far more than half of the population, it was natural that writers who sided with the proletariat against the bourgeoisie should use, in their criticism of the bourgeois regime, the standard of the peasant and petty bourgeois, and from the standpoint of these intermediate classes, should take up the cudgels for the working class. Thus arose petty-bourgeois

---

7   This applies chiefly to Germany, where the landed aristocracy and squirearchy have large portions of their estates cultivated for their own account by stewards, and are, moreover, extensive beetroot-sugar manufacturers and distillers of potato spirits. The wealthier British aristocracy are, as yet, rather above that; but they, too, know how to make up for declining rents by lending their names to floaters or more or less shady joint-stock companies. [Engels, 1888 German edition]

Socialism. Sismondi was the head of this school, not only in France but also in England.

This school of Socialism dissected with great acuteness the contradictions in the conditions of modern production. It laid bare the hypocritical apologies of economists. It proved, incontrovertibly, the disastrous effects of machinery and division of labour; the concentration of capital and land in a few hands; overproduction and crises; it pointed out the inevitable ruin of the petty bourgeois and peasant, the misery of the proletariat, the anarchy in production, the crying inequalities in the distribution of wealth, the industrial war of extermination between nations, the dissolution of old moral bonds, of the old family relations, of the old nationalities.

In its positive aims, however, this form of Socialism aspires either to restoring the old means of production and of exchange, and with them the old property relations, and the old society, or to cramping the modern means of production and of exchange within the framework of the old property relations that have been, and were bound to be, exploded by those means. In either case, it is both reactionary and Utopian.

Its last words are: corporate guilds for manufacture; patriarchal relations in agriculture.

Ultimately, when stubborn historical facts had dispersed all intoxicating effects of self-deception, this form of Socialism ended in a miserable hangover.

C. GERMAN OR "TRUE" SOCIALISM The Socialist and Communist literature of France, a literature that originated under the pressure of a bourgeoisie in power, and that was the expressions of the struggle against this power, was introduced into Germany at a time when the bourgeoisie, in that country, had just begun its contest with feudal absolutism.

German philosophers, would-be philosophers, and beaux esprits (men of letters), eagerly seized on this literature, only forgetting, that when these writings immigrated from France into Germany, French social conditions had not immigrated along with them. In contact with German social conditions, this French literature lost all its immediate practical significance and assumed a purely literary aspect. Thus, to the German philosophers of the Eighteenth Century, the demands of the first French Revolution were nothing more than the demands of "Practical Reason" in general, and the utterance of the will of the revolutionary French bourgeoisie signified, in their eyes, the laws of pure Will, of Will as it was bound to be, of true human Will generally.

The work of the German literati consisted solely in bringing the new French ideas into harmony with their ancient philosophical conscience, or rather, in annexing the French ideas without deserting their own philosophic point of view.

This annexation took place in the same way in which a foreign language is appropriated, namely, by translation.

It is well known how the monks wrote silly lives of Catholic Saints over the manuscripts on which the classical works of ancient heathendom had been written. The German literati reversed this process with the profane French literature. They wrote their philosophical nonsense beneath the French original. For instance, beneath the French criticism of the economic functions of money, they wrote "Alienation of Humanity," and beneath the French criticism of the bourgeois state they wrote "Dethronement of the Category of the General," and so forth.

The introduction of these philosophical phrases at the back of the French historical criticisms, they dubbed "Philosophy of Action," "True Socialism," "German Science of Socialism," "Philosophical Foundation of Socialism," and so on.

The French Socialist and Communist literature was thus completely emasculated. And, since it ceased in the hands of the German to express the struggle of one class with the other, he felt conscious of having overcome "French one-sidedness" and of representing, not true requirements, but the requirements of Truth; not the interests of the proletariat, but the interests of Human Nature, of Man in general, who belongs to no class, has no reality, who exists only in the misty realm of philosophical fantasy.

This German socialism, which took its schoolboy task so seriously and solemnly, and extolled its poor stock-in-trade in such a mountebank fashion, meanwhile gradually lost its pedantic innocence.

The fight of the Germans, and especially of the Prussian bourgeoisie, against feudal aristocracy and absolute monarchy, in other words, the liberal movement, became more earnest.

By this, the long-wished-for opportunity was offered to "True" Socialism of confronting the political movement with the Socialist demands, of hurling the traditional anathemas against liberalism, against representative government, against bourgeois competition, bourgeois freedom of the press, bourgeois legislation, bourgeois liberty and equality, and of preaching to the masses that they had nothing to gain, and everything to lose, by this bourgeois movement. German Socialism forgot, in the nick of time, that the French criticism, whose silly echo it was, presupposed the existence of modern bourgeois society, with its corresponding economic conditions of existence, and the political constitution adapted thereto, the very things whose attainment was the object of the pending struggle in Germany.

To the absolute governments, with their following of parsons, professors, country squires, and officials, it served as a welcome scarecrow against the threatening bourgeoisie.

It was a sweet finish, after the bitter pills of flogging and bullets, with which these same governments, just at that time, dosed the German working-class risings.

While this "True" Socialism thus served the government as a weapon for fighting the German bourgeoisie, it, at the same time, directly represented a reactionary interest, the interest of German Philistines. In Germany, the petty-bourgeois class, a relic of the sixteenth century, and since then constantly cropping up again under the various forms, is the real social basis of the existing state of things.

To preserve this class is to preserve the existing state of things in Germany. The industrial and political supremacy of the bourgeoisie threatens it with certain destruction—on the one hand, from the concentration of capital; on the other, from the rise of a revolutionary proletariat. "True" Socialism appeared to kill these two birds with one stone. It spread like an epidemic.

The robe of speculative cobwebs, embroidered with flowers of rhetoric, steeped in the dew of sickly sentiment, this transcendental robe in which the German Socialists wrapped their sorry "eternal truths," all skin and bone, served to wonderfully increase the sale of their goods among such a public.

And on its part German Socialism recognised, more and more, its own calling as the bombastic representative of the petty-bourgeois Philistine.

It proclaimed the German nation to be the model nation, and the German petty Philistine to be the typical man. To every villainous meanness of this model man, it gave a hidden, higher, Socialistic interpretation, the exact contrary of its real character. It went to the extreme length of directly opposing the "brutally destructive" tendency of Communism, and of proclaiming its supreme and impartial contempt of all class struggles. With very few exceptions, all the so-called Socialist and Communist publications that now (1847) circulate in Germany belong to the domain of this foul and enervating literature.[8]

2. Conservative or Bourgeois Socialism

A part of the bourgeoisie is desirous of redressing social grievances in order to secure the continued existence of bourgeois society.

To this section belong economists, philanthropists, humanitarians, improvers of the condition of the working class, organisers of charity, members of societies for the prevention of cruelty to animals, temperance fanatics, hole-and-corner reformers of every imaginable kind. This form of socialism has, moreover, been worked out into complete systems.

We may cite Proudhon's *Philosophie de la Misère* as an example of this form.

---

8   The revolutionary storm of 1848 swept away this whole shabby tendency and cured its protagonists of the desire to dabble in socialism. The chief representative and classical type of this tendency is Mr Karl Gruen. [Engels, 1888 German edition]

The Socialistic bourgeois want all the advantages of modern social conditions without the struggles and dangers necessarily resulting therefrom. They desire the existing state of society, minus its revolutionary and disintegrating elements. They wish for a bourgeoisie without a proletariat. The bourgeoisie naturally conceives the world in which it is supreme to be the best; and bourgeois Socialism develops this comfortable conception into various more or less complete systems. In requiring the proletariat to carry out such a system, and thereby to march straightway into the social New Jerusalem, it but requires in reality, that the proletariat should remain within the bounds of existing society, but should cast away all its hateful ideas concerning the bourgeoisie.

A second, and more practical, but less systematic, form of this Socialism sought to depreciate every revolutionary movement in the eyes of the working class by showing that no mere political reform, but only a change in the material conditions of existence, in economical relations, could be of any advantage to them. By changes in the material conditions of existence, this form of Socialism, however, by no means understands abolition of the bourgeois relations of production, an abolition that can be affected only by a revolution, but administrative reforms, based on the continued existence of these relations; reforms, therefore, that in no respect affect the relations between capital and labour, but, at the best, lessen the cost, and simplify the administrative work, of bourgeois government.

Bourgeois Socialism attains adequate expression when, and only when, it becomes a mere figure of speech.

Free trade: for the benefit of the working class. Protective duties: for the benefit of the working class. Prison Reform: for the benefit of the working class. This is the last word and the only seriously meant word of bourgeois socialism.

It is summed up in the phrase: the bourgeois is a bourgeois—for the benefit of the working class.

3. Critical-Utopian Socialism and Communism

We do not here refer to that literature which, in every great modern revolution, has always given voice to the demands of the proletariat, such as the writings of Babeuf and others.

The first direct attempts of the proletariat to attain its own ends, made in times of universal excitement, when feudal society was being overthrown, necessarily failed, owing to the then undeveloped state of the proletariat, as well as to the absence of the economic conditions for its emancipation, conditions that had yet to be produced, and could be produced by the impending bourgeois epoch alone. The revolutionary literature that accompanied these first movements of the proletariat had necessarily a reactionary character. It inculcated universal asceticism and social levelling in its crudest form.

The Socialist and Communist systems, properly so called, those of Saint-Simon, Fourier, Owen, and others, spring into existence in the early undeveloped period, described above, of the struggle between proletariat and bourgeoisie (see Section I. Bourgeois and Proletarians).

The founders of these systems see, indeed, the class antagonisms, as well as the action of the decomposing elements in the prevailing form of society. But the proletariat, as yet in its infancy, offers to them the spectacle of a class without any historical initiative or any independent political movement.

Since the development of class antagonism keeps even pace with the development of industry, the economic situation, as they find it, does not as yet offer to them the material conditions for the emancipation of the proletariat. They therefore search after a new social science, after new social laws, that are to create these conditions.

Historical action is to yield to their personal inventive action; historically created conditions of emancipation to fantastic ones; and the gradual, spontaneous class organisation of the proletariat to an organisation of society especially contrived by these inventors. Future history resolves itself, in their eyes, into the propaganda and the practical carrying out of their social plans.

In the formation of their plans, they are conscious of caring chiefly for the interests of the working class, as being the most suffering class. Only from the point of view of being the most suffering class does the proletariat exist for them.

The undeveloped state of the class struggle, as well as their own surroundings, causes Socialists of this kind to consider themselves far superior to all class antagonisms. They want to improve the condition of every member of society, even that of the most favoured. Hence, they habitually appeal to society at large, without the distinction of class; nay, by preference, to the ruling class. For how can people, when once they understand their system, fail to see in it the best possible plan of the best possible state of society?

Hence, they reject all political, and especially all revolutionary action; they wish to attain their ends by peaceful means, necessarily doomed to failure, and by the force of example, to pave the way for the new social Gospel.

Such fantastic pictures of future society, painted at a time when the proletariat is still in a very undeveloped state and has but a fantastic conception of its own position, correspond with the first instinctive yearnings of that class for a general reconstruction of society.

But these Socialist and Communist publications contain also a critical element. They attack every principle of existing society. Hence, they are full of the most valuable materials for the enlightenment of the working class. The practical measures proposed in them—such as the abolition of the distinction between town and country, of the family, of the carrying on of industries for the account of private individuals, and of the wage system, the proclamation of social harmony, the conversion of the function of the state into a mere superintendence of production—all these proposals point solely to the disappearance of class antagonisms which were, at that time, only just cropping up, and which, in these publications, are recognised in their earliest indistinct and undefined forms only. These proposals, therefore, are of a purely Utopian character.

The significance of Critical-Utopian Socialism and Communism bears an inverse relation to historical development. In proportion as the modern class struggle develops and takes definite shape, this fantastic standing apart from the contest, these fantastic attacks on it, lose all practical value and all theoretical justification. Therefore, although the originators of these systems were, in many respects, revolutionary, their disciples have, in every case, formed mere reactionary sects. They hold fast by the original views of their masters, in opposition to the progressive historical development of the proletariat. They, therefore, endeavour, and that consistently, to deaden the class struggle and to reconcile the class antagonisms. They still dream of experimental realisation of their social Utopias, of founding isolated "phalansteres," of establishing "Home Colonies," or setting up a "Little Icatia"[9]—duodecimo editions of the New Jerusalem—and to realise all these castles in the air, they are compelled to appeal to the feelings and purses of the bourgeois. By degrees, they sink into the category of the reactionary [or] conservative Socialists depicted above, differing from these only by more systematic pedantry, and by their fanatical and superstitious belief in the miraculous effects of their social science.

They, therefore, violently oppose all political action on the part of the working class; such action, according to them, can only result from blind unbelief in the new Gospel.

The Owenites in England, and the Fourierists in France, respectively, oppose the Chartists and the Réformistes.

IV. Position of the Communists in Relation to the Various Existing Opposition Parties

Section II has made clear the relations of the Communists to the existing working-class parties, such as the Chartists in England and the Agrarian Reformers in America.

---

9   Phalanstères were Socialist colonies on the plan of Charles Fourier; Icaria was the name given by Cabet to his Utopia and, later on, to his American Communist colony. [Engels, 1888 English Edition] "Home Colonies" were what Owen called his Communist model societies. Phalanstères was the name of the public palaces planned by Fourier. Icaria was the name given to the Utopian land of fancy, whose Communist institutions Cabet portrayed. [Engels, 1890 German Edition]

The Communists fight for the attainment of the immediate aims, for the enforce-ment of the momentary interests of the working class; but in the movement of the present, they also represent and take care of the future of that movement. In France, the Communists ally with the Social-Democrats[10] against the conservative and rad-ical bourgeoisie, reserving, however, the right to take up a critical position in regard to phases and illusions traditionally handed down from the great Revolution.

In Switzerland, they support the Radicals, without losing sight of the fact that this party consists of antagonistic elements, partly of Democratic Socialists, in the French sense, partly of radical bourgeois.

In Poland, they support the party that insists on an agrarian revolution as the prime condition for national emancipation, that party which fomented the insur-rection of Cracow in 1846.

In Germany, they fight with the bourgeoisie whenever it acts in a revolutionary way, against the absolute monarchy, the feudal squirearchy, and the petty bourgeoisie.

But they never cease, for a single instant, to instill into the working class the clearest possible recognition of the hostile antagonism between bourgeoisie and proletariat, in order that the German workers may straightway use, as so many weapons against the bourgeoisie, the social and political conditions that the bour-geoisie must necessarily introduce along with its supremacy, and in order that, after the fall of the reactionary classes in Germany, the fight against the bourgeoisie itself may immediately begin.

The Communists turn their attention chiefly to Germany, because that country is on the eve of a bourgeois revolution that is bound to be carried out under more advanced conditions of European civilisation and with a much more developed pro-letariat than that of England was in the seventeenth, and France in the eighteenth century, and because the bourgeois revolution in Germany will be but the prelude to an immediately following proletarian revolution.

In short, the Communists everywhere support every revolutionary movement against the existing social and political order of things.

In all these movements, they bring to the front, as the leading question in each, the property question, no matter what its degree of development at the time.

Finally, they labour everywhere for the union and agreement of the democratic parties of all countries.

The Communists disdain to conceal their views and aims. They openly declare that their ends can be attained only by the forcible overthrow of all existing social con-ditions. Let the ruling classes tremble at a Communistic revolution. The proletarians

---

10   The party then represented in Parliament by Ledru-Rollin, in literature by Louis Blanc, in the daily press by the Réforme. The name of Social Democracy signifies, with these its inventors, a section of the Democratic or Republican Party more or less tinged with socialism. [Engels, 1888 English Edition]

have nothing to lose but their chains. They have a world to win. WORKING MEN OF ALL COUNTRIES, UNITE!

Questions

1. What is the relationship between the bourgeoisie and the proletariat?

2. What does Marx think of capitalism?

3. How do the social conditions of Marx's time differ from earlier times?

4. How does Marx's vision of the relationship between work and those who control the means of production differ from today's?

5. Consider what Marx advocates in the *Manifesto*; what specifically (if anything) is undesirable?

Further Reading

Carver, Terrell, ed. *The Cambridge Companion to Marx*. Cambridge: Cambridge University Press, 1991.

Husami, Ziyad. "Marx on Distributive Justice." *Philosophy and Public Affairs*, vol. 8, 1978, pp. 27–64.

Marx, Karl. *Karl Marx: Selected Writings*. 2nd ed. Edited by David McLellan. Oxford: Oxford University Press, 2000.

Singer, Peter. *Marx: A Very Short Introduction*. Oxford: Oxford University Press, 2000.

Wolff, Jonathan. *Why Read Marx Today?* Oxford: Oxford University Press, 2002.

Wolff, Robert Paul. *Understanding Marx*. Princeton, NJ: Princeton University Press, 1984.

9.

"THE SOCIAL RESPONSIBILITY OF BUSINESS IS TO INCREASE ITS PROFITS"

MILTON FRIEDMAN

About This Reading

In the past forty years or so, there has been a movement in business ethics that is often referred to as corporate social responsibility or *CSR*. The basic view is that businesses should respect both the spirit and the letter of the law. Businesses should include in their decision-making the social as well as economic goods that may flow from their actions. Doing so expands the notion of a stakeholder beyond that of just the shareholders.

In stark relief to this view is that of Milton Friedman, who holds that a business's primary responsibility is to its shareholders. It is the job of the corporation to maximize profits while doing business within the letter of the law. While individuals may use the profits they receive to do charitable work, Friedman argues that it is dangerous for unelected, unaccountable individuals to provide (or be required to provide) social goods. Such requirements would lead us down a slippery slope to a state-controlled, planned economy.

When I hear businessmen speak eloquently about the "social responsibilities of business in a free-enterprise system," I am reminded of the wonderful line about the Frenchman who discovered at the age of 70 that he had been speaking prose all his life. The businessmen believe that they are defending free enterprise when they declaim that business is not concerned "merely" with profit but also with promoting desirable "social" ends; that business has a "social conscience" and takes seriously its responsibilities for providing employment, eliminating discrimination, avoiding pollution and whatever else may be the catchwords of the contemporary crop of reformers. In fact they are—or would be if they or anyone else took them seriously—preaching pure and adulterated socialism. Businessmen who talk this way are unwitting puppets of the intellectual forces that have been undermining the basis of a free society these past decades.

The discussions of the "social responsibilities of business" are notable for their analytical looseness and lack of rigor. What does it mean to say that "business" has responsibilities? Only people can have responsibilities. A corporation is an artificial person and in this sense may have artificial responsibilities, but "business" as a whole cannot be said to have responsibilities, even in this vague sense. The first step toward clarity in examining the doctrine of the social responsibility of business is to ask precisely what it implies for whom.

Presumably, the individuals who are to be responsible are businessmen, which means individual proprietors or corporate executives. Most of the discussion of social responsibility is directed at corporations, so in what follows I shall mostly neglect the individual proprietors and speak of corporate executives.

In a free-enterprise, private-property system, a corporate executive is an employee of the owners of the business. He has direct responsibility to his employers. That responsibility is to conduct the business in accordance with their desires, which generally will be to make as much money as possible while conforming to the basic rules of the society, both those embodied in law and those embodied in ethical custom. Of course, in some cases his employers may have a different objective. A group of persons might establish a corporation for an eleemosynary purpose—for example, a hospital or a school. The manager of such a corporation will not have money profit as his objective but the rendering of certain services.

In either case, the key point is that, in his capacity as a corporate executive, the manager is the agent of the individuals who own the corporation or establish the eleemosynary institution, and his primary responsibility is to them.

Needless to say, this does not mean that it is easy to judge how well he is performing his task. But at least the criterion of performance is straightforward, and the persons among whom a voluntary contractual arrangement exists are clearly defined.

Of course, the corporate executive is also a person in his own right. As a person, he may have many other responsibilities that he recognizes or assumes voluntarily—to his family, his conscience, his feelings of charity, his church, his clubs, his city, his country. He may feel impelled by these responsibilities to devote part of his income to causes he regards as worthy, to refuse to work for particular corporations, even to leave his job, for example, to join his country's armed forces. If we wish, we may refer to some of these responsibilities as "social responsibilities."

But in these respects he is acting as a principal, not an agent; he is spending his own money or time or energy, not the money of his employers or the time or energy he has contracted to devote to their purposes. If these are "social responsibilities," they are the social responsibilities of individuals, not of business.

What does it mean to say that the corporate executive has a "social responsibility" in his capacity as businessman? If this statement is not pure rhetoric, it must mean that he is to act in some way that is not in the interest of his employers. For example, that he is to refrain from increasing the price of the product in order to contribute to the social objective of preventing inflation, even though a price increase would be in the best interests of the corporation. Or that he is to make expenditures on reducing pollution beyond the amount that is in the best interests of the corporation or that is required by law in order to contribute to the social objective of improving the environment. Or that, at the expense of corporate profits, he is to hire "hardcore" unemployed instead of better qualified available workmen to contribute to the social objective of reducing poverty.

In each of these cases, the corporate executive would be spending someone else's money for a general social interest. Insofar as his actions in accord with his "social responsibility" reduce returns to stockholders, he is spending their money. Insofar as his actions raise the price to customers, he is spending the customers' money. Insofar as his actions lower the wages of some employees, he is spending their money.

The stockholders or the customers or the employees could separately spend their own money on the particular action if they wished to do so. The executive is exercising a distinct "social responsibility," rather than serving as an agent of the stockholders or the customers or the employees, only if he spends the money in a different way than they would have spent it.

But if he does this, he is in effect imposing taxes, on the one hand, and deciding how the tax proceeds shall be spent, on the other.

This process raises political questions on two levels: principle and consequences. On the level of political principle, the imposition of taxes and the expenditure of tax proceeds are governmental functions. We have established elaborate constitutional, parliamentary and judicial provisions to control these functions, to assure that taxes are imposed so far as possible in accordance with the preferences and desires of the public—after all, "taxation without representation" was one of the battle cries of the American Revolution. We have a system of checks and balances to separate the legislative function of imposing taxes and enacting expenditures from the executive function of collecting taxes and administering expenditure programs and from the judicial function of mediating disputes and interpreting the law.

Here the businessman—self-selected or appointed directly or indirectly by stockholders—is to be simultaneously legislator, executive, and jurist. He is to decide whom to tax by how much and for what purpose, and he is to spend the proceeds—all this guided only by general exhortations from on high to restrain inflation, improve the environment, fight poverty and so on and on.

The whole justification for permitting the corporate executive to be selected by the stockholders is that the executive is an agent serving the interests of his principal. This justification disappears when the corporate executive imposes taxes and spends the proceeds for "social" purposes. He becomes in effect a public employee, a civil servant, even though he remains in name an employee of a private enterprise. On grounds of political principle, it is intolerable that such civil servants—insofar as their actions in the name of social responsibility are real and not just window-dressing—should be selected as they are now. If they are to be civil servants, then they must be elected through a political process. If they are to impose taxes and make expenditures to foster "social" objectives, then political machinery must be set up to make the assessment of taxes and to determine through a political process the objectives to be served.

This is the basic reason why the doctrine of "social responsibility" involves the acceptance of the socialist view that political mechanisms, not market mechanisms, are the appropriate way to determine the allocation of scarce resources to alternative uses.

On the grounds of consequences, can the corporate executive in fact discharge his alleged "social responsibilities?" On the other hand, suppose he could get away with spending the stockholders' or customers' or employees' money. How is he to know how to spend it? He is told that he must contribute to fighting inflation. How is he to know what action of his will contribute to that end? He is presumably an expert in running his company—in producing a product or selling it or financing it. But nothing about his selection makes him an expert on inflation. Will his holding down the price of his product reduce inflationary pressure? Or, by leaving more spending power in the hands of his customers, simply divert it elsewhere? Or, by forcing him to produce less because of the lower price, will it simply contribute to shortages? Even if he could answer these questions, how much cost is he justified in imposing on his stockholders, customers and employees for this social purpose? What is his appropriate share and what is the appropriate share of others?

And, whether he wants to or not, can he get away with spending his stockholders', customers' or employees' money? Will not the stockholders fire him? (Either the present ones or those who take over when his actions in the name of social responsibility have reduced the corporation's profits and the price of its stock.) His customers and his employees can desert him for other producers and employers less scrupulous in exercising their social responsibilities.

This facet of "social responsibility" doctrine is brought into sharp relief when the doctrine is used to justify wage restraint by trade unions. The conflict of interest is naked and clear when union officials are asked to subordinate the interest of their members to some more general purpose. If the union officials try to enforce wage restraint, the consequence is likely to be wildcat strikes, rank-and-file revolts and the emergence of strong competitors for their jobs. We thus have the ironic phenomenon that union leaders—at least in the U.S.—have objected to Government interference with the market far more consistently and courageously than have business leaders.

The difficulty of exercising "social responsibility" illustrates, of course, the great virtue of private competitive enterprise—it forces people to be responsible for their own actions and makes it difficult for them to "exploit" other people for either selfish or unselfish purposes. They can do good—but only at their own expense.

Many a reader who has followed the argument this far may be tempted to remonstrate that it is all well and good to speak of Government's having the responsibility to impose taxes and determine expenditures for such "social" purposes as controlling pollution or training the hardcore unemployed, but that the problems are too urgent to wait on the slow course of political processes, that the exercise of social responsibility by businessmen is a quicker and surer way to solve pressing current problems.

Aside from the question of fact—I share Adam Smith's skepticism about the benefits that can be expected from "those who affected to trade for the public good"—this argument must be rejected on grounds of principle. What it amounts to is an assertion that those who favor the taxes and expenditures in question have failed to persuade a majority of their fellow citizens to be of like mind and that they are seeking to attain by undemocratic procedures what they cannot attain by democratic procedures. In a free society, it is hard for "evil" people to do "evil," especially since one man's good is another's evil.

I have, for simplicity, concentrated on the special case of the corporate executive, except only for the brief digression on trade unions. But precisely the same argument applies to the newer phenomenon of calling upon stockholders to require corporations to exercise social responsibility (the recent G.M. crusade for example). In most of these cases, what is in effect involved is some stockholders trying to get other stockholders (or customers or employees) to contribute against their will to "social" causes favored by the activists. Insofar as they succeed, they are again imposing taxes and spending the proceeds.

The situation of the individual proprietor is somewhat different. If he acts to reduce the returns of his enterprise in order to exercise his "social responsibility," he is spending his own money, not someone else's. If he wishes to spend his money on such purposes, that is his right, and I cannot see that there is any objection to his doing so. In the process, he, too, may impose costs on employees and customers. However, because he is far less likely than a large corporation or union to have monopolistic power, any such side effects will tend to be minor.

Of course, in practice the doctrine of social responsibility is frequently a cloak for actions that are justified on other grounds rather than a reason for those actions.

To illustrate, it may well be in the long-run interest of a corporation that is a major employer in a small community to devote resources to providing amenities to that community or to improving its government. That may make it easier to attract desirable employees, it may reduce the wage bill or lessen losses from pilferage and sabotage or have other worthwhile effects. Or it may be that, given the laws about the deductibility of corporate charitable contributions, the stockholders can contribute more to charities they favor by having the corporation make the gift than by doing it themselves, since they can in that way contribute an amount that would otherwise have been paid as corporate taxes.

In each of these—and many similar—cases, there is a strong temptation to rationalize these actions as an exercise of "social responsibility." In the present climate of opinion, with its widespread aversion to "capitalism," "profits," the "soulless corporation" and so on, this is one way for a corporation to generate goodwill as a by-product of expenditures that are entirely justified in its own self-interest.

It would be inconsistent of me to call on corporate executives to refrain from this hypocritical window-dressing because it harms the foundations of a free society. That would be to call on them to exercise a "social responsibility"! If our institutions, and the attitudes of the public make it in their self-interest to cloak their actions in this way, I cannot summon much indignation to denounce them. At the same time, I can express admiration for those individual proprietors or owners of closely held corporations or stockholders of more broadly held corporations who disdain such tactics as approaching fraud.

Whether blameworthy or not, the use of the cloak of social responsibility, and the nonsense spoken in its name by influential and prestigious businessmen, does clearly harm the foundations of a free society. I have been impressed time and again by the schizophrenic character of many businessmen. They are capable of being extremely farsighted and clearheaded in matters that are internal to their businesses. They are incredibly shortsighted and muddleheaded in matters that are outside their businesses but affect the possible survival of business in general. This shortsightedness is strikingly exemplified in the calls from many businessmen for wage and price guidelines or controls or income policies. There is nothing that could do more in a brief period to destroy a market system and replace it by a centrally controlled system than effective governmental control of prices and wages.

The shortsightedness is also exemplified in speeches by businessmen on social responsibility. This may gain them kudos in the short run. But it helps to strengthen the already too prevalent view that the pursuit of profits is wicked and immoral and must be curbed and controlled by external forces. Once this view is adopted, the external forces that curb the market will not be the social consciences, however highly developed, of the pontificating executives; it will be the iron fist of Government bureaucrats. Here, as with price and wage controls, businessmen seem to me to reveal a suicidal impulse.

The political principle that underlies the market mechanism is unanimity. In an ideal free market resting on private property, no individual can coerce any other, all cooperation is voluntary, all parties to such cooperation benefit or they need not participate. There are no values, no "social" responsibilities in any sense other than the shared values and responsibilities of individuals. Society is a collection of individuals and of the various groups they voluntarily form.

The political principle that underlies the political mechanism is conformity. The individual must serve a more general social interest—whether that be determined by a church or a dictator or a majority. The individual may have a vote and say in what is to be done, but if he is overruled, he must conform. It is appropriate for some to require others to contribute to a general social purpose whether they wish to or not.

Unfortunately, unanimity is not always feasible. There are some respects in which conformity appears unavoidable, so I do not see how one can avoid the use of the political mechanism altogether.

But the doctrine of "social responsibility" taken seriously would extend the scope of the political mechanism to every human activity. It does not differ in philosophy from the most explicitly collectivist doctrine. It differs only by professing to believe: that collectivist ends can be attained without collectivist means. That is why, in my book *Capitalism and Freedom*, I have called it a "fundamentally subversive doctrine" in a free society, and have said that in such a society, "there is one and only one social responsibility of business—to use its resources and engage in activities designed to increase its profits so long as it stays within the rules of the game, which is to say, engages in open and free competition without deception or fraud."

Questions

1. What practices is Friedman concerned with?

2. What is the problem with thinking that businesses have social responsibilities beyond increasing profits? In principle? In consequence?

3. Is there something beyond profits with which businesses should be concerned?

4. In what way does Friedman allow for businesses to act as if they have social responsibilities beyond merely increasing profits?

Further Reading

André, R. "Assessing the Accountability of the Benefit Corporation: Will This New Gray Sector Organization Enhance Corporate Social Responsibility?" *Journal of Business Ethics*, vol. 110, 2012, pp. 133–50.

B Corporations at www.bcorporation.net/what-are-b-corps

eBay v. Newmark at www.delawarelitigation.com/uploads/file/int51%281%29.pdf

Hiller, J.S. "The Benefit Corporation and Corporate Social Responsibility." *Journal of Business Ethics*, vol. 118, 2013, p. 287.

Narveson, Jan. *The Libertarian Idea*. Peterborough, ON: Broadview Press, 2001.

Roark, Eric. *Removing the Commons: A Lockean Left-Libertarian Approach to the Just Use and Appropriation of Natural Resources*. Lanham: Lexington Books, 2013.

10.
"THE WHY'S OF BUSINESS REVISITED"

RONALD F. DUSKA[1]

About This Reading

What is the purpose of business? A traditional claim for the purpose of business is that businesses exist to maximize profits. This argument is made elsewhere in this book (see the article by Milton Friedman). Ronald Duska takes another look at the question of what the purpose of business is. This is an important question, because as Duska points out, we can judge the success of a business based on what the purpose of that business is. If the purpose of business is to maximize profits, then the standard by which to judge all businesses is the amount of profit generated by that business. However, there is an alternative view regarding the purpose of business. Duska distinguishes motives from purposes and argues that, while the motive of a business may be to maximize profit, the purpose of a business is the production of goods and services.

"'The limits of my language are the limits of my world' (Ludwig Wittgenstein). By this he meant that the language we speak constrains and delimits the world of thoughts and possibilities that is open to us ... To paraphrase Heidegger, we do not have our language so much as it has us."[2]

"The business of business is business." (Popular saying)

"That's just business." (Another popular saying)

---

1   I need to thank Norman Bowie and Nicholas Rongione, who read various versions of this essay, for their helpful comments.
2   Terrence Ball, "What's Wrong with Values," *The New Oxford Review*, May 1996, pp. 6 and 7.

"What's happening ... is that people are coming to grips with *the fact that* the
point of business is to make a profit."[3]

There is dispute about the purpose of a for-profit corporation. The most common
belief about the purpose of business, articulated or not, seems to be that the primary
purpose of business is to maximize profit. Think what is implied when one says,
"The business of business is business"; "That's just business"; or "The bottom line
is ..." Don't these ways of speaking indicate that the point of business is to make a
profit? Don't they indicate acquiescence in the belief that that's just the way things
are? People are in business to make a profit, so whatever needs to be done, no matter
what, is "just business." Business activities are justified by the pursuit of black ink
on the bottom line.

There are, of course, those who believe that the primary purpose of business is to
provide goods and services. But this belief does not seem to be very commonly held,
nor is it embodied in any pithy sayings or popular maxims. The first position seems
obvious, and is readily defended against the second by appealing to the fact that in
our corporate world, when people invest money, they don't usually ask what goods
or services the companies they invest in produce, but rather inquire what return on
their investment the company pays. Those who defend the position that the primary
purpose of business is the production of goods and services cannot point to any
readily observable trait of human beings that would incentivize people to invest for
the sake of society. The most that we hear is: "Being socially responsible is good for
business"; "Good ethics is good business,"[4] or "Emphasizing customer service is the
best way to improve the bottom line." All of these of course return us to the increasing
of profits as the ultimate end or primary purpose of business.

But why is what people take to be the purpose of business an important consideration? It is important because what we conceive as the purpose of something
will determine when that something is acting appropriately. The purpose determines the way the thing should operate, and hence, in a manner of speaking, the
responsibilities of the thing. The purpose furnishes us with a criterion of evaluation.
For example, a knife has an end or purpose. What makes a knife a good knife is
how well it "fulfills its purpose," i.e. cuts. Similarly, a business is designed for some

---

3   Albert Dunlap in his first remark in a discussion at the Occidental Grill, a restaurant in Washington, D.C.
"Forum," *Harper's Magazine*, May 1996.
4   Aristotle says, "Every art or inquiry aims at some good," *Nicomachean Ethics*. Whether a business is
good, then, is determined by what good business activity aims at. If what business aims at is increasing profit,
then the good business will be the one which increases profit. But Aristotle distinguishes between what
has the aspect of good, or appears good (profit certainly can be viewed as a good or having good aspects)
and what true good is, that which brings real happiness. This is the good we *should* aim at. The trick is to
use our practical reason to sort out which apparent goods are really good.

purpose and what makes it a good business is determined by how well it fulfills its purpose. If its main purpose is to maximize profits, then a business with a good bottom line which maximizes profits is a good business. The responsibility of those running the business is to make it a good business, or in other words, do what is necessary to maximize profits. If, on the other hand, we view the main purpose as providing goods and services, then we will view the primary responsibility to be the production of quality goods, and the better the quality of those goods and services, the better the business. We can see the hold the profit-maximizing view has on us if we reflect on how often we justify the most harmful behavior, such as layoffs or business closings, by appealing to the maximization purpose in saying, "That's just business." The profit of the bottom line justifies whatever behavior is necessary to improve the bottom line.

Given the logic of the language of "purpose," if Heidegger and Wittgenstein are right, and we do not have our language so much as it has us, we should expect to be held captive by our ordinary way of conversing about business, which entails the profit maximizing view. And we are. We are held captive to such an extent that even those who critique the dominant view fall under its spell. To take some examples, note how Laura Nash, who would otherwise be a proponent of the production of goods and services as the point of business, talks about the purpose of business in an unguarded moment. "The good corporation is expected to avoid perpetrating irretrievable social injury while focusing on its purpose as a profit-making organization."[5] Or note how Tom Donaldson in a discussion format talks of the purpose of business: "The fundamental purpose of a business is to make a profit for its owners, but I would say that's not its only purpose."[6]

This dominant view, though, is not neutral. No view of purpose is. Such a view legitimates the institutional practices of business, and in this case does so to such an extent that even if we are opposed to the practices we do not have the language to critique them. So we are faced with an anomaly—even those who would claim that the purpose of business is to provide goods and services slip into talk about business which legitimizes some of the behavior they would not approve of in theory.

---

5   Laura Nash, "Ethics without the Sermon," *Harvard Business Review*, November-December, 1981, p. 89. Nash is not alone. I have heard other colleagues slip into that kind of talk.

6   Tom Donaldson, "Transcript of a Discussion by the Panel of Judges, American Business Ethics Awards," November 16, 1993. Published in *Chapter Handbook for Ethical Guidance & Professional Standards Committee*, American Society of CLU and ChFC, 1996. One might object that we should not be held as strictly accountable for what we say in the context of a discussion as for what we put in print. To begin, I am not holding either Nash or Donaldson accountable. I think, however, that what we say in informal settings indicates our general unreflective viewpoint, and that is precisely the point I am trying to make. This way of thinking is part of our culture and language. It is the way we talk, and hence it reflects our underlying outlooks.

How widespread is this maximization of profits view? The fact that it shows up in our ordinary discourse is clear enough. But it also shows up in our learned discourse. Notice how in a standard financial management text, chosen at random, the goal of the firm is taken for granted.

> We believe that the preferable goal of the firm should be the maximization of shareholder wealth, by which we mean maximization of the price of the existing common stock.[7]

Here the goal or purpose of the firm is maximizing shareholder wealth as contrasted with maximizing profits, a popular distinction in business school discussions. The authors take some to task who hold that the purpose of business is profit maximization.

> In microeconomics courses, profit maximization is frequently given as the goal of the firm. Profit maximization stresses the efficient use of capital resources, but it is not specific with respect to the time frame over which profits are to be measured ... In microeconomics, profit maximization functions largely as a theoretical goal, with economists using it to prove how firms behave rationally to increase profit. Unfortunately, it ignores many real-world complexities.

Here the authors stress the new in-vogue concept of maximizing shareholder value over profit maximization. Yet this difference need not deter us. Whether we call the goal "the maximization of shareholder wealth" or "maximization of profits," it is structurally the same for our purposes. The primary goal of business is not the production of a product but the accumulation of wealth brought about by means of the production of products.

We see, then, that the view that the primary purpose of business is to maximize value is the dominant view—so much so that what "Chainsaw" Dunlap has said, "people are coming to grips with *the fact that* the point of business is to make a profit," is perilously close to the truth. The only amendment we would make to Dunlap's point is that people are not so much coming to grips with the fact that the point of business is to make a profit as they are acquiescing in the acceptance of the belief. However to the extent that this belief is unreflectively accepted, it becomes as intractable as a fact. That is disturbing, for to believe something is a fact means thinking there is nothing that can be done about it, and that kills the will to change it, because what

7   Arthur J. Keown, David F. Scott Jr., John D. Martin and J. William Petty, *Basic Financial Management*, seventh edition, Prentice Hall, 1996, pp. 2–3.

is, is. Hence, the sigh of resignation in the statements: "That's just business. That's the way things are ... there's nothing that can be done about it."

I want to argue that the maximization view, be it the maximization of profit or shareholder wealth, is wrongheaded and that it gains its credibility only by confusing and/or conflating two quite different things, motives (or subjective reasons) for actions with (objective) purposes for the action. I also want to show that if we make a distinction between motives (which explain) and purposes (which justify), we are logically impelled to reject the view that the purpose of business is the pursuit of profit. (That's the way the tool is working, but that's not what it was invented for.)

In offering this way of seeing the issue, I am simply retracing the steps of my own thinking process. I am convinced the view is wrongheaded and that it gains its power from the failure to distinguish between motives and objective purposes, because it was a view I once held. At the time, trying to show that employees owed no loyalty to a corporation, I claimed the following:

> A business or corporation does two things in the free enterprise system. It produces a good or service and makes a profit. The making of a profit, however, is the primary function of a business as a business, for if the production of the good or service were not profitable the business would go out of business ... The cold hard truth is that the goal of profit is what gives birth to a company and forms that particular group.[8]

Those claims about the purpose of business seemed obvious to me. What I came to realize is that while they expressed the popular belief about the purpose of business, and relied on assumptions commonly made, on reflection they are not obviously true. The mistake I made was not being clear about the differences between purposes, and motives.

The concepts of purposes and motives and their relationships and differences are well discussed in philosophy. In most of the philosophical psychology literature numerous telling distinctions among the notions of goals, purposes, ends, intentions, motives, causes or reasons are made, while in most of the business ethics and corporate responsibility literature with which I am familiar, there seems to be an uncritical use of a whole host of those related terms. However, I think it would be wise if we leave aside the concepts of goals, intentions, causes and reasons, and narrow our focus on the differences between purposes and motives, because purposes and motives, while they both provide answers to the question "Why?", function in quite different ways.

---

8   "Whistleblowing and Employee Loyalty," in Desjardin & McCall, *Contemporary Issues in Business Ethics*, pp. 297–98.

There are two different answers to the question "Why?" when addressed to human actions: the justificatory and the explanatory. To cite a purpose for doing something is to attempt to justify it and give a legitimating reason. To cite a motive for doing something is to give a psychological explanation. Hence, the question, "Why did you give the money to the poor?" can be answered by the justifying purpose, "To alleviate his hunger," or by the psychological motive explanation, "Because I needed to or wanted to."

In making our distinction, let's specify a bit more clearly what we mean by a purpose and a motive. Suppose we conceive of the purpose of something as the "what for" of that thing. Such a "what for" is crucial for defining the nature of the thing or activity, because we do not fully understand what some things or activities are unless we understand what they are for. For example, a hollowed out ebony cylinder one inch long and one and a half inches in diameter is indeed a piece of hollowed out wood, but with all that empirical data we don't understand what it *is* until we know what *it's for*. We understand what it is, what the "nature" of this artifact is when we understand what it's for, in this case, holding napkins. (To be sure, artifacts are conventions, and hence it may appear a little strange talking of their "natures," but then corporations and the business system are conventions and we don't seem to think it strange to talk about the nature of corporations.) At any rate the example shows how the purpose of something is the "what a thing is for," and how a full understanding of something requires knowing what its purpose is.[9]

Motives, however, are quite different from purposes. Motives are individual psychological forces which "move" (hence, "emotive") individuals to behave in certain ways. Even though both a purpose (the what for) and a motive can be given as an answer to the question "Why?" with respect to an action being done, the purposes for acting are not the same as the motives for acting. To confuse the purpose with the motive would be like confusing the purpose of a train, to get people from place to place, with what drives the train, the engine. The engine is analogous to the motive, since it moves the train.

There are other examples that can be given of the difference. The purpose of the practice of almsgiving is to aid the poor. Yet Kant among others has shown that there

---

9 Those familiar with Aristotle of course will see this as an account of the four causes: the material, formal, efficient and final. For Aristotle, the final cause was the purpose, or the "what for," and one's knowledge of anything was incomplete unless it was knowledge of all of the causes. Hence the question "What is business?" from Aristotle's point of view cannot be answered without an account of its purpose, and a correct account cannot be given if we have the purpose wrong. Note also that this introduction of purposes, or teleology, makes knowledge of things more than a purely empirical enterprise, and necessarily an enterprise with a value dimension.

can be any number of *motives* for helping the poor, such as getting public acclaim or getting a tax write-off.[10]

Scholastic philosophers employed the difference between purpose and motive with respect to the institution of marriage. The primary purpose of marriage as an institution according to the scholastics was held to be the procreation and education of children. When the purpose of procreation got tied to a prohibition of premarital sex, it led many to believe that the purpose of marriage was to legitimate sexual activity. But one does not need to get married to have sex, only, on some accounts, to make it morally permissible. So the desire for sexual fulfillment cannot be the primary purpose of marriage. But if one thought that sex outside of marriage was sinful and could lead to eternal damnation, the desire for legitimate sex became a powerful *motive* to get married, but nonetheless not the reason for getting married.[11]

A final example is education. The purpose of education would seem to be the development of the person's mind or some such. All too often today though we turn the purpose of education into something like getting a job. But that is not the purpose of education; rather it is a desirable side effect. Education like anything else can have multiple effects. But the effects don't determine the purpose. Primarily education is for human fulfillment and secondarily it may help one make a living. (Plato, by the way, in dividing goods into three kinds—those good as means only, those good in themselves, and those good in themselves and as means—maintains that the last kind, those good as both means and ends, are the best.) The fact that any number of students have turned their education into a means of getting a job shows what happens when we neglect to make the distinction between purposes and motives.

A typical conversation with business students might go like this. "Why are you studying accounting?"

"So I can get a good job."

"But why accounting?"

"It pays well."

"But other fields pay well."

There are all sorts of ways to make money, and wanting to make money is certainly acceptable as a *motive*, but the purpose of the practice of accounting is not to make money, any more than the purpose of the practice of medicine is to make money. Medicine's purpose is to minister to the sick. These examples should help to

---

10   Note that when we start investigating individual motives and confuse them with the purposes, we almost always end up with some sort of egoistic self-interested account of the purpose. That may be because we keep looking for a psychological answer to the question "Why be moral?" when there is no answer.

11   One should note here, that the scholastics ingeniously, for their purposes, turned motives into secondary purposes. There would be no procreation without desire. But the child needs protection. Hence the purpose of the drive was a species purpose. A secondary purpose of marriage then was to give an outlet for sexual desire.

make it clear that our motives for doing something may or may not accord with the purpose of the activity. Further, we should see that by turning motives into purposes we get involved in turning means into ends, the converse of using the end to justify the means. In that way the production of goods and services are the means used for the sake of making money. But even if that is so, and it is unacceptable, how does that show that the "what for" of business is the production of goods and services. For that we need a separate argument.

To begin that argument we need to note that social practices have their own purposes independent of the motives of the persons engaged in the practices. Turning to business as a practice, we see that it is a conventional practice, i.e. one designed by human beings, not something natural. As a practice it is a "form of life," to use Wittgenstein's phrase, and has a set of rules and expected ways of behaving which have developed with some end or purpose in mind. (Whose mind is a problem for a different paper.) But is that purpose the making of a profit or the providing of goods and services?

If a purpose is a what for, the what for must be the what for of some conscious being or beings. Business is a societal practice, a developed conventional form of life. To begin, no society or group would create a social institution unless that institution was seen as promoting some good for the society or group. For example, our society does not sanction the creation of groups to manufacture and distribute heroin, or create pornographic films which exploit children, because they do not see these activities as having any redeeming social value. Hence, it stands to reason that the purpose of any societally constructed system or institution has to do with an end that is compatible with some social good (good of the whole through its parts) which may or may not be compatible with any specific individual's interest. If this is so, society instituted business and its practices and rules, by which we mean the competitive profit-motivated free enterprise system, to help itself (society) develop and survive. Hence business is instituted to be beneficial to society. The claim is made, from Adam Smith on down, that a competitive profit-motivated free enterprise system is a very efficient *means* of bringing about a laudable goal—benefit to society. If business were seen as harmful, society would close it down.

While our system of business as it has developed is not the only way to produce goods and services, it is argued that it is the most efficient. The somewhat regulated capitalist economic system which our society permits, is permitted because it is seen as a very productive if not the most productive economic system. However, this capitalist system ingeniously centers around rules governing the distribution of profits. Profits are distributed in such a way as to incentivize or motivate the entrepreneur. But profits are merely the means for achieving the purpose of business, and as the means should not usurp the ultimate goal of business any more than sexual fulfillment should override the procreation of children as the goal of marriage. Thus, if we keep our distinction in mind, it is clear that profit is not the purpose of business, but is only the motive for doing business.

But how did such an obvious fact get forgotten? A full answer to such a question is beyond the scope of this paper.[12] Still one can speculate that whatever caused the rise of the theory, it was aided by the ambiguous use of the word "intention" in Adam Smith's famous passage about the invisible hand. Let us examine the passage.

> As every individual, therefore, endeavors as much as he can both to employ his capital in the support of domestic industry, and so to direct that industry that its produce may be of the greatest value, every individual necessarily labors to render the annual revenue of the society as great as he can. He generally indeed, neither intends to promote the public interest, nor knows how much he is promoting it ... and by directing that industry in such a manner as its produce may be of the greatest value, he intends only his own gain, and he is in this, as in many other cases, led by an invisible hand to promote *an end which was no part of his intention.* (Italics Mine) Nor is it always the worse for society that it was no part of it. By pursuing his own interest he frequently promotes that of the society more effectually than when he really *intends* to promote it. I have never known much good done by those who affected to trade for the public good. It is an affectation, indeed, not very common among merchants, and very few words need be employed in dissuading them from it.[13]

This passage of Smith contains two elements. First it gives a psychological account of why an individual would be motivated to work. Second, he *justifies* such motivation by predicting that it will lead to "an end (read "purpose") that is no part of his intention (read "motive")." "He generally indeed, neither intends to promote the public interest, nor knows how much he is promoting it ... he intends only his own gain, and he is in this led by an invisible hand to promote an end which was no part of his intention." If for "intention" we read "'motivated by," then what Smith says is that even though the business person is not motivated to promote the public interest, in being motivated by his own interest he succeeds in bringing it about anyway. But the purpose of all this is clearly to advantage the public interest, and as Smith says consumer oriented and limited by justice.[14] The fact that the public interest is served by self-interested motivation is serendipitous, a boon such as Plato thought

---

12   I would venture, if pressed, to explain it by two factors: 1) an attempt to rationalize the acceptability of acquisitiveness; and 2) an attempt to make being virtuous less difficult. Cf. the contemporary counterpart, Gauthier's *Morals by Agreement.*

13   Adam Smith, *The Wealth of Nations,* ed. Edwin Canan (Random House, 1937), p. 14.

14   Cf. P. Werhane, *Adam Smith and His Legacy for Modern Capitalism* (Oxford, 1991), esp. Ch. 3.

was the best good, a means that is also good in itself, self-satisfaction bringing about a good end, the public good.

But the word "intention" as Smith uses it has a subjective sense, which can also refer to a "whatfor" as in what is your intention or reason for doing this? Hence while Smith uses "intention" in a subjective sense and as a motive, later readings of "intention" turn it into an objective societal purpose.[15] It is not Smith so much as his economic followers such as Friedman who deny that the purpose of the baker is to bake bread, insisting that the what for of his action is his own interest. But if we keep in mind our earlier distinction between subjective and objective the baker's action has an objective intention, to produce bread (the purpose), and a subjective intention to make money spurred by the desire for money (the motivation).[16]

The problem of course is that turning the means, self-interested motivation, into a purpose, opens a Pandora's box. Legitimizing such a means unleashes what the theologians call "greed." The "rational maximizer" can become the greedy, grasping, acquisitive, profit-motivated, bottom-line-oriented entrepreneur, who feels no responsibility to the public welfare, because whatever he does leads to the public welfare. The benefits of utilizing the profit motive are obvious, but so are the undesirable externalities.

Contemporary defenders of the classical theory of corporate social responsibility such as Milton Friedman and other current defenders of the "invisible hand" utilize the conflation to make their point that the primary responsibility or function

---

15   Intentions are often associated with subjective purposes, as in: "my intention (or purpose) in doing that"; "my reason for doing that"; "my motive for doing that." But subjective intentions are closer to what I have called motives than objective intentions of acts. It is not only possible but necessary to distinguish between the objective intention of an act and the subjective intention. Similarly we could talk about a subjective purpose and an objective purpose. But we don't seem to. We talk of whys: The subjective why, which is a motive, and the objective why, which is a purpose. If we simply think of a subjective intention as the individual's subjective motive for doing something, the personal psychological cause, then we can distinguish it from a possible objective intention, an intention which looks very much like what we will call a purpose, a non-subjective reason for doing something. At any rate, individualism and subjectivism, to an extent, cause us to conflate motives and purposes. So an individual can talk of "my purpose in doing this" or "my intention in doing this" or "what motivated me to do this." But this conflation is a mistake which leads to all sorts of intellectual and ethical mischief.

16   The conflation of these two meanings of intention, coupled with the rise of individualism, a social contract view of society, and an egoistic reductivism, i.e. a social science requirement to explain all human actions in terms of measurable individual units of self-interest, allowed the ambiguity not only to remain undetected but to seemingly disappear. The confusion is rampant, and my hunch is that this conflation of purposes and motives is the result of an egoistic reductivist tendency found especially in the literature of economics and in the concept of the rational self-interested maximizer. After all, the reductivist society cannot be anything other than a collection of individuals with their own individual intentions or motives, and what are individual intentions and motives except self-interested concerns? But that is a topic for another paper. Whatever the cause of the confusion, that there is confusion seems obvious enough.

of business is to make a profit. But to make the theory tenable, we depend on an individualistic, reductivistic view of human nature and purposes and a naive belief in the "invisible hand."

The rest of the story is fairly obvious. Aside from appeals to liberty and autonomy, this type of appeal to an "invisible hand" is the most popular defense of the institution of business as we know it. It provides a formula which in essence states that the business person should keep in mind as a goal, the single-minded, self-interested pursuit of profit. From that formula, theoreticians such as Milton Friedman argue functionally that since business is a system set up to make a profit, a good business person will be one who performs the profit-making function well. Further, according to the principle of the division of labor, since business has as its function to perform in society as a whole, and government and labor have their different functions, if each part fulfills its respective functions, society as a whole will be better off. Hence, as Smith and his supporters like Friedman maintain, the "end" of "public interest" need not be a part of the business person's intention.

But even here, the ambiguity should be unpacked, for, as is well known, Smith and Friedman legitimate the self-interested motives by a consequentialist justification.[17] Smith's contention provides Friedman and others with a reason to say that the "primary and only responsibility of business is to use its resources and engage in activities designed to increase its profits so long as it stays within the rules of the game, which is to say, engages in open and free competition without deception and fraud."[18]

The Utilitarian structure of the argument is simple enough to see. The activity or practice of self-interested pursuits is justified because of the good that will accrue to society if such a profit oriented system is adopted. In short, the greatest good for the greatest number will be served if the market, driven by self-interest, is allowed to operate. Hence, we get a utilitarian justification of an egoistic stance. Look out for your own concerns and society as a whole will be better off.

That may be true, most of the time. In fact that seems to be what thinkers such as Gauthier are trying to show.[19] But the sticking point is those times when the pursuit of self-interest does not lead to the good of the whole, but is at the expense of others. At that time what is the proper thing to do? Pursue profits or concern oneself with lessening the cost to others? If one would argue that because societal benefit is the purpose of business, one is obliged to concern oneself with others, how would one motivate such behavior? After all looking out for others is hard to do. Why, in the

---

17   While the Smith quote contains the core of a consequentialist defense of the self-interested pursuit of profit found in the competitive free market, it would probably be anachronistic to refer to it as a "Utilitarian" defense of capitalism.

18   Friedman, "The Social Responsibility of Business Is to Increase Its Profits," *New York Times Magazine*, September 13, 1970.

19   Cp. David Gauthier, *Morals by Agreement* (Oxford, 1986).

sense of what motivation exists to look out for others? But that is the same as the problem of "What self-interested motives are there for being moral?" Depending on the definitions of moral and self-interested here, the answer may be "no motives." But that, too, is the topic of another paper which would address the difficulties of psychological and ethical egoism.[20]

Counter to those who adopt a Friedmanian stance, if we say that the purpose of business is to provide goods and services, while the motive is making a profit, then the responsibility of the manager or agent of the business is not simply to pursue profits, but to pursue them regulated by the demands of the public interest. Of course to determine what those demands are is another area beyond the scope of this paper.

We have tried to indicate that if we confuse purpose with motives for doing, and reduce the former to the latter, we make it impossible to give a theoretical ground for legitimate restraints on business, other than those required by a Kantian formalism. However, business, construed as an artifact created for the sake of society, specifically for the production of goods and services, is construed in such a way that the values are implied. A good business will be one which fulfills its purposes, which aims at the betterment of society, in this case through production of goods and services.

There is of course, an obvious objection to all of this. What if the "good" or "service" a business produces is not so good. Here I think we have some difficult issues, but also some solvable ones. Why do we prohibit in the United States the manufacture and distribution of cocaine? There is certainly a market for it and the producers make a good profit. In one sense, if the only constraint on business were profit maximization, and if business were to be judged on the basis of its efficiency, what better case study of an efficient operation than cocaine production and distribution could be found, since it continues to be profitable in spite of the fact that entire governments attempt to impede its production and distribution. U.S. society has determined that though cocaine appears as a good to some, a subjective good, it is not good for society and has banned its production. Defenders of the maximization view have a hard time dealing with those interferences, which may be why Friedman is a proponent at least of legalizing marijuana. Still the question who's to say what is a good or not will be raised. But that is another issue. Suffice it to say, the direction one must go in addressing it is the direction a number of people concerned with the social responsibility of business go, and that is to evaluate businesses not simply on their efficiency and market value, but on how well they fulfill their purpose, i.e. provide goods and services.

---

20   For the time being, James Rachel's marvelous essay on egoism will have to suffice. Cf. Rachel, "Egoism and Moral Skepticism," in *A New Introduction to Philosophy*, ed. Steven M. Cahn (Harper & Row, 1971).

In conclusion, to the extent that maximizing profits becomes a legitimation of greedy practices we have an erosion of the ethical climate of the business environment. To the extent that we allow phrases such as "that's business" to legitimate cutthroat competition, we have an unethical climate. One of the most insidious mistakes made in discussing business ethics is that made in viewing the only responsibility of business to be maximizing profits.

That is a mistake, because business is a social institution, i.e. an invention of society. The first humans did not have an institution called business. In order for such an institution to come into existence, human beings had to invent a whole set of categories for identifying the goods and burdens of the world such as property, cost, profits, etc., as well as an entire set of rules governing the "fair" distribution of them. But the only way society would legitimate those business operations would be if those operations were seen as benefiting society by providing goods and services. A society which put up with practices that did not help but harmed it would be irrational. No sane society would permit a system that did it more harm than good. The appeal to profit was a means to motivate more production, but it was not the purpose of the production. As we said, to confuse the motive, literally the moving force, with the purpose of something is like confusing the engine of a train with the purpose of a train. The purpose of business is to provide goods and services, the motivating force is the reward of profit for individuals. But the means of motivation in some way became confused with the purpose of business. But to make maximizing profits of paramount concern rather than putting the horse before the cart, turns the horse into the cart.

Questions

1. What are the two competing views identified by Duska regarding the purpose of business?

2. Why does it matter what the purpose of business is?

3. How do "purpose" and "motive" differ?

4. What argument does Duska offer in favor of his view?

5. What is the problem, according to Duska, with the other view?

Further Reading

Carroll, Archie B. "Corporate Social Responsibility: Evolution of a Definitional Construct." *Business & Society*, vol. 38, no. 3, 1999, pp. 268–95.

Carroll, Archie B. "The Pyramid of Corporate Social Responsibility: Toward the Moral Management of Organizational Stakeholders." *Business Horizons*, vol. 34, no. 4, 1991, pp. 39–48.

Freeman, R. Edward. *Strategic Management: A Stakeholder Approach*. Cambridge: Cambridge University Press, 2010.

Friedman, Milton. *Capitalism and Freedom*. Chicago: University of Chicago Press, 2009.

Garriga, Elisabet, and Domènec Melé. "Corporate Social Responsibility Theories: Mapping the Territory." *Journal of Business Ethics*, vol. 53, no. 1, 2004, pp. 51–71.

11.
"THE PROFIT MOTIVE"

ANTONY FLEW[1]

About This Reading

The pursuit of profit is sometimes identified with a selfish motive—where others do not matter. If this is the case, then those with the profit motive are to be distrusted as looking out only for themselves. Flew questions the assumption that the profit motive is something to be avoided. He makes the case that being motivated by profit is no different from being motivated by other goals that are very similar to profit. For example, employees are often motived by what we might call a "salary motive." The question then emerges, how does the salary motive differ morally from the profit motive? Given that we typically take these other motives to be morally unproblematic, why do we care about the profit motive?

I. Two Fundamental Suggestions

We hear much talk of the (private) profit motive; and many suggestions that, because (private) profit is a defining characteristic essential to capitalism, therefore any such economic system must be inherently more selfish and hard-nosed than actual or possible rivals. For instance: in the summer of '72 *The Times* of London reported that Archbishop Camara of Brazil had asked a meeting of members of both Houses of Parliament: "Why do you not help lay bare the serious distortions of socialism

1   The first version of this paper was written for presentation to a seminar of the Foundation for Business Responsibilities and published in 1972 as one of their semi-private pamphlets. I am grateful to the Foundation, both for their original sponsorship, and for their willingness to permit the wider publication of this drastically revised and extended version. I am also grateful to those who on that and other occasions offered criticisms both orally and in writing. Of these I have to mention particularly: first, Professor David Wiggins, who unwittingly confirmed my conviction that the sort of thing which I have to say very much needs saying; and, second, Dr. David Lloyd Thomas, who laboured to reveal the weaknesses which I have now tried to remedy.

such as they exist in Russia and China? And why do you not denounce, once and for all, the intrinsic selfishness and heartlessness of capitalism?"[2]

A. I want to start by responding with another question: "Why do we never hear of the rent motive or the wages motive?" Perhaps the classical distinction between profit and rent is outmoded. But, if it is proper to speak of a profit motive, it should surely be equally proper to speak of a wages motive. And, if it is proper to say that those who work for wages are stirred by the wages motive; then it must be not merely proper but positively refined to say that those whose wages are paid at longer intervals, and called a salary or even compensation, are inspired by, respectively, the salary motive and the compensation motive.[3] By parity of reasoning we shall then have to admit into our economic psychology the fixed interest motive, the top price motive, and the best buy motive. And so on, and on and on.

My first general suggestion is that it is radically misguided thus to insist upon applying to psychology a categorical system originally developed in, and appropriate to, economics. A good way to become seized both of the nature and of the misguidedness of such insistence is to contemplate, and to relish, one of the most bizarre and delightful of those high theoretical fantasies which adorn *A Treatise of Human Nature*. For there, in the section "Of the Probability of Causes," Hume concludes that, upon his then principles, "a man, who desires a thousand pound [sic], has in reality a thousand or more desires, which uniting together, seem to make only one passion; tho' the composition evidently betrays itself upon every alteration of the object, by the preference he gives to the larger number, if superior only by an unite."[4]

Noticing that suggestive "or more," one is tempted to go on to urge: that before decimalization the desire for a thousand pounds was—"in reality"—two hundred

---

2   "Waiting for a Sign from the Egoists" (June 27, 1972). Later in the same week the *Catholic Herald* (June 30, 1972) reported other meetings at which the archbishop—described by Cardinal de Roy, president of the Pontifical Commission for Justice and Peace, as "one of the great voices of our time"—"called on British Catholics to fight the forces of capitalist imperialism." It is a pity that this great voice thus insists on inserting the qualification "capitalist" into his denunciations of imperialism. By so doing the archbishop is bound to suggest to any attentive reader: either that he believes that there is no such thing as a socialist empire; or that he disapproves of empires only when the imperial power has not yet nationalized all the means of production, distribution, and exchange. If it is the former, then he is subject to the commonest and most damaging of contemporary delusions—wilful blindness to the realities of the Great Russian empire of what Maoists rightly call the "new Tsars." If it is the latter, then he must be the bearer of a most curiously perverted conscience—nonetheless perverted for being in many quarters nowadays, in the descriptive sense, normal.
3   Compare Bernard Mandeville in *The Fable of the Bees*, ed. Philip Harth (Harmondsworth, Middlesex: Penguin, 1970):
      "And, when folks understood their cant
      "They changed that for 'emolument';
      "Unwilling to be short or plain,
      "In any thing concerning gain ..." (p. 66).
4   Hume, *A Treatise of Human Nature*, 1(iii)12:141 in the Selby-Bigge edition (Oxford: Clarendon Press, 1896).

and forty thousand old penny desires; that now it has diminished to a mere hundred thousand new pence hankerings; and that a desire for a thousand piastre pounds must, by parity of reasoning, really be an American billion of almost indiscernible atomic yens. The mind boggles at the unfolding vista of possible implications of other currency differences and equivalences for the psychology of the notorious gnomes of Zurich and the infamous money changers of Beirut! But enough is enough to indicate the nature of my first general objection to the economic psychology implicit in all this loose talk about the profit motive.

B. My second general suggestion is that no one—not even an archbishop—has any business simply to assume that the desire to make a (private) profit is always and necessarily selfish and discreditable; notwithstanding that the corresponding desires to obtain a wage, or a salary, or a retirement income, are—apparently—not. No doubt all these various desires are interested; in the sense that those who are guided by any of them are—in the immortal words of Mr. Damon Runyon—"doing the best they can." But, precisely because this does apply equally to all, we can find no ground here for condemning one and not the others.

This neglected fact is awkward for the denouncers. For no one, surely, is so star-ry-eyed as to believe that any system of economic organization can dispense with all such interested motives. If, therefore, one such system is upon this particular ground to be condemned as "intrinsically selfish and heartless," then, by the same token, all must be. Yet that, of course, is precisely not what is wanted by those who thus denounce capitalism root and branch, and as such; while tolerantly discounting as more or less "serious distortions" whatever faults they can, however reluctantly, bring themselves to recognize in the socialist countries.

The further fundamental mistake here is that of identifying the interested with the selfish. This is wrong. For, though selfish actions are perhaps always interested, only some interested actions are also selfish. To say that a piece of conduct was self-ish is to say more than that it was interested, if it was. The point is that selfishness is always and necessarily out of order. Interestedness is not, and scarcely could be.

For example: when my daughters eagerly eat their dinners they are, I suppose, pursuing their own interests. But it would be monstrous to denounce them as selfish hussies, simply on that account. The time for denunciation could come only after one of them had, for instance, eaten someone else's dinner too; or refused to make some sacrifice which she ought to have made. Again, even when my success can be won only at the price of someone else's failure, it is not always and necessarily selfish for me to pursue my own interests. The rival candidates competing for some coveted job are not selfish just because they do not all withdraw in order to clear the way for the others.

The upshot, therefore, is that it will not do to dismiss any one economic system as "intrinsically selfish and heartless": simply because that system depends upon and engages interested motives; or even simply because it allows or encourages people to pursue their own interests in certain situations of zero sum conflict. If there is something peculiarly obnoxious about wanting to make a (private) profit, it will have to be something about making a (private) profit, rather than something about just wanting to acquire some economic good; or even about competing to acquire scarce economic goods in any zero sum conflict situation, as such.

II. Three Popular Aristotelian Misconceptions

That it is indeed essentially scandalous to make a profit—and hence, presumably, also scandalous to wish to do so—is an idea both as old as the Classical Greek philosophers and as topical as—for instance—tomorrow's Labour party political broadcasts. Consider what was said by the one who has had, and albeit mainly through Aquinas and Hegel continues to have, by far the greatest influence.

The economic thought of Aristotle is to be found mainly in the *Politics*.[5] It is altogether characteristic that he takes as normative whatever he believes to be—as it were—the intention of nature. By the way: it should be salutary for those inclined to accept that principle to see where it can lead. For instance, after discussing slavery, Aristotle concludes: "It is thus clear that, just as some are by nature free, so others are by nature slaves, and for these latter the condition of slavery is both beneficial and just."[6] Again: "as nature makes nothing purposeless or in vain, all animals must have been made by nature for the sake of men. It also follows that the art of war is in some sense a natural mode of acquisition. Hunting is a part of that art; and hunting ought to be practised, not only against wild animals, but also against those human beings who are intended by nature to be ruled by others and refuse to obey that intention. War of this kind is naturally just."[7]

These remarks well illustrate Aristotle's characteristic appeal to nature and to its alleged intentions. We should not after this be surprised that for Aristotle the supposed ideal universal provider is not—as it would be today—the state, but nature: "On a general view, as we have already noticed, a supply of property should be ready to hand. It is the business of nature to furnish subsistence for each being brought into the world; and this is shown by the fact that the offspring of animals always gets nourishment from the residuum of the matter that gives it its birth."[8]

A. It is significant, and entirely consistent with this providential assumption, that Aristotle goes on to emphasise acquisition rather than production: "The natural

---

5   *The Politics of Aristotle*, trans. Ernest Barker (Oxford: Clarendon Press, 1948).
6   Ibid., 1(v)11:1255A 1–3.
7   Ibid., 1(viii)12:1256B 20–26. I have smoothed the translation here.
8   Ibid., 1(x)3:1258A 33–36. No one seems to have anticipated me in noticing these sentences as a respectably Classical formulation of the shabby doctrine that the world owes us a living.

form, therefore, of the art of acquisition is always, and in all cases, acquisition from fruits and animals. That art ... has two forms: one which is connected with ... trade, and another which is connected with the management of the household. Of these two forms, the latter is necessary and laudable; the former is a method of exchange which is justly censured, because the gain in which it results is not naturally made, but is made at the expense of other men."[9]

Aristotle's point is that trade is in essence exploitation. The acquisitions of the trader must, Aristotle thinks, be made at the expense of that trader's trading partner; whereas the only creditable acquisitions are those achieved from non-human nature direct. Shorn of these notions of what is and is not in accord with the intentions of nature, Aristotle's is the same thesis—and the same misconception—as we find in John Ruskin: "Whenever material gain follows exchange, for every plus there is a precisely equal minus."[10]

Despite its august sponsorship, and its hardy perennial appeal, a moment's thought will show that this contention must be wrong. We have, therefore, a welcome opportunity here to quote once again A.E. Housman's blistering comment: "A moment's thought would have shown him this. But thought is a painful process. And a moment is a long time."

The crux is that trade is a reciprocal relationship. If I am trading with you it follows necessarily that you are trading with me. Trade is also, for both parties, necessarily voluntary. Nothing which you may succeed in seizing from me by force can, by that token, be either acquired or relinquished in trade. So, if any possible advantage of trade to the trader could be gained only at the expense of some corresponding disadvantage to his trading partner, it would appear that in any commercial exchange at least one party must be either a fool, or a masochist, or a gambler.

But, of course, as all must recognize when not either by theory or by passion distracted, the truth is that the seller sells because, in his actual situation, he would rather receive the price than retain the goods, while the buyer buys because, in his actual situation, he would rather pay the price than be without the goods. Ruskin was, therefore, diametrically wrong. It is of the essence of trade: not that any advantage for one party can be achieved only at the expense of the other; but that no deal is made at all unless, whether rightly or wrongly, both parties believe that they stand to gain thereby—or at least both prefer the deal actually made to any available alternative deal, and to no deal at all.

Certainly one of the trading partners, or even both, may be mistaken or in some other way misguided in his decision to deal. Certainly too the actual situation of either party, the situation in which it seems better to him to make the deal than not,

---

9   Ibid., 1(x)4:1258A 37–1258B 2.
10   John Ruskin, *Unto This Last* (London: G.A. Allen, 1899), p. 131.

may be in many ways unfair or unfortunate.[11] But all this is contingent, and hence to the present question irrelevant. This question is: "What is and is not essential to the very idea of trade?" Mutually satisfactory sex is a better model here than poker played for money. For in the former the satisfactions of each depend reciprocally upon those of the other; whereas the latter really is a zero sum game in which your winnings precisely equal, because they are, my losses.

One temptation to conclude that trade necessarily involves a zero sum confrontation lies in the fact that both buyers and sellers would often, if they had to, pay more or accept less than they do. Obviously it is in such a situation possible to regard either the more which might have been got or the less which might have been given as an advantage forfeited by one trading partner to the other. But this, which is perhaps often the case, certainly is not so always. And both buyer and seller may be, and I imagine typically are, simultaneously in similar situations with regard to such forfeited possible advantages. So it cannot be correct to infer, as a general conclusion, that all the gains of trade must always be achieved by one trading partner at the expense of the other.

Another less intellectual, but in practice more powerful, temptation lies in the unlovely human inclination rather to attend with eager jealousy to the gains of others than to find some modest contentment in one's own; to forget that the deal was to your advantage in order to resent that it was to his also.[12] Yet, surely, he would not—as you so ungraciously insist—"have made his profits out of you," had it not also been the case that you saw some advantage to yourself in your dealings with him?

In general, I suggest, and it is a reflection which has a relevance far wider than its present occasion, economic arrangements are best judged by results. Concentrate on the price and quality of the product. Do not officiously probe the producer's purity

---

11   This important reservation is developed in, for instance, E.J. Mishan, *21 Popular Economic Fallacies* (Harmondsworth, Middlesex: Penguin, 1971), pp. 95–97. But it is unfortunate that Mishan gets off on the wrong foot by saying that, if I am forced at pistol point to drink castor oil, then "I may be said to have chosen to do it of my own free will...." What he should have said is that the man who thus acts not of his own free will but under compulsion, nevertheless acts; and hence, in the most fundamental senses, does have a choice and could have done other than he in fact did. See, for instance, my "Is There a Problem of Freedom?" in *Phenomenology and Philosophical Understanding*, ed. E. Pivcevic (Cambridge: Cambridge University Press, 1975), secs. 3(a) and 3(b).

12   Compare Mandeville again: "Few men can be persuaded that they get too much by those they sell to, how extraordinary soever their gains are, when at the same time there is hardly a profit so inconsiderable, but they'll grudge it to those they buy from" (p. 113). Typically, such meanness of spirit both encourages, and is compounded by, the intellectual fault of confusing markup over costs of acquisition with profit on risk capital employed. Much attention is given nowadays to the unappealing motives which people may have for wishing to preserve existing social arrangements. It could be an unusually instructive exercise in fair mindedness to devote a comparable measure of attention to the perhaps equally unappealing motives which their opponents may have for wishing to revolutionize those arrangements.

of heart. If, nevertheless, we are to consider motives, then this envy which resents that others too should gain, and maybe gain more than us, must be accounted much nastier than any supposed "intrinsic selfishness" of straight self-interest. Some might even discern the hand of Providence at work when it appears that, for thus putting the resentment-of-profit-motive first, "the Envious Society" of the United Kingdom pays a heavy price in forfeited economic growth.

Let us, however, conclude the present subsection not with snide moralizing but with a gesture of Roman piety. Adam Smith wrote: "It is not from the benevolence of the butcher, the brewer, or the baker that we expect our dinner, but from their regard for their own interest. We address ourselves, not to their humanity but to their self-love, and never talk to them of our own necessities but of their advantages. Nobody but a beggar chooses to depend chiefly upon the benevolence of his fellow citizens."[13]

B. Aristotle's next contribution is equally unfortunate, and has been equally important. Immediately after the last passage quoted earlier he continues: "The trade of the usurer is hated most, and with most reason.... Currency came into existence merely as a means of exchange; usury tries to make it increase. This is the reason why interest is called by the word we commonly use [the word *tokos*, which in Greek also means offspring]; for as the offspring resembles its parent, so the interest bred by money is like the principal which breeds it, and it may be called 'currency the son of currency.' Hence we can understand why, of all modes of acquisition, usury is the most unnatural."[14]

Usury is now, thanks first to Aristotle and still more to his medieval successors, such a bad word that it may not be at once obvious just what it is to which Aristotle is objecting. It is not only to excessive or, as we should now say, usurious fixed interest. Nor is it only to all fixed interest as such, which was the prime target of those medieval successors.[15] He objects, rather, to any money return upon any money investment. It is, he thinks, against nature for money to breed money.[16]

The moment Aristotle's point is appreciated, it becomes quite clear that both his objection and his supporting reason are superstitious and muddled. For a sum of money is the substantial equivalent of any of the goods or collections of goods which it might buy. There can, therefore, be nothing obnoxiously unnatural about

---

13   Adam Smith. *The Wealth of Nations*, 1(i):13 of vol. 1 in the Everyman edition (New York: Dent & Dutton, 1910).

14   *Aristotle*, 1(x)4-S:1258B 2–8.

15   See R.H. Tawney, *Religion and the Rise of Capitalism* (Harmondsworth, Middlesex: Penguin Books, 1938): "Medieval opinion, which has no objection to rent or profits, provided that they are reasonable—for is not everyone in a small way a profit-maker?—has no mercy for the debenture-holder. His crime is that he takes a payment for money which is fixed and certain, and such a payment is usury" (p. 55).

16   *Aristotle* 1(ix)8.

receiving a money return upon an investment in money, unless it would be equally obnoxious and unnatural to ask for some return either in money or in kind for the use of the goods themselves.

Before proceeding to the Aristotelian source of yet a third perennially popular misconception, take time out to notice two corollaries. First, it must be psychologically unilluminating to speak of any money motive; and, by the same token, still more unilluminating to try to develop a complete economic psychology upon a basis of a series of economic distinctions between various mercenary motives. For that someone wants to make a profit or to earn a wage tells us nothing of what he wants the money for. Almost any desire can take the form of a desire for money. It is obvious that this is a necessary consequence of the essential nature of money as a conventional instrument of exchange. Aristotle himself elsewhere makes this point about money. But he misses its present application. Second, and consequently, it must be wrong to hope that the abolition of money, or the reduction of the range of goods which money can buy, might by itself reduce greed and competition for those goods. Certainly it is tautologically true that the profit motive, the fixed interest motive, the wages motive, and all the other factitious motives mischievously listed in IA above, are mercenary. All, that is, are defined in terms of the acquisition of money. It might therefore seem that totally to abolish money, or to reduce its importance as a means of acquisition, must be to abolish or at least to weaken, all mercenary motives.

In an appropriately empty sense this no doubt is true. Yet, unless these changes happened to be accompanied by something quite different, an enormous transformation of present human nature, people would presumably continue to pursue, and to compete for, whatever it was which they had always wanted, but which money could not now buy. In a word: if cars are not on sale for money, but are available as a perquisite of high office, then this fact will by itself tend only to increase the already surely sufficiently ferocious competition for such privileged official places. The abolition of money might make us less mercenary. It would not by itself even begin to make us less materialistic or less competitive.

C. A third perennially popular misconception about the profit motive also apparently originates in Aristotle. For his difficult and unsteady distinction between two forms of the art of acquisition[17]—acquisition for household use and acquisition for financial gain—is, surely, ancestor of the evergreen false antithesis between production for profit and production for use.[18]

_____

17 Ibid., 1(viii)–(x).

18 Not to be too polemically topical, consider John Strachey's pamphlet *Why You Should Be a Socialist* (London: Gollancz, 1944). In one form or another this achieved an immense circulation in the thirties and forties. Strachey wrote: "One of the familiar phrases of the moment is to say that under capitalism (cont'd)

The antithesis is false for the very obvious reason that there can be no profit in producing what no one has any wish to buy, and presumably, to use.[19] Certainly, what ordinary people want to buy may not be what their actual or supposed superiors believe that they need; and hence ought to want. (The word here is, or used to be, "candyfloss"; candyfloss being taken as typical of all the things which our moral and intellectual superiors consider it wrong for us lesser creatures to want to buy, or for entrepreneurs to make and to sell.) Certainly too, folk may want and—much more seriously—may both need and want, what they lack the money to buy; and what, because they do both need and want it, they ideally ought to be able to buy. Again, the market may not always offer the range of options which you or I might like to be making our choices between.[20] But none of this justifies any general opposition: between, on the one hand, the profit motive and the profit system; and, on the other hand, the satisfaction of human needs. The true and relevant antithesis here is quite different. It is that between a command and a market economy; and it is significant that while the individual is himself the prime authority on what he wants, his needs, or his alleged needs, are in principle determined as well, or better, by others.

Nor will it do to argue—what is in fact more often assumed than argued—that: where, and in so far as, it is a contingently necessary condition of the production of anything that its production should be profitable to the producing firm; there, and to that extent, the profit motive provides the only reason why that product actually is produced and sold. This argument is on two different counts invalid.

First, it overlooks the most typical case. For motives—if it really is motives we are considering—are notoriously apt to be mixed. Dostoevski was not exaggerating much when he said: "No one ever acts from a single motive." That this is indeed one of a lady's motives by no means precludes that she has other motives also. A man may invest his capital in a bassoon factory both because he wants a profitable investment; and because he wants to popularize bassoon-playing; and because he wants to infuriate his unmusical aunt. Indeed conduct often is fully overdetermined, in the sense that the agent has two or more reasons either or any one of which would have been sufficient to secure his action.

Second, that something has one necessary condition does not preclude that it has other necessary conditions also. Allow that the firm will ultimately be shut

---

production is carried on for profit, while under socialism it is carried on for use; that socialism is planned production for use. What is meant by this phrase?" (p. 68).

19   That so obvious an objection seems never to occur to the often able people for whom this false antithesis remains a treasured catchword is one good reason for challenging the smug leftist assumption that left-wingers are, unlike their opponents, constitutionally questioning and critical. No doubt there have been times and places where this was indeed true. But observation of, for instance, the contemporary British student body can show that it is by no means a universal truth!

20   See, for instance, the Mishan reference given in n. 11 above.

down if it continues to run at a loss. So it will be if, for instance, no one is prepared to work for it or to buy from it. Say then that these further considerations are effective only in so far as they affect profitability. This is, no doubt, with appropriate qualifications, true. Yet that it is true, and that profitability is thus affected by other considerations, is itself the decisive reason why there cannot be a radical disjunction between profitability and all such other considerations.

Two other equally common, and equally unsound moves are to argue: either, from premises about the putative purposes of institutions, to conclusions about the motives of those who work within and for those institutions; or, from premises about the intentions of agents, to conclusions about the actual consequences of their actions. That this ministry or this state corporation was purportedly established solely to serve the public provides no guarantee: either that successive ministers, directors, civil servants, and other employees are oriented similarly; or that its actual operations are beneficial. Nor, similarly, are we entitled to infer: either, from the fact that the successive ministers supporting, say, the Concord project have been virginally untainted by any private mercenary motives, the conclusion that the public money poured into this has been well spent; or, conversely, from the fact that the shareholders of, say, Marks and Spencer have hoped for profits (and have not, so far, been disappointed) the conclusion that the operations of that firm have not in fact been in the public interest also.[21]

III. The Alleged Wickedness of Investment Income

What is constantly presented as a revulsion against the profit motive unfortunately may, and in fact often does, blind people to all other considerations; including sometimes other considerations which ought to weigh far more heavily than any preferences between rival economic arrangements. For example: while I was working on the present paper I happened to read Max Beloff's critical notice of Margaret Cole's *The Life of G.D.H. Cole*.[22] In this book Cole's widow confesses: "Douglas, like so many more of us, saw in Soviet Russia the negation of the immoralities of industrial capitalism and the system of private profit ..."; and, "It cost him a good deal of mental suffering towards the end of his life to admit that 'democratic centralism' and Stalinism in Russia had produced horrors which outweighed the advantages

---

21　It would be mean not to share the surely too good to be true story of the demonstration occurring during the Prague Spring—before the arrival of the friendly neighbourhood tanks of imperial normalization. A banner was, it is said, unfurled: "We want Marks and Spencer, not Marx and Engels!"
22　Margaret Cole, *The Life of G.D.H. Cole* (London: Macmillan Co., 1972).

of their having abolished private profit. Even then he was apt to maintain that the Americans, who had retained private profit, were much worse."[23]

Probably the most powerful of the sources of this revulsion against "the profit motive" is one which I have not so far mentioned. It is the desire to have done with every kind of investment income; and, what it is a mistake to think is the same thing as this, the drive to insist that all income must be earned.[24] Adequately to consider these aspirations would require a second paper. Some may wish that this was that paper. But all I can, or need, say in the present consideration of the profit motive is enough to show that such commitments demand something much more extensive by way of justification than a visceral revulsion against "the (private) profit motive." They cannot by themselves justify, what the present paper is attacking, a concentrated hostility to this as opposed to any or all the others indicated in IA above.

The fundamental objection may be either to deriving income from any form of (private) ownership or, more particularly, to deriving income from (private) ownership of the means of production. In each case the postulated motives fall under the ban in as much as they are desires to do what is thought to be wrong. In the first case these clearly should include the debenture as well as the profit motive. Indeed, since there is no relevant reason for distinguishing the ownership of real property here, and since all income from any kind of property constitutes rent for the use of that property, the proper enemy would be not the profit but—in this comprehensive sense of *rent*—the rent motive.

In the second case the suggestion is that to derive income from the ownership of the means of production—though not perhaps from ownership as such—is essentially exploitative. Too often it is suggested further that to end this one kind of putative exploitation must be to end all exploitation.[25]

23   The passages are quoted at pp. 64 and 66 of *Encounter* for February 1972. I should myself like to have seen in both Coles somewhat more concern for the victims of their pet nostrums; even if that did leave rather less for the husband's distress in recognizing his wilfully self-blinded imperceptions.
24   You need to be a bit careful about the common denunciatory equation of investment with unearned income. Mr. Brian Barry, for instance, in his *The Liberal Theory of Justice* (London: Oxford University Press, 1973) dismisses the whole subject in a peremptory sideswipe: "and of course get rid of unearned income" (p. 115). Yet Barry certainly does not want to prohibit all welfare payments which have not been either earned or insured for by the recipients. And does he really want to insist that any interest paid on a person's own savings from earned income must be in real terms—as thanks to high taxation and high inflation it now often is—either nil or negative? Karl Marx in his *Critique of the Gotha Programme* was, by contrast, careful to make "funds for those unable to work" one of the first charges on the budget for his socialist state (K. Marx and F. Engels, *Selected Works* [Moscow: Foreign Languages Publishing House, 1969], 1: 21).
25   Thus Strachey urged: "But the term *exploitation* has an exact meaning. It describes precisely the process by which those who own the means of production draw off almost all the wealth.... They eat food, wear clothes, and live in houses produced by other men's labour and offer no product of their own labour in exchange. That is exploitation" (p. 36). It should be sobering to compare a sentence from Robert Conquest's *The Great Terror* (London: Macmillan Co., 1968): "For what it is worth, the evidence seems to

A. As regards the first form of objection, it is hard to see how one could defend the total rejection in principle of the acceptance of rent for the use of (private) property if once one had conceded any rights to (private) property at all. On another occasion I should like to consider the implication of such a total repudiation of all (private) property. But now it is sufficient to suggest that few people are in practice prepared in a cool hour to advocate a complete abandonment of all private property; and, consequently, of the acceptance of any rent for the use of it. This being so, the other objections to such rent, and to the factitious rent motive, presumably reduce to objections either to the amount of the rent, or to the actual distribution of the property, or to having private property in certain sorts of goods; rather than as such to private property itself, or to rent for the use of it.

B. As regards the second contention—that to derive income from the private ownership of the means of production, distribution, and exchange is immoral—it is difficult to discern how, if private ownership of such property is immoral, its collective ownership by any groups less than the whole human race is to be appropriately justified. For citizens of the better endowed socialist states, and members of the better endowed collective farms and other cooperatives both inside and outside these states, are all deriving, from their collective ownership of these endowments, advantages which they surely did not earn by their own toil, and which are certainly not available to less fortunate collective owners in the same or other countries. If these inequalities are in principle unacceptable, then the moral must be that proclaimed long ago by Gratian: "The use of all the things which there are in this world ought to be common to all men."[26]

Suppose, however, that they are not wholly unacceptable. And who of us— whether socialist or anti-socialist—is really prepared to abandon all the privileged endowments of a still relatively rich country in favour of a universal and conscientiously egalitarian poverty? Then the objection to private profit and the private profit motive becomes, it seems, an objection not to the profit but to the privacy. And that is a very different story. For the objection now is not to acquisitiveness, or to excess, or even to exploitation. It is to what is individual and private rather than public and collective.[27] And here we see again what may be to some a somewhat less acceptable face of socialism.

---

be that Stalin really believed that the abolition of incomes from capital was the sole necessary principle of social morality, excusing any other action whatever" (p. 67).

26   Gratian, *Decretum*, quoted by R.H. Tawney, p. 45.

27   George Schwartz in his *Bread and Circuses* (London: *Sunday Times*, 1959) quotes a sensible statement to the Supreme Soviet on August 18, 1953, by the future power station manager Malenkov: "Many enterprises which are still running at a loss exist in industry, enterprises in which production costs are higher than the prices laid down ... factories, enterprises and mines which we are running at a loss ... living at the expense of leading enterprises ..." (p. 65).

Questions

1. What are rent/wage/salary motives?

2. How does being selfish differ from being self-interested?

3. Can voluntary exchanges be exploitative?

4. Is usury wrongful?

5. Does a profit motive differ from a salary motive?

Further Reading

Goldman, Alan H. "Business Ethics: Profits, Utilities, and Moral Rights." *Philosophy and Public Affairs*, vol. 9, 1980, pp. 260–86.

Gond, Jean-Pascal, Guido Palazzo, and Kunal Basu. "Reconsidering Instrumental Corporate Social Responsibility through the Mafia Metaphor." *Business Ethics Quarterly*, vol. 19, no. 1, 2009, pp. 57–85.

McCarty, Richard. "Business and Benevolence." *Business and Professional Ethics Journal*, vol. 7, no. 2, 1988, pp. 63–83.

Nordal, Salvör. "Self-Interest, Deregulation and Trust." *Etikk I Praksis: Nordic Journal of Applied Ethics*, vol. 3, no. 2, 1 Jan. 2009, pp. 53–63.

Primeaux, Patrick, and John Stieber. "Profit Maximization: The Ethical Mandate of Business." *Journal of Business Ethics*, vol. 13, no. 4, 1994, pp. 287–94.

Richardson, Benjamin J, and Wes Cragg. "Being Virtuous and Prosperous: SRI's Conflicting Goals." *Journal of Business Ethics*, vol. 92, 2010, pp. 21–39.

12.

"NOXIOUS MARKETS"

DEBRA SATZ

About This Reading

When discussing business ethics, we often accept certain things as givens. We assume, for example, the existence of a market in a particular good, and then proceed to question what rules or principles should govern interactions within that market. But rarely do we ask the more fundamental question of whether a market in a particular good ought to exist.

In some cases there is little debate about the morality of a market. Markets in Apple TVs, Rokus, or LED televisions don't (all things considered) raise ethical questions. On the other hand, sometimes the very existence of a market may be morally problematic. The market in health insurance in the United States is one example. For many the question is simply whether the market operates efficiently or provides the payment or services that were covered in the policy. Others may argue that health care is a right, and thus allowing the market to determine who has or doesn't have access to insurance is unjust. But this judgment depends upon our being able to determine what things should or should not be for sale. According to Debra Satz, we can determine which types of markets are objectionable by appealing to the four parameters she outlines in this selection.

Abstract Markets versus Noxious Markets

What is wrong with markets in everything? What is it about the nature of particular exchanges that concerns us, to the point that markets in some goods appear to be clearly undesirable? How should our social policies respond to such markets? Where and for what reasons is it appropriate to regulate a market, and when should we seek to block it? [...]

Several brief clarifications about my scope and aims here. First, [...] my project does not involve an overall assessment of "the market system."[1] Markets allow people to accomplish many important social and individual tasks under modern conditions of interdependence and diversity. The point of my inquiry is not to raise general questions about the market system or about markets in the abstract. Rather, I am concerned here with the differing characteristics of very particular market exchanges: in human body parts, child labor, toxic waste, sex, and life-saving medicines. Markets in these goods provoke reservations even among those who are otherwise great enthusiasts about the market system.

Second, I put aside questions concerning the rationing of essentials in cases of extreme scarcity, "tragic choices," as they are referred to in the legal literature.[2] These are cases in which no amount of money or effort will produce enough of urgently needed goods. Market allocations in tragic choice cases raise distinct considerations from the examples considered here, as such cases do for all the alternative systems of allocation, including those using lottery, age, or merit.

[...M]arket failures (including externalities), distributional equality, and the importance of access to specific goods are important considerations in assessing markets.[3] Yet my underlying theory about the limits of markets also differs. I argue for a more nuanced view of the idea of market failure, one that takes into account how markets shape our relationships with others in ways that go beyond the idea of unabsorbed economic costs. A market exchange based in desperation, humiliation, or begging or whose terms of remediation involve bondage or servitude is not an exchange between equals. On my view, lurking behind many, if not all, noxious markets are problems relating to the *standing* of the parties before, during, and after the process of exchange.

I will also argue [...] that some markets are noxious and need to be blocked or severely constrained if the parties are to be equals in a particular sense, as citizens in a democracy. In making this argument I draw on the writings of Adam Smith and the other classical political economists [...]. Recall that these thinkers recognized that markets require certain background conditions—specification of and enforcement of entitlements and property rights—in order to support relations of freedom and equality. The markets of the classical political economists were

---

1   See also Kanbur, "On Obnoxious Markets," for discussion of the distinction between abstract and particular markets.
2   Calabresi and Bobbitt, *Tragic Choices*.
3   See also Treblicock, *The Limits*; Kanbur, "On Obnoxious Markets." Treblicock's approach to markets stresses externalities, information failures, and coercion; Kanbur's account stresses extreme individual outcomes, weak agency, and distributional inequality, where extreme outcomes and inequality are characterized in terms of welfare economics.

populated not by the abstract individuals with given wants that tend to characterize contemporary economic theory, but by landless peasants and wasteful landlords and by impoverished workers who stood in asymmetrical power relations with their employers. Moreover, agents' preferences, capacities, and relationships were understood to be shaped by the structure and nature of particular markets. Like these theorists, the approach to markets I defend recognizes market heterogeneity and stresses the need to consider other values besides efficiency and distributional equality narrowly conceived. But, [...] I think we should reject the main contemporary alternative arguments for limiting markets based on the social meaning of goods. As I see it, a major problem with noxious markets is not that they represent inferior ways of valuing goods (as those who link the limits of markets to social meanings claim) but that they undermine the conditions that people need if they are to relate as equals. At any rate, so I shall argue.

Noxious Markets: The Basic Parameters

I begin with a characterization of four parameters in terms of which we can differentiate the markets that people find especially objectionable from other types of markets. Several of these parameters are *internal* to the perspective of economics in that scoring high on them will often undermine efficiency. However, there are also political and moral rationales for limiting noxious markets. That is why the addition of more markets is not always the appropriate response to a noxious market. In some cases our goal should be to curtail a particular noxious market, not to make it work better.[4]

The first two parameters characterize the *consequences* of particular markets.

1. Some markets produce extremely *harmful outcomes.* That is, the operation of some markets leads to outcomes that are deleterious, either for the participants themselves or for third parties.[5] Consider market exchanges that lead to the depletion of the natural resource base of a country or to the fueling of a genocidal civil war. Or consider a stock market transaction that wipes out a person's resources.

Of course, many markets have harmful outcomes without eliciting our revulsion; we think that the ups and downs of prices come with the territory. But some market outcomes are so negative, so extremely harmful that they almost always

---

4   This appeal to moral and political rationales for limiting markets makes my approach distinct from those of Michael Treblicock and Ravi Kanbur. Although I draw on some of their insights in formulating my parameters, I offer a particular way of thinking about harmful outcomes and externalities that is tied to a theory of equality.

5   Of course, as I have stressed, many markets *promote* access to goods and services, decreasing their price and making them more available to more people than do other systems of distribution.

evoke a strong reaction. How harmful is that? Following up on a suggestion by Ravi Kanbur, we might consider as a natural starting point for answering this question a market whose operation leaves a person destitute.[6] For example, a grain market whose operation leaves some people starving because they cannot afford the price at which grain is set through supply and demand is bound to make us feel uncomfortable.

Yet markets can also be extremely harmful to individuals in ways that go beyond destitution. Amartya Sen usefully distinguishes between two types of interests that people have: *welfare interests* concern a person's overall good, and *agency interests* concern a person's ability to participate in deciding matters that bear on that good.[7] These interests are interdependent, but they are distinct. (A benign dictator, for example, could meet all my basic welfare interests.) We can define a set of *basic* interests for people, interests in minimum levels of well-being and agency, and define extremely harmful market outcomes as outcomes that leave these basic interests unsatisfied. The idea of basic interests is meant to capture the idea that there are universal features of an adequate and minimally decent human life, a "line beneath which no one is to be allowed to sink."[8]

2. In addition to leading to extreme individual harms, certain markets can also be *extremely harmful for society*. The operation of these markets can undermine the social framework needed for people to interact *as equals*, as individuals with equal standing. There are, of course, running disagreements among philosophers concerning the meaning of "interact as equals," as well as the scope of this ideal. I take the content of this ideal to be given by the preconditions necessary for individuals to make claims on one another and interact without having to beg or to push others around. Markets help enable this ideal, as the basis of market claims is reciprocal self-interest of the parties.[9] But they can also undermine it. Consider

---

6   Kanbur, "On Obnoxious Markets," 44.
7   Sen, *On Ethics and Economics.*
8   Shue, *Basic Rights*, 18. The language of human rights tries to capture the idea of some universal basic interests whose protection is especially urgent.
9   Adam Smith stressed this point in his famous remarks on the human tendency "to truck, barter, and exchange":

> When an animal wants to obtain something ... it has no other means of persuasion but to gain the favor of those whose services it requires. A puppy fawns upon its dam, and a spaniel endeavors by a thousand attractions to engage the attention of his master who is at dinner, when it wants to be fed by him. Man sometimes uses the same arts with his brethren, and ... endeavors by very servile and fawning attention to obtain their good will.... But man has almost constant occasion for the help of his brethren, and it is in vain for him to expect it from their benevolence only. He will be more likely to prevail if he can ... show them that it is for their own advantage to do for him what he requires of them.... It is not from the benevolence of the butcher, the brewer, or the baker that we expect our dinner, but from their regard to their own

markets that operate to undermine the capacities that a person needs to claim her rights or to participate in society; this is a problem with child labor markets and bonded labor [...]. Or consider that particular markets may condition people to be docile or servile, shape them into passive accepters of a status quo. Whereas contemporary economics sees the capacities and preferences of agents in a market as givens, particular markets—think of media, education, and caregiving—shape us. Moreover they may shape us in ways that are in tension with a society of equals.

A special case is a market that is harmful for the standing of the parties as equal citizens in a democracy. This case ratchets up from the more minimal notion of equal standing: it has to do with the equality of individuals as co-deliberants and co-participants in making laws that apply to themselves. This kind of equality presupposes additional constraints on markets and their scope. Recall James Tobin: "Any good second year graduate student in economics could write a short examination paper proving that voluntary transactions in votes would increase the welfare of the sellers as well as the buyers."[10] Nevertheless the legitimacy of the democratic process depends on the prohibition of such transactions. I will discuss this case later in this chapter.

The next two parameters characterize the *sources* of particular markets, the underlying condition of the market agents:

3. Some markets are characterized by *very weak or highly asymmetric knowledge and agency* on the part of market participants. The Pareto efficiency results assume that agents are fully aware of the consequences of their actions and have complete information about the goods exchanged.[11] But, as is widely noted by economists and others, in most circumstances these assumptions do not hold. Agency failures can occur because some of the direct participants lack important knowledge or because the market has serious indirect effects on people who are not involved in the market transactions.[12] If one or both of the parties to a contract are mistaken about the material facts or about the future consequences of their contract, we cannot assume that the exchange is a Pareto improvement.

All real markets, of course, involve imperfect information. But in some cases this imperfect information is apt to produce extremely harmful consequences. This

---

interest. We address ourselves, not to their humanity, but to their self-love.... Nobody but a beggar chooses to depend chiefly upon the benevolence of his fellow-citizens. (*Wealth of Nations*, 118–19) Elizabeth Anderson's article "Ethical Assumptions" reminded me of the importance of this quotation.

10 Tobin, "On Limiting," 269.

11 In Milton Friedman's words, "The possibility of coordination through voluntary cooperation rests on the elementary—yet frequently denied—proposition that both parties to an economic transaction benefit from it, *provided the transaction is bilaterally voluntary and informed*" (*Capitalism*, 13).

12 Kanbur, "On Obnoxious Markets," discusses agency failures.

may be most likely in cases where there is a significant time lag between the initiation and the completion of a transaction.[13] It is hard to predict one's future preferences. Consider the case of a woman selling her ability to have a child. In this case we might suspect that a woman who has never been pregnant cannot really know the consequences of selling the right to the child she bears.

Of course the fact that a contract has potential risks for an agent does not mean that the contract should not bind the agent, or else most contracting would fail. Nevertheless information failures are relevant to our assessment of particular markets in the face of harmful outcomes; in particular such failures serve to block justifications of a market transaction that appeal simply to the fact that it was chosen. Thus if agency is weak in surrogacy contracts, and a surrogate is now devastated by the thought of giving up the child she has borne, we will be less likely to think that we can justify enforcement of the contract simply on the basis that there was an agreement.

Although the majority of troubling markets characterized by weak agency involve extremely harmful outcomes, it is possible to be concerned by such markets even in the absence of harms. In this category would fall product markets that target young children; markets involving the production, purchase, and dissemination of information that fail to present relevant alternative points of view about a pressing political issue; and markets whose products are based on deception, even when there is no serious harm.[14]

Agency problems also arise in markets in which one of the affected parties is not directly involved in the transaction but depends on others to transact for her. In such cases we cannot be certain that the party herself actually benefits from the transaction. In the majority of cases of child labor, for example, parents are transacting on behalf of the children whose time and labor are traded. Many forms of child labor give little or no benefit to the working child and in some cases significantly interfere with the child's ability to grow up into a healthy functioning adult.[15] Other markets in which some of the affected parties are not directly involved as participants include markets in a nation's important scarce natural resources (such as timber in a rain forest), which can affect subsequent generations and others around the globe.

4. Some markets reflect the *underlying* extreme *vulnerabilities* of one of the transacting parties. Rousseau wrote that no citizen should "be wealthy enough to

---

13   I discuss commercial surrogacy in chapter 5 of Satz, *Why Some Things Should Not Be for Sale*.

14   Industry spending on advertising to children under the age of twelve has exploded in the past decade, increasing from a mere $100 million in 1990 to more than $2 billion in 2000. See http://mediasmarts.ca/ digital-media-literacy/media-issues/marketing-consumerism/how-marketers-target-kids

15   See chapter 7 of Satz, *Why Some Things Should Not Be for Sale*.

buy another, and none poor enough to be forced to sell himself."[16] When people come to the market with widely varying resources or widely different capacities to understand the terms of their transactions, they are unequally vulnerable to one another. In such circumstances the weaker party is at risk of being exploited. For example, when a desperately poor person agrees to part with an asset at a fire sale price, even if the exchange improves his well being we are rightly concerned with the fact that his circumstances made him willing to accept an offer for his asset that no one with a decent alternative would ever accept. When a person enters a contract from a position of extreme vulnerability he is likely to agree to almost any terms that are offered. Other examples of markets that exploit the vulnerability of transacting agents include markets in urgently needed goods where there is only a small set of suppliers and markets where the participants have highly unequal needs for the goods being exchanged.[17]

Some markets not only *reflect* the different and unequal underlying positions of market agents but may also *exacerbate* them by the way they operate. For example, in Bangladesh a recent famine arose when the price of the main food, rice, rose very rapidly and became too expensive for the poor to purchase. By contrast, rich households were insulated from the risks of rising prices because they generally receive rice from their tenants as payment for the use of land so that they have rice for their own needs and surplus to sell.[18]

So we have two dimensions regarding the source of a market and two dimensions regarding the consequences of a market that can be used to think about the acceptability of particular markets (see Table 1).

High scores along one of these dimensions, or several of them together, can make any market appear "noxious" to us. Consider the market in diamonds, whose sale is used to fund brutal civil wars. Many people find such a market abhorrent. On the analysis offered here, the best way to understand our negative reaction to this market has to do with its *extremely harmful* outcome—prolonging a bloody civil war in which thousands or tens of thousands die, hence the term "*blood* diamonds"—and with the *weak agency* of so many who are affected by the markets that fuel that war.[19] Our discomfort with such markets doesn't seem to have anything to do with the social meaning of diamonds and little to do with the underlying income inequality of buyers and sellers.

16   Rousseau, *Social Contract*, 34.
17   See White, *The Civic Minimum*, for an illuminating discussion of market vulnerability.
18   See Crow, *The Diversity of Markets*.
19   Again, see Kanbur, "On Obnoxious Markets," for illustrations.

TABLE 1: WHAT MAKES A MARKET NOXIOUS?

Source: Weak Agency	Source: Vulnerability
Inadequate information about the nature of and/or consequences of a market; others enter the market on one's behalf	Markets in a desperately needed good with limited suppliers; markets with origins in poverty and destitution; markets whose participants have very unequal needs for goods being exchanged
Outcome: Extreme Harms for Individual	**Outcome: Extreme Harms for Society**
Produces destitution; produces harm to the basic welfare and/or agency interests of the individual	Promotes servility and dependence; undermines democratic governance; undermines other regarding motivations

At the same time, although in theory markets in any good can become noxious, markets in some goods are much more likely to score higher than others on these parameters. Consider the case of markets in goods that no one but the desperate would ever exchange. Some people think that desperation is a characteristic feature of kidney markets [...].

A number of these parameters are easily incorporated within the approaches of contemporary economics; for example, concerns with harmful outcomes and information failures can be captured in the perspectives of welfare and neoclassical economics. Several authors, notably Ravi Kanbur and Michael Treblicock, have done this, showing that economic theory itself has available resources for dealing with many problematic markets. Nevertheless markets raise questions of political philosophy as well as of economics. Markets can damage important relationships people have with one another by allowing people to segment and opt out of a common condition. A central feature of most noxious markets on my approach has to do with their effects on the relationships between people, particularly the horizontal relationship of equal status. For two people to have equal status they need to see each other as legitimate sources of independent claims and they need to each have the capacity to press their claims without needing the other's permission to do so. This requires that each have rights and liberties of certain kinds as well as very specific resources, such as a level of education.

Equal status stands opposed to the ideas of caste, hereditary privilege, and unequal birthright. It insists that all individuals have an equal moral worth. Although it is perhaps possible to interpret this idea of equal status in economic terms, it is not easy to see how this would be done. Equal income and wealth by themselves do not entail equal status, as I stressed in my discussion of people with disabilities who have been marginalized from social positions and from public spaces.

Why not let people enter into labor contracts that involve bondage or contracts that grant labor bondage as remediation in the case of default? These were once common practices; later I will show that such practices are compatible with both libertarian choice theory and welfare economics.[20] But those who think that the problem with a market in bonded labor is its incompatibility with a conception of equal human status have reason to prohibit such contractual arrangements.

Equal Status in a Democracy

Social rights in their modern form imply an invasion of contract by status, the subordination of market price to social justice, the replacement of the free bargain by the declaration of rights.[21]

The preconditions for equal status as citizens in a democracy are more demanding than those needed for people to interact in horizontal relationships based on their reciprocal self-interest and equal moral worth. According to the conception of citizenship developed by the British social theorist T.H. Marshall, citizenship not only includes formal legal freedoms, but also a set of social rights with respect to health care, education, housing, and a decent minimum of income. These latter rights, he claimed, are needed to make one a full member of one's society. I think Marshall is correct: an equal right to vote has little effective meaning if some voters are too badly educated to read a ballot; citizenship means little for the destitute if society is so structured that they have no opportunity to share in society's benefits.

According to Marshall's view, the status of equal citizenship requires that all have (1) equal basic political rights and freedoms, including rights to speech and participation in the political process; (2) equal rights and freedoms within civil society, including rights to own property; and (3) equal rights to a threshold of economic welfare and to "share to the full in the social heritage and to live the life of a civilized being according to the standards prevailing in the society."[22]

---

20 I write "compatible with," not "entailed by," because welfare economists need not embrace bonded labor. But insofar as a libertarian thinks that all rights are alienable, the permissibility of labor bondage may well be entailed by it.

21 Marshall, "Citizenship," 122.

22 Ibid., 78. I discuss the implications of Marshall's view of citizenship for education in Satz, "Equality."

Marshall viewed citizenship as a given status, not a privilege that depends on individual virtue or achievement. Citizenship gives to all within its ambit a single set of rights, irrespective of their wealth or family origin. While markets can be supportive of equal citizenship understood in this sense, whether or not they are so depends on the background circumstances, property rights, and regulations within which they operate. Someone who is desperately poor might agree to an exchange that requires her to function as an around-the-clock domestic servant or to bond her labor to obtain a loan at usurious rates that she can never hope to repay. The fate of such a person may be little different from that of a serf under feudalism.

In thinking about the preconditions of equal citizenship, it is important to think in terms of general social practices and not acts. For example, there may seem to be no problem with allowing a single person to work for whatever wages and hours she chooses, yet the existence of minimum wages and maximum hours laws may be necessary to preserve a threshold of economic welfare "according to the standards prevailing in the society,"[23] and to enhance the bargaining power of the poorest people in society to protect them from exploitation and abuse. Or consider another example: even if it makes sense in an individual instance for a poor family to put its children to work, when child labor is adopted as a widespread social practice it drives down adult wages, making it virtually impossible for poor parents to refrain from sending their children to work. Rather than seeing a person's market choices as exogenous variables, the choices we actually have open to us may depend on other market choices being blocked.[24]

The transfer of income and wealth will not always be sufficient to maintain the conditions for citizen's equality; here the insights of specific egalitarians like Michael Walzer, Elizabeth Anderson, and Michael Sandel are important. Consider the case of distributing primary and secondary school education through a market. Lack of education is an extremely harmful outcome in terms of democratic citizenship: a very poorly educated person will be incompetent as a juror and a voter and have little or no access to the basic opportunities and liberties associated with full membership in her society. But giving money, even a great deal of money, to a child who has not been educated will not compensate for her lack of education, even if cash is what she (as an adult) now herself prefers. Not only does it not replace the personal and social development that education might have enabled for her, but it does not turn her into a citizen who can participate competently and meaningfully in democratic self-governance. (Nor can we be sure that if money were transferred to a parent he would choose to use that money to keep his children in school. While

---

23   Marshall, "Citizenship," 78.
24   If there is paternalism involved in such cases, it is a form of *collective paternalism*: we restrict the choices open to us in order to maintain the choices that we need to protect ourselves from serious harm to our society.

some data suggest that many parents do keep their children in school when they have enough money to feed their families, some parents are selfish or shortsighted, perhaps lacking information about education's true costs and benefits because they had little formal education themselves.)

These are all reasons for *not* distributing primary and secondary education solely through a market system, but enforcing it as a mandatory requirement. If our concern is with avoiding outcomes that undermine the conditions for citizens to interact as equals, then there is a powerful argument for guaranteeing access to a certain level of goods—education, health care, opportunities, rights, liberties, and physical security—even if some citizens would prefer to trade and sell these goods, or the opportunity to access these goods, to the highest bidder. While markets can supplement the supply of these goods in many cases, my point is that access to these goods should not depend only on individual preferences or income. The conditions for equal citizenship cannot be cashed out in terms of a generic good like money or utilitarian welfare; in addition to some level of income, they require that some goods be distributed in kind and that, in some cases, the distribution be more or less equal.

At the same time I would not defend the distribution of education or health care in terms of the idea that these goods are corrupted through sale. A public right to education is in theory compatible with the existence of a complementary or supplementary private education system.[25] Instead my argument draws on Marshall's suggestion that some goods function as prerequisites for *full inclusion* in society, for counting as an equal member. A person who lacks a certain level of education or access to medical care or physical security is not only ill-equipped to navigate her own life and values, but also faces substantial impediments to participation in the economy and to participating in public debates about social choices. Such a person is vulnerable to exploitation and manipulation by others and dependent on luck or the will of benefactors to meet her basic needs.

In addition to supplementing market distributions in goods such as education and health care, we may have reason to *block certain market exchanges altogether* if citizens are to be equals. Consider votes in a democracy. No one defends the outright sale of voting, even though it can be argued that such sale is consistent with efficiency and freedom.[26] The interesting question is why. I think there are two main answers to this question, associated with two different ideals of democratic citizenship.

---

25 Vast inequalities in education, however, may undermine democratic society. See Satz, "Equality," for discussion.

26 Perhaps some libertarians would gladly engage in vote buying and selling, but they are unlikely to find many followers.

The first answer points out that the regulative idea of democracy is that citizens are equals engaged in a common cooperative project of governing themselves together. Thus citizens participate with others on an equal footing in deciding on the laws and policies that will govern them. A market in votes would have the predictable consequence of giving the rich disproportionate power over others since the poor would be far more likely than the rich to sell their political power. Indeed one rationale for secret ballots is to make contracts about votes unenforceable, thus protecting the poor and vulnerable from pressure to sell. If political, regulatory, judicial, and legal decision mechanisms were literally up for sale, this would concentrate political power in the hands of a few.

A second answer pushes in a more republican direction, interpreting democracy not merely as government among equals but as a means of determining the common good.[27] On this view of democracy, *votes are acts of political co-deliberation*. Even if a vote market were not monopolized by the rich, we would still have a reason to proscribe vote trading on the grounds that voting is not about the aggregation of private interests; it is an act undertaken only after collectively deliberating about what is in the common good. Distributing votes according to preferences views citizens as consumers, not co-deliberators.

Both conceptions of democracy require that some markets be blocked and others be highly regulated. Both conceptions would block markets in votes, judicial offices, legislative offices, and voluntary slavery. Moreover, both conceptions would regulate markets governing the production and distribution of political information and markets governing access to legislative office and the opportunities associated with political influence, although to varying degrees.[28] But these two conceptions might well differ on the treatment of military service as a market good. On the republican conception of democracy, there is something deeply troubling about the ways in which today's volunteer army shares some attributes with a mercenary army. Rather than seeing military service as an obligation of citizenship, today's soldiers are drawn from a small segment of the population that is largely working class.

Just as democracies made up of equal citizens require blocks on markets in votes or people, a related argument might be made that some markets need to be blocked or highly regulated if people are to develop the *capacities* that they need to participate effectively in civil and political society. Human beings are malleable in a way that goods such as apples are not.[29] We do not usually need to worry about the

---

27   See Sandel, *What Money Can't Buy*, for discussion of a republican view of democracy.

28   See Rawls, *Theory of Justice*, for discussion of the *fair* distribution of political liberties. See also Brighouse, "Egalitarianism and Equal Availability."

29   Labor markets may be highly constitutive in their effects on the parties involved. As we saw, Adam Smith conjectured that a worker who spends her life engaged in menial, servile tasks in which she has no voice or authority is not likely to develop the capacities she needs to function as an active citizen. (Nor is she likely,

noneconomic effects of a market on the apples exchanged,[30] but we do need to worry about whether a particular kind of market produces or supports passivity, alienation, or a ruthless egoism. Labor markets may be structured so as to accustom people to being pushed around and managed by others. Widespread markets in women's reproductive or sexual capacities (including quid pro quo sexual harassment contracts) might amplify gender inequalities by entrenching and deepening negative stereotypes about women.[31] Unregulated education markets are compatible with children being treated as and raised as servile dependents. We need to pay special attention to cases like these, for they pose potential threats to the stable reproduction of democratic citizenship over time. Indeed the democratic state has an interest in withholding its support from institutions that cultivate subordination and servitude, even if those institutions are not strictly illegal.

Regulating Markets, Blocking Markets

How should we decide what approach to take to a noxious market? Obviously which policies it makes sense to adopt depends on the source of the market's noxiousness, which of the four parameters is in play. We need to tailor our response to the particular problems with that market. For example, if weak agency is the problem with a particular market, then we may want to undertake measures that increase information. If underlying vulnerability is a problem, we may want to redistribute income or create supplementary alternatives to market provision. Regulating a market is often the best way to address a market's noxiousness. At the same time, some problems with a market may be best addressed by closing off the ability of agents to trade in that market at all. Some markets undermine the social context in which people are able to interact on terms of equality.

In such cases we need to address not merely distributions, but also the underlying property rights of the transacting agents. To illustrate this, let's look briefly at child labor [...]. In our world child labor often arises on the basis of destitution. But even in a world without destitution child labor would be problematic. Although many libertarian economists often view freedom as the freedom to participate in the market, they are often blind to the fact that individuals are not born with all the required capacities for exercising agency and making choices (including market choices) already developed. The achievement of even a minimal threshold level of decision-making powers requires support from a variety of sources, including parents

---

given the chance, to be a loyal employee. Indeed a large body of research shows that high worker effort and loyalty require substantial departures from the treatment of labor as a pure commodity.)

30 Although see Pollan, *The Omnivore's Dilemma*, on the effects of large-scale industrial food production on the quality of the food that is produced.

31 See chapters 5 and 6 of Satz, *Why Some Things Should Not Be for Sale*.

and the state: nurturing, help in developing the capacities for understanding and weighing alternatives, help in developing the ability to see oneself as an agent worthy of having choices, and attaining an adequate level of education. Child labor fails to promote and often blocks the development of these capacities.

Cases: The Titanic and Toxic Waste

With my framework in mind, I'd like to [discuss...] the *Titanic's* market in safety and Larry Summers' memo advocating a market in toxic waste.

Beginning with the *Titanic*, [...] individuals booking passage were allowed to buy tickets with or without the guarantee of access to a lifeboat in the event of an emergency. Their market choices can be understood as a function of their preferences given their resources and their information. In the case of the actual *Titanic*, there was weak agency (based on faulty information about the ship's "unsinkability") and extremely harmful individual outcomes (drowning when the ship went down). These considerations give us good grounds for treating the distribution of safety according to ticket price aboard the *Titanic* as an instance of a noxious market.

But suppose that we increased agency and redistributed income so that all could easily afford the price of a first-class ticket on the boat. Is there any reason why it might make sense to prefer a more constrained system for the distribution of safety, whereby all are prevented from making choices that they would take as individuals if those options were available? [...] I don't think that paternalism gives us a strong reason to forbid people from making decisions to forgo access to lifeboats on the *Titanic*.

A commitment to equal citizenship, however, does presuppose that there are some rights that individuals cannot contract away. This is because, if these rights were contracted away, some individuals would be subject to servitude and subordination. Employers, for example, could demand that their employees travel in the cheapest possible manner, even if that means forgoing a lifeboat. And other individuals would find themselves placed in situations where they would have to treat people as less than equal, pushing them out of the lifeboat, for example.

Note, however, that protecting people from humiliating subordination and servitude can be secured in this example by providing a floor of provision, a (literal?) safety net, compatible with large (market-generated) inequalities above the floor. [...] In his discussion of the *Titanic* example Thomas Schelling concludes that it is the *inequality* aboard the ship that is problematic, not the inadequate safety floor: "Those who risk their lives at sea and cannot afford a safe ship should perhaps not be denied the opportunity to entrust themselves to a cheaper ship without lifeboats;

but if some people cannot afford the price of passage with lifeboats, and some people can, they should not travel on the same ship."[32]

Schelling seems to be suggesting that if we allow a market to distribute safety, then we must ensure that it gives the same safety to everyone; or at least to everyone within the community. We have already seen that there is an argument that connects equal provision of votes and basic political rights to democratic citizenship. But it seems puzzling to conclude that we need to equalize specific goods such as safety for the sake of such citizenship.

I can think of two basic reasons that democratic societies might want to secure the equal provision of certain specific goods. The first reason is that inequalities in some goods, such as education or political influence, sit too uneasily with the idea that we are each other's equals. For example, it may be hard to maintain that conviction if excesses of privileged schooling impose great differences on children's future lives. Education is simply too important to participation and inclusion in society's institutions, and relative inequalities can confine the worst off to occupy lowly positions. Significant educational inequalities in the quality of K-12 education do not seem fair, because they suggest that some children matter a great deal less to society than others. Of course, there are disagreements about such cases and about how much educational inequality is compatible with a democratic society. But my point is that there are instances in which inequalities in some goods affront the idea that people are the equals of their neighbors: they reek of caste-like privileges. Sometimes the goods that affront equality may be conventionally determined, as Michael Walzer argued. For example, many Americans would look with great distaste on the idea of a market in positions on ticket lines at movie theaters, even if the introduction of such a market did not change their own relative position on the line. The fact that everyone irrespective of income has to wait his or her own turn on the line for a movie is a convention that has come to symbolize our equality. (If you doubt this, just try to buy your way into the line.)

The second reason concerns the effects of markets on the aggregation of interests, an effect that we saw invoked by the republican conception of democratic citizenship. Markets enable people to opt out of relationships with particular producers and to take up new relationships, to find new ways of satisfying their preferences. Albert Hirschman used the term "exit" to describe this function that markets provide, and it is an important mechanism for enhancing freedom as well as economic improvement (because exit signals dissatisfaction, at least relative to available alternatives).[33] Hirschman counterposed "exit" with "voice," by which he had in mind trying to

---

32 Schelling, *Choice and Consequence*, 115–16.
33 Hirschman, *Exit*.

change another person's behavior by directly alerting him to a problem. But we might think of another function of voice; as in the case of voting, voice can play an important role in shaping and forming common interests.[34] Exit via a market might sometimes enhance common interests (as when consumers withdraw their support for a shoddy product), but it might also diminish the possibility of forming or satisfying those common interests.

Recent research by Susanna Loeb on school financing provides a good illustration of this phenomenon.[35] Among the funding models for education that she considers is one in which school districts receive a uniform per pupil funding grant from the state and then are allowed to raise unlimited additional funds. Although this system looks attractive because it allows voters to pursue their preferred spending levels while maintaining a minimum funding level for all students, Loeb argues that it may not be sustainable because the high-wealth districts may lose their incentive to support state funding. People in these districts might be rationally motivated to vote for politicians who support lower levels of state provision since much of their aid is based on their own fund-raising and local taxes. In that case the ability of those who are left to provide for public education on the basis of state provision would decline.

As this example shows, the stratification and sorting inevitably produced by a market can be especially problematic in cases where one person's prospects for attaining some important good is closely connected to another person's decisions. This is especially true in a representative form of government. For example, we may suspect that when officials can insulate their own children from the effects of poor public schooling or unsafe neighborhoods they may find it easier to support cuts to state budgets in those areas than they would if their own families were directly affected by such cuts.

In a recent paper on risk and safety and the "*Titanic* puzzle" I am concerned with here, Jonathan Wolff cites work by John Adams showing that the initial effect of mandating seatbelts for car drivers but not for passengers was an *increase* in the number of passenger deaths.[36] Because the drivers were now safer, they took more risks, which fell on others for whom the risks had not changed. Wolff points out that this analysis also applies to the case of safety aboard ships:

> If the Captain was assured of a place in the lifeboat, or even that the people he most cared about were assured of their place, then he may well have steered a riskier course than otherwise. This is an analogue to the familiar problem of "moral hazard" in insurance, reducing people's incentives to take

---

34   Wolff, "Market Failure."
35   Loeb, "Estimating."
36   Adams, *Risk*, 121.

care. This may well be why the Captain is supposed to go down with the ship, or, at least, be the last one off.[37]

When decision makers can buy private solutions for themselves in education, police protection, and even garbage collection, this may have problematic consequences for the public provision of these goods. To the extent that this is true, it may be that the best way to ensure that the public's interests are taken into account is to give both the public and the decision maker the same interests. At any rate, as this example shows, we need to be attentive to the effects of markets on motivations that affect actions. Sometimes allowing people to sort and segment into diverse groups will undermine the solidarity that is needed to provide for a public good.

Mandating the equal provision of goods is at least theoretically compatible with having those goods supplied to a large extent through regulated markets. Moreover banning a market will sometimes have costs in terms of other values people care about; there will be trade-offs. As I have repeatedly stressed, markets are engines of growth and have important roles to play with respect to our equality and freedom. In some cases the requirements of equal citizenship will push us to a floor of provision, not strict equality in the distribution of the good. In other cases that may not be so; we may care about the ceiling as well as the floor because we want to constrain the amount of inequality to maintain a healthy democracy. Often empirical considerations will be paramount, such as the effects of the inequality on the prospects of those worst off. Some markets trade in things that no democratic society can countenance; others need to be regulated, constrained, or supplemented with other mechanisms if the preconditions for a democratic society are to be maintained.

Summer['s toxic waste memo...] argued that trade in toxic waste would benefit the poor countries and indeed make both the less developed countries and the developed countries better off. The exchange appears to be a Pareto improvement. Why, then, did the public release of the memo occasion such uproar? Why did so many people view the proposed market as clearly noxious? How does the framework in this chapter throw light on the public response? There are three reasons for thinking that a toxic waste market is noxious.

In the first place, there is the unequal *vulnerability* of the bargaining positions of the rich and poor countries. Trade in toxic waste holds up a mirror to global inequality. Because of that disparity the rich countries are able to exploit the vulnerabilities of the less developed countries (LDCs). Critics might suspect that, were they not so poor, the LDCs would not consent to the transfer of toxic waste to their lands, or perhaps they would hold out for better terms.[38]

---

37 Wolff, "Market Failure."
38 See also Kanbur, "On Obnoxious Markets," 52.

In the second place, there is likely to be *weak agency*. Many poor countries are run by corrupt governments that do not represent the interests of their citizens. When accepting toxic waste in exchange for money, the interests of these citizens, or at the least the poorest and most vulnerable citizens, might well be neglected. As Daniel Hausman and Michael McPherson note in their discussion of it, Summers' memo implicitly applies the Pareto criterion to the rich and poor nations as a whole.[39] This is, as they write, a "cheat": if we apply the Pareto criterion to individuals, some individuals, very poor individuals within the LDCs into whose neighborhoods the waste is likely to be dumped, might be made very much worse off by the trade.[40] In addition to the weak agency of the poor, the leaders of these countries (as well as the leaders of the rich countries) may not have adequate knowledge about the long-term effects of storing toxic waste.

Vulnerability and weak agency concern the *sources* of an international market in toxic waste. But we may also worry about the *consequences* of such a market. So in the third place there is the possibility for extremely *harmful outcomes to individuals.* Shipping and storing toxic waste, at least some forms of it, are likely to have very bad consequences.[41] Many people might die or suffer in terms of their health. For other forms of toxic waste there may be a risk of serious future harm. If this is so, then future generations, who are not themselves parties to the agreement, might bear the costs of extremely harmful outcomes. Additionally, if toxic waste is exported to poor countries that have less capacity to monitor and regulate pollution, this may lead to more pollution, and even more harm, overall than would be the case if the waste stayed in the developed world.

On the other hand, it is hard to *directly* connect such markets to the idea of harmful social outcomes, that is, to the undermining of equal status. At the same time, we might wonder if the readiness of country A to transfer toxic waste to country B fails to show equal concern and respect for the citizens of country B. Would citizens be as likely to transfer toxic waste to those in their own backyard, that is, to themselves? (Similar concerns, of course, can be raised about the location of toxic waste facilities in wealthy countries, which tends to be in very poor neighborhoods.)

The Limits of My Approach

My account analyzes noxious markets in terms of extremely harmful outcomes for individuals and for society (including the special case of equal status in a democratic society), weak agency (including incomplete information), and vulnerabilities that

39   See Hausman and McPherson, *Economic Analysis,* 200.
40   Ibid., 201.
41   Kanbur, "On Obnoxious Markets."

give some people significant power over others. It grounds a moral distinction between types of markets, but one that is not primarily based on the special nature of certain goods, but on considerations that cut across goods. (Thus on my account credit or housing markets may become more objectionable than sex markets.) But my account is also limited in certain crucial respects.

First, as I have emphasized, we cannot immediately conclude from the fact that a market is noxious that we ought legally to ban it. Even if a market interfered with or failed to promote certain values, banning it might be worse overall from the point of view of those same values. Our policy response must depend on what the alternative to a market is likely to be, as well as on the particular problematic parameters in play. Some markets are simply incompatible with securing the equality of status of individuals and should be prohibited; some are incompatible with equality of status in a democracy of equal citizens; others require regulation, including redistribution of income and property. Many markets are noxious only in a given context; instead of changing the market we might try to change the context. Even in cases where there do not seem to be good reasons in favor of allowing a particular market, it may be impractical to ban it. For example, in the case of drug markets such as for heroin and cocaine, where the transaction costs are low and the market exchange is easy to enforce,[42] a rich black market can and does exist even in the presence of state attempts to block such markets. Thus, although there will be cases in which we will want to ban the particular noxious market, in other cases it will make sense to respond to a noxious market by legislating a safety net, or by educational policies designed to increase information, or by mechanisms aimed at increasing accountability, or by tax-and-transfer schemes to reduce inequality. And sometimes we will simply want to ensure that nonmarket mechanisms for providing a good exist side by side with market mechanisms.

Second, some of the parameters I have appealed to can conflict with each other or with other values. People will have different views of the appropriate trade-offs between the different parameters, as well as between these parameters and other values. For example, people will disagree about whether to prioritize increasing agency or decreasing vulnerability.

Third, I have not settled on exactly how to operationalize these values; for example, I have not here specified a numerically precise interpretation of how much underlying vulnerability market agents must have for a market to become noxious. The characterizing parameters plainly admit of degrees, and there is room for reasonable disagreement as to when a particular market is no longer acceptable. Further, context matters a great deal for the noxiousness of any particular market.

---

42 Such markets are easy to enforce because market exchange is close to instantaneous in time, and there are effective private sanctions for noncompliance.

Consider large inequalities of wealth produced by a labor market. These inequalities might be blocked from translating into extremely harmful outcomes for equal citizenship in a democratic society by laws regulating the financing of political campaigns, by ensuring a fair distribution of educational resources so that wealth does not translate into a fixed intergenerational caste, and by regulations aimed at securing a high enough minimum income so that no one is impoverished.

Fourth, it should be evident that my account is sensitive to changing circumstances so that markets that are currently noxious may emerge under other conditions as perfectly acceptable (or the reverse).

Fifth, it must be admitted that other accounts of noxious markets are possible [...]. Some may wish to question placing so much moral weight on our intuitive reactions to particular markets as I have done, pointing out that people were once horrified by the idea of life insurance. Perhaps many of our reactions are little more than an irrational repugnance at that which we dislike. Still others may find particular markets objectionable that do not seem to run afoul of any of the criteria that I have proposed, for example, a market in supermodel eggs or Nobel Prize-winner's sperm or a market in a good whose sale violates their deeply held religious values.[43] By contrast, my account focuses on widely shared values—preventing extreme harm and vulnerability—as well as considerations that democratic citizens, with differing moral frameworks and conceptions of life, have reason to find especially problematic.

My analysis in this chapter has implications for the role of markets in theories of equality. Egalitarians should focus on more than the distribution of things, but also attend to the people who have those things and their relationships with one another. Many markets are rightly celebrated as mechanisms of freedom and efficiency, yet some markets traffic in things that no decent society should allow its members to be without, some deepen objectionable hierarchies of class and privilege, and some undermine democratic values. In thinking about the scope of markets we need to pay attention not only to the distributive outcomes of different markets but also to the relationships between people that these markets enable and support.[44] Ultimately, these questions about the limits of markets are not merely questions of costs and benefits but of how we define our society, of who we are and what we care about.

---

43 Eric Rakowski raised the example of supermodel eggs in conversation. A Web auction site purported to sell the eggs of beautiful female models to the highest bidder. Although the website was later exposed as a fraud, the site got bids of up to $42,000, proving that some people were willing to be part of such a market.
44 It is important to keep in mind that many allocative decisions are shaped neither by government nor by the market. These include distribution through gift, lottery, merit, the intrafamily regulation of work and distribution, and other principles such as seniority and need.

Unfortunately, many proponents and critics of markets have operated on a high level of abstraction in which all markets function in more or less the same way. But different markets have particular features and raise different moral concerns. [...

Questions

1. Should markets be allowed in all areas?

2. What constitutes a "noxious" market?

3. Why might noxious markets be morally problematic?

4. How does Satz think that we should respond to noxious markets?

Further Reading

Fabre, Cécile. Review of Debra Satz, *Why Some Things Should Not Be for Sale: The Moral Limits of Markets. Ethics: An International Journal Of Social, Political, and Legal Philosophy*, vol. 121, no. 2, 2011, pp. 469–75.

McMillan, John. *Reinventing the Bazaar: A Natural History of Markets*. New York: W.W. Norton & Company, 2003.

Sandel, Michael. "What Money Can't Buy: The Moral Limits of Markets." *European Journal of Philosophy*, vol. 24, no. 4, 2016, pp. 999–1003.

Stout, Lynn A. *The Shareholder Value Myth: How Putting Shareholders First Harms Investors, Corporations, and the Public*. San Francisco: Berrett-Koehler Publishers, 2012.

References

Adams, John. *Risk*. London: University College London Press, 1995.

Anderson, Elizabeth. "Ethical Assumptions of Economic Theory: Some Lessons from the History of Credit and Bankruptcy." *Ethical Theory and Practice* 7 (2004): 347–60.

Brighouse, Harry. "Egalitarianism and Equal Availability of Political Influence." *Journal of Political Philosophy*, vol. 4, no. 2 (1996): 118–41.

Calabresi, Guido, and Philip Bobbitt. *Tragic Choices: The Conflicts Society Confronts in the Allocation of Tragically Scarce Resources*. New York: Norton, 1978.

Crow, Ben. *The Diversity of Markets: How the Grain Train Shapes Wealth and Poverty in Rural South Asia*. London: Macmillan, 2001.

Friedman, Milton. *Capitalism and Freedom*. Chicago: University of Chicago Press, 1962.

Hausman, Daniel, and Michael McPherson. *Economic Analysis and Moral Philosophy*. Cambridge: Cambridge University Press, 1996.

Hirschman, Albert O. *Exit, Voice and Loyalty: Responses to Decline in Firms, Organizations and States*. Cambridge, MA: Harvard University Press, 1970.

Kanbur, Ravi. "On Obnoxious Markets." In *Globalization, Culture and the Limits of the Market: Essays in Economics and Philosophy*, ed. Stephen Cullenberg and Prasanta Pattanaik. New Delhi: Oxford University Press, 2004.

Loeb, Susanna. "Estimating the Effects of School Finance Reform: A Framework for a Federalist System." *Journal of Public Economics* 80 (2001): 225–47.

Marshall, T.H. "Citizenship and Social Class." In *Class, Citizenship and Social Development: Essays by T.H. Marshall*. Chicago: University of Chicago Press, 1977.

Pollan, Michael. *The Omnivore's Dilemma: A Natural History of Four Meals*. New York: Penguin, 2006.

Rawls, John. *A Theory of Justice*. Revised ed. Cambridge, MA: Harvard University Press, 1999.

Rousseau, J.J. *Social Contract and Discourses*. London: J.M. Dent. (Originally published in 1762.)

Sandel, Michael J. *What Money Can't Buy: The Moral Limits of Markets*. Tanner Lectures on Human Values, vol. 21, ed. Grete B. Peterson. Salt Lake City: University of Utah Press, 2000.

Satz, Debra. "Equality, Adequacy, and Education for Citizenship." *Ethics* 117, no. 4 (2007): 623–48.

——— *Why Some Things Should Not Be for Sale: The Moral Limits of Markets*. New York: Oxford University Press, 2010.

Schelling, Thomas. *Choice and Consequence*. Cambridge, MA: Harvard University Press, 1984.

Sen, Amartya. *On Ethics and Economics*. Oxford: Blackwell Publishing, 1987.

Shue, Henry. *Basic Rights: Subsistence, Affluence and U.S. Foreign Policy*. Princeton, NJ: Princeton University Press, 1996.

Smith, Adam. *Wealth of Nations: Books I-III* (Harmondsworth: Penguin, 1970), p. 119.

Tobin, James. "On Limiting the Domain of Inequality." *Journal of Law and Economics* 13, no. 2 (1970)" 263–77.

Treblicock, Michael. *The Limits of Freedom of Contract*. Cambridge, MA: Harvard University Press, 1997.

White, Stuart. *The Civic Minimum: On the Rights and Obligations of Economic Citizenship*. Oxford: Oxford University Press, 2002.

Wolff, Jonathan. "Market Failure, Common Interests, and the Titanic Puzzle." In *Egalitarianism: New Essays on the Nature and Value of Equality*, ed. K. Lippert-Rasmussen and N. Holtung. Oxford: Oxford University Press, 2007.

III.
THE CONDUCT OF BUSINESS

13.

"IS BUSINESS BLUFFING ETHICAL?"

ALBERT Z. CARR

About This Reading

It is common to defend certain practices in business by dismissing them as "just business." The idea behind this phrase is that there are practices in business that are distinct from other concerns that might exist outside a business decision. Carr argues that business is analogous to the game of poker, where certain allowances are simply part of the game. Thus business, according to Carr, should also be viewed as a game. This means that certain actions that may be problematic in other contexts are entirely appropriate in business practices.

A respected businessman with whom I discussed the theme of this article remarked with some heat, "You mean to say you're going to encourage men to bluff? Why, bluffing is nothing more than a form of lying! You're advising them to lie!"

I agreed that the basis of private morality is a respect for truth and that the closer a businessman comes to the truth, the more he deserves respect. At the same time, I suggested that most bluffing in business might be regarded simply as game strategy—much like bluffing in poker, which does not reflect on the morality of the bluffer.

I quoted Henry Taylor, the British statesman who pointed out that "falsehood ceases to be falsehood when it is understood on all sides that the truth is not expected to be spoken"—an exact description of bluffing in poker, diplomacy, and business. I cited the analogy of the criminal court, where the criminal is not expected to tell the truth when he pleads "not guilty." Everyone from the judge down takes it for granted that the job of the defendant's attorney is to get his client off, not to reveal the truth; and this is considered ethical practice. I mentioned Representative Omar Burleson, the Democrat from Texas, who was quoted as saying, in regard to the ethics of Congress, "Ethics is a barrel of worms"[1]—a pungent summing up of the problem of deciding who is ethical in politics.

---

1 *The New York Times*, March 9, 1967.

I reminded my friend that millions of businessmen feel constrained every day to say *yes* to their bosses when they secretly believe *no* and that this is generally accepted as permissible strategy when the alternative might be the loss of a job. The essential point, I said, is that the ethics of business are game ethics, different from the ethics of religion.

He remained unconvinced. Referring to the company of which he is president, he declared: "Maybe that's good enough for some businessmen, but I can tell you that we pride ourselves on our ethics. In 30 years not one customer has ever questioned my word or asked to check our figures. We're loyal to our customers and fair to our suppliers. I regard my handshake on a deal as a contract. I've never entered into price fixing schemes with my competitors. I've never allowed my salesmen to spread injurious rumors about other companies. Our union contract is the best in our industry. And, if I do say so myself, our ethical standards are of the highest!"

He really was saying, without realizing it, that he was living up to the ethical standards of the business game—which are a far cry from those of private life. Like a gentlemanly poker player, he did not play in cahoots with others at the table, try to smear their reputations, or hold back chips he owed them.

But this same fine man, at that very time, was allowing one of his products to be advertised in a way that made it sound a great deal better than it actually was. Another item in his product line was notorious among dealers for its "built-in obsolescence." He was holding back from the market a much-improved product because he did not want it to interfere with sales of the inferior item it would have replaced. He had joined with certain of his competitors in hiring a lobbyist to push a state legislature, by methods that he preferred not to know too much about, into amending a bill then being enacted.

In his view these things had nothing to do with ethics; they were merely normal business practice. He himself undoubtedly avoided outright falsehood—never lied in so many words. But the entire organization that he ruled was deeply involved in numerous strategies of deception.

Pressure to Deceive

Most executives from time to time are almost compelled, in the interests of their companies or themselves, to practice some form of deception when negotiating with customers, dealers, labor unions, government officials, or even other departments of their companies. By conscious misstatements, concealment of pertinent facts, or exaggeration—in short, by bluffing—they seek to persuade others to agree with them. I think it is fair to say that if the individual executive refuses to bluff from time to time—if he feels obligated to tell the truth, the whole truth, and nothing but the truth—he is ignoring opportunities permitted under the rules and is at a heavy disadvantage in his business dealings.

But here and there a businessman is unable to reconcile himself to the bluff in which he plays a part. His conscience, perhaps spurred by religious idealism, troubles him. He feels guilty; he may develop an ulcer or a nervous tic. Before any executive can make profitable use of the strategy of the bluff, he needs to make sure that in bluffing he will not lose self-respect or become emotionally disturbed. If he is to reconcile personal integrity and high standards of honesty with the practical requirements of business, he must feel that his bluffs are ethically justified. The justification rests on the fact that business, as practiced by individuals as well as by corporations, has the impersonal character of a game—a game that demands both special strategy and an understanding of its special ethics.

The game is played at all levels of corporate life, from the highest to the lowest. At the very instant that a man decides to enter business, he may be forced into a game situation, as is shown by the recent experience of a Cornell honor graduate who applied for a job with a large company:

This applicant was given a psychological test which included the statement, "Of the following magazines, check any that you have read either regularly or from time to time, and double-check those which interest you most: *Reader's Digest, Time, Fortune, Saturday Evening Post, The New Republic, Life, Look, Ramparts, Newsweek, Business Week, U.S. News & World Report, The Nation, Playboy, Esquire, Harper's, Sports Illustrated*."

His tastes in reading were broad, and at one time or another he had read almost all of these magazines. He was a subscriber to *The New Republic*, an enthusiast for *Ramparts*, and an avid student of the pictures in *Playboy*. He was not sure whether his interest in *Playboy* would be held against him, but he had a shrewd suspicion that if he confessed to an interest in *Ramparts* and *The New Republic*, he would be thought a liberal, a radical, or at least an intellectual, and his chances of getting the job, which he needed, would greatly diminish. He therefore checked five of the more conservative magazines. Apparently it was a sound decision, for he got the job. He had made a game player's decision, consistent with business ethics.

A similar case is that of a magazine space salesman who, owing to a merger, suddenly found himself out of a job:

This man was 58, and, in spite of a good record, his chance of getting a job elsewhere in a business where youth is favored in hiring practice was not good. He was a vigorous, healthy man, and only a considerable amount of gray in his hair suggested his age. Before beginning his job search he touched up his hair with a black dye to confine the gray to his temples. He knew that the truth about his age might well come out in time, but he calculated that he could deal with that situation when it arose. He and his wife decided that he could easily pass for 45, and he so stated his age on his resume.

This was a lie; yet within the accepted rules of the business game, no moral culpability attaches to it.

The Poker Analogy

We can learn a good deal about the nature of business by comparing it with poker. While both have a large element of chance, in the long run the winner is the man who plays with steady skill. In both games ultimate victory requires intimate knowledge of the rules, insight into the psychology of the other players, a bold front, a considerable amount of self-discipline, and the ability to respond swiftly and effectively to opportunities provided by chance.

No one expects poker to be played on the ethical principles preached in churches. In poker it is right and proper to bluff a friend out of the rewards of being dealt a good hand. A player feels no more than a slight twinge of sympathy, if that, when—with nothing better than a single ace in his hand—he strips a heavy loser, who holds a pair, of the rest of his chips. It was up to the other fellow to protect himself. In the words of an excellent poker player, former President Harry Truman, "If you can't stand the heat, stay out of the kitchen." If one shows mercy to a loser in poker, it is a personal gesture, divorced from the rules of the game.

Poker has its special ethics, and here I am not referring to rules against cheating. The man who keeps an ace up his sleeve or who marks the cards is more than unethical; he is a crook, and can be punished as such—kicked out of the game or,—in the Old West, shot.

In contrast to the cheat, the unethical poker player is one who, while abiding by the letter of the rules, finds ways to put the other players at an unfair disadvantage. Perhaps he unnerves them with loud talk. Or he tries to get them drunk. Or he plays in cahoots with someone else at the table. Ethical poker players frown on such tactics.

Poker's own brand of ethics is different from the ethical ideals of civilized human relationships. The game calls for distrust of the other fellow. It ignores the claim of friendship. Cunning deception and concealment of one's strength and intentions, not kindness and open heartedness, are vital in poker. No one thinks any the worse of poker on that account. And no one should think any the worse of the game of business because its standards of right and wrong differ from the prevailing traditions of morality in our society.

Discard the Golden Rule

This view of business is especially worrisome to people without much business experience. A minister of my acquaintance once protested that business cannot possibly function in our society unless it is based on the Judeo-Christian system of ethics. He told me:

> I know some businessmen have supplied call girls to customers, but there are always a few rotten apples in every barrel. That doesn't mean the rest of the fruit isn't sound. Surely the vast majority of businessmen are ethical. I myself am acquainted with many who adhere to strict codes of ethics based fundamentally on religious teachings. They contribute to good causes. They participate in community activities. They cooperate with other companies to improve working conditions in their industries. Certainly they are not indifferent to ethics.

That most businessmen are not indifferent to ethics in their private lives, everyone will agree. My point is that in their office lives they cease to be private citizens; they become game players who must be guided by a somewhat different set of ethical standards.

The point was forcefully made to me by a Midwestern executive who has given a good deal of thought to the question:

> So long as a businessman complies with the laws of the land and avoids telling malicious lies, he's ethical. If the law as written gives a man a wide-open chance to make a killing, he'd be a fool not to take advantage of it. If he doesn't, somebody else will. There's no obligation on him to stop and consider who is going to get hurt. If the law says he can do it, that's all the justification he needs. There's nothing unethical about that. It's just plain business sense.

This executive (call him Robbins) took the stand that even industrial espionage, which is frowned on by some businessmen, ought not to be considered unethical. He recalled a recent meeting of the National Industrial Conference Board where an authority on marketing made a speech in which he deplored the employment of spies by business organizations. More and more companies, he pointed out, find it cheaper to penetrate the secrets of competitors with concealed cameras and microphones or by bribing employees than to set up costly research and design departments of their own. A whole branch of the electronics industry has grown up with this trend, he continued, providing equipment to make industrial espionage easier.

Disturbing? The marketing expert found it so. But when it came to a remedy, he could only appeal to "respect for the golden rule." Robbins thought this a confession of defeat, believing that the golden rule, for all its value as an ideal for society, is simply not feasible as a guide for business. A good part of the time the businessman is trying to do unto others as he hopes others will not do unto him.[2] Robbins continued:

> Espionage of one kind or another has become so common in business that it's like taking a drink during Prohibition—it's not considered sinful. And we don't even have Prohibition where espionage is concerned; the law is very tolerant in this area. There's no more shame for a business that uses secret agents than there is for a nation. Bear in mind that there already is at least one large corporation—you can buy its stock over the counter—that makes millions by providing counterespionage service to industrial firms. Espionage in business is not an ethical problem; it's an established technique of business competition.

"We Don't Make the Laws"

Wherever we turn in business, we can perceive the sharp distinction between its ethical standards and those of the churches. Newspapers abound with sensational stories growing out of this distinction:

- We read one day that Senator Philip A. Hart of Michigan has attacked food processors for deceptive packaging of numerous products.[3]

- The next day there is a Congressional to-do over Ralph Nader's book, *Unsafe at Any Speed*, which demonstrates that automobile companies for years have neglected the safety of car-owning families.[4]

- Then another Senator, Lee Metcalf of Montana, and journalist Vic Reinemer show in their book, *Overcharge*, the methods by which utility companies elude regulating government bodies to extract unduly large payments from users of electricity.[5]

---

2   See Bruce D. Henderson, "Brinkmanship in Business," *HBR* March–April 1967, p. 49.
3   *The New York Times*, November 21, 1966.
4   New York, Grossman Publishers, Inc., 1965.
5   New York, David McKay Company, Inc., 1967.

These are merely dramatic instances of a prevailing condition; there is hardly a major industry at which a similar attack could not be aimed. Critics of business regard such behavior as unethical, but the companies concerned know that they are merely playing the business game.

Among the most respected of our business institutions are the insurance companies. A group of insurance executives meeting recently in New England was startled when their guest speaker, social critic Daniel Patrick Moynihan, roundly berated them for "unethical" practices. They had been guilty, Moynihan alleged, of using outdated actuarial tables to obtain unfairly high premiums. They habitually delayed the hearings of lawsuits against them in order to tire out the plaintiffs and win cheap settlements. In their employment policies they used ingenious devices to discriminate against certain minority groups.[6]

It was difficult for the audience to deny the validity of these charges. But these men were business game players. Their reaction to Moynihan's attack was much the same as that of the automobile manufacturers to Nader, of the utilities to Senator Metcalf, and of the food processors to Senator Hart. If the laws governing their businesses change, or if public opinion becomes clamorous, they will make the necessary adjustments. But morally they have in their view done nothing wrong. As long as they comply with the letter of the law, they are within their rights to operate their businesses as they see fit.

The small business is in the same position as the great corporation in this respect. For example:

> In 1967 a key manufacturer was accused of providing master keys for
> automobiles to mail-order customers, although it was obvious that some
> of the purchasers might be automobile thieves. His defense was plain and
> straightforward. If there was nothing in the law to prevent him from selling
> his keys to anyone who ordered them, it was not up to him to inquire as
> to his customers' motives. Why was it any worse, he insisted, for him to sell
> car keys by mail, than for mail-order houses to sell guns that might be used
> for murder? Until the law was changed, the key manufacturer could regard
> himself as being just as ethical as any other businessman by the rules of the
> business game.[7]

Violations of the ethical ideals of society are common in business, but they are not necessarily violations of business principles. Each year the Federal Trade Commission orders hundreds of companies, many of them of the first magnitude,

---

6   *The New York Times*, January 17, 1967.
7   Cited by Ralph Nader in "Business Crime," *The New Republic*, July 1, 1967, p. 7.

to "cease and desist" from practices which, judged by ordinary standards, are of questionable morality but which are stoutly defended by the companies concerned.

In one case, a firm manufacturing a well-known mouthwash was accused of using a cheap form of alcohol possibly deleterious to health. The company's chief executive, after testifying in Washington, made this comment privately:

> We broke no law. We're in a highly competitive industry. If we're going to stay in business, we have to look for profit wherever the law permits. We don't make the laws. We obey them. Then why do we have to put up with this "holier than thou" talk about ethics? It's sheer hypocrisy. We're not in business to promote ethics. Look at the cigarette companies, for God's sake! If the ethics aren't embodied in the laws by the men who made them, you can't expect businessmen to fill the lack. Why, a sudden submission to Christian ethics by businessmen would bring about the greatest economic upheaval in history!

It may be noted that the government failed to prove its case against him.

Cast Illusions Aside

Talk about ethics by businessmen is often a thin decorative coating over the hard realities of the game:

> Once I listened to a speech by a young executive who pointed to a new industry code as proof that his company and its competitors were deeply aware of their responsibilities to society. It was a code of ethics, he said. The industry was going to police itself, to dissuade constituent companies from wrongdoing. His eyes shone with conviction and enthusiasm.

> The same day there was a meeting in a hotel room where the industry's top executives met with the "czar" who was to administer the new code, a man of high repute. No one who was present could doubt their common attitude. In their eyes the code was designed primarily to forestall a move by the federal government to impose stern restrictions on the industry. They felt that the code would hamper them a good deal less than new federal laws would. It was, in other words, conceived as a protection for the industry, not for the public.

> The young executive accepted the surface explanation of the code; these leaders, all experienced game players, did not deceive themselves for a moment about its purpose.

The illusion that business can afford to be guided by ethics as conceived in private life is often fostered by speeches and articles containing such phrases as, "It pays to be ethical," or, "Sound ethics is good business." Actually this is not an ethical position at all; it is a self-serving calculation in disguise. The speaker is really saying that in the long run a company can make more money if it does not antagonize competitors, suppliers, employees, and customers by squeezing them too hard. He is saying that oversharp policies reduce ultimate gains. That is true, but it has nothing to do with ethics. The underlying attitude is much like that in the familiar story of the shopkeeper who finds an extra $20 bill in the cash register, debates with himself the ethical problem—should he tell his partner?—and finally decides to share the money because the gesture will give him an edge over the s.o.b. the next time they quarrel.

I think it is fair to sum up the prevailing attitude of businessmen on ethics as follows:

> We live in what is probably the most competitive of the world's civilized societies. Our customs encourage a high degree of aggression in the individual's striving for success. Business is our main area of competition, and it has been ritualized into a game of strategy. The basic rules of the game have been set by the government, which attempts to detect and punish business frauds. But as long as a company does not transgress the rules of the game set by law, it has the legal right to shape its strategy without reference to anything but its profits. If it takes a long-term view of its profits, it will preserve amicable relations, so far as possible, with those with whom it deals. A wise businessman will not seek advantage to the point where he generates dangerous hostility among employees, competitors, customers, government, or the public at large. But decisions in this area are, in the final test, decisions of strategy, not of ethics.

The Individual & the Game

An individual within a company often finds it difficult to adjust to the requirements of the business game. He tries to preserve his private ethical standards in situations that call for game strategy. When he is obliged to carry out company policies that challenge his conception of himself as an ethical man, he suffers.

It disturbs him when he is ordered, for instance, to deny a raise to a man who deserves it, to fire an employee of long standing, to prepare advertising that he believes to be misleading, to conceal facts that he feels customers are entitled to know, to cheapen the quality of materials used in the manufacture of an established

product, to sell as new a product that he knows to be rebuilt, to exaggerate the cura-
tive powers of a medicinal preparation, or to coerce dealers.

There are some fortunate executives who, by the nature of their work and circumstances, never have to face problems of this kind. But in one form or another the
ethical dilemma is felt sooner or later by most businessmen. Possibly the dilemma is
most painful not when the company forces the action on the executive but when he
originates it himself—that is, when he has taken or is contemplating a step which is in
his own interest but which runs counter to his early moral conditioning. To illustrate:

- The manager of an export department, eager to show rising sales, is
  pressed by a big customer to provide invoices which, while containing
  no overt falsehood that would violate a U.S. law, are so worded that the
  customer may be able to evade certain taxes in his homeland.

- A company president finds that an aging executive, within a few years of
  retirement and his pension, is not as productive as formerly. Should he be
  kept on?

- The produce manager of a supermarket debates with himself whether to
  get rid of a lot of half-rotten tomatoes by including one, with its good side
  exposed, in every tomato six-pack.

- An accountant discovers that he has taken an improper deduction on his
  company's tax return and fears the consequences if he calls the matter
  to the president's attention, though he himself has done nothing illegal.
  Perhaps if he says nothing, no one will notice the error.

- A chief executive officer is asked by his directors to comment on a rumor
  that he owns stock in another company with which he has placed large
  orders. He could deny it, for the stock is in the name of his son-in-law and
  he has earlier formally instructed his son-in-law to sell the holding.

Temptations of this kind constantly arise in business. If an executive allows
himself to be torn between a decision based on business considerations and one
based on his private ethical code, he exposes himself to a grave psychological strain.

This is not to say that sound business strategy necessarily runs counter to ethical
ideals. They may frequently coincide; and when they do, everyone is gratified. But
the major tests of every move in business, as in all games of strategy, are legality and
profit. A man who intends to be a winner in the business game must have a game
player's attitude.

The business strategist's decisions must be as impersonal as those of a surgeon performing an operation—concentrating on objective and technique, and subordinating personal feelings. If the chief executive admits that his son-in-law owns the stock, it is because he stands to lose more if the fact comes out later than if he states it boldly and at once. If the supermarket manager orders the rotten tomatoes to be discarded, he does so to avoid an increase in consumer complaints and a loss of goodwill. The company president decides not to fire the elderly executive in the belief that the negative reaction of other employees would in the long run cost the company more than it would lose in keeping him and paying his pension.

All sensible businessmen prefer to be truthful, but they seldom feel inclined to tell the *whole* truth. In the business game truth-telling usually has to be kept within narrow limits if trouble is to be avoided. The point was neatly made a long time ago (in 1888) by one of John D. Rockefeller's associates, Paul Babcock, to Standard Oil Company executives who were about to testify before a government investigating committee: "Parry every question with answers which, while perfectly truthful, are evasive of *bottom* facts."[8] This was, is, and probably always will be regarded as wise and permissible business strategy.

For Office Use Only

An executive's family life can easily be dislocated if he fails to make a sharp distinction between the ethical systems of the home and the office—or if his wife does not grasp that distinction. Many a businessman who has remarked to his wife, "I had to let Jones go today" or "I had to admit to the boss that Jim has been goofing off lately," has been met with an indignant protest. "How could you do a thing like that? You know Jones is over 50 and will have a lot of trouble getting another job." Or, "You did that to Jim? With his wife ill and all the worry she's been having with the kids?"

If the executive insists that he had no choice because the profits of the company and his own security were involved, he may see a certain cool and ominous reappraisal in his wife's eyes. Many wives are not prepared to accept the fact that business operates with a special code of ethics. An illuminating illustration of this comes from a Southern sales executive who related a conversation he had had with his wife at a time when a hotly contested political campaign was being waged in their state:

> I made the mistake of telling her that I had had lunch with Colby, who gives me about half my business. Colby mentioned that his company had a

---

8   Babcock in a memorandum to Rockefeller (Rockefeller Archives).

stake in the election. Then he said, "By the way, I'm treasurer of the citizens' committee for Lang. I'm collecting contributions. Can I count on you for a hundred dollars?"

Well, there I was. I was opposed to Lang, but I knew Colby. If he withdrew his business I could be in a bad spot. So I just smiled and wrote out a check then and there. He thanked me, and we started to talk about his next order. Maybe he thought I shared his political views. If so, I wasn't going to lose any sleep over it.

I should have had sense enough not to tell Mary about it. She hit the ceiling. She said she was disappointed in me. She said I hadn't acted like a man, that I should have stood up to Colby.

I said, "Look, it was an either-or situation. I had to do it or risk losing the business."

She came back at me with, "I don't believe it. You could have been honest with him. You could have said that you didn't feel you ought to contribute to a campaign for a man you weren't going to vote for. I'm sure he would have understood."

I said, "Mary, you're a wonderful woman, but you're way off the track. Do you know what would have happened if I had said that? Colby would have smiled and said, 'Oh, I didn't realize. Forget it.' But in his eyes from that moment I would be an oddball, maybe a bit of a radical. He would have listened to me talk about his order and would have promised to give it consideration. After that I wouldn't hear from him for a week. Then I would telephone and learn from his secretary that he wasn't yet ready to place the order. And in about a month I would hear through the grapevine that he was giving his business to another company. A month after that I'd be out of a job."

She was silent for a while. Then she said, "Tom, something is wrong with business when a man is forced to choose between his family's security and his moral obligation to himself. It's easy for me to say you should have stood up to him—but if you had, you might have felt you were betraying me and the kids. I'm sorry that you did it, Tom, but I can't blame you. Something is wrong with business!"

This wife saw the problem in terms of moral obligation as conceived in private life; her husband saw it as a matter of game strategy. As a player in a weak position, he felt that he could not afford to indulge an ethical sentiment that might have cost him his seat at the table.

Playing to Win

Some men might challenge the Colbys of business—might accept serious setbacks to their business careers rather than risk a feeling of moral cowardice. They merit our respect—but as private individuals, not businessmen. When the skillful player of the business game is compelled to submit to unfair pressure, he does not castigate himself for moral weakness. Instead, he strives to put himself into a strong position where he can defend himself against such pressures in the future without loss.

If a man plans to take a seat in the business game, he owes it to himself to master the principles by which the game is played, including its special ethical outlook. He can then hardly fail to recognize that an occasional bluff may well be justified in terms of the game's ethics and warranted in terms of economic necessity. Once he clears his mind on this point, he is in a good position to match his strategy against that of the other players. He can then determine objectively whether a bluff in a given situation has a good chance of succeeding and can decide when and how to bluff, without a feeling of ethical transgression.

To be a winner, a man must play to win. This does not mean that he must be ruthless, cruel, harsh, or treacherous. On the contrary, the better his reputation for integrity, honesty, and decency, the better his chances of victory will be in the long run. But from time to time every businessman, like every poker player, is offered a choice between certain loss or bluffing within the legal rules of the game. If he is not resigned to losing, if he wants to rise in his company and industry, then in such a crisis he will bluff—and bluff hard.

Every now and then one meets a successful businessman who has conveniently forgotten the small or large deceptions that he practiced on his way to fortune. "God gave me my money," old John D. Rockefeller once piously told a Sunday school class. It would be a rare tycoon in our time who would risk the horse laugh with which such a remark would be greeted.

In the last third of the twentieth century even children are aware that if a man has become prosperous in business, he has sometimes departed from the strict truth in order to overcome obstacles or has practiced the more subtle deceptions of the half-truth or the misleading omission. Whatever the form of the bluff, it is an integral part of the game, and the executive who does not master its techniques is not likely to accumulate much money or power.

Questions

1. What is the poker analogy of business ethics?

2. Is it ever justifiable to bluff about the relative health of one's company?

3. Do all people in business assume they are engaging in a kind of game?

4. If it was explicitly stated that deception could be assumed in any negotiation that was about to take place, could negotiations proceed?

5. What are some of the objections that could be raised against Carr's view of business?

Further Reading

Beach, John. "Bluffing: Its Demise as a Subject Unto Itself." *Journal Of Business Ethics*, vol. 4, 1 June 1985, pp. 191–96.

Globerman, Steven. "The Social Responsibility of Managers: Reassessing and Integrating Diverse Perspectives." *Business and Society Review: Journal of the Center for Business Ethics at Bentley College*, vol. 116, no. 4, 2011, pp. 509–32.

Van Wyk, Robert N. "When Is Lying Morally Permissible? Casuistical Reflections on the Game Analogy, Self-Defense, Social Contract Ethics." *Journal of Value Inquiry*, vol. 24, no. 2, 1 April 1990, pp. 155–68.

14.
"THE BUSINESS OF ETHICS"

NORMAN CHASE GILLESPIE

About This Reading

Is business a game? While Albert Carr argues that it is—drawing an analogy between business and poker—Norman Gillespie disagrees. While Carr does make a compelling argument for viewing business as a game of poker, Gillespie notes that Carr has left out of his analysis several important ways in which this analogy is inappropriate.

Carr's analysis of business as a game of poker views it from the perspective of the players and the strategies they employ. Assuming everyone understands that they are participants in a game, then deception, bluffing, putting on a bold front, and understanding the psychology of the other players are all legitimate tactics. But, as Gillespie notes, these are not the only aspects of a game. There are also the elements that are taken for granted. For example, when one plays poker, it is generally only the player's money that is at stake. If she loses a hand, the loss is wholly hers. Yet this is not the case with those doing business. An owner or CEO not only risks his or her own well-being, but also that of those who don't have a seat at the table. Investors, managers, line workers, maintenance workers, and receptionists all have a stake in the company. Consequently, a bad night of business-poker can result in harm to a number of non-players.

In addition to questioning the strength of the poker analogy, Gillespie also questions the assumptions underlying this approach to business ethics. Is it really the case that if something is not illegal, then it is morally acceptable? Do businesses have to take advantage of legal opportunities since others may? Does the fact that a practice is widespread entail that it is morally acceptable? By raising these issues, Gillespie questions the moral force of the poker-analogy approach to business ethics.

It is the business of ethics to tell us what are our duties, or by what test we may know them.—John Stuart Mill, *Utilitarianism*

The public image of business does not always inspire public confidence, since it is often assumed that talk of ethics in business is only talk, not something that makes a difference in practice. Business executives are pragmatic individuals, accustomed to dealing with their environment as they find it and not inclined to question how things ought to be. That frame of mind reinforces the public image of business as impervious to moral imperatives.

That image is often only confirmed in the press, for instance, by such articles as those of Albert Carr, which embrace the purest kind of moral conventionalism: That which is generally done in business sets the standard of ethical conduct, so that an executive acts ethically as long as he or she conforms to the general practice. Carr goes so far as to maintain that misrepresentation in business is as ethical as bluffing in poker, and that only needless concern and anxiety will result from applying the ordinary moral standards of society to the conduct of business.[1] On this score, I believe Carr is completely mistaken.

This paper will argue that ordinary moral standards do apply to business decisions and practices and will explain *how* they apply. This should result in a clearer picture of the relationship between business and ethics—what it is now and what it ought to be. Carr, in setting forth the conventionalist position, argues:

(1) Business, like poker, is a form of competition.

(2) In this competition, the rules are different from what they are in ordinary social dealings.

(3) Anyone who abides by ordinary moral standards instead of the rules of business is placed at a decided disadvantage. Therefore,

(4) It is not unethical or immoral to abide by the current rules of business. (These rules are determined in part by what is generally done in business and in part by legal statutes governing business activities.)

In support of this position, three reasons might be offered:

(1) If a business practice is not illegal, it is thereby ethically acceptable.

---

1   Albert Carr advocates conventionalism in *Business as a Game* (New York, 1968); "Is Business Bluffing Ethical?" *Harvard Business Review* (January-February, 1968) pp. 143–53; and reiterates it in "Can an Executive Afford a Conscience?" *Harvard Business Review* (July-August, 1970), pp. 58–64. In defending himself against the criticism that he is condoning unethical behavior, Carr insists that an executive who acts according to prevailing business practices "is guilty of nothing more than conformity; he is merely playing the game according to the rules." "Showdown on Business Bluffing," *Harvard Business Review* (May-June, 1968), p. 169.

(2) If a businessman does not take advantage of a legal opportunity, others will surely do so.

(3) If a practice is so widespread as to constitute the norm, everyone expects conformity.

The claim that it is ethically correct to do something because it is not illegal is, of course, one of the conventionalist's weakest arguments, since it should be obvious that legality does not establish morality—it may not be illegal for a teacher to favor some students over others for nonacademic reasons, yet it is clearly unethical. When one speaks of ethics in business, it is to establish what business practices ought to be. The law, as written, does not settle that issue. The other two reasons, however, may appear to have some merit and require more detailed analysis.

Business as a Game

Suppose that such things as industrial espionage, deception of customers, and shading the truth in published financial statements are common enough to be of broad concern, in effect comprising some de facto state of business affairs. What bearing would such a state have upon what is moral or ethical in conducting business? Would the existence of such "rules of the game" relieve owners, managers, and employees of otherwise appropriate ethical obligations? Or, would such behavior merely be a matter of business strategy and not a matter *of* ethics?

The obvious fallacy in the "business-as-a-game" idea is that, unlike poker, business is not a game. People's lives, their well-being, their plans, and their futures often depend upon business and the way it is conducted. Indeed, people usually exchange part of their lives (i.e., the portion spent earning money) for certain goods and services. They have the right not to be misled or deceived about the true nature of those goods or services. Similarly, elected officials have a duty to legislate and act for the good of their country (or state). It can hardly be right for business executives to frustrate them in the performance of that duty by providing them with evasive answers or by concealing relevant facts.

The Price of Duty

So, the poker analogy, while informative of the way things are, seems to have no bearing at all on the way they *ought* to be in business. Why, then, do so many people adopt the conventionalist position that "business is business and, when in business, do as the others do"? Some take that position for essentially the same reason Yossarian offers to justify his conduct in the novel *Catch 22*. (Yossarian has refused to fly any more combat missions and when asked, "But suppose everybody on our side felt that way?" he replies, "Then I'd be a damn fool to feel any other way. Wouldn't!?")[2] If everyone were refusing to fly, Yossarian says, he would be a fool to fly. In business, the position would be: If everyone is bluffing, an individual would be a fool not to do the same. On this point, Yossarian and the conventionalist are correct, but not because there are special rules (or special ethics) for airplane gunners and people in business. The reason, instead, is that our ordinary moral reasoning does, indeed, make allowance for just such cases. In other words, the idea that there is something ethically distinctive about a situation in which a person in business may find himself or herself is sound. But it is sound because ordinary moral reasoning allows for such circumstances, not because there are special ethical rules for people in business comparable to the rules of poker. The sort of considerations I have in mind all involve the *cost* of doing what would normally be one's duty. There are at least three ways in which a normal or ordinary duty may cease to be so because the cost is too high. The first of these is widely recognized: Sometimes the *moral cost* of obeying a standard moral rule is too great, so one must make an exception to that rule. If the only way to save someone's life is by telling a lie, then one should normally lie. If treating an accident victim involves breaking a promise to meet someone on time, then one should normally be late. In a variety of circumstances obeying a moral rule might require breaking some other, more urgent, moral duty. In these circumstances, the more urgent duty dictates an exception to the lesser rule. The second way in which an ordinary duty may cease to be a duty is when the *cost to the individual* of fulfilling that duty is too high. For example, when driving an automobile, one normally has the duty not to run into other cars, and one also has the general duty not to harm or injure other persons. But suppose one is driving down a steep mountain road and the brakes fail. One might have a choice among three options: cross into the oncoming lane of traffic, go off the cliff on one's right, or drive into the car in front. In such a case, a driver would not act wrongly by choosing the third option, even though there is a way in which the duty of not injuring others and not driving into other people's cars can be met, namely, by going off the cliff. In these circumstances, the cost to the individual of meeting the duty is simply too high, and virtually no one would blame the driver or condemn the action as morally wrong if he or she drove into the back of the car ahead rather than going off the cliff. The third way in which a normal duty may turn out not to be a duty is the kind of situation described by Yossarian. If everyone else is not doing what ought to be done, then one would be a fool to act differently. This third consideration does not obviate all duties, for example, just because everyone else is committing murder does not make it right

---

2   Joseph Heller, *Catch 22* (New York, Dell, 1961), chapter 9.

for you to do so, but it does apply to those cases in which the *morally desirable state of affairs can be produced only by everyone, or virtually everyone, doing his or her part.* With respect to such a duty, for example, jury duty, one person alone cannot accomplish anything; one can only be placed at a disadvantage vis-à-vis everyone else by doing what everyone ought to do but is not doing. This sort of situation can be described as a "state of nature situation,"[3] and by that I mean a situation in which certain moral rules are generally disobeyed either by everyone or by the members of a well-defined group.

In dealing with such situations, the fact that other people can be expected to act in certain ways is morally relevant in that it creates a special sort of moral dilemma. If one does what everyone ought to do but is not doing, then one will, in all likelihood, be at a disadvantage. The morally questionable behavior of others creates the circumstances in which one finds oneself and in those circumstances it may be necessary to fight fire with fire and resist deception with deception. But replying in kind only prolongs the state of nature situation, so one's primary goal should be to attempt to change the situation. No one ought to take unfair advantage of others, but no one is obligated to let others take unfair advantage of him or her. It is absolutely essential to note, in connection with such situations, that people are not doing what they ought to be doing. The conventionalist recognizes that simple application of ordinary moral rules to such situations is inadequate. But it is a mistake to conclude (1) that ordinary rules do not apply *at all* to such cases, and (2) that business has its own distinctive set of rules that determines one's duties in such circumstances. Both points are incorrect because (1) the ordinary rules help define the situation as one in which people are not doing what they ought to be doing (we apply the ordinary moral rules to such cases and find that they are not being generally observed), and (2) the considerations that are relevant in determining one's duties in such circumstances do not constitute a special set of factors that are relevant only in business. The mitigating considerations apply generally and are an important part of ordinary moral reasoning.

When virtually everyone is not doing what ought to be done, it affects what we can morally expect of any one individual. That person does not have a duty to "buck the tide" if doing so will cause the individual substantial harm or not do any good. But, in conjunction with everyone else, the person *ought to be* acting differently. So the tension one may feel between what one does and what one ought to do is quite real and entirely appropriate.

In the conventionalist argument, these two considerations—the cost to the individual and what everyone else is doing—recur again and again: It is right to lie about one's age and one's magazine preferences when doing otherwise will prevent you from

---

3   Marcus A. Singer uses this term in *Generalization in Ethics* (New York: Knopf, 1961), pp. 153, 156–57.

getting a job; right to engage in industrial espionage because everyone else is doing it; right to sell a popular mouthwash with a possibly deleterious form of alcohol in it because cigarettes are sold to the public; and right to sell master automobile keys through the mails (to potential criminals) because guns are sold.[4]

Of these four examples, the last two seem to me to be clearly wrong since neither the high cost to the individual of doing otherwise nor the existence of a general practice has been established. Industrial espionage, however, is a good illustration of a "state of nature situation," and if (1) one does it to others who are doing the same, and (2) it is necessary to "fight fire with fire," for the sake of survival, then it would not be morally wrong. For the job applicant, the conditions themselves are morally dubious, so here, too, it may be a case of fighting fire with fire for the sake of personal survival. But notice, in each of these examples, how distasteful the action in question is; most of us would prefer not to engage in such activities. The point is that conditions may be such that the cost of not engaging in them may be so great that an individual caught in such circumstances is blameless. At the same time, however, we do feel that *the circumstances* should be different.

The second consideration, distinct from the cost to the individual, is that one person doing what everyone ought to do (but is not doing) will accomplish nothing. This can be the case even where the individual cost is insignificant. To take a homely example, suppose there were a well-defined path across the local courthouse lawn as the result of shortcuts taken across it. It would not cost anyone very much to walk around instead of across the lawn, but if one knows his fellow citizens and knows that the path is there to stay, then walking around will accomplish nothing. So one may as well take the path unless, of course, one decides to set an example of how others ought to be acting. Since it costs so little, it might well be a good idea to set such an example. This would be one small way at least of trying to change the situation.

Although one's primary goal ought to be to change the situation, that statement, like all claims about what one ought to do, is subject to the moral precept that individuals have a duty to do only what they can do. So, if it is impossible for one individual to change the situation, that person does not have a duty to change it. What is true is that the situation ought to be different, but to make it so may require the combined efforts of many people. All of them collectively have the duty to change it, so this is not a duty that falls solely or directly on the shoulders of any one person. For the individual executive, then, the question is primarily one of what he or she in conjunction with others can accomplish. Secondarily, it is a question of the likely personal cost to the executive of instituting or proposing needed changes.

---

4   Examples from Carr's "Is Business Bluffing Ethical?" pp. 144, 146, 148.

A Role for the Individual Executive

At the very least, executives should not *thwart* the impetus for change on the ground that business sets its own ethical standards. Everyone has a legitimate interest in the way business is run, and Better Business Bureaus and legislative inquiries should be viewed as important instruments serving that interest. We know on the basis of ordinary moral rules that in certain business environments a new way of acting is a desirable goal. If no one else will join in the promotion of that goal, then the individual executive can, as the poet said, "only stand and wait." But according to that same poet, John Milton, "They also serve who only stand and wait."

The essential difference between the conventionalist position and ordinary moral reasoning comes out most clearly in the following example, provided by Carr in defense of his position. A businessman, Tom, is asked by an important customer in the middle of a sales talk to contribute to the election campaign of a candidate Tom does not support. He does so, and the talk continues with enthusiasm. Later, Tom mentions his action to his wife, Mary, and she is furious. They discuss the situation and the conversation concludes with her saying, "Tom, something is wrong with business when a man is forced to choose between his family's security and his moral obligation.... It's easy for me to say you should have stood up to him—but if you had, you might have felt you were betraying me and the kids. I'm sorry you did it, Tom, but I can't blame you. Something is wrong with business."

Carr comments that, "This wife saw the problem in terms of moral obligation as conceived in private life; her husband saw it as a matter of game strategy." Those who would refuse to make the contribution "merit our respect—but as private individuals, not businessmen."[5]

What Tom did was not morally wrong in those circumstances, but not for the reasons cited in Carr's paper. There is something wrong with *the situation* in which Tom found himself. It *ought not be the case* that one has to choose between one's family and being honest about one's political preferences. Carr fails to recognize this and either misses or ignores entirely the fact that Mary makes precisely this point: She does not blame her husband or say that he did the wrong thing in those circumstances; what she says, instead, is that *something* is *wrong with business* when a person has to act as her husband did. It is business and the way it is conducted that ought to be changed. The conventionalist position simply blocks out such an issue: It nowhere considers how business ought to be. It merely says that "the way it is" is all that need be taken into account in deciding what would be ethical.

An analogous situation exists in connection with the financing of political campaigns. No one blames candidates for taking contributions from lobbyists and other

---

5   Ibid., pp. 152–53.

individuals since they need the money to run for office. But many people do think that the system ought to be changed. In other words, the current practices are not as honest or ethical as they ought to be. Now, how can the conventionalist handle such a claim? It seems obvious that he cannot, since he systematically rules out applying ordinary moral standards to business practices. But the correct position is that these standards do apply, and sometimes we find they are not being put into practice. In precisely those cases, the general practice ought to change.

The Need for Change

There is a most important difference, then, between asking "What are the individual duties of a person doing business?" and "What are the ways in which business ought to be conducted?" Both are an essential part of the ethics of business but the conventionalist simply ignores the second question in attempting to answer the first. The answers to the second question can be found, for the most part, by consulting our ordinary moral standards of how people ought to act vis-à-vis one another. When we find that business is not as moral as we would like it to be, that *does* have some bearing upon the answer to the first question. But, as I have argued in this paper, ordinary moral reasoning is prepared to take those facts into account. It is not at all necessary to postulate a special ethical outlook or a distinctive set of ethical rules for business in order to explain the ethical relevance of such phenomena to the individual businessman.

Ordinary moral reasoning, then, is far richer than mere conventionalism, and the factors it takes into account are relevant in many managerial and executive decisions. Ethics can be subtle, as well as realistic, and conventionalism is unrealistic when it obscures the moral imperative for change.

Questions

1. Why does Gillespie disagree with the idea that if everyone is acting as if business is a game, this means that everyone should act in that way?

2. In what ways does the gambling done by a businessperson differ from the gambling done in a game of poker?

3. In what ways is the poker analogy an inappropriate model of business ethics?

4. Describe a situation in which Gillespie thinks we might be exempt from behaving morally.

Further Reading

Gichure, Christine Wanjiru. "A Different Kind of Capital: Qualities That Add Value to the Ends of Business and Leadership (Review of Alejo José G. Sison's *The Moral Capital of Leaders: Why Virtue Matters*)." *Business Ethics Quarterly*, vol. 16, no. 1, 1 Jan. 2006, pp. 95–102.

Koehn, Daryl. "Business and Game-Playing: The False Analogy." *Journal of Business Ethics*, vol. 16, nos. 12–13, 1 Sept. 1997, pp. 1447–52.

Sullivan, Roger J. "A Response to 'Is Business Bluffing Ethical'." *Business and Professional Ethics Journal*, vol. 3, 1 Dec. 1984, pp. 1–18.

Varelius, Jukka. "Allhoff on Business Bluffing." *Journal of Business Ethics*, vol. 65, no. 2, 1 May 2006, pp. 163–71.

15.
"CORPORATE MORAL AGENCY"

PETER A. FRENCH[1]

About This Reading

The idea of corporations as persons dates back to the early 1800s. The United States Constitution does not mention corporations, and consequently the nature of these institutions has developed through a series Supreme Court rulings. This change began with the 1844 ruling in *Louisville, Cincinnati, and Charleston Railroad v. Letson*, which held that corporations were "citizens" of the states where they were incorporated. While this ruling expanded corporate power within states, it was still difficult for corporations to sue or be sued in federal court unless all its shareholders resided in that state. In 1853 the *Marshall v. Baltimore and Ohio Railroad* decision extended Letson, when it held that for the purposes of law, shareholders would be considered citizens of the company's home state. This made it easier for a corporation to sue or be sued in federal court.

It was not until the 1886 decision in *County of Santa Clara v. Southern Pacific Railroad* that we see the beginnings of corporate "personhood." In the Santa Clara case, the court ruled that the 14th Amendment to the Constitution applied to corporations. Given that the amendment states that no State shall "deprive any *person* of life, liberty, or property, without due process of law; nor deny to any *person* within its jurisdiction the equal protection of the laws" [emphasis added], later courts would appeal to the idea of corporations as persons by citing this case.

The Supreme Court rulings from 1886 to the present have continued to expand the rights of the corporate person. These rulings would attribute to corporations the right to protection from unlawful search and seizure, due process, double jeopardy, freedom of speech, and even freedom of religion.

---

1   Peter A. French runs the Lincoln Center for Applied Ethics and teaches philosophy at Arizona State University.

The recognition that corporations are persons by the legal system raises several philosophical and ethical questions. To say that someone has a right to freedom of speech or freedom of religion implies that the person can have beliefs he or she wants to exercise or ideas he or she wishes to express. In other words, right holders can have *intentions*, that is, they can form ideas or beliefs and then be determined to act in certain ways. While this seems obvious when talking about people, how can a corporation *intend* anything? Do corporations have beliefs? Unlike many who view corporations as merely legal fictions, Peter French argues that corporations can in fact have intentions, and if they can have intentions, then they should be accorded moral personhood.

1

In one of his *New York Times* columns of not too long ago Tom Wicker's ire was aroused by a Gulf Oil Corporation advertisement that "pointed the finger of blame" for the energy crisis at all elements of our society (and supposedly away from the oil company). Wicker attacked Gulf Oil as the major, if not the sole, perpetrator of that crisis and virtually every other social ill, with the possible exception of venereal disease. I do not know if Wicker was serious or sarcastic in making all of his charges; I have a sinking suspicion that he was in deadly earnest, but I have doubts as to whether Wicker understands or if many people understand what sense such ascriptions of moral responsibility make when their subjects are corporations. My interest is to argue for a theory that accepts corporations as members of the moral community, of equal standing with the traditionally acknowledged residents—biological human beings—and hence treats Wicker-type responsibility ascriptions as unexceptionable instances of a perfectly proper sort without having to paraphrase them. In short, I shall argue that corporations should be treated as full-fledged moral persons and hence that they can have whatever privileges, rights, and duties as are, in the normal course of affairs, accorded to moral persons.

2

There are at least two significantly different types of responsibility ascriptions that I want to distinguish in ordinary usage (not counting the laudatory recommendation, "He is a responsible lad"). The first type pins responsibility on someone or something, the who-dun-it or what-dun-it sense. Austin has pointed out that it is usually used when an event or action is thought by the speaker to be untoward. (Perhaps we are more interested in the failures rather than the successes that punctuate our lives.)

The second type of responsibility ascription, parasitic upon the first, involves the notion of accountability. "Having a responsibility" is interwoven with the notion "Having a liability to answer," and having such a liability or obligation seems to imply (as Anscombe has noted) the existence of some sort of authority relationship either between people, or between people and a deity, or in some weaker versions between people and social norms. The kernel of insight that I find intuitively compelling is that for someone to legitimately hold someone else responsible for some event, there must exist or have existed a responsibility relationship between them such that in regard to the event in question the latter was answerable to the former. In other words, a responsibility ascription of the second type is properly uttered by someone Z if he or she can hold X accountable for what he or she has done. Responsibility relationships are created in a multitude of ways, e.g., through promises, contracts, compacts, hirings, assignments, appointments, by agreeing to enter a Rawlsian original position, etc. The "right" to hold responsible is often delegated to third parties; but importantly, in the case of moral responsibility, no delegation occurs because no person is excluded from the relationship: moral responsibility relationships hold reciprocally and without prior agreements among all moral persons. No special arrangement needs to be established between parties for anyone to hold someone morally responsible for his or her acts or, what amounts to the same thing, every person is a party to a responsibility relationship with all other persons as regards the doing or refraining from doing of certain acts: those that take descriptions that use moral notions.

Because our interest is in the criteria of moral personhood and not the content or morality, we need not pursue this idea further. What I have maintained is that moral responsibility, although it is neither contractual nor optional, is not a class apart but an extension of ordinary, garden-variety responsibility. What is needed in regard to the present subject, then, is an account of the requirements in *any* responsibility relationship.

3

A responsibility ascription of the second type amounts to the assertion that the person held responsible is the cause of an event (usually an untoward one) and that the action in question was intended by the subject or that the event was the direct result of an intentional act of the subject. In addition to what it asserts, it implies that the subject is liable to account to the speaker (who the speaker is or what the speaker is, a member of the "moral community," a surrogate for that aggregate). The primary focus of responsibility ascriptions of the second type is on the subject's intentions rather than, though not to the exclusion of, occasions.

4

For a corporation to be treated as a responsible agent it must be the case that some things that happen, some events, are describable in a way that makes certain sentences true, sentences that say that some of the things a corporation does were intended by the corporation itself. That is not accomplished if attributing intentions to a corporation is only a shorthand way of attributing intentions to the biological persons who comprise, for example, its board of directors. If that were to turn out to be the case, then on metaphysical if not logical grounds there would be no way to distinguish between corporations and mobs. I shall argue, however, that a corporation's CID Structure (the Corporate Internal Decision Structure) is the requisite redescription device that licenses the predication of corporate intentionality.

It is obvious that a corporation's doing something involves or includes human beings' doing things and that the human beings who occupy various positions in a corporation usually can be described as having reasons for *their* behavior. In virtue of those descriptions they may be properly held responsible for their behavior, *ceteris paribus*. What needs to be shown is that there is sense in saying that corporations and not just the people who work in them, have reasons for doing what they do. Typically, we will be told that it is the directors, or the managers, etc. that really have the corporate reasons and desires, etc., and that although corporate actions may not be reducible without remainder, corporate intentions are always reducible to human intentions.

5

Every corporation must have an internal decision structure. The CID Structure has two elements of interest to us here: (1) an organizational or responsibility flow chart that delineates stations and levels within the corporate power structure and (2) corporate decision recognition rule(s) (usually embedded in something called "corporate policy"). The CID Structure is the personnel organization for the exercise of the corporation's power with respect to its ventures, and as such its primary function is to draw experience from various levels of the corporation into a decision-making and ratification process. When operative and properly activated, the CID Structure accomplishes a subordination and synthesis of the intentions and acts of various biological persons into a corporate decision. When viewed in another way the CID Structure licenses the descriptive transformation of events seen under another aspect as the acts of biological persons (those who occupy various stations on the organizational chart) as corporate acts by exposing the corporate character of those events. A functioning CID Structure *incorporates* acts of biological persons. For illustrative purposes, suppose we imagine that an event E has at least two aspects, that is, can be described in two nonidentical ways. One of those aspects is "Executive X's doing y" and one is "Corporation C's doing z." The corporate act and the individual act may have different properties: indeed they have different causal ancestors though they are causally inseparable.

Although I doubt he is aware of the metaphysical reading that can be given to this process, J.K. Galbraith rather neatly captures what I have in mind when he writes in his recent popular book on the history of economics:

> From [the] interpersonal exercise of power, the interaction ... of the participants, comes the *personality* of the corporation.[2]

I take Galbraith here to be quite literally correct, but it is important to spell out how a CID Structure works this "miracle."

In philosophy in recent years we have grown accustomed to the use of games as models for understanding institutional behavior. We all have some understanding of how rules of games make certain descriptions of events possible that would not be so if those rules were nonexistent. The CID Structure of a corporation is a kind of constitutive rule (or rules) analogous to the game rules with which we are familiar. The organization chart of, for example, the Burlington Northern Corporation distinguishes "players" and clarifies their rank and the interwoven lines of responsibility within the corporation. The Burlington chart lists only titles, not unlike King, Queen, Rook, etc. in chess. What it tells us is that anyone holding the title "Executive Vice President for Finance and Administration" stands in a certain relationship to anyone holding the title "Director of Internal Audit" and to anyone holding the title "Treasurer," etc. Also it expresses, or maps, the interdependent and dependent relationships that are involved in determinations of corporate decisions and actions. In effect, it tells us what anyone who occupies any of the positions is vis-à-vis the decision structure of the whole. The organizational chart provides what might be called the grammar of corporate decision-making. What I shall call internal recognition rules provide its logic.[3]

---

2 John Kenneth Galbraith, *The Age of Uncertainty* (Boston: Houghton Mifflin, 1977), p. 261.
3 By "recognition rule(s)" I mean what Hart, in another context, calls "conclusive affirmative indication" that a decision or act has been made or performed for corporate reasons. H.L.A. Hart, *The Concept of Law* (Oxford: Clarendon Press, 1961), Chap. VI.

Recognition rules are of two sorts. Partially embedded in the organizational chart are the procedural recognitors: we see that decisions are to be reached collectively at certain levels and that they are to be ratified at higher levels (or at inner circles, if one prefers the Galbraithean model). A corporate decision is recognized internally not only by the procedure of its making, but by the policy it instantiates. Hence every corporation creates an image (not to be confused with its public image) or a general policy, what G.C. Buzby of the Chilton Company has called the "basic belief of the corporation,"[4] that must inform its decisions for them to be properly described as being those of that corporation. "The moment policy is side-stepped or violated it is no longer the policy of that company."[5]

Peter Drucker has seen the importance of the basic policy recognitors in the CID Structure (though he treats matters rather differently from the way I am recommending). Drucker writes:

> Because the corporation is an institution it must have a basic policy. For it must subordinate individual ambitions and decisions to the *needs* of the corporation's welfare and survival. That means that it must have a set of principles and a rule of conduct which limit and direct individual actions and behavior.[6]

6

Suppose, for illustrative purposes, we activate a CID Structure in a corporation. Wicker's favorite, the Gulf Oil Corporation. Imagine then that three executives X, Y, and Z have the task of deciding whether or not Gulf Oil will join a world uranium cartel (I trust this may catch Mr. Wicker's attention and hopefully also that of Jerry McAfee, current Gulf Oil Corporation president). X, Y, and Z have before them an Everest of papers that have been prepared by lower echelon executives. Some of the reports will be purely factual in nature, some will be contingency plans, some will be in the form of position papers developed by various departments, some will outline financial considerations, some will be legal opinions, and so on. Insofar as these will all have been processed through Gulf's CID Structure system, the personal reasons, if any, individual executives may have had when writing their reports and recommendations in a specific way will have been diluted by the subordination of individual inputs to peer group input even before X, Y, and Z review the matter. X, Y, and Z take a vote. Their taking of a vote is authorized procedure in the Gulf CID

---

4   G.C. Buzby, "Policies—A Guide to What a Company Stands For," *Management Record* (March 1962), p. 5.
5   Ibid.
6   Peter Drucker, *Concept of the Corporation* (New York: John Day Co., 1946/1972), pp. 36–37.

Structure, which is to say that under these circumstances the vote of X, Y, and Z can be redescribed as the corporation's making a decision: that is, the event "X Y Z voting" may be redescribed to expose an aspect otherwise unrevealed that is quite different from its other aspects, e.g., from X's voting in the affirmative.

But the CID Structure, as already suggested, also provides the grounds in its nonprocedural recognitor for such an attribution of corporate intentionality. Simply, when the corporate act is consistent with the implementation of established corporate policy, then it is proper to describe it as having been done for corporate reasons, as having been caused by a corporate desire coupled with a corporate belief and so, in other words, as corporate intentional.

An event may, under one of its aspects, be described as the conjunctive act "X did a (or as X intentionally did a) and Y did a (or as Y intentionally did a) and Z did a (or as Z intentionally did a)" (where a = voted in the affirmative on the question of Gulf Oil joining the cartel). Given the Gulf CID Structure—formulated in this instance as the conjunction of rules: when the occupants of positions A, B, and C on the organizational chart unanimously vote to do something and if doing that something is consistent with an implementation of general corporate policy, other things being equal, then the corporation has decided to do it for corporate reasons—the event is redescribable as "the Gulf Oil Corporation did j for corporate reasons f" (where j is "decided to join the cartel" and f is any reason [desire + belief] consistent with basic policy of Gulf Oil, e.g., increasing profits) or simply as "Gulf Oil Corporation intentionally did j." This is a rather technical way of saying that in these circumstances the executives voting are, given its CID Structure, also the corporation deciding to do something, and that regardless of the personal reasons the executives have for voting as they do, and even if their reasons are inconsistent with established corporate policy or even if one of them has no reason at all for voting as he does, the corporation still has reasons for joining the cartel: that is, joining is consistent with the inviolate corporate general policies as encrusted in the precedent of previous corporate actions and its statements of purpose as recorded in its certificate of incorporation, annual reports, etc. The corporation's only method of achieving its desires or goals is the activation of the personnel who occupy its various positions. However, if X voted affirmatively purely for reasons of personal monetary gain (suppose he had been bribed to do so), that does not alter the fact that the corporate reason for joining the cartel was to minimize competition and hence pay higher dividends to its shareholders. Corporations have reasons because they have interests in doing those things that are likely to result in realization of their established corporate goals regardless of the transient self-interest of directors, managers, etc. If there is a difference between corporate goals and desires and those of human beings, it is probably that the corporate ones are relatively stable and not very wide ranging, but that is only because corporations can do relatively fewer things than human beings, being confined in action predominately to a limited socioeconomic sphere. It is, of course, in a corporation's interest that its component membership view the corporate purposes as instrumental in the achievement of their own goals. (Financial reward is the most common way this is achieved.)

It will be objected that a corporation's policies reflect only the current goals of its directors. But that is certainly not logically necessary nor is it in practice totally true for most large corporations. Usually, of course, the original incorporators will have organized to further their individual interests and/or to meet goals which they shared. But even in infancy the melding of disparate interests and purposes gives rise to a corporate long-range point of view that is distinct from the intents and purposes of the collection of incorporators viewed individually. Also corporate basic purposes and policies, as already mentioned, tend to be relatively stable when compared to those of individuals and not couched in the kind of language that would be appropriate to individual purposes. Furthermore, as histories of corporations will show, when policies are amended or altered it is usually only peripheral issues and matters of style that are involved. Radical policy alteration constitutes a new corporation. This point is captured in the incorporation laws of such states as Delaware. ("Any power which is not enumerated in the charter or which cannot be inferred from it is *ultra vires* [beyond the legal competence] of the corporation.") Obviously underlying the objection is an uneasiness about the fact that corporate intent is dependent upon policy and purpose that is but an artifact of the sociopsychology of a group of biological persons. Corporate intent seems somehow to be a tarnished, illegitimate, offspring of human intent. But this objection is a form of the anthropocentric bias that pervades traditional moral theory. By concentrating on possible descriptions of events and by acknowledging only that the possibility of describing something as an agent depends upon whether or not it can be properly described as having done something for a reason, we avoid the temptation of trying to reduce all agents to human referents.

The CID Structure licenses redescriptions of events as corporate and attributions of corporate intentionality, while it does not obscure the private acts of executives, directors, etc. Although X voted to support the joining of the cartel because he was bribed to do so, X did not join the cartel: Gulf Oil Corporation joined the cartel. Consequently, we may say that X did something for which he should be held morally responsible, yet whether or not Gulf Oil Corporation should be held morally responsible for joining the cartel is a question that turns on issues that may be unrelated to X's having accepted a bribe.

Of course Gulf Oil Corporation cannot join the cartel unless X or somebody who occupies position A on the organization chart votes in the affirmative. What that shows, however, is that corporations are collectivities. That should not, however, rule out the possibility of their having metaphysical status and being thereby full-fledged moral persons.

This much seems to me clear: We can describe many events in terms of certain physical movements of human beings and we also can sometimes describe those events as done for reasons by those human beings, but further we also can sometimes describe those events as corporate and still further as done for corporate reasons that are qualitatively different from whatever personal reasons, if any, component members may have for doing what they do.

Corporate agency resides in the possibility of CID Structure-licensed redescription of events as corporate intentional. That may still appear to be downright mysterious, although I do not think it is, for human agency, as I have suggested, resides in the possibility of description as well. On the basis of the foregoing analysis, however. I think that grounds have been provided for holding corporations *per se* to account for what they do, for treating them as metaphysical persons *qua* moral persons.

A.A. Berle has written:

> The medieval feudal power system set the "lords spiritual" over and against the "lords temporal." These were the men of learning and of the church who in theory were able to say to the greatest power in the world: "You have committed a sin: therefore either you are excommunicated or you must mend your ways." The lords temporal could reply: "I can kill you." But the lords spiritual could retort: "Yes that you can, but you cannot change the philosophical fact." In a sense this is the great lacuna in the economic power system today.[7]

I have tried to fill that gap by providing reasons for thinking that the moral world is not necessarily composed of homogeneous entities. It is sobering to keep in mind that the Gulf Oil Corporation certainly knows what "You are held responsible for payment in full of the amount recorded on your statement" means. I hope I have provided the beginnings of a basis for an understanding of what "The Gulf Oil Corporation should be held responsible for destroying the ecological balance of the bay" means.

Questions

1. What is a CID structure?

2. How can we distinguish between a corporate action and a personal action?

3. How can we distinguish between the actions of a corporation and the actions of a mob?

---

7   A.A. Berle, "Economic Power and the Free Society," *The Corporate Take-Over*, ed. Andrew Hacker (Garden City, N.Y.: Doubleday, 1964), p. 99.

4. Can corporations really be held accountable (punished) for their actions (in a manner analogous to human beings)?

5. Are corporate structures representative of how day-to-day decisions are made in corporations?

Further Reading

Arnold, Denis G. "Corporate Moral Agency." *Midwest Studies in Philosophy*, vol. 30, 1 Jan. 2006, pp. 279–91.

Davidson, Donald. "Agency." In *Agent, Action, and Reason*, edited by R. Binkley, R. Bronaugh, and A. Marras. Toronto: University of Toronto Press, 1971, pp. 1–37.

Gans, David H., and Douglas T. Kendall. "A Capitalist Joker: The Strange Origins, Disturbing Past, and Uncertain Future of Corporate Personhood in American Law." *The John Marshall Law Review*, vol. 44, issue 3, 2011, pp. 643–99.

Gibson, Kevin. "Toward an Intermediate Position on Corporate Moral Personhood." *Journal of Business Ethics*, vol. 101, no. 1, 2011, pp. 71–81.

Gorr, Michael. "Agency and Causation." *Journal for the Theory of Social Behaviour*, vol. 9, 1 March 1979, pp. 1–14.

Nemetz, Patricia L. "The Good, the Bad, and the Ugly of Corporate Personhood and Corporate Political Spending: Implications for Shareholders." *Business and Society Review: Journal of the Center for Business Ethics at Bentley College*, vol. 121, no. 4, 1 Dec. 2016, pp. 569–91.

16.

"CORPORATE MORAL AGENCY

THE CASE FOR

ANTHROPOLOGICAL BIGOTRY"

JOHN R. DANLEY

About This Reading

In the previous chapter, Peter French argued for full moral personhood for
corporations based on the idea that corporations can be said to be intentional
beings, that is, beings cable of determining their own actions independently of
the people who run the corporation. According to John Danley, French's view
of the corporation fails to recognize the extent to which corporations differ
from actual human beings.

    According to Danley, corporations are "*personae fictae*" or fictional peo-
ple, which is a legal distinction, not a moral one. Only real people can be held
morally accountable for their actions. Corporations cannot "intend" anything,
and corporate actions are—in Danley's account—simply a reflection of the
actions of the real human beings running a company. To support this view,
Danley systematically responds to each of French's arguments for corporate
personhood. In the end, Danley concludes that we should embrace a different
model of the corporation—one that views the corporation as being a machine.

In "Corporate Moral Agency," Peter A. French argues for a position, increasingly
popular, which would accept "corporations as members of the moral community,
of equal standing with the traditionally acknowledged residents—biological human
beings." This is but one implication of accepting the claim that one can legitimately
ascribe moral responsibility to corporations. To put the matter somewhat differently,
again in French's words, "corporations should be treated as full-fledged moral persons

and hence ... have whatever privileges, rights, and duties as are, in the normal course of affairs, accorded to moral persons."

Unwilling to rest content with the usual assaults on prejudices against real persons based on race, creed, sex, religion, or national origin, French is among those[1] seeking to open yet another new front. The struggle is now being extended beyond real persons to eliminate discrimination against a particular class of *personae fictae*, fictitious persons, namely the corporation. Before too hastily endorsing this new "corporate" liberation movement let us pause for reflection. If after serious consideration we do vote to admit these peculiar entities into our rather exclusivist and elitist community of moral beings, we should insist on their having equal standing with the rest of us run-of-the-mill featherless bipeds. After all, what moral neighborhood worthy of the name would allow second-class citizens? After examining the case for admission, however, I find myself driven to the uncomfortable position of defending apartheid, biological apartheid that is, of defending anthropological bigotry. I contend that corporations should not be included in the moral community; they should not be granted full-fledged moral status. Within this emotionally charged atmosphere it is tempting to employ the standard *ad hominems* of bigotry ("Think of the value of your property"; or, "Before you know it your daughter will bring a corporation home to dinner"; "What about the children?"; and so forth), but I will attempt to ward off these temptations. My claim is that the corporatist programs of the kind represented by French would seriously disturb the logic of our moral discourse. Indeed, the corporatist position, while offering no substantial advantages, would entail the reduction of biological persons to the status of second-class citizens. Let us turn now to the dispute.

There is little doubt that we often speak of corporations as being responsible for this or that sin or charitable act, whether of microscopic or cosmic proportions. The question is what we mean when we speak in that way. Sometimes all we mean is that the corporation is the cause of such and such. In these instances we are isolating a cause for an event or state of affairs, an exercise not much more (or less) troublesome than saying "The icy pavement caused the accident." The debate revolves around a fuller sense of "responsibility," a sense which includes more than the idea of "causing to happen." In this richer sense, we ascribe responsibility only if the event or state of affairs caused was also intended by the agent.

When the concept of responsibility is unpacked in this fashion, the traditionalists appear to have victory already in hand. Whatever else we may say of them, collective entities are surely not the kinds of things capable of intending. Individuals within

---

1   Those who apparently espouse this view to some degree include Norman Bowie and Tom L. Bauchamp in *Ethical Theory and Business* (Englewood Cliffs, NJ: Prentice-Hall, 1979), e.g., chap. 1 and comments on p. 128; and Christopher Stone in *Where the Law Ends* (New York: Harper, Colophon, 1975).

the corporation can intend, lust, have malice aforethought, and so forth, but the corporation cannot. Traditionalists, like myself, maintain that only persons, that is, entities with particular physical and mental properties, can be morally responsible. Corporations lack these. For the traditionalists, to speak of corporations being responsible is simply elliptical for speaking of certain individuals within the corporation being responsible. On this point, and perhaps this one alone, I do not believe Milton Friedman[2] to be in error.

Undaunted by this venerable line of reasoning, the corporatists proceed to press their case. Although it is French's view that I am treating, I am concerned not so much with the details of his argument as with the general outlines of the corporatist position. Using French's theory as representative, however, provides us with one of the most forceful, sophisticated theories developed. French has worked for years in the area of collective responsibility.[3] His strategy is to accept the traditionalists' analysis of "responsibility," and then to attempt to show that some sense can be made of ascribing "intentions" to a corporation.

The key to making some sense of corporate "intentions" is what French calls the Corporate Internal Decision Structure, the CID. The CID is that which allows one, "licenses" one, to redescribe the actions of certain individuals within a corporation as actions of the corporation. Although the notion is complicated, a CID contains two elements which are particularly relevant:

1. an organization or responsibility flow chart delineating stations and levels within the corporate power structure and

2. corporate decision recognition rules.

As French puts it, the organizational chart provides the grammar for corporate decision making; the recognition rules provide the logic. The purpose of the organizational chart is to locate which procedures will count as decisions for the corporation, and who may or must participate in those procedures. The recognition rules, we are informed, are of two sorts. The first sort is procedural recognitors, "partially embedded in the organizational chart." What these amount to, it seems, are directives more explicit than those contained in the chart, expanding upon it. The second sort of recognition rules is expressed primarily in corporate policy.

Employing the cumbersome apparatus of the CID, some acts may now be described in two non-identical ways, or so it is claimed.

---

2   See *Capitalism and Freedom* (Chicago: University of Chicago Press, 1962), pp. 133–36.
3   One of French's earliest works is "Morally Blaming Whole Populations," which appears in *Philosophy, Morality, and International Affairs* (New York: Oxford University Press, 1974) ed. Virginia Held et al., pp. 266–85.

One of those ... is "Executive X's doing y" and one is "Corporation C's doing z." The corporate act and the individual act may have different properties: indeed, they have different causal ancestors though they are causally inseparable.

The effect of this, of course, is that when certain individuals as specified by the organizational chart, engage in certain procedures as specified by the organizational chart and some recognition rules, and act in accordance with other recognition rules (corporate policy), then French claims we can re-describe the action as a corporate act, an intentional corporate act. It is critical to the corporatist position that the two descriptions are non-identical. Saying that "Corporation C did z" is not reducible to the statement that "Executives X, Y, and Z, voted to do y," even though y and z are the same. Since they are non-identical the traditionalist is supposedly prevented from ascribing responsibility only to these individuals. The acts of the individuals are necessary for a corporate act but not identical with it.

Like a child with a new toy, one is strongly inclined by the glitter of this technical hardware to dismantle it, to try to find out how it all works, to see whether it really fits together, to see how and whether it can handle hard cases. To be sure, there are some problems which one can detect immediately. Let me mention two. First of all, it is unclear what French means by an organizational chart. Since his examples are those of nice neat black lines and boxes on a page, like the ones found in business textbooks and corporate policy manuals, one is left with the impression that this is what he has in mind. If so, there are severe difficulties. Most everyone is aware of the extent to which corporate reality departs from the ethereal world of black lines and boxes. Will French maintain that any decisions made by the managers of corporations which do not conform to the organizational chart are not decisions of the corporation? Biting the bullet here may be the best course but it is probable that most decisions are not strictly corporate decisions then. Few corporations act at all, if this criterion is used. French needs a more positivistic interpretation[4] of the organizational chart, one which would insure that the flow chart realistically captured the actual procedures and personages holding the powers. The difficulty with this modification, however, is that the CID begins to lose its function as a normative criterion by which to determine which acts are corporate acts and which are not. The positivistic interpretation would mean that a corporate act is whatever some powerful person within the corporation manages to get others in the corporation to perform, or gets others outside to accept as a corporate act. That will not work at

---

4   The positivistic interpretation is suggested by, among other things, French's references to Austin and H.L.A. Hart. The distinction between organizational chart and recognition rules also resembles the positivistic distinction between secondary and primary rules.

all. The CID appears nestled upon the familiar horns of a dilemma. At least more work is necessary here.

There is a second difficulty. A basic component of the CID must be the corporate charter. Recently the general incorporation charters have become little more than blank tablets for the corporation to engage in business for "any lawful purpose," although some aspects of the organizational chart and a few recognition rules are delineated. Even these permissive rules of recognition have pertinence for French. Suppose every aspect of the CID was followed except that the board of directors voted unanimously to engage the corporation in some unlawful activity. According to the charter, a part of the CID, this is not possible. One could not redescribe such an act as a corporate act. The result of this is that corporations can never act illegally. Unlike the Augustinian doctrine that for fallen man it is not possible not to sin, the French doctrine appears to be that for the corporation it is not possible to sin at all.

These are but two of many queries which might be addressed to French's proposal. However, it is not my concern to dwell on such technical points here, lest we be distracted from the larger issue. Suppose, for the sake of argument, that we accept some mode of redescribing individual acts such that one could identify these acts as constituting a corporate intentional act. Accept French's. Would that establish the corporatist case? I think not. French tips his hand, for instance, when he writes that what "needs to be shown is that there is sense in saying that corporations, and not just the people who work in them, have reasons for doing what they do." But, obviously, French needs to show much more. All that is established by a device which redescribes, is that there is *a sense* in saying that corporations have intentions. The significant question is whether that sense of "intend" is the one used by the traditionalists when explicating "responsibility," and when denying that corporations can have intentions. The traditionalists can easily, and quite plausibly, claim that the corporatist is equivocating on "intend." The sense in which a corporation intends is much different from that in which a biological person intends. The corporatist has further laid the foundation for this charge by finding it necessary to construct the apparatus so that the sense of "intend" involved can be made clear. The more clearly this sense of "intend" is articulated, the more clearly it diverges from what we usually mean by "intend." The arbitrariness of constructing a sense of "intend" should be evident when we consider the possibility of ascribing intentions to numerous other entities, such as plants, animals, or machines. One could go to extraordinary lengths to provide a sense for attributing intentionally to many of these. Yet, few would contend that it was very similar to what we mean in attributing "intention" to humans.

Consider a computer programmed to play chess which learns from previous mistakes. There is a sense in which the computer intends to respond P-K4 to my king pawn opening, but is this the same sense of "intend" as when I intended P-K4?

Furthermore, even ascribing an intention to the computer by no means entails that we would be ready to ascribe responsibility to it. The point is that it remains for the corporatist to demonstrate the relationship between the sense of "intend" and the sense involved in ascriptions of responsibility to humans. Hence, a rather difficult task remains for the corporatist before the case is made.

Thus far I have established only that the corporatist has failed to establish the position. I must admit that I am not entirely enamored of the preceding line of argument. The dispute smacks of the theological controversies concerning whether "wisdom" or "goodness" when attributed to God have the same sense as when predicated of humans. Nonetheless, the corporatist has moved the debate in this direction by attempting to equate two markedly different senses. There are, fortunately, other factors to be considered in evaluating the corporatist position. These factors appear when one expands the focus of attention beyond the narrow conditions for ascribing "responsibility," and begins to examine the concept as it functions in the broader context of moral discourse.

Much hangs in the balance when ascribing "responsibility." Affixing responsibility is a prelude to expressing approbation or disapprobation—praise or blame. When the agent responsible is praised, that is the final move in the moral game. (Morality never pays very well.) But, when the responsibility is affixed and the agent in question is blameworthy, that is far from the end of the matter. In this case, affixing responsibility and expressing disfavor is itself a prelude to many further permissible or obligatory moves. Minimally, the blameworthy party is expected to express regret or remorse. More importantly, the agent may be required to pay compensation or be subject to punishment. Ascribing responsibility opens the door for these major moral moves. (There are other door openers as well, for example, the notion of cause in strict liability.) Any understanding of the concept of responsibility is incomplete without incorporating the role it plays in relation to these other moral moves. It is this which is lacking from the previous discussion of "intend." Such an analysis cannot be provided here. What can be done, however, is to sketch briefly how ascribing responsibility to corporations effectively blocks these moves, sundering many of the threads which tie "responsibility" so intimately with concepts like remorse, regret, compensation, or punishment. Let me elaborate.

An indication of the consequences of admitting the corporation into the moral community have been foreshadowed by admission into the legal corpus as a person. That legacy is an odious one, marred by an environment within which the corporation has enjoyed nearly all of the benefits associated with personhood while shouldering but few of the burdens or risks. Much the same would result from admission into the moral world. That legacy is not solely to be explained by jaundiced justices or bad judicial judgments, but is a natural consequence of attempting to pretend that the corporation is just another pretty face. While the law early began holding the corporation liable (read: responsible) for certain specified acts, and the scope of things for which it was liable has dramatically increased over the years, there has been a hesitancy to judge that corporations could be subject to most criminal statutes. One of the major stumbling blocks was just the one which is the subject of this paper. It was clear that many of the criminal statutes required criminal intent, or a criminal state of mind, and unable to locate the corporate mind, it was judged that the corporation was not subject to these. The relevance of proposals such as French's is that the justices would now have a method of determining when the corporation acts with intent, with malice aforethought, with premeditation or out of passion. What I am anxious to bring to light, however, is that these proposals offer no advantage over the traditionalist view and in fact create further problems. Consider now the moral moves involved in extracting compensation from, or punishing, a guilty person. How is one to make these moral moves against a corporate person? One cannot. An English jurist put the point well in an often-quoted quip to the effect that corporations have no pants to kick, no soul to damn. We may concur with the sentiment of that jurist who concluded that "by God they ought to have both," but they have neither, although French has given them a surrogate soul, the CID.

The corporation cannot be kicked, whipped, imprisoned, or hanged by the neck until dead. Only individuals of the corporation can be punished. What of punishment through the pocketbook, or extracting compensation for a corporate act? Here too, the corporation is not punished, and does not pay the compensation. Usually one punishes the stockholders who in the present corporate climate have virtually no control over corporate actions. Or, if the corporation can pass on the cost of a fiscal punishment or compensation, it is in the end the consumer who pays for the punishment or compensation. If severe enough, hitting the pocketbook may result in the reduction of workforce, again resting the burden on those least deserving, more precisely, on those not responsible at all. Sooner or later, usually sooner, someone hits upon the solution of punishing those individuals of the corporation most directly responsible for the corporate act. There are also moral difficulties associated with this alternative. For example, many top executives are protected through insurance policies, part of the perks of the job. That would be satisfactory if the intent is simply to compensate, but it neutralizes any deterrent or retributive effect. But let us pass over these considerations and examine more closely these recommendations to "go inside" the corporation to punish an individual, whether stockholder, employee, agent, manager, or director of the corporation.

For the traditionalist there is little difficulty. The traditionalist recognizes the corporation as a legal fiction which for better or worse may have equal protection under the law of other persons, but the traditionalist may accept those legal trappings as at best a useful way of treating the corporation for legal purposes. After all, morally the corporation is not responsible; only individuals are. As long as those within the corporation pay for the deed, there is no theoretical difficulty.

What of the corporatist's position? The single advantage is that the adoption of the position would mean that some sense could be made of pointing an accusing finger or raising a fist in moral outrage at a fictitious person, a behavior which might otherwise appear not only futile but ridiculous. In the new corporatist scheme the behavior would no longer be ridiculous, only futile. The disadvantages, on the other hand, are apparent when one attempts to follow the responsibility assignment with the normally attendant moral moves as I have just shown. Either those moves are blocked entirely, since one may find no method by which to punish, or the moves are diverted away from the genuine culprit (the fictitious moral agent) and directed toward someone inside the corporation (non-fictitious moral agent). Either alternative is unacceptable. The former would entail that some citizens of the moral community, namely corporate persons, were not subject to the full obligations of membership. That reduces biological members to the status of second-class citizens, shouldering as they do all the burdens. The latter alternative, "going inside," is equally offensive. This alternative means that biological agents are sacrificed vicariously for the sins of the corporation. This solution not only reduces the biological agents to second-class citizens, but would make scapegoats or, worse, sacrificial lambs, of them. Thus would the admission of the corporation into the moral community threaten to disturb the logic associated with the ascription of responsibility.

In addition to these problems, the corporatists face other theoretical obstacles. It is not clear that "going inside" a corporation is often, if ever, intelligible, given the analysis of a corporate act. To counter the traditionalist's claim that only individuals are responsible, French claims that the corporate act is not identical with the acts of individuals in the corporation. Given this, how is it possible now to reverse that claim and hold individuals responsible for something which they did not do? All they did at most was to vote for the corporation to do something, or to pay for something to be done on behalf of the corporation. The claim that individual acts and corporate acts are not identical opens the door to criminalless crime, a possibility admitted openly by French in another earlier paper. French there notes that a collective entity may be responsible yet no individual in that collectivity be responsible. Far from being an extreme case, that outcome may include all corporate acts. As mentioned above, such an alternative is unacceptable. But, again, can one make intelligible going inside to make one or more individuals responsible? In order to do so the corporatist must shift ground and concede that the individual acts and the corporate acts are identical, or perhaps that the individuals, by voting on a course of illegal or immoral action, coerced the hapless corporation to go along with the deed.

Although I have offered what I take to be a satisfactory defense of the traditionalist position, I would like to close by suggesting an alternative model for viewing the corporation. An alternative is needed because the corporatist's model has largely succeeded in warping many of our intuitions and is reinforced not only by legal idioms, but by managerial vocabulary. In many a corporatist's eye the corporation is an organism, and perhaps even much like a biological person. It has a brain, nerve receptors, muscle, it moves, reproduces, expands, develops, grows, in some periods the "fat is cut off," processes information, makes decisions, and so on. It adjusts to the environment. Such a metaphor may be useful but we have now begun to be victimized by the metaphorical model. Unfortunately, reformers have found it useful to accept that language and that model. It is useful to personify and then to vilify. The model, I fear, stands behind many attempts to endow the corporation with moral agency and personhood.

A more adequate model, especially for those who are reform-minded, I would maintain provides a different perspective from which to view contemporary trends. The corporation is more like a machine than an organism.[5] Like machines they are human inventions, designed by humans, modified by humans, operated by humans. Like many machines they are controlled by the few for the benefit of the few. They are no longer simple, easily understandable, organizations, but as complicated as the latest piece of electronic hardware. It takes years of training to learn how to operate and direct one. Like machines they are created, yet they create and shape humans.

If a complicated machine got out of hand and ravaged a community, there seems something perverse about expressing our moral outrage and indignation to the machine. More appropriately, our fervor should be addressed to the operators and to the designers of the machine. They, not the machines, are morally responsible. To ascribe responsibility to such machines, no matter how complicated, is tantamount to mistaking the created for the creator. This mystification is a contemporary form of animism. Such is the case for anthropological bigotry.

Questions

1. Do you think that Danley is correct when he claims that punishing corporations often results in punishing those least responsible for the corporate wrongdoing?

2. If we take the CID structure seriously, would it be impossible for a corporation to ever do anything immoral?

---

5 Although I do not follow Ladd's argument, one good example of taking this alternative model seriously is demonstrated in his "Morality and the Ideal of Rationality in Formal Organizations," in *Monist*, vol. 54 (October 1970), pp. 488–516.

3. Does treating a corporation as a moral person make it easier or more difficult to hold it accountable for its wrongdoings?

4. What does Danley mean when he states that if we treat corporations as persons, then it is possible to have crimes without criminals?

5. What is the Machine Model of the corporation?

Further Reading

Corlett, J. Angelo. "French on Corporate Punishment: Some Problems." *Journal of Business Ethics*, vol. 7, no. 3, 1988, pp. 205–10.

Ewin, Robert E. "The Moral Status of the Corporation." *Journal of Business Ethics*, vol. 10, 1991, pp. 749–56.

French, Peter A. "The Corporation as a Moral Person." *American Philosophical Quarterly*, vol. 16, no. 3, 1979, pp. 207–15.

Manning, Rita C. "Corporate Responsibility and Corporate Personhood." *Journal of Business Ethics*, vol. 3, no. 1, 1984, pp. 77–84.

Moore, Geoff. "Corporate Moral Agency: Review and Implications." *Journal of Business Ethics*, vol. 21, no. 4, 1999, pp. 329–43.

17.

"THE FOURTH WAVE

THE ETHICS OF CORPORATE DOWNSIZING"

JOHN ORLANDO

About This Reading

It is common for companies to increase profits or share prices through down-sizing. This is the practice of laying off workers, and it happens for a variety of reasons. A typical view of corporations, specifically, is that it is shareholders that matter the most (consider also "Managing for Stakeholders" in this volume), in particular when compared to employees. This generates a motive to downsize whenever the stock price of a company is in trouble or falls below a certain point. In this article, Orlando considers several arguments that are used to justify a preference for shareholders over employees. He then considers several arguments against downsizing in general.

The Issue[1]

A survey of contemporary business ethics literature leads one to believe that the primary ethical questions facing businesses today concern topics such as affirmative action, sexual harassment, and the environment. While these are without a doubt weighty concerns, many workers, especially manufacturing workers, would place corporate downsizing—the closing of whole plants or divisions in order to increase profits—at the head of their list of ethically contentious business practices. Though the issue has provoked considerable debate in the popular press, the philosophical community has largely ignored it.

---

1 I would like to thank Kristin Novotny, Robert Pepperman Taylor, Alan Wertheimer, Don Loeb, David Christenson, and a reviewer at *Business Ethics Quarterly* for their helpful comments on earlier drafts of this work. For those scratching their heads over the title, note that agriculture has been called the first wave in industrial development, manufacturing the second wave, and information the third wave (of course, "wave" has two meanings in the title).

This oversight is curious given that downsizing is arguably the major business trend of our era. A 1988 survey of 1,200 personnel managers indicated that 35 percent of the respondents worked for a company that had downsized within the past 12 months.[2] While there is evidence that the wave has begun to crest, news reports demonstrate that the practice is still common.[3] More importantly, downsizing is now considered normal practice by the business community at large.

The statistics on downsizing's human costs are sobering. One study found that 15 percent of downsized workers lost their homes, and another that the suicide rate among laid-off workers is 30 times the national average.[4] Despite the rosy picture of the economy painted by the popular media, where attention is constantly drawn to the growth of the stock market, evidence suggests that trends such as downsizing have led to a general decline in employee earnings, as well as a widening of the gulf between rich and poor in America.[5] Added to this is the fact that since the loss of jobs is concentrated in a relatively small geographic area, these closings affect the entire community. Businesses that rely upon workers' spending will feel the pinch, often leading to secondary layoffs. Consequently, communities as a whole have been devastated by such closings.[6] Downsizing also carries with it serious nonquantifiable harms. News of mass layoffs sends psychological tremors across the nation, leading to general worker apprehension about job security and less job satisfaction.[7] Worse yet, the anxiety of unemployment often leads to psychological symptoms such as depression, or expresses itself through a variety of unpleasant behaviors: i.e., crime, domestic violence, child abuse, and alcohol and drug abuse.[8]

---

2   Richard L. Bunning, "The Dynamics of Downsizing," *Personnel Journal* 69, 1. 9 (Sep 1990), p. 69.

3   The very day these words were written, Xerox announced it would cut 10,000 jobs, despite enjoying a 20 percent jump in profits this year. *Burlington Free Press*, March 25, 1998, 5A, by Ben Dobbin of *The Associated Press*.

4   Bunning, op. cit., p. 70.

5   Interview with Secretary of Labor Robert Reich in *Challenge*, July/August 1996, p. 4. Reich notes that while the *average* wage is up, the *median* wage (the wage of the individual in the middle) is down. The discrepancy is due to the unprecedented rise in compensation for top executives during the 1980s and 1990s.

6   Downsizing by the auto industry in the 1970s and 1980s caused Flint, Michigan's unemployment rate to climb to the highest in the United States, and its crime rate to rise accordingly. *Facts About the Cities*, ed. Allan Carpenter (New York: H.W. Wilson Co., 1992).

7   Harvey M. Brenner, *Mental Illness and the Economy* (Cambridge, Harvard University Press, 1973); Ralph Catalano and David Dooley, "Economic Predictors of Depressed Mood and Stressful Life Events in a Metropolitan Community," *Journal of Health and Social Behavior* 18 (1977): 292–307; Jean Hartley, Dan Jacobson, Bert Klandennans, and Tinka van Vuuren, *Job Insecurity Coping with Jobs at Risk* (Newbury Park Sage, 1991); and John R. Reynolds, "The Effects of Industrial Employment Conditions on Job-Related Distress," *Journal of Health and Social Behavior*, June 1997, pp. 105–18.

8   David Dooley, Ralph Catalano, and Karen S. Rook, "Personal and Aggregate Unemployment and Psychological Symptoms," *Journal of Social Issues* 44 (1988): 107–23; David Dooley, Ralph Catalano, (cont'd)

Though the business ethics literature contains a wealth of discussion on the question of whether corporate managers have obligations to parties besides shareholders—a theoretical issue having a central bearing on downsizing's ethical status—these discussions have generally fallen short of practical application, with downsizing serving as a case in point. No wonder Andrew Stark laments that business ethics writing is without much value to the manager on the front lines of the corporate decision-making process.[9] Stark finds today's academic discussions too, well, academic—obsessed with abstract speculation to the exclusion of practical directives.[10] This is due, I believe, to two reasons. One, those who defend the view that firms have duties to parties other than shareholders—the stakeholder theory—fail to distinguish between different groups of stakeholders. Since each party is in a unique position in relation to the firm, the firm may have different duties to each. Thus, the blanket pronouncement that firms have duties to stakeholders says little about a firm's duty to individual stakeholders. I propose that we can circumvent this problem, and hence make considerable moral headway, if we narrow our focus to a particular group, in this case to workers. Two, abstract principles, even if they can be agreed upon, are often too vague to apply clearly to individual cases. I shall demonstrate that greater consensus can be reached if the debate is shifted to situations analogous to the ones actually faced by business managers.

The lack of engagement with downsizing on the part of the philosophical community has effectively left the debate in the hands of the popular press, and to journals specifically tailored to the business community. But the writers in these publications generally fail to appreciate the complexity of the issues that must be addressed in order to evaluate downsizing's ethical status. Because they normally lack a background in ethical theorizing, those who voice opposition to downsizing have usually articulated and defended their positions poorly. This has left defenders of the practice with rather easy targets, allowing them to dismiss downsizing's critics with a quip or a platitude. Thus, the discussion has remained on a superficial level, with critics of the practice finding themselves marginalized to the periphery

---

and Georjeanna Wilson, "Depression and Unemployment. Panel Findings from the Epidemiologic Catchment Area Study," *American Journal of Community Health* 22 (1994): 745–65.

9   "What's the Matter with Business Ethics?" *Harvard Business Review* 71, no. 3, pp. 38–48. See also Joseph H. Monast's discussion of the piece in "What Is (and Isn't) the Matter With 'What's the Matter ...'," in *Business Ethics Quarterly* 4, no. 4 (Oct. 1994): 499–512.

10   This problem is by no means unique to business ethics literature. While the volume of paper devoted to explorations of liberalism's foundations could insulate a room addition, the pieces that apply these theoretical principles to practical matters would barely serve as an adequate coaster. Even Ronald Dworkin, who has done as much as anyone to advance understanding of liberalism's foundations, laments that political philosophy has had little impact on public debate of concrete issues because it has rarely been oriented toward those debates. See Dworkin, *Life's Dominion* (New York: Knopf, 1993).

of the political arena.[11] Moreover, the ethics instructor who wishes to the cover the issue in her course finds a dearth of material from which to choose.[12] The ethical questions raised by downsizing are far too important for the philosophical community to remain on the sidelines of this debate; it is high time for a philosophically rigorous critique of the practice. Since downsized workers themselves have no real platform from which to air their concerns, those with the background and means to do so carry a special obligation to present their case to the public.

I will argue that acts of downsizing are very often morally wrong. I will begin by demonstrating that the business ethics literature has yet to identify a morally relevant distinction between the situation of the shareholder and that of the worker in relation to the corporation. This means that the corporate manager has no naturally greater duty to shareholders than to workers. I will make my case by examining, and dismissing, the various arguments advanced for privileging the interests of shareholders above all other parties. I then advance arguments against the moral permissibility of acts of downsizing. I will finish with a few words about how the concerns I raise might provide direction for future investigations into the ethical status of related practices, such as the replacement of full-time workers with part-time help.

The Moral Equality of Workers and Shareholders

Property Rights

First, it must be understood that one cannot justify the position that shareholder concerns take precedence over all other groups simply by appeal to the fact that the shareholders are the legal owners of the corporation. In that case, all one has done is provide a definition of the term *share holder*: one has yet to provide a morally relevant reason for privileging the interests of that group. This is analogous to arguing that abortion is impermissible after viability because that is the point where the fetus could survive outside of the womb.

The natural tack at this point is to assert that a legal owner has property rights that allow her to dispose of her property in any manner she sees fit.[13] But this

---

11　Perhaps the only congressional official to demonstrate any serious concern for the issue is Bernard Sanders, Vermont's representative to the House of Representatives.

12　This paper in fact arose out of an interest in covering the issue of downsizing in an ethics course, but discovering no philosophical works on which to situate the discussion.

13　See Gillian Brock, "Meeting Needs and Business Obligations: An Argument for the Libertarian Skeptic," *Journal of Business Ethics* 15, no. 6 (June 1996): 695–704; J.M. Elegido, "Intrinsic Limitations of Property Rights," *Journal of Business Ethics* 14, no. 5 (May 1995): 411–19; and Jeff Nesteruk and David T. Risser, "Conceptions of the Corporation and Ethical Decision Making in Business," *Business and Professional Ethics Journal* 2, no. 1, pp. 73–89.

justification skews the issue in the shareholder's favor by appealing to a paradigm that does not apply in the case of corporate ownership. The term *property rights* conjures up images of property for personal *use*, not *profit*. For instance, property rights advocates normally worry about laws that place restrictions on the use of one's homestead, such as laws regulating the appearance of one's home. Similarly, militia groups who dig in and take shots at ATF officials never barricade themselves in their businesses, but rather their homes. We may harbor a deep-seated intuition that property is sacred, but that intuition is tied to property with which we are in some respect intimately connected, such as a home.

To avoid glossing over the distinction between property for private use and property for profit, we will need to narrow our inquiry to an example of property for profit. Imagine that I own an apartment which I have rented to a couple for ten or fifteen years (think Fred and Ethel from "I Love Lucy"). I discover that I can make more money by dividing up the apartment and renting it to college students. My intuition is that I have a responsibility to the people who rent from me. At the very least, I should assure the couple, who might be frightened about the prospect of being thrown into the street, that I will not have them leave until they have procured similar housing elsewhere at a similar cost. I would also feel obligated to insure [sic] that their transition is as easy as possible by, for instance, helping them move. Moreover, the purpose of the money will have a bearing on the moral status of the act. The act is far easier to justify if it is needed to pay for my wife's extended medical care, than if it merely allows me to buy a longer sailboat. Thus, the general appeal to property rights breaks down when the property in question is for profit, and when we turn to scenarios closer to the practice of downsizing itself.

Fiduciary Duties

Many theorists and business managers defend the moral superiority of shareholders on grounds that corporate managers are bound by a fiduciary duty to their shareholders which trumps any competing duties.[14] The burden of proof is then taken to fall on the shoulders of those arguing against this position to demonstrate that the

---

14   See John R. Boatright,"Fiduciary Duties and the Shareholder-Management Relation. Or, What's So Special About Shareholders?" *Business Ethics Quarterly* 4, no. 4 (October 1994): 393–407; Kenneth E. Goodpaster, "Business Ethics and Stakeholder Analysis," *Business Ethics Quarterly* 1, no. 1. pp. 53–71; Kenneth E. Goodpaster and Thomas E. Holloran, "In Defense of a Paradox," *Business Ethics Quarterly* 4, no. 4 (1994): 423–29; John Hasnas, "The Normative Theories of Business Ethics: A Guide for the Perplexed," *Business Ethics Quarterly* 8, no. 1, pp. 19–42; David Rockefeller, "America after Downsizing," *Vital Speeches of the Day* 63, no. 2, (November 1996): 40–43; Eugene Rostow, "To Whom and for What Ends Are Corporate Managers Responsible?" in *The Corporate Manager and Modern Society*, ed. Edward S. Mason (New York: Atheneum, 1975).

manager has equally strong duties to others as well. Set this way, the objectors can only meet the duty to shareholders with a similar fiduciary duty to others, thus proposing what Kenneth E. Goodpaster terms a "multi-fiduciary" theory of managerial responsibility.[15] Goodpaster considers the position incoherent because it saddles the corporate manager with conflicting responsibilities, much like a lawyer forced to represent both sides of a civil suit at once.

But this characterization of the issue misconstrues the lines of justification for the duties of an agent in a fiduciary relationship. The fiduciary duty does not establish the obligations of the agent; it is rather prior considerations pertaining to the nature of the relationship that determine the parameters of that duty. For instance, the fiduciary duty of a lawyer to her client is not the same as that of a realtor to his client. Thus, the fiduciary duty itself cannot establish the agent's obligations, since the obligations differ in the two cases. This means that we must look to the particularities of the relationship to identify the contours of the manager's duty to her shareholders. The term *fiduciary duty* is merely a label for whatever obligations the manager owes to the shareholder; it does not create those duties, and thus cannot justify them.

One important factor determining the nature of an agent's fiduciary duty is the reason why the principal requires the protection of that duty. That is, from what is the individual being protected? For example, much of the duty of a lawyer to her client involves not releasing information about the client to others. This can be justified on grounds that in order to mount an adequate defense, the client must feel free to speak candidly about his case. Thus a lawyer's fiduciary duty to her client in criminal cases can be thought of as protecting the client from the state by insuring the best possible defense. However, the fiduciary duty of the real estate broker is not of this sort, as here the protection is not from others, but rather from the real estate broker himself. The danger is that by knowing the seller's intentions and financial situation, a broker might collude with a potential buyer, or an agent acting on behalf of that buyer, to rig an offer for a quick commission. Similar considerations have led to the recent creation of the "buyer's broker" relationship. In the classic real estate relationship, the buyer's agent works not for the buyer, but for the seller's broker, something not always understood by the buyer. For this reason, the buyer's agent is technically obligated to provide information about the buyer's intentions and financial position to the seller's broker if asked. This obviously undermines the buyer's position. To correct the problem, a buyer working with a realtor can now sign a contract that places the realtor in a fiduciary relationship which obligates the realtor to refrain from divulging any information that might undermine the buyer's negotiating position. In both instances, prior considerations serve to establish the requirements and boundaries of the fiduciary duty.

---

15 Goodpaster, op. cit.

There is considerable evidence that the fiduciary duty of a corporate manager has been historically justified as a means of protecting the owner from that manager. The legal justification of this duty can be traced to the 1741 court ruling in *The Charitable Corporation v. Sir Robert Sutton*, where the court ruled that managers of corporations were "most properly agents of those who employ them." Interestingly, the suit was brought against the managers of The Charitable Corporation for "self-dealing by executives, theft, failure of inventory control, and a huge unmet financial commitment."[16] Notice that the neglect of managerial duty cited involved not benevolent contributions to others, but rather acting in their *own* interest.

This theme re-emerged in the famous exchange between Merrick Dodd and A. Berle in the 1930s, which has been credited with initiating the debate about corporate social responsibility. Berle was arguing that managerial powers were held in trust by the stockholders as the sole beneficiary of the corporate enterprise, while Dodd was defending the position that these powers were held in trust by the entire community.[17] However, Berle was arguing his position on grounds that shareholders require such protection in order to defend themselves from managers who would divert profits into their own pockets. Again, the protection is from the managers, and not from other beneficiaries of the managers' actions. More recently, the American Law Institute printed a Principles of Corporate Governance, which included the stipulation that "By assuming his office, the corporate director commits allegiance to the enterprise and acknowledges that the best interests of the corporation and its shareholders must prevail over any individual interest *of his own*."[18]

Hence, there is good reason to believe that the legal basis of fiduciary duties of corporate managers to shareholders has been construed as the obligation to not advance their own interests against those of the shareholders. Adopting this view of the fiduciary relationship would mean that when a corporate manager takes into account the interests of stakeholders, even where that comes at the expense of profits, this does not conflict with a manager's fiduciary duty to shareholders.

Risk

Ian Maitland provides two justifications for the position that corporate managers have duties to shareholders over those to other parties. The first appeals to the fact that shareholders have vested capital in the corporation. Why is this fact morally relevant? According to Maitland, shareholders have taken a risk in placing their money

---

16   Goodpaster and Holloran, op. cit., p. 425.
17   Dodd, "For Whom Are Corporate Managers Trustees?" *Harvard Business Review* 45, no. 7 (May 8, 1932): 1145–63, and Berle, "Corporate Powers as Powers in Trust," *Harvard Legal Review* 44 (1931): 1049.
18   Goodpaster and Holloran, op. cit., p. 434: emphasis added.

in the hands of the corporation, and are thereby due compensation in the form of having their interests given privilege over those of other parties. Maitland states that:

> As a practical matter, no stakeholder is likely to agree to bear the risk asso-
> ciated with the corporation's activities unless it gets the commitment that
> the corporation will be managed for its benefit. That is logical because the
> stockholder alone stands to absorb any costs of mismanagement.[19]

It is strange, however, to think that the worker who loses his job has not absorbed any costs of mismanagement. Maitland's point must be that while workers stand to lose their jobs due to corporate mismanagement, they only lose future potential earnings, whereas shareholders lose something they have placed into the corporation. However, workers too have placed something at risk when accepting a job. At the very least, the worker has bypassed other possible job opportunities, opportunities which may have turned out to be financially more rewarding. Also, some have gone to school in the hopes of pursuing a career in the field, thereby investing substantial sums of money (or accruing substantial debt) in the process. Even more importantly, many workers have purchased homes in the expectation of a steady income, and in this manner have risked their homes on the corporation. We can also add to our list the various ways in which workers plant roots in the community, which are disrupted when they are forced to relocate, such as placing their children in local schools or having their spouses accept jobs. While the worker's investment in a corporation is not of the same sort as the shareholder's, it constitutes a risk nevertheless, and so the worker's position is not dissimilar to that of the shareholder. The only difference between the risks taken by the two parties is one of degree, and the degree of that risk will depend upon the particular situation of each individual.

Contracts

Maitland's second argument is that corporations are fundamentally a "freely chosen ... nexus ... of contracts" between its stakeholders, which establish both the "rights" and the "obligations" of each party.[20] These contracts stipulate that the worker will give the corporation her labor in return for a fixed wage, while the shareholder will receive all of the profits of the corporation in return for investing capital in it. When third parties tinker with that arrangement, they violate the right of self-determination of

---

19   Ian Maitland, "The Morality of the Corporation. An Empirical or Normative Disagreement?" *Business Ethics Quarterly* 4, no. 4 (1994): 445–57.
20   Maitland, op. cit., p. 449.

the members of the contract, who have determined the terms of the contracts under "free," "voluntary," and "uncoerced" bargaining circumstances.[21]

But Maitland cannot possibly mean that such contracts are explicit, for no such document was signed by either shareholders or employees. He must therefore mean that some sort of implied contract exists between all parties involved. For example, as a teacher, I never explicitly state that I will not allow a student's membership in a morally repellent organization to bias the grades I give him, but this is certainly implied by the nature of our relationship.

However, Maitland's picture of the corporation simply does not square with reality. It turns out that most shareholders expect corporate managers to take into account the interests of other constituencies when making decisions about the welfare of the corporation.[22] More importantly, shareholders tend to think of themselves not as owners of the corporation, but rather as investors in it.[23] This rings true, for imagine that I were to describe a friend as a part-owner of a major corporation. My listener would assume that the person owns a substantial percentage of that corporation's shares, and thus has a say in its operations. But if I were to clarify that my friend has one thousand dollars invested in a mutual fund with one percent of its holdings in Microsoft, my listener would now take the comment as a rather weak joke. For the vast majority of shareholders, dabbling in the stock market is thought of as one means among many of investing one's money, something chosen for its high rate of return, not in order to become a corporate owner. Thus, it is hard to understand how the investor can be acting under the assumption of an unstated contract between himself, management, and the company's employees. On the other side, employees have traditionally assumed that taking a job meant having it for life as long as they perform their duties well.[24] Given these considerations, if we are basing such contracts on the implicit understandings and expectations of the parties involved, the evidence actually points in the very opposite direction to which Maitland argues.

Finally, one can raise serious doubts about the assertion that the worker/manager/shareholder relationship has been established under "free, voluntary, and uncoerced" circumstances. For one, the parties are by no means in an equal bargaining position. Despite Maitland's insistence that the disgruntled employee can always "fire his boss by resigning,"[25] employees often find that they have very few job options given their skills, the labor market, and the costs of moving to another area. Shareholders, however, have thousands of companies from which to choose,

---

21 Maitland, op. cit., p. 450.
22 Larry D. Sonderquist and Robert P. Vecchio, "Reconciling Shareholders' Rights and Corporate Responsibility New Guidelines for Management," *Duke Law Journal* (1978): 840, reproduced in Boatright, p. 398.
23 Boatright, op. cit., p. 397.
24 Reich, op. cit.
25 Maitland, op. cit., p. 451.

and a variety of mechanisms specifically designed to make movement in and out of the stock market as easy as possible. Maitland does acknowledge this imbalance, but claims that the situation "presumably reflects the preferences of stakeholders as expressed in the marketplace."[26] But the view that current corporate structure emerged as a result of market forces is implausible. It is far more likely that this structure is a result of unquestioned social assumptions, passed from generation to generation, about how companies should be organized. It simply does not occur to the average worker living in the United States that this structure is negotiable, and thus the worker does not attempt to express preferences for alternate models.

Other People's Money

Milton Friedman also advances two arguments against the position that corporations have a responsibility to parties other than shareholders. Friedman's first objection is that "the corporation is an instrument of the stockholders who own it," meaning that the manager is acting with other people's money, and thus serving the public interest at the expense of profits is an impermissible use of that money.[27] Another way to put it is that any action that diminishes profits to aid other parties constitutes a "tax" on the shareholders' income.

However, such a use of the shareholders' income is only impermissible if it is unauthorized, and as I have noted, most shareholders expect managers to take into account considerations beyond maximizing profits. Moreover, shareholders in a modern corporation can withdraw their money from that corporation with a simple phone call, and thus the manager who announces his intention to act for the public good gives shareholders plenty of time to remove their money before such a "tax" is levied. More importantly, it is a generally accepted principle that moral duties "transfer through" from principal to agent, such that if it is morally forbidden for me to do something, then it is forbidden for me to enlist an agent to act on my behalf. Thus, an act of downsizing cannot be morally justified in virtue of the fact that it is done in the interests of the shareholders of the corporation, since if it is wrong for the shareholder to perform that act, then it is equally wrong for the manager to do so for them. The fact that a manager is an agent of others cannot itself make the action morally right, and therefore the moral status of the act will turn on other considerations.[28]

---

26   Ibid.

27   Friedman, "The Social Responsibility of Business Is to Increase Its Profits," *New York Times Magazine*, September 1970, reprinted in *Ethical Theory and Business*, ed. Tom L. Beauchamp and Norman E. Bowie (Englewood Cliffs, N.J.: Prentice-Hall, 1979), pp. 136–38.

28   I owe this insight to Don Loeb.

Private vs. Public

Friedman's second objection is that requiring corporations to act in the social interest disrupts the private/public distinction which is at the heart of the free market system. Care for the public welfare, the objection goes, is properly the function of the state acting through officers specifically appointed for the task, not of businesspersons trained in other fields. Note that Friedman need not be against public welfare measures in principle, only those that place the burden of caring for the public welfare on the shoulders of corporations.

But this point can be met with at least two responses. First, one might argue with Dodd that corporations are best thought of as entities permitted to exist by the state because they serve the public good, not because individuals have a right to enrich themselves through them.[29] Of course, corporate activities can end up doing both, but the issue concerns what justifies their existence, and in fact there is considerable historical evidence that corporations were originally conceived as a means of advancing the public good. Thus, the objection requires a defense of the position that corporations must only be run for the private good of their owners. Second, the objection cannot be applied to the case at hand. Downsizing concerns a corporation terminating the employment of its workers. Thus, unlike providing food and shelter to those in need, there is no public sector analogue to the service being demanded of corporations. Unless Friedman is willing to concede that the government should be in the business of hiring all laid-off workers, which of course would eventually lead to a nearly entirely state-run economy—the very antithesis of the free market—then he will need to acknowledge that the business of employing people falls precisely on the private sector whenever possible.

Friedman also objects to the social responsibility position on grounds that it transfers too much decision-making power to the government, again disrupting the public/private split. In his mind, government interference in corporate profit-seeking objectives constitutes "police state" tactics.[30] However, Friedman is conveniently forgetting the fact that the free market system which he so cherishes requires active intervention by the government in order to exist. For instance, if Friedman owned a corporation that had recently released a very popular home video game that was subsequently copied down to the last detail by a rival company, he would likely turn to the government for protection, since one of the government's corporate life-sustaining activities is copyright protection. Similarly, if a radio or television station tries to broadcast on a competitor's frequency, the FCC will prevent it from doing so since

---

29   Dodd, op. cit., p. 1148.
30   Friedman, op. cit., p. 137. Of course, the view that regulations designed to improve the general welfare of the population constitute "police state" tactics would only be held by someone not actually living in one.

the FCC issues licenses to stations guaranteeing them sole access to their frequency. Once we add to this list the ordinary protections such as police, fire, and disaster relief (not to mention the billions of tax dollars spent on various "corporate welfare" programs), it becomes apparent that one cannot simply label any government intervention into business activities unjust. To do so mistakenly assumes a situation of complete non-intervention by the government as one's moral baseline. But this assumption is untenable because the free market requires government support in a variety of ways. The government can thereby demand certain concessions to the community welfare in return. Ironically, Friedman illustrates his own position with a prime example of this point. He attacks price controls on businesses on grounds they would lead to "the destruction of the free-enterprise system and its replacement by a centrally controlled system," and furthermore, would not even be effective because "what determines the average level of prices and wages is the amount of money in the economy."[31] But the primary factor determining the amount of money in the economy is the federal reserve interest rate, a government function supported by taxpayer money.

I have argued that no philosophically sound argument has yet been advanced for privileging the interests of shareholders over those of workers simply by virtue of the fact that they are shareholders. This is not to say that no such argument may someday appear, but rather that in the absence of compelling reasons to the contrary, we must assume that the worker has an equal moral standing as the shareholder since they are, after all, both humans. Cast in this manner, the burden of proof in the debate runs contrary to what has been up to now believed by its participants. It has been tacitly assumed that it is the job of those arguing for the moral status of non-shareholders to establish their position, perhaps due to the earlier-mentioned view of fiduciary duties. But one of our most deeply felt convictions is that two human beings have equal moral status until morally relevant considerations can distinguish between them. Thus, it is really on the shoulders of those arguing for privileging the interests of the shareholders to make their case. This, I have argued, they have yet to do, leaving us to default to the presumption of equality.

The Utilitarian Argument

I now wish to examine the utilitarian defense of downsizing. It seems to me that once the moral equality of workers and shareholders has been granted, the only considerations that could justify acts of downsizing would be consequentialist in nature. At the very least, arguments currently advanced to justify acts of downsizing, when they do not rely upon the premise of a moral superiority of shareholders, have

---

31   Friedman, op. cit., p. 137.

been utilitarian. Thus, if I can establish that the utilitarian case has yet to be made, I will have demonstrated that we have yet to find an adequate defense of downsizing.

Ronald Lieber argues for the rather startling claim that not only does the country as a whole benefit from downsizing, but so too do the downsized workers themselves. He begins by noting that 80 percent of the shares in Fortune 500 companies are held by personal stock holdings and retirement plans. Since nearly all retirement plans invest in mutual funds, the workers of these companies themselves own the shares.[32] The remainder of his argument is sketched out in an accompanying graphic entitled "Virtuous Circle." It begins at the top with an inquisitive-looking figure, representing a worker, investing in a 401K. We next see a stern-faced figure representing a mutual fund manager "put[ting] the screws to the company he invests in." The third step involves the blank-faced (or perhaps contemplative) figure of the company's CEO laying off sad-looking employees. This is followed by a graph containing a long flat arrow which suddenly shoots upward at the angle of anti-aircraft weaponry, representing the fact that Wall Street responds favorably to the news of these layoffs, and the company's stock soars. Finally, the stock increase drives up the value of the 401K account and we come full circle to find the formerly glum looking employees gleefully smiling with dollar signs in their eyes.

Lieber, of course, ignores the fact that these employees are out of a job. It is highly unlikely that the lost wages made up for the increase in the value of the 401Ks, especially since mutual funds tend to diversify their holdings; thus, the rise in the fund's value is likely to be minimal. In fact, there is no reason to assume that the employee's 401Ks have any money at all invested in that particular company. Perhaps Lieber is assuming that all former employees will soon find similar work elsewhere, but this optimism is certainly unwarranted.

Notice how Lieber is arguing that every single individual is made better off by downsizing, a claim so strong it would be surprising to find it defensible. But the classical utilitarian model does not require such bold conclusions, for utilitarianism is generally construed as the principle that the act which maximizes total utility is morally right. Thus, Lieber could argue that downsizing benefits the majority of the population, and though it leaves some individuals by the wayside, the benefit to the whole outweighs the harm to the few. The entire economy, it might be argued, is becoming more efficient. Moreover, the stock market has skyrocketed, benefiting all those who have investments in mutual funds.

But there is reason to doubt whether downsizing has generated a net gain in utility. A group of researchers recently concluded a fifteen-year study which found that when acts of downsizing are not accompanied by careful restructuring of the corporation—in other words, when people are simply laid off in order to lower costs

---

32　Ronald B. Lieber, "Who Owns the 500? You Do," *Fortune*, April 29, 1996, pp. 264–66.

of production without thought of how the remaining employees will sustain levels of productivity—downsizing has always hurt the corporation in the long run.[33] Reich also notes that the downsizing trend has caused a general drop in employee loyalty in the United States.[34] Workers are far less likely to go the extra mile for firms who treat them as disposable cogs in the corporate machine. While loyalty is not easily quantifiable, and thus does not show up in a corporate ledger, it will affect the company's overall performance.

Second, the benefits from the performance of the stock market are by no means spread evenly across the board. Recall Lieber's claim that 80 percent of the stock in Fortune 500 companies is held by personal stock holdings and retirement plans. This does not tell us how stock is divided between the two groups. Since the category "personal stock holdings" includes the wealthy, the benefits of the stock market might be primarily distributed to a relatively small group of investors. Thus, the trend might be benefiting a few at the expense of the many. This view is supported somewhat by the aforementioned claim that the median wage of workers has declined in the past few years, while the fortunes of the very wealthy have grown considerably.[35] It has also been argued that higher wages and economic security for workers increases profits for the shareholders, as it increases the consumption of goods that companies produce.[36]

But even if the case could be made that downsizing improves the overall health of the economy, there would still be a gap between this fact and the conclusion that overall utility has risen. If the argument were to terminate at this point, it would be assuming that one can equate well-being with financial gain; however, far more things go into determining one's well-being. For instance, it is indisputable that the anxiety from job loss has a profoundly negative influence upon one's psychic health. The harm of unemployment cannot simply be measured by the total loss of income; it produces fear for one's own well-being as well as the well-being of one's family, not to mention the anxiety experienced by those other groups themselves. When these factors are taken into account, it becomes clear that utilitarian considerations do not

33 Wayne F. Cascio, interview on National Public Radio, November 14, 1997.

34 Reich, op. cit.

35 It was recently reported that Bill Gates made eighteen *billion* dollars in 1996, including 2.5 billion dollars in one day, bringing his personal fortune to an eye-popping thirty-five billion dollars. See Randall E. Stross's aptly titled, "Bill Gates: The Richest Man Ever," *Fortune*, August 4, 1997, pp. 38–40. Those interested in keeping abreast of Gates's fortune can receive up-to-the-minute updates on a web site entitled "Bill Gates' Personal Wealth Clock," http://www.webho.com/WealthClock (which lists his wealth at 40.1 billion dollars on August 1, 1997). [Editor's Note: This link no longer works; for an up-to-date count on the current wealth of Bill Gates, do a web search on "Bill Gates personal wealth counter."]

36 Dodd, op. cit. p. 1152. It is perhaps telling that this argument was made in the nineteen-thirties, as there is one theory that the Great Depression was caused by a long-term drop in wages for the average worker, leading to an economy which could not purchase what it made.

clearly point in favor of downsizing. It might in fact be determined that downsizing improves net utility in the long run, but the empirical evidence is inconclusive. Our position on the issue, therefore, will need to be informed by other considerations.

Arguments against Downsizing

Harming Some to Benefit Others

Up to this point I have argued only that defenders of downsizing have failed to establish that downsizing is morally permissible. Here I will present reasons for thinking that downsizing is often morally wrong. The first argument appeals to the widely held intuition that it is wrong to subject individuals to certain types of harms in order to benefit others. Consider the following example: a town has recently experienced a rash of murders, such that people are afraid to go out at night, or concern themselves with anything but the most critical of functions.[37] Let us further assume that the sheriff of this town knows who has committed the murders and that the murderer has died in his sleep. But the sheriff cannot prove to the town that this individual is guilty (the townspeople would just assume that the sheriff is making up the story in order to shirk his duties). However, there is a drifter passing through town that the sheriff knows can be framed for the murders. Our sheriff performs the utilitarian calculations and determines that the gain in a feeling of security for the town outweighs the harm of going to jail for this one individual, and so frames him for the killings.

Here the individual is subjected to a great harm in order to produce a proportionally lesser benefit to others. I take it that no one would consider the act morally acceptable. This illuminates the widespread moral intuition that causing a great harm for a lesser benefit, even to a great number of people, cannot be morally justified. Most people would even consider it wrong to incur a great harm to a few in order to produce a great benefit to the many, such as removing the eyes from a sighted man and implanting them in two blind persons so that they can now see (with only a drop off in peripheral vision and depth perception distinguishing them from those with two eyes). There are even some who believe that no amount of harm to an individual can be justified on grounds that it will benefit others, since harms and benefits are incommensurable commodities.[38] Given that statistics demonstrate that downsizing often leads to the loss of home and even suicide, it seems hard to deny that at least some downsized workers incur a significant harm from the practice. On the other

---

37   I owe this example to Marcus Singer.
38   See Frances M. Kamm, *Morality, Mortality: Death and Whom to Save from It* (Oxford, Oxford University Press, 1993).

side, since investors in a large corporation tend to diversify their assets, they incur only a minor benefit when any one stock price rises. Thus, if the act of downsizing is not done as a means of saving the corporation—preventing more workers from losing their jobs—but rather to increase profits, it involves causing a great harm for a minor benefit.

We can also draw a distinction within the practice of downsizing which will serve to amplify its wrongfulness in certain circumstances. Ask yourself if there is a difference in the moral status of the following two acts: First, a country involved in a just war bombs the other side's munitions factory in order to end the war, knowing that the bombing will also destroy a grade school bordering the factory and thus killing ten children. Second, a country in a just war bombs the school where the leaders of the opposing country send their kids in order to get them to end the war (accidentally destroying the neighboring munitions factory in the process). Most people would agree that the latter act is far worse than the former. The best way to explain this intuition is that in the latter act, the death of the children is a means to ending the war, while in the former it is an unfortunate byproduct of that means. The children in the second act are being *used* in a way that they are not being used in the former act.

Now consider the case where a CEO downsizes under the knowledge that the mere news of these layoffs will be greeted favorably by the stock market, and thus cause stock prices to rise (as Lieber himself notes), as opposed to the case where downsizing will improve profits by increasing productivity. Here the very act which harms the workers—the loss of their jobs—itself produces the benefit to shareholders. Harm is not a simple byproduct of an act which independently brings benefit, but rather is the means to that benefit. This grates even more deeply against our intuitions that it is wrong to use individuals for others' benefit.

Legitimate Expectations

We might also approach the issue from the perspective of the legitimate expectations of the individuals involved. To illustrate this notion, consider the possibility that the federal government repeals the home interest tax break without any other modifications in the tax code. While I see no reason why homeowners, and not renters, deserve such a break, one could question the action on grounds that homeowners have made plans under the assumption that this break would continue. Those who lose their homes because of the change in the tax laws would have a legitimate complaint, even though there was never a written guarantee that current tax laws would remain forever unchanged. Similarly, workers have made plans under the assumption of a continued source of income. These are not simply plans for leisure activities such as vacations, but rather plans which impinge upon their fundamental well-being as well as the well-being of their families. There are, however, no similar expectations on the part of the shareholder. For one, shareholders know that stock prices are volatile and that they take a risk when entering the market. Thus, no reasonable investor backs her home on the future performance of her securities. Investors may expect a certain average rate of return, but this is over the long term and they budget accordingly. They do not bank important items such as their homes on the assumption of the continued unprecedented rates of return seen in the past few years. Surely, these returns are treated as "icing on the cake," and thus if preserving jobs will diminish returns to the levels historically expected from the market, no critical expectations are thwarted. Also, as mentioned earlier, shareholders tend to consider the companies in which they invest to have obligations to parties other than themselves. Hence, one cannot plead that shareholders entered the market expecting that the company would be run solely for their own benefit.

Fairness

We may also appeal to the work of John Rawls to provide critical perspective on the issue.[39] Rawls is, of course, best known for his mechanism of the "original position" as a means of generating principles of justice. However, this hypothetical construct has been much maligned on grounds that it is unclear what would emerge from such a radically foreign situation from our own. In order to avoid this objection, I will draw upon what I consider his more central intuition: that the arbitrary conditions of one's situation ought not to count against one's life prospects. The idea here is that the individual does not deserve the rewards or punishments that come via things for which she is not responsible. At the very least, these factors include genetic endowments and the social institutions of the society in which she lives.

This seems to me a very strong intuition, one that can account for a wide variety of common moral responses. Consider, for instance, the indignation fans often feel toward professional athletes who receive an exorbitant degree of compensation for their efforts. Physical talents have a considerable genetic component, meaning that much of a top athlete's skill is due to choosing his parents more wisely than the average person. Moreover, these people were lucky enough to be born in a society that happens to value their particular skills, also not something for which they can claim credit. While they might have worked hard to develop their natural talents, there is no reason to think that they have put in more effort than the less talented; and any differences in effort are certainly not great enough to merit the incredible differences in compensation.

---

39   John Rawls, *A Theory of Justice* (Cambridge: Cambridge University Press, 1971).

To apply the principle here, we would first note that the worker who loses his job does so through no fault of his own. Someone fired due to incompetence is not downsized. Downsizing does not involve a surgical removal of all employees in a firm whose work is not up to snuff; instead, whole divisions are removed by virtue of their overall profitability, with no effort made to determine if individual members of those divisions are at fault. In fact, if a division or plant is unprofitable it is most likely due to mismanagement on the part of those running the corporation. This is perhaps one of the reasons why downsized workers feel betrayed, as no attempt is made by management to judge their actual job performance. Downsized workers find themselves harmed due to forces outside of their control. Moreover, these forces have conspired to selectively harm them, since upper management tends to be insulated from these harms, by devices such as receiving a sizable "golden parachute" when dismissed.[40] True, there are a variety of ways in which natural and social forces reward and punish arbitrarily, but this does not make those harms permissible or release us from obligations to mitigate them.

On the other side, shareholders have done nothing to merit the sharp gains that downsizing produces. Perhaps they are owed good faith efforts at sound management by the corporation in virtue of their investment, but they cannot claim to deserve the special increases in the value of their investments due solely to laying off workers. The fact that we happen to live in a world where canning large numbers of workers is a quick means of increasing profits is not any of their doing. Note also that those shareholders who have invested through mutual funds have not themselves chosen to invest in this particular firm. These investors most likely have little idea as to which stocks their mutual funds actually hold, since one of the appeals of these funds is that they allow individuals to enter the market without the need to concern themselves with the intricacies of investing, or the day-to-day fluctuations of the market.

This argument may also be recast at the level of public policy. Many people have wondered if Rawls's second principle of justice—that rewards must be distributed so as to maximally advantage the worst-off individual—would so disrupt the economy that it would be impractical to apply. Nevertheless, one could yet appeal to it as an ethical ideal, and judge particular public policy initiatives on the basis of whether their net result is to move us toward, or away from, this goal. That is, the fact that downsizing redistributes income in a manner that moves the United States away from satisfying the second principle of justice provides reason for regulating it. While we may not be able to approximate an ideally just society, we are compelled to at the very least avoid actions which exacerbate an already unfair situation.

---

40   For instance, Michael Ovitz, second in command at Disney, got a ninety million dollar check with his pink slip. See "Executive Pay," *CQ Researcher* 7, no. 26, July 11, 1997, p. 603.

Applying the Results and Related Concerns

In essence, I have argued for two theses in this work. First, the question of the ethical status of an act of downsizing will turn not on theoretical questions of the general responsibilities of corporate managers, but rather empirical considerations pertaining to the actual situation of the worker and shareholder. That is, features intrinsic to the worker/manager/shareholder relationship, the focus of most business ethics literature, will not help to resolve the issue of the morality of an act of downsizing. Business managers will need to examine the actual situations of their shareholders and workers, as well as that of the company, in order to ascertain if a decision to downsize is morally permissible. While this grants that some acts of downsizing may be morally permissible, simply establishing that corporate managers cannot lay claim to a special duty to shareholders which trumps any competing duties cuts against the grain of much of corporate America's current philosophy. For instance, in a speech to business representatives, David Rockefeller argued that corporations "have a responsibility to society beyond that of maximizing profits for shareholders." Yet he quickly qualified this position by stating that "let me add, before they come to retract my Chicago degree, that making profits must come first."[41] While many business persons would agree that corporations have some obligations to persons besides shareholders, all but the most socially conscious would likely consider anathema the position that these obligations stand on equal footing with obligations to shareholders.

The second thesis concerns the general methodology of most business ethics literature. The business ethics community's concern with debating the relative merits of general principles concerning business responsibilities, such as property rights and fiduciary duties, provides little aid in resolving the particular ethical dilemmas that business managers face. Even if agreement can be reached on these principles, they are often too vague to point in any particular direction when applied to a particular issue. The business ethics community would thus do better to focus instead on particular issues, and approach these issues by constructing structurally similar analogies to the situation under debate, where greater consensus can be built on the ethical status of these situations.

How might the corporate manager apply the insights gathered here to a particular situation? First and foremost, an act of downsizing that prevents the collapse of the corporation can be justified on grounds that the organism is saved by amputating a limb. However, we must keep in mind that bankruptcy does not always mean the complete shutting down of shop. Bankruptcy courts make every effort to find a way of restructuring the debts of the corporation to keep it in business. In fact, corporations have been known to use bankruptcy as a means of avoiding a court settlement.

41   Rockefeller, op. cit.

But an act of downsizing that merely increases profits, which seems increasingly the case, requires a careful analysis of the harms and benefits it will incur to the parties involved. For a small firm, such as a fast-food franchise with a single proprietor, the owner may be at greater risk than her employees. The owner most likely has a large percentage of her personal fortune wrapped up in the company, whereas the workers are usually (but not always) high school students just earning extra spending money. However, with a large corporation, the results are likely to be quite different. It bears mention that the corporate entity is grounded in the principle that a separation exists between the corporation and the personal finances of its owners, a device created specifically to minimize the risk to shareholders. Thus, the owner of a corporation is not personally liable for its debts; if IBM dissolves, shareholders need not fear that IBM's creditors will come knocking at their doors. Legal protection to the share-holder is built into the corporation's charter. More importantly, since investors tend not to risk money that is required for their sustenance, their losses do not normally affect their immediate well-being. By contrast, the worker who banks his home on his job places his immediate well-being, as well as the well-being of his family, in far greater peril. Finally, investors today diversify their assets through mutual funds which own shares in thousands of corporations. Thus, losses from one stock create only a minor shift in the fund's overall value. This means that acts of downsizing can cause great harm to a few for a minor benefit to the many, something which I have argued is not morally permissible. Also, one can argue that the sole proprietor who has nursed the business from the ground up merits greater consideration than the mutual fund investor who may not even know that he or she owns shares in the corporation. Moreover, the worker who has purchased a home, and started a family, based on the assumption of the continued source of income, is deserving of greater consideration than the investor who finds that unprecedented gains in the stock market allow him to extend his vacation to Aruba by a week.

Finally, the conceptual tools that I have developed here could be applied to other related practices as well, such as the explosion in CEO compensation. It is not coincidental that the downsizing wave has corresponded with an inordinate rise in CEO compensation, since businesses have been linking more and more of the CEO's compensation to stock earnings.[42] In 1980, CEO compensation was 42 times that of the average worker; by 1995, the number had grown to 141. The 1996 Jury Award for CEO compensation went to Lawrance M. Coss, head of the Greentree Corporation, who received one hundred million dollars in 1996.[43] The following sequence is not at

---

42 Brett Chase, "Investors Suing Greentree over CEO's Compensation," *American Banker* 162, no. 26, February 7, 1997, p. 5. The reason for this, as it turns out, is that companies can claim the compensation they pay to executives in the form of stock options as a tax deduction.

43 Chase, op. cit. Incidentally, Greentree is a corporation that specializes in making high-interest loans to mobile home owners who, due to their financial situation, are unable to get financing elsewhere. It was

all uncommon: a corporation with sagging profits hires a new CEO. The CEO's contract provides a few-hundred-thousand-dollar base salary and a bonus for increases in the share price. The CEO immediately dismisses whole divisions of the firm, even going so far as to cut the firm nearly in half. The stock market, as Lieber reports, reacts favorably to the news, and the company's share price rises, bringing a windfall in the many millions to the CEO (something Lieber neglects to mention). What are we to say about this practice? To put it baldly, but I think not inaccurately, the skill needed to lay off people is not terribly impressive, nor is it in short supply. It is hard to argue that the CEO deserves this level of compensation. Importantly, as noted earlier, if the corporate manager's fiduciary duty to his shareholders means anything, it entails that the manager is violating his duty when he runs the corporation for his own benefit. Thus, when an act of downsizing is initiated by corporate managers for the intent of enriching themselves, it runs contrary to the CEO's duties. Of course, this intent might be hard to establish in practice, but there is no reason in principle why courts couldn't take a variety of pieces of evidence together as indicating sufficient evidence of a CEO's intentions. In fact, such cases are now being brought up in civil courts (the CEO of Greentree being one).[44] Moreover, the very fact that CEOs can enrich themselves in this manner raises a conflict of interest (and possible violation of insider trading laws), which the government might have reason to regulate.[45]

Another major trend in business is the practice of replacing full-time employees with part-time help, in jobs which pay only a fraction of that of full-time positions and provide no benefits at all. While employers have always used part-time help, more and more employees are finding that these positions are the only ones available to them, and are thus becoming permanent part-time employees. Ironically, academia provides a prime example of this movement, and it is curious that many academics who claim to be concerned for the working class feel no compulsion to speak out on behalf of their own underemployed colleagues. The fact that younger faculty members often lack the opportunities that were available to older faculty members raises serious concerns of fairness. Finally, the practice of moving jobs overseas in pursuit of cheaper labor begs for philosophical scrutiny.[46]

Why has the philosophical community ignored the issue of corporate downsizing? Perhaps this is due to the perception that challenges to the practice would

---

reported that Travelers Group chief Sanford I. Weill collected 220 million dollars in stock options in 1997 (*Burlington Free Press*, March 30, 1998).

44　Chase, op. cit.

45　"Executive Pay," op. cit. One example that raises an eyebrow concerns Albert J. "Chainsaw Al" Dunlap, famous for cutting up companies and moving on, who made 70 million dollars in 1998 (*Burlington Free Press*, March 30, 1998).

46　The Labor Department has certified that NAFTA has resulted in at least 132,972 lost jobs. *Burlington Free Press*, July 10, 1997.

strike at the heart of the free market system, and thus would likely emanate from a Marxist, or other similarly passé philosophical systems. But I hope to have demonstrated that the issue can be tackled with garden-variety moral intuitions, ones that appeal to nothing more exotic than principles pertaining to the fundamental moral equality of humans. These arguments may provoke objections, but they are intended to initiate discussion on a topic long in need of careful examination.

Questions

1. What are the empirical effects of downsizing?

2. What arguments does Orlando address to make the case for the moral equality of shareholders and workers?

3. What arguments does Orlando offer to make the independent case for the wrongness of downsizing?

4. Should shareholders and workers be seen as having different relationships to a company?

Further Reading

De Meuse, Kenneth P., Thomas J. Bergmann, and Paul A. Vanderheiden. "Corporate Downsizing: Separating Myth from Fact." *Journal of Management Inquiry*, vol. 6, no. 2, 1997, pp. 168–76.

Hopkins, Willie E., and Shirley A. Hopkins. "The Ethics of Downsizing: Perceptions of Rights and Responsibilities." *Journal of Business Ethics*, vol. 18, no. 2, 1999, pp. 145–55.

McMahon, Thomas F. "Lifeboat Ethics in Business." *Business Ethics Quarterly*, vol. 10, no. 1, 2000, pp. 269–76.

Van Buren, Harry J. "The Bindingness of Social and Psychological Contracts: Toward a Theory of Social Responsibility in Downsizing." *Journal of Business Ethics*, vol. 25, no. 3, 2000, pp. 205–19.

18.
"DECENCY MEANS MORE THAN 'ALWAYS LOW PRICES'
A COMPARISON OF COSTCO TO
WALMART'S SAM'S CLUB"

WAYNE F. CASCIO

About This Reading

An intuitive argument for companies paying low wages is the affordability of their products. Walmart is typically assumed to embody such an approach. It is through low wages that Walmart is able to keep prices so low, or so the argument goes. Walmart is the largest retailer in the world, and yet part of that company, the Sam's Club warehouse portion of the business, is not the market leader in its area (warehouse stores). The top warehouse retailer is Costco, and this is the case even though Costco has fewer stores than Sam's Club. Additionally, Costco employees are in a better position in terms of wages and benefits than Walmart employees. This seems to be a violation of the seemingly intuitive idea that low prices require low wages. In this article, Wayne Cascio explains how Costco has managed to maintain its place as the market leader while maintaining employee wages and benefits. Assuming that the same model would work for Walmart, the natural question is, are the practices of Walmart morally justifiable?

It is also interesting to note that Walmart seems to have recently increased its externalized costs. Cascio references a recent study that claims that one 200-person Walmart store results in costs to federal taxpayers of over $470,000. A more recent *Mother Jones* article cites a new study by the same group that finds the cost to taxpayers is currently between $900,000 and $1.74 million for a 300-person store. This is a startling increase.

EXECUTIVE OVERVIEW Wal-Mart's emphasis on "Always low prices. *Always*" has made it the largest retail operation in history. However, this unrelenting mission has also created a way of doing business that draws substantial criticism regarding the company's employment practices, relationships with suppliers, and the company's impact on local economies. This paper focuses on a company that delivers low prices to consumers, but in a fundamentally different way than its competitor, Wal-Mart. That company is warehouse-retailer Costco. In the following sections we will begin by providing some background on the company, including its history, its business model, its ethical principles, core beliefs, and values. Then we will consider some typical Wall Street analysts' assessments of this approach, followed by a systematic comparison of the financial performance of Costco with that of Sam's Club, a warehouse retailer that is part of Wal-Mart.

To be sure, Wal-Mart wields its awesome power for just one purpose: to bring the lowest possible prices to its customers. Sam Walton, affectionately known as "Mr. Sam" by Wal-Mart associates, embodied a number of admirable values that he instilled in the company he founded: hard work, discipline, modesty, unpretentiousness, and frugality. By all accounts he also wanted his employees to be motivated, inspired, and happy to work for Wal-Mart. At the same time, however, he was driven, tireless, and determined to drive a hard bargain (Walton, 1992). His brilliance lay in his ability to execute a singularly powerful idea: Sell stuff that people need every day, just a little cheaper than everyone else, sell it at that low price all the time, and customers will flock to you. Wal-Mart's mission is found as a slogan printed on every Wal-Mart bag: "Always low prices. *Always*." Wal-Mart's obsessive focus on that single core value created what has become the largest and most powerful company in history.

The company espouses those same core values today, but ironically, their application is quite different from that in the 1960s, the 1970s, even the 1980s. Today, the very characteristics that allowed Wal-Mart to prosper and grow are the source of unrelenting criticism. As Fishman (2006) notes, the company's core values seem to have become inverted, for they now sometimes drive behavior that is not only exploitative, but in some cases illegal as well. Consider the pressure on store managers to control labor costs. As noted in its 2005 annual report (pp. 45, 46), Wal-Mart is a defendant in numerous class-action lawsuits involving employment-related issues as varied as failure to pay required overtime to hourly employees, challenges to exempt (from overtime) status by assistant store managers, and allegations of gender-based discrimination in pay, promotions, job transfers, training, job assignments, and health-care coverage.

There is another aspect of the Wal-Mart effect that is more troubling, and it concerns how Wal-Mart gets those low prices: low wages for its employees, unrelenting pressure on suppliers, products cheap in quality as well as price, offshoring jobs [...]. "Wal-Mart has the power to squeeze profit-killing concessions from suppliers, many of whom are willing to do almost anything to keep the retailer happy, in part because Wal-Mart now dominates consumer markets so thoroughly that they have no choice ... Wal-Mart's price pressure can leave so little profit that there is little left for innovation ... [As a result] decisions made in Bentonville routinely close factories as well as open them" (Fishman 2006, p. 89).

This paper focuses on a company that is already more than "always low prices." That company is warehouse-retailer Costco—one that may provide an alternative to the Wal-Mart model by delivering low prices to consumers, but not at the cost of employees' wages or quality of life. In the following sections we will begin by providing some background on the company, including its history, its business model, its ethical principles, core beliefs, and values. Then we will consider some typical Wall Street analysts' assessments of this approach, followed by a systematic comparison of the financial performance of Costco with that of Sam's Club, a warehouse retailer that is part of Wal-Mart.

Costco, a Brief History

The company's co-founder and chief executive officer, Jim Sinegal, is the son of a coal miner and steelworker. In 1954, as an 18-year-old student at San Diego Community College, a friend asked him to help unload mattresses for a month-old discounter called Fed-Mart. What he thought would be a one-day job turned into a career. He rose to executive vice-president for merchandising, and became a protégé of Fed-Mart's chairman, Sol Price. Mr. Price is credited with inventing the idea of high-volume warehouse stores that sell a limited number of products.

Sol Price sold Fed-Mart to a German retailer in 1975, and was fired soon after. Mr. Sinegal then left and helped Mr. Price start a new warehouse company, Price Club. Its huge success led others to enter the business: Wal-Mart started Sam's Club, Zayre's started BJ's Wholesale Club, and in 1983 a Seattle entrepreneur, Jeffrey Brotman, helped Mr. Sinegal to found Costco Wholesale Corporation (Greenhouse 2005). The company began with a single store in Issaquah, Washington, outside of Seattle. At the end of fiscal 2005, as the fourth largest retailer in the United States and the ninth largest in the world, it had a total of 460 warehouses in 37 U.S. states, Puerto Rico, and several additional countries: Canada, Mexico, the United Kingdom,

Taiwan, South Korea, and Japan (Costco Wholesale Corp. annual report 2005). Costco and Price Club merged in 1993.

Business Model

Costco's business model is based on that of Sol Price: sell a limited number of items, keep costs down, rely on high volume, pay workers well, have customers buy memberships, and aim for upscale shoppers, especially small-business owners. In addition, don't advertise—that saves two percent a year in costs.

Consider one key feature of the business model: sell a limited number of items. A typical Costco store stocks 4,000 types of items, including perhaps just four brands of toothpaste. A Wal-Mart, in contrast, typically stocks more than 100,000 types of items, and may carry 60 sizes and brands of toothpaste. Narrowing the number of options increases the sales volumes of each, allowing Costco to squeeze deeper and deeper bulk discounts from suppliers. Among warehouse retailers, Costco is number one in market share, accounting for about half of the sales in the industry. Sam's Club is number two, with 642 stores, and about 40 percent of the market. Sam's Club, however, is not a typical runner-up: it is part of the Wal-Mart empire, which, with $315.6 billion in 2005 sales, dwarfs Costco's sales of $52.9 billion in the same year (*Fortune 500* 2006).

In terms of memberships and target customers, at the end of fiscal 2005 Costco had 45.3 million loyal members, each paying $45 per year to join, with an 86 percent renewal rate. Executive memberships are available both to business and individual members, for an annual fee of $100, and there were 4.2 million of those at the end of fiscal 2005. The Executive Membership program offers members additional savings and benefits on various business and consumer services offered by Costco (Costco Wholesale Corp. Annual Report 2005). The average annual income of Costco's customers is $74,000, with 31 percent earning over $100,000 (Greenhouse 2005).

Ethical Principles, Core Beliefs, and Values

In their most recent letter to shareholders, cofounders Jeff Brotman and Jim Sinegal wrote: "We remain committed to running our company and living conscientiously by our Code of Ethics every day: to obey the law; take care of our members; take care of our employees; respect our suppliers; and reward you, our shareholders" (Costco Wholesale Corp. Annual Report 2005, p. 5). Note the modern-day heresy in Costco's numbered code of ethics: taking care of customers and employees takes precedence over rewarding shareholders. As we will see below, this has not escaped the critical appraisal of Wall Street analysts.

In contrast to Wal-Mart, which believes, as many other companies do, that shareholders are best served if employers do all they can to hold down costs, including the costs of labor, Costco's approach is decidedly different. In terms of how it treats its workers, Mr. Sinegal says, "It absolutely makes good business sense. Most people agree that we're the lowest-cost provider. Yet we pay the highest wages. So it must mean we get better productivity. It's axiomatic in our business—you get what you pay for" (Shapiro 2004, p. 5).

Wages at Costco start at $10 an hour, rising to $18.32, excluding *twice*-a-year bonuses of between $2,000 and $3,000 for those at the top wage for more than a year. Its average hourly wage is $17 an hour. Wal-Mart does not share its wage scale, and does not break out separately the pay of its Sam's Club workers, but the average pay of a full-time worker at Wal-Mart is $10.11 an hour (Coleman-Lochner 2006). The pay scale of unionized grocery clerks in the Puget Sound area, very good jobs as far as retail goes, provides a further comparison. Those jobs start at $7.73 an hour and top out at $18 (Shapiro 2004).

Labor costs at Costco are expensive, accounting for about 70 percent of the company's total cost of operations, and they are more than 40 percent higher than those at Wal-Mart. So how can the company compete based on cost leadership and still pay such high wages? According to co-founder Sinegal: "It's just good business. I mean obviously anyone who is a business person thinks about the importance of people to their operation. You've got to want to get the very best people that you can, and you want to be able to keep them and provide some job security for them. That's not just altruism, it's good business" (Frey 2004, p. 3).

Turning over Inventory Faster Than People

Costco's wages help keep turnover unusually low, 17 percent overall and just 6 percent after the first year. In contrast, turnover at Wal-Mart is 44 percent per year, close to the retail-industry average (Frontline 2004). "We're trying to turn our inventory faster than our people," says Mr. Sinegal. "Obviously it's not just wages that motivate people. How much they are respected, and whether they feel they can have a career at a company, are also important" (Shapiro 2004, p. 5).

Toward that end, Costco also has some rules about discipline and promotion. An employee with more than two years of service cannot be fired without the approval of a senior company officer. (It used to be that only one of the cofounders, Sinegal or Brotman, could issue this approval.) The company also requires itself to promote internally for 86 percent of its openings in top positions. "In truth, it turns out to be 98 percent" according to Mr. Sinegal (Shapiro 2004, p. 5). By comparison, and this is also very high, 76 percent of all store managers at Wal-Mart started their careers in hourly positions (Wal-Mart 2005 annual report).

Costco's chief financial officer, Richard Galanti, speaks the same language. "One of the things Wall Street chided us on is that we're too good to our employees ...

We don't think that's possible." In his office, he keeps a memo from Sol Price, dated August 8, 1967, posted on his bulletin board. It reads: "Although we are all interested in margin, it must never be done at the expense of our philosophy." To Galanti, there is an object lesson in that approach with respect to employee relations: "Costco is not going to make money at the expense of what's right" (Shapiro 2004, p. 6).

Costco's senior vice president for human resources, John Matthews, echoes the same sentiment. "When Jim [Sinegal] talks to us about setting wages and benefits, he doesn't want us to be better than everyone else. He wants us to be demonstrably better" (Greenhouse 2005, p. 2).

The View from Wall Street Analysts

How is Costco's treatment of employees received on Wall Street? Not everyone is happy with this business strategy. Some Wall Street analysts argue that Mr. Sinegal is overly generous, not only to Costco's customers, but to its employees as well. They worry that the company's operating expenses could get out of hand. In the opinion of Deutsche Bank Securities, Inc. analyst Bill Dreher, "At Costco, it's better to be an employee or a customer than a shareholder" (Holmes & Zellner 2004, p. 76). Sanford C. Bernstein & Co. analyst Ian Gordon argued similarly: "Whatever goes to employees comes out of the pockets of shareholders" (Shapiro 2004, p. 1).

Another Sanford C. Bernstein & Co. analyst, Emme Kozloff, faulted Mr. Sinegal for being too generous to his employees. She noted that when analysts complained that Costco's workers were paying just 4 percent toward their health-care costs, he raised that percentage only to 8 percent, when the retail average is 25 percent. "He has been too benevolent," she said. "He's right that a happy employee is a productive, long-term employee, but he could force employees to pick up a little more of the burden" (Greenhouse 2005, p. 2). She added, "Their benefits are amazing, but shareholders get frustrated from a stock perspective" (Zimmerman 2004, p. 3).

Like other companies, public and private, small and large, surging health-care costs forced Costco to move aggressively to control expenses. The increase in Costco employees' contribution to 8 percent was the company's first increase in employee health premiums in eight years. According to CEO Jim Sinegal, the company held off from boosting premiums for as long as it could, and it did not give in until it had lowered its earnings forecast twice (Zimmerman 2004).

Analyst Bill Dreher agrees with Emme Kozloff. "From the perspective of investors, Costco's benefits are overly generous. Public companies need to care for shareholders first. Costco runs its business like it is a private company" (Zimmerman 2004, p. 1). According to Mr. Dreher, Costco's unusually high wages and benefits contribute to investor concerns that profit margins at Costco aren't as high as they should be.

Analyst Ian Gordon also noted another Costco sin: it treats its customers too well. Its bargain-basement prices are legendary, and, as a result, customers flock to its stores. At about the same time that these analysts were commenting on Costco, the company was planning to add staff at checkouts in order to shorten lines. While business schools often teach that caring for customers is a cardinal rule for business success, Wall Street tended to put a different spin on the company's customer-care initiative, as analyst Gordon noted: "It was spending what could have been share-holders' profit on making a better experience for customers" (Shapiro 2004, p. 1).

What is Costco's response to this criticism? According to CEO Sinegal: "On Wall Street they're in the business of making money between now and next Thursday. I don't say that with any bitterness, but we can't take that view. We want to build a company that will still be here 50 and 60 years from now" (Greenhouse 2005, p. 2).

If shareholders mind Mr. Sinegal's philosophy, it is not obvious. Figure 1 shows a 5-year comparison of the performance of Costco's and Wal-Mart's common stock, as of May 1, 2006. Based on an index value of 100 on May 1, 2001, Costco's stock has risen 55 percent during that time period, while Wal-Mart's has fallen 10 percent. According to Forbes.com, on May 20, 2006, Costco shares traded at 24.8 times expected earnings. At Wal-Mart the multiple was 17.4. According to analyst Dreher, Costco's share price is so high because so many people love the company. "It's a cult stock" (Greenhouse 2005, p. 2).

If anything, Costco's approach shows that when it comes to wages and benefits, a cost leadership strategy need not be a race to the bottom. In the words of CEO Sinegal, "We pay much better than Wal-Mart. That's not altruism, that's good business" (Shields 2005). The contrast is stark and the stakes are high. Which model of competition will predominate in the United States? As we shall see below, Costco's magic lies in its ability to lift productivity, to compete on employee smarts, management savvy, and constant innovation, rather than to skimp on pay and benefits.

Although it is heresy to today's Wall Street analysts, Abraham Lincoln said in his First Annual Message to Congress, December 3, 1861, "Labor is prior to, and independent of, capital. Capital is the fruit of labor and could not exist if labor had not first existed. Labor is the superior of capital and deserves much the higher consideration" (Abraham Lincoln Research Site 2006).

Unfortunately, most companies that compete based on cost-leadership take the low road on wages and benefits, yet Costco shows that treating employees justly and humanely turns out to be very good business indeed. Will Costco's model work in all situations? Probably not. Wharton professor (and *AMP editor*) Peter Cappelli argued this point recently, when he said, "It's absolutely not true that all those companies that are not being nice to their employees are simply stupid. Nor is it just about good guys and bad guys. There are systematic reasons people adopt the practices they do

... Companies that compete on price don't necessarily need the same level of skills in their workers as do their higher-end counterparts" (Shapiro 2004, pp. 2, 3).

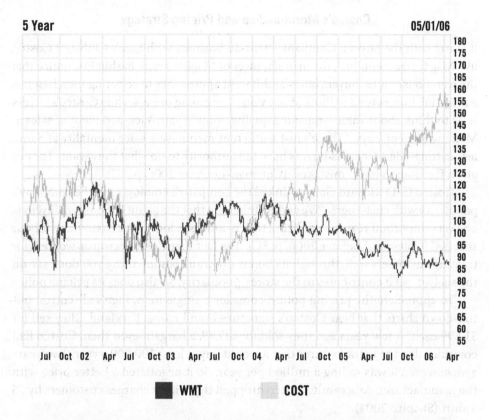

5 Year   **05/01/06**

WMT   COST

Figure 1: Five-year comparison of the performance of Costco and Wal-Mart common stock. May 1, 2001 through May 1, 2006. At May 1, 2001, the index value for each stock was 100.

Fair enough. Even among companies that adopt a low-price strategy, like Sam's Club and Costco, there are important differences in the kinds of customers they serve, the merchandise they sell, and, by extension, in the skill sets of employees they hire. Costco is the largest purveyor of fine wines in the world. It also sells state-of-the-art electronics and Tiffany-style jewelry. Last year it sold 90,000 karats of diamonds, some for more than $250,000 (Goldberg & Ritter 2005; Shapiro 2004). Make no mistake: there is a socio-economic element to Costco's success.

In contrast, Sam's Club stocks few upper-end items. There are no coats over $100, no jewelry over $3,000. Gourmet cheeses and other staples of *la dolce vita* are hard to find (Shapiro 2004). Yet Sam's Club and Costco compete fiercely on lower-cost merchandise. In our next section, therefore, we will consider a fundamental question—namely, why do customers shop at Costco?

Costco's Merchandise and Pricing Strategy

It starts with the buyers. Companies that do business with Sam's Club and Costco, like Mag Instrument, Inc., the manufacturer of Maglite brand flashlights, notice that the warehouse clubs' buyers have far different approaches to selecting merchandise. Sam's Club buyers tend to think about value—meaning price—while Costco's buyers tend to think about value—meaning quality. John Wyatt, Vice-president of sales at Mag Instrument, says, "There's just a different mentality, a safer mentality at Sam's, less cutting-edge. Costco's buyers have full authority to do what they want. They're given freedom to make mistakes" (Coleman-Lochner 2006, p. 8C).

Costco CFO Richard Galanti linked the company's employees to the company's popularity with customers. "We certainly believe that the quality of our employees is one very important reason—realizing they're ambassadors to the customer—for our success" (Coleman-Lochner 2006, p. 8C). The fact that Costco rewards workers for treating customers well, through its bonus program, is something you don't see on the shelves, yet it contributes to the stores' popularity. So also does its pricing policy.

To appreciate the pricing policy, consider a single item, men's all-cotton button-down shirts that bear Costco's signature brand name, Kirkland. They sell for $12.99 each. A few years ago they sold for $17.99, a bargain even then. Costco had committed to the manufacturer that it would buy at least 100,000 a year. Two years ago, however, it was selling a million per year. So it negotiated a better price with the manufacturer. As a result, Costco dropped the price it charges customers by $5 a shirt (Shapiro 2004).

Acknowledging the temptation to charge a little more, CEO Sinegal asks, "Who the hell's going to notice if you charge $14.99 instead of $12? Well, we're going to know. It's an attitudinal thing—you always give the customer the best deal" (Shapiro 2004, p. 9). That is the essence of Costco's pricing strategy: wow consumers with unbelievably low prices so they keep coming in.

In fact, Costco sets a strict cap on its profit margin per item: 14 percent for all goods except Kirkland-brand items, which have a 15 percent cap. Department stores typically mark up items by 30 percent or more. That cap on markup stays the same no matter how great the demand or how limited the supply. As with Kirkland-brand shirts, the more people want an item, the cheaper it becomes. Costco gets away with this because of volume (Shapiro 2004).

CEO Sinegal is famous for his ferocious attention to detail, price, and focus on the customer. As he has said, "We're very good merchants and we offer value. The traditional retailer will say, 'I'm selling this for $10. I wonder whether I can get

$10.50 or $11.' We say, 'We're selling it for $9. How do we get it down to $8?' We understand that our customers don't come and shop with us because of the Santa Claus or the piano player. They come and shop with us because we offer great values" (Greenhouse, 2005, p.2).

Relations with Suppliers

Fishman (2006 this issue), and others (Welch & Welch 2006) have described Wal-Mart's legendary squeeze plays on its suppliers. Costco takes a slightly different, but no less tough, approach toward its suppliers. It simply warns suppliers not to offer other retailers lower prices than Costco gets.

When a frozen-food supplier mistakenly sent Costco an invoice meant for Wal-Mart, Mr. Sinegal discovered that Wal-Mart was getting a better price. Costco has not brought that supplier back. Costco has to be flinty, because the competition is so fierce. Says Mr. Sinegal, "We have to be competitive against the biggest competitor in the world. We cannot afford to be timid" (Greenhouse 2005, p. 3).

Nor can Costco allow personal relationships to get in the way. As an example, consider what happened when Starbucks did not pass on savings from a drop in coffee-bean prices. Although Mr. Sinegal is a friend of Starbucks Chairman Howard Schultz, Mr. Sinegal warned that he would remove Starbucks coffee from his stores unless it cut its prices. Starbucks relented. According to Tim Rose, Costco's Senior Vice-President for food merchandizing, "Howard said, 'Who do you think you are, the price police?'" Mr. Sinegal replied emphatically that he was (Greenhouse 2005, p. 4).

To sum up the previous two sections, a reasonable conclusion is that Costco offers high quality merchandise at low prices, and it does not hesitate to lean on its suppliers—all of its suppliers—to ensure that it is getting as good a deal as any other retailer. What it sacrifices in margin it makes up in volume. Such frugality extends to the chief executive officer's pay, but when it comes to Costco employees, generous benefits and accommodation to labor unions set Costco apart from almost any other retailer.

CEO Pay and Employee Benefits at Costco

For the last three years, CEO Sinegal has received a salary of $350,000, excluding stock options. That is very low for a CEO of a $52 billion-per-year business. By comparison, the typical CEO of a large American company makes more than 430 times the pay of the average worker (NBC Nightly News 2006). In a 2005 interview with ABC News Mr. Sinegal said, "I figured that if I was making something like 12 times more than the typical person working on the floor, that was a fair salary." Of course, as a co-founder of the company, Sinegal owns a lot of Costco stock—more than $150 million worth. He's rich, but only on paper (Goldberg & Ritter 2005).

In terms of employee benefits, Costco contributes generously to its workers' 401(k) plans, starting with 3 percent of salary the second year, and rising to 9 percent after 25 years. Its insurance programs absorb most dental expenses. Costco workers pay 8 percent of their health premiums. Full-time workers are eligible for health insurance after three months, and part-timers after six months. The retail-industry average is 23 percent (Coleman-Lochner 2006). Eighty-five percent of Costco employees have health-insurance coverage, compared to less than half at Wal-Mart and Target (Greenhouse 2005).

Perhaps Chief Financial Officer Richard Galanti best sums up Costco's philosophy of employee relations. "From day one, we've run the company with the philosophy that if we pay better than average, provide a salary people can live on, have a positive environment and good benefits, we'll be able to hire better people, they'll stay longer, and be more efficient" (Zimmerman 2004, pp. 2–3).

In return for all of its largesse, Costco does enjoy low employee turnover, as we mentioned earlier, but it also reaps a less obvious benefit: low inventory shrinkage. Shrinkage is a combination of employee theft, shoplifting, vendor fraud, and administrative error. Of these four components, employee theft is by far the largest contributor. How much does shrinkage cost? A 2002 study by Ernst & Young of 55 of the largest and most successful American retailers operating an average of 1,076 stores with mean revenues of approximately $8.8 billion, revealed that the average loss was 1.7 percent of sales, or roughly $19 million annually (Ernst & Young 2003). At a national level that amounts to more than $31 billion, costing the average family of four more than $440 a year in higher prices ("Retail theft" 2002). Costco's inventory shrinkage is the lowest in the industry, well below 0.20 percent of sales for fiscal 2005 (Costco Wholesale Corp. annual report 2005). That also keeps prices low for consumers.

Health-Care Insurance at Wal-Mart and Target

As of February, 2006, Wal-Mart's own count indicates that 46 percent of its employees are enrolled in company health plans. With an average income of $20,000 a year, they spend 8 percent of their income on health care insurance, nearly twice the national average (Gogoi & Berner 2006). They also pay 33 percent of their health-care insurance premiums (Coleman-Lochner 2006). To make matters worse, a *CBS News* report of an internal Wal-Mart memo from the fall of 2005 indicated that 46 percent of the children of Wal-Mart workers were uninsured or on public health care ("Unions protest" 2006).

In response, Wal-Mart has announced improvements to its health-care insurance offerings, effective May 13, 2006. While full-time employees wait 180 days to be eligible for health-insurance coverage, part timers (those who work fewer than

34 hours a week) will be eligible after one year of working at the company, down from two years previously. (The average wait in the retail industry is less than 90 days, Coleman-Lochner 2006.) Part-timers also will be able to add their children to their coverage for the first time. In addition, the company cut co-pays on some generic medicines from $10 to $3 and offers 20 percent discounts on prescription drugs otherwise not covered. These changes will affect more than 150,000 part-time workers (Gogoi & Berner 2006).

In April 2006, Target Corporation changed its health-care plan so that its 300,000 employees are responsible for more of the costs, and it is considering eliminating its traditional health insurance entirely. Under its new plans, Target will make annual contributions of $400 for individual workers and $800 for families. Monthly premiums will drop to as little as $20 for individuals, but deductibles will be as high as $5,000. The other alternative is an employer funded health-reimbursement account that is not portable. Premiums paid by workers are higher, but deductibles are lower (Zimmerman 2006).

These moves are an attempt to reign in rising health-care costs. According to the Kaiser Family Foundation, health-care premiums paid by workers and their employers jumped 73 percent between 2000 and 2005 (Zimmerman 2006). Comparisons to Wal-Mart and Target, two of Costco's major competitors, bring the generosity of Costco's health care benefits into even starker relief.

Relations with Unions

When 70,000 employees of the nation's three largest grocery chains, Kroger, Safeway, and Albertson's, went on strike in Southern California in 2004, Costco avoided the fray, quietly renegotiating a separate contract with its union employees there. The three-year deal, which was ratified by more than 90 percent of the workers, included higher wages and increased company contributions to employee pension plans.

In contrast, the strike at the supermarket chains lasted four months before a settlement was reached on February 29, 2004. It resulted in cuts in wages and benefits for new workers, thereby creating a two-tier system in which new workers coming in do not have the same wages and benefits as older workers (Frontline 2004).

About 13 percent of Costco's employees belong to unions (in California, Maryland, New Jersey, New York, and Virginia), and they work at warehouses that were previously Price Club locations (Frey 2004). The relative labor peace is symbolic of the company's relations with its employees. According to Rome Aloise, an international union representative for the Teamsters, Costco is one of the better companies he deals with. "They gave us the best agreement of any retailer in the country." The contract guarantees employees at least 25 hours of work a week, and requires that at least half of a store's employees be full time (Greenhouse 2005).

Wal-Mart takes a different tack. Its official stance, as stated on its Website, Walmartfacts.com, is as follows:

> Our Wal-Mart union stance is simple. There has never been a need for a Wal-Mart union due to the familiar, special relationship between Wal-Mart associates and their managers. Wal-Mart has encouraging and advantageous relationships with both our loyal and happy associates on the floor of each Wal-Mart facility and our wonderful managerial staff. There has yet to be a standard in Wal-Mart union history for a union to be needed.

According to the *Los Angeles Times*, at the first sign of union activity, Wal-Mart managers are supposed to call a hotline, prompting a visit from a special team from Wal-Mart headquarters. Wal-Mart spokesperson Mona Williams told the *Times* that such teams do exist, but that their purpose is merely to help managers respond effectively and legally to union-organizing activity. Judges have ruled in cases across the country that Wal-Mart has illegally influenced employees seeking to organize (Frontline 2004).

A few Wal-Mart employees have succeeded in organizing. A Wal-Mart store in Jonquière, Canada was certified as a union shop, represented by the United Food & Commercial Workers (UFCW), in August 2004. Two months later, just as the UFCW and Wal-Mart representatives were preparing to begin mandatory contract negotiations, Wal-Mart Canada issued an ominous press release from its headquarters near Toronto. "The Jonquière store is not meeting its business plan, and the company is concerned about the economic viability of the store." In February 2005, before a collective-bargaining agreement was reached, Wal-Mart closed the store (Bianco 2006).

In 2000, 10 butchers at a Wal-Mart Supercenter in Jacksonville, Texas, voted to join a union. Less than a month later, Wal-Mart switched to pre-packaged meats, eliminating jobs for butchers from its stores nationwide (Frontline 2004).

Having examined business models, pricing strategies, and employment policies at Costco and some of its competitors, it is appropriate to look at their relative financial and operating performance in the marketplace. To do that, we will compare some relevant operating and financial-performance statistics of warehouse retailer Sam's Club, a business unit of Wal-Mart, to those of Costco.

Costco versus Sam's Club: A Test of High- and Low-Wage Strategies

All data in this section come from the 2005 annual reports of Costco and Wal-Mart, unless otherwise noted. In 2005 Costco employed approximately 67,600 workers at its 338 warehouses in the United States, while Sam's Club employed approximately

110,200 at its 551 U.S. warehouses.[1] In terms of wages alone, a Costco employee earned, on average, $35,360 ($17 per hour). The average Sam's Club employee earned $21,028 ($10.11 per hour).[2] Labor rates at Costco are therefore more than 40 percent higher than those at Sam's Club. One important effect of high-versus-low wages is on employee turnover, and the financial effects of such turnover. These effects are quite different at Costco and Sam's Club.

The fully loaded cost of replacing a worker who leaves (separation, replacement, and training costs), depending on the level of the job, typically varies from 1.5 to 2.5 times the annual salary paid for that job, excluding lost productivity (Cascio 2000). To be extremely conservative, let us assume that the fully loaded cost to replace an hourly employee at Costco or Sam's Club costs only 60 percent of his or her annual salary.

If a Costco employee quits voluntarily, the fully loaded cost to replace him or her is therefore $21,216. If a Sam's Club employee leaves, the cost is $12,617. At first glance it may look like the low-wage strategy at Sam's Club yields greater savings in turnover. But wait. Employee turnover at Costco is 17 percent per year (11,492 employees), excluding seasonal workers (Coleman-Lochner 2006). At Sam's Club it is more than 2.5 times higher, 44 percent a year (48,488 employees) (Frontline 2004). The total annual cost to Costco is therefore $21,216 x 11,492 = $243.81 million, while the total annual cost to Sam's Club is $12,617 x 48,488 = $611.77 million.

Of course the overall costs and numbers of employees who leave at Sam's Club is higher, because it employs more people. If Costco had an annual employee-turnover rate equivalent to that of Sam's Club (44 percent), that is, 29,744 employees who leave, its annual cost would be $631.05 million. Costco's opportunity savings (costs not incurred) therefore are $387.24 million *per year*.[3] Averaged over the total number of employees at each firm, however, the per-employee cost at Sam's Club is still higher, $5,274.41 versus $3,628.11 at Costco. High employee-turnover rates are expensive any way you look at it.

Wages are not the only distinguishing characteristic between the two retailers. At Costco, 85 percent of employees are covered by the company's health care insurance plan, with the company paying an average of $5,735 per worker. Sam's Club

---

1   These figures were derived under the assumption that each warehouse at Sam's Club and Costco employs an average of 200 workers. In 2005 Costco had 338 warehouses in the United States. In 2005 Sam's Club had 551 U.S. warehouses.
2   The average wage rate for Costco employees was reported in Coleman-Lochner (2006). The average wage rate for Sam's Club employees is based on the average wage rate for Wal-Mart's hourly workers. The company does not identify the pay rate of Sam's Club employees separately. Annual wages are computed by multiplying 2,080 (40 hours per week X 52 weeks) times the average employee's hourly wage in each company.
3    $631.05 million (costs that would be incurred with a 44 percent turnover rate) minus $243.81 million (costs actually incurred with a 17 percent turnover rate) = $387.24 million.

covers 47 percent of its workers, at an average annual outlay of $3,500 (Greenhouse 2005; Holmes & Zellner 2004). Fully 91 percent of Costco's employees are covered by retirement plans, with the company contributing an average of $1,330 per employee, versus 64 percent of employees at Sam's Club, with the company contributing an average of $747 per employee (Holmes & Zellner 2004).

In return for all of its generosity, Costco gets one of the most loyal and productive workforces in all of retailing. While Sam's Club's 110,200 employees generated some $37.1 billion in U.S. sales in 2005, Costco did $43.05 billion in U.S. sales with 38 percent fewer employees. As a result, Costco generated $21,805 in U.S. operating profit per hourly employee, compared to $11,615 at Sam's Club.[4]

Costco's productive workforce more than offsets its higher costs. Labor and overhead costs at Costco (selling, general, and administrative expenses, or SG&A) were 9.73 percent of sales in 2005. Wal-Mart does not break out SG&A at Sam's Club, but it is likely higher than at Costco, but lower than Wal-Mart's 17 percent of sales. By comparison, it was 24 percent at Target Stores (Holmes & Zellner 2004). Costco's motivated employees also sell more: $886 of sales per square foot, versus only $525 of sales per square foot at Sam's Club, and $461 at BJ's Wholesale Club, its other primary club rival.[5]

These figures illustrate nicely the common fallacy that labor rates equal labor costs. Costco's hourly labor rates are more than 40 percent higher than those at Sam's Club ($17 versus $10.11), but when employee productivity is considered (sales per employee), Costco's labor costs are lower than those at Sam's Club (5.55 percent at Costco versus 6.25 percent at Sam's Club).[6]

---

4   Wal-Mart measures the profit of each of its segments, of which Sam's Club is one, as "segment operating income," which is defined as income from continuing operations before net income expense, income taxes, and minority interest (Wal-Mart 2005 annual report, p. 48). Sam's Club's operating income for 2005 was $1.28 billion. At Costco, it was $1.474 billion. When Sam's Club's operating income is divided by the number of employees (110,200) it equals $11,615.25. When Costco's operating income is divided by the number of employees (67,600) it equals $21,804.73.

5   In its 2005 annual report, Costco reported that each of its warehouses averaged $124 million in sales, and that each warehouse averaged 140,000 square feet. Wal-Mart's 2005 annual report showed Sam's Club's total square footage as 70.7 million, with $37.119 billion in sales. Information for BJ's Wholesale Club for 2005 comes from the 5-year financial-information summary presented at the following website: http://www.bjsinvestor.com/factsheet.cfm.

6   These figures were computed as follows. Costco generates $636,849 in annual sales per employee, and it pays each employee an average of $35,360 in wages. That is 5.55 percent of the sales generated. Sam's Club generates $336,660 in annual sales per employee, and it pays each employee an average of $21,028 in wages. That is 6.25 percent of the sales generated.

Conclusions

As Holmes and Zellner (2004) noted, "Given Costco's performance, the question for Wall Street shouldn't be why Costco isn't more like Wal-Mart. Rather, why can't Wal-Mart deliver high shareholder returns and high living standards for its workforce?" Says Costco CEO James Sinegal: "Paying your employees well is not only the right thing to do, but it makes for good business" (p. 77).

To make its high-wage strategy pay off, however, Costco is constantly looking for ways to increase efficiency, such as by repackaging goods into bulk items to reduce labor, speeding up Costco's just-in-time inventory and distribution system, and boosting sales per square foot. Nor have rivals been able to match Costco's innovative packaging or merchandising mix. For example, Costco was the first wholesale club to offer fresh meat, pharmacies, and photo labs.

Defenders of Wal-Mart's low-wage strategy focus on the undeniable benefits its low prices bring to consumers, but the broader question is this: Which model of competition will predominate in the United States? While shareholders may do just as well with either strategy over the long run, it is important to note that the cheap-labor model is costly in many ways. It can lead to poverty and related social problems, and transfer costs to other companies and taxpayers, who indirectly pay the health-care costs of all the workers not insured by their frugal employers.

Fishman [...] described the extent to which Wal-Mart shifts the burden of payments for health care to taxpayers in Georgia and Tennessee. Those are not the only states where this has occurred. According to a study by the Institute for Labor and Employment at the University of California, Berkeley, California, taxpayers subsidized $20.5 million for medical care for Wal-Mart employees in that state alone (Chase 2003).

At a broader level, the Democratic Staff of the Committee on Education and the Workforce estimates that one 200-person Wal-Mart store may result in a cost to federal taxpayers of $420,750 per year—about $2,103 per employee (Democratic Staff 2004). Those additional public costs stem from items such as the following for qualifying Wal-Mart employees and their families: free and reduced lunches, housing assistance, federal tax credits and deductions for low-income families, additional federal health-care costs of moving into state children's health-insurance programs, and low-income energy assistance.

If a large number of employers adopted the same low-wage strategy, their policies would certainly reduce the wages of U.S. workers, along with their purchasing power and standards of living. Such a low-wage strategy would crimp consumer spending, and constrict economic growth. In that sense, Wal-Mart is a problem, but also an opportunity (Fishman 2006, [...]). Consumer sentiment may provide some encouragement. Thus, in a recent survey (*USA Today* 2005), 89 percent of consumers said they would be willing to spend "a little extra" for products that are produced by companies that pay workers good wages and have good working conditions. Only 10 percent of respondents answered "no" to that item, and 1 percent were unsure. Costco's strategy of combining high wages and benefits with innovative ideas and a productive workforce shows that consumers, workers, and shareholders all can benefit from a cost-leadership strategy.

References

Abraham Lincoln Research Site. 2006 Retrieved from http://home.att.net/rjnorton/Lincoln78. html on May 20, 2006.

Bianco, A. 2006. "No union, please, we're Wal-Mart." *Business Week*, February 13: 78–81.

Cascio, W.F. 2000. *Costing human resources: The financial impact of behavior in organizations* (4th ed.). Cincinnati, OH: South Western.

Chase, S. 2003. "The true cost of shopping at Wal-Mart." December 19: *Now with Bill Moyers*, Transcript.

Coleman-Lochner, L. 2006. "Costco service key to outpacing rival Sam's Club." *The Denver Post*, March 4: 1C, 8C.

Costco Wholesale Corporation. 2005. *Annual report, 2005.* Retrieved from www.Costco.com on April 8, 2006.

Democratic Staff of the Committee on Education and the Workforce. 2004. "Everyday low wages: The hidden price we all pay for Wal-Mart." In F.J. Bonello (Ed.), *Taking sides: Clashing views on economic issues* (12th ed., 2006, pp. 162–78). Dubuque, Iowa: McGraw-Hill/Dushkin.

Ernst & Young. 2003. "Ernst & Young estimates retailers lose $46 billion annually to inventory shrinkage." Retrieved from www.clear-vu.com/industrynews.cfm?newssel9 on May 21, 2006.

Fishman, C. In press. "Wal-Mart and the decent society: Who knew shopping was so important?" *Academy of Management Perspectives*.

Fishman, C. 2006. *The Wal-Mart Effect.* New York: Penguin.

Fortune 500. 2006. "Fortune 500: America's largest corporations." *Fortune*, April 17: F-1–F-20.

Frey, C. 2004. "Costco's love of labor: Employees' well-being key to its success." *Seattle Post-Intelligencer*, March 29. Retrieved from www.seattlepi.nwsource.com on May 1, 2006.

Frontline. 2004. "Is Wal-Mart good for America?" November 16. Retrieved from www.pbs. org/wgbh/pages/frontline/shows/walmartftransform/protest.html on October 19, 2005.

Gogoi, P., & Berner, R. 2006. "Wal-Mart puts on a happy face." *Business Week Online*, April 19. Retrieved from www.businessweek.com/investor/content/apr2006 on May 10, 2006.

Goldberg, A.B., & Ritter, B. 2005. "Costco CEO finds pro-worker means profitability." *ABC News*, December 2. Retrieved from http://abcnews.go.com/2020 on April 24, 2006.

Greenhouse, S. 2005. "How Costco became the anti-Wal-Mart." *The New York Times*, July 17. Retrieved from www.nytimes.com/2005/07/17/business/yourmoney/17costco.html on May 1, 2006.

Holmes, S., & Zellner, W. 2004. "The Costco way." *Business Week*, April 12. pp. 76, 77.

NBC Nightly News. 2006. CEO pay. April 20.

Retail theft and inventory shrinkage. 2002. Retrieved from http://retailindustry.about.com/od/statistics_loss_prevention/1/aa021126a.htm on May 21, 2006.

Shapiro, N. 2004. "Company for the people." *Seattle Weekly*, December 15. Retrieved from www.seattleweekly.com/generic/show_print.php on May 1, 2006.

Shields, M. 2005. "Treating workers justly pays off." *CNN.com*, September 5, 2005. Retrieved from http://cnn.worldnews.com on May 1, 2006.

"Unions protest Wal-Mart health care." 2006. Retrieved from www.cbsnews.com/stories. 2006/04/26/ap/business on May 1, 2006.

USA Today. 2005. "Consumers willing to support workers." October 13: 1B.

Wal-Mart Corporation. 2005. *2005 annual report.* Retrieved from www.Walmart.com on April 8, 2006.

Walmartfacts.com. 2006. "Wal-Mart union." Retrieved from http://www.walmartfacts.com/wal-mart-union.aspx on May 21, 2006.

Walton, S. (with Huey, J.). *Sam Walton: Made in America.* New York: Bantam Books, 1992.

Welch, J., & Welch, S. 2006. What's right about Wal-Mart. *Business Week*, May 1: 112.

Zimmerman, A. 2004. "Costco's dilemma: Is treating employees well unacceptable for a publicly-traded corporation?" *The Wall Street Journal*, March 26. Retrieved from www.reclaimdemocracy.org/articles_2004/costco_employee_benefits_walmart.html on May 1, 2006.

Zimmerman, A. 2006. "Target transfers more health costs to its employees." *The Wall Street Journal*, May 20: p. A7.

Questions

1.   What is the status of Walmart in today's market?

2.   What are the empirical differences between Costco and Walmart/Sam's Club that are relevant for the author's argument?

3.   What explains how Costco can pay employees so much more, yet maintain similar prices and a better market share?

4.   What is the justification offered by Costco's CEO for the treatment of employees?

Further Reading

Auger, Pat, Paul Burke, Timothy M. Devinney, and Jordan J. Louviere. "What Will Consumers Pay for Social Product Features?" *Journal of Business Ethics*, vol. 42, no. 3, 2003, pp. 281–304.

Creyer, Elizabeth H. "The Influence of Firm Behavior on Purchase Intention: Do Consumers Really Care about Business Ethics?" *Journal of Consumer Marketing*, vol. 14, no. 6, 1997, pp. 421–32.

Moriarty, Jeffrey. "Justice in Compensation: A Defense." *Business Ethics: A European Review*, vol. 21, no. 1, 2012, pp. 64–76.

Sinegal, Jim, W. Michael Hoffman, and Thomas Albert Kennedy. *Costco: How Our Ethics Evolved over the First 30 Years.* Center for Business Ethics, Bentley University, 2015.

Trudel, Remi, and June Cotte. "Does Being Ethical Pay?" *Wall Street Journal*, 12 May 2008, https://www.wsj.com/articles/SB121018735490274425, accessed 19 April 2018.

IV.
BUSINESS, THE INDIVIDUAL,
AND SOCIETY

19.

"THE MORAL SIGNIFICANCE OF EMPLOYEE LOYALTY"

BRIAN SCHRAG

About This Reading

It is common in business to assume that employees owe a duty of loyalty to their employer. This is often the starting place for talking about the issue of whistle blowing. Schrag considers the issue of loyalty more broadly. He begins with a vignette about a company that fostered a great deal of loyalty in its employees. He argues that employee loyalty can be a double-edged sword, bringing both benefits and potential pitfalls to both employee and employer. Lastly, he considers the possible obligations that employers might have due to peoples' natural inclination to be loyal to the organizations that employ them.

ABSTRACT Expectations and possibilities for employee loyalty are shifting rapidly, particularly in the for-profit sector. I explore the nature of employee loyalty to the organization, in particular, those elements of loyalty beyond the notion of the ethical demands of employee loyalty. I consider the moral significance of loyalty for the employee and whether the development of ties of loyalty to the work organization is in fact a good thing for the employee or for the employer. I argue that employees have a natural inclination to extend loyalty to the organization and that organizations consequently have an obligation to make clear to employees the degree to which the organization will recognize and reward employee loyalty.

Introduction

The business literature features a considerable debate these days over how to encourage employee loyalty.[1] That, of course, presumes that employee loyalty is a good thing. In this essay I want to think briefly about the nature of employee loyalty in an organizational setting, whether it is good for employees and whether it is good for the organization or corporation. This paper is not intended to be an exhaustive account of the concept of employee loyalty. In particular, I will not dwell on the question of employees' ethical duties of loyalty to their organization, although that topic has been much discussed. Some assume that the moral significance of employee loyalty lies primarily in an account of the "demands of loyalty," the nature and moral grounds, content and limits of duties incurred by employee loyalty.[2] I do not. Much of the discussion of employee loyalty has focused on personal loyalties within the organization, but in this paper I wish to attend to employee loyalty to the organization itself. I begin with a short narrative to focus and illustrate some of the points I will make.

Loyalty at RCA

In 1940, RCA Corporation opened an electronics plant in Bloomington, Indiana, designed to produce radios. This event marked the beginning of a 58-year relationship with employees, located in the same set of plants, in the same location in Bloomington for the entire period. (RCA had moved to Bloomington from Camden, New Jersey, to avoid a nasty labor problem. In 1936–37, RCA management had threatened Camden workers with plant relocation if they voted in a union. The result of the gradual relocation to Indiana was an eventual loss of 10,000 jobs for Camden.)[3]

RCA employees took great pride in their association with a manufacturing leader. Bloomington workers were proud to recite a litany of RCA accomplishments at the

---

1   See, for example, Linda Stroh and Anne Reilly, "Rekindling Organizational Loyalty: The Role of Career Mobility," *Journal of Career Development* 24 (1997): 39–54; and Douglas Hall and Jonathan Moss, "The New Protean Career Contract Helping Organizations and Employees Adapt," *Organizational Dynamics* (Winter 1998), pp. 22–37.

2   For an excellent early discussion of the ethical obligations of employee loyalty and a review of some of the literature on that topic, see John H. Fielder, "Organizational Loyalty," *Business and Professional Ethics Journal* 11 (1992): 71–90. See also Marcia Baron, *The Moral Status of Loyalty* (Chicago: Kendall/Hunt, 1984), and Karen Hanson, "The Demands of Loyalty," *Idealistic Studies* 16 (1986): 195–204.

3   See Jefferson Cowie, *Capital Moves: RCA's Seventy-Year Quest for Cheap Labor* (Ithaca: Cornell University Press, 1999). Cowie provides a detailed account of a 70-year history of RCA management's decisions to move RCA from Camden, New Jersey, to Bloomington, Indiana, to Memphis, Tennessee, and finally to Juarez, Mexico. Cowie argues that over a 70-year period, RCA demonstrated a pattern of using plant locations and the threat of plant relocations in an effort to find and keep docile workers who did not develop a sense of ownership in the corporation.

Bloomington plant: RCA produced the first black and white televisions there in 1949. In 1954 the first mass-produced color televisions in the nation were manufactured in Bloomington. By 1965, the plant employed 8,300. In 1981, it produced the first videodisc players.

In 1969, RCA set up its first plant in Juarez, Mexico. In 1986, GE bought out RCA, and in 1987, GE sold its RCA division to Thomson SA, a state-owned French conglomerate. In 1990, as the 50 millionth color TV rolled off the assembly lines, Bloomington was the color television capital of the world. At the time, Thomson's chairman assured employees that the plant would be a key player in the future of television manufacturing and that the Bloomington operation was not just a pawn waiting to be moved across some border. However, he did warn them that the company was subject to the forces of competition.

In 1993, Thomson set up a second plant in Juarez, where assembly workers were paid 50 cents an hour, compared to $11.29 in Bloomington. Bloomington workers agreed to salary freezes in exchange for Thomson's promise not to move to Mexico. Wages at the Bloomington plant then slid from among the highest in Bloomington to the lowest. In 1997, Thomson announced that it would close the Bloomington plant in 1998 and move its operations to Mexico.

Janice was hired at RCA in 1956 and worked there for 38 years. The plant was a family affair: an aunt, two sisters, and eventually Janice's son all worked there. (For her son, it was a dream come true to carry on the family tradition in a work relation he had grown up trusting and respecting.) Janice took great pride in the company, her job, and the products she helped produce. She has an RCA satellite dish and four television sets in her home, which is filled with RCA memorabilia she has collected and proudly displayed over the years. She was proud of the grandfather clock and jewelry given her for 25, 30, and 35 years of service to the corporation. She was stunned to learn of the plant closing just as she retired. All her family and friends would lose their jobs. Her reaction is a sense of betrayal. "I am realizing, after all these years, they don't really care about us."

Nelda began working at RCA 31 years ago at age 17. She has been a proud and loyal employee. She believed in the value of the firm's products. For 30 years, she drove to work 100 miles a day round trip, five days a week on narrow, hilly, winding two-lane roads. (These roads can be very dangerous in the wet and icy weather that is present for a considerable portion of the year.) She made getting to work a priority, no matter what the weather. In 1994 she and a few co-workers won a quality leadership award for inventing a technique that improved the assembly line process for color TVs.

When the plant closing was announced, many expected that Nelda and her co-workers would refuse to show up the next day. They did show up, however, and they surpassed their quota for the shift. As Nelda put it, "We're from the old school.

We are paid a day's wage for a day's work and that is what we have always done. We all went in, did our job and did it well."

Working at the plant has been her life. Co-workers are like family, a support network. She lost her job 12 years before she expected to retire, and with it she lost $140,000 in retirement benefits (two-thirds of her expected retirement). Her comment on commuting since the closing was announced: "I am no longer going to risk my life to get to work. What do they care?"[4]

Although this vignette draws on the experience of blue-collar workers, these reflections on employee loyalty are not restricted to that category of employees. White-collar employees, managers, and professionals could recount similar experiences, and the issues I wish to consider arise equally for them. For example, in a recent study of 686 managers in Fortune 500 companies in an environment of ruthless downsizing, respondents indicated that their loyalty to their corporation had declined over the past few years. These were persons identified not as victims of downsizing but as the "survivors" of those activities, as up-and-coming managers with an average age of 37 and a master's degree.[5]

My focus in this paper will be on employee loyalty, not employer loyalty. However, I will argue that the nature and value of employee loyalty has moral implications for employer loyalty. I will suggest why an organization's indifference to employee loyalty is morally unacceptable, even though there may be good reasons why an employer's reciprocity of loyalty in terms of unlimited job security may not always be possible.

The Nature of Employee Loyalty

The philosopher John Ladd argues that loyalty, in its broadest sense, can be understood as "wholehearted devotion to an object."[6] The object of loyalty can be a person, a group of persons, an organization (a church, a college, a firm), a cause, or a country. What can constitute the *object* of loyalty for an employee is worth some reflection.

The Object of Loyalty

As John Haughey notes, within a business firm, the object of one's loyalty might be one's direct supervisor, one's manager or management in general, one's coworkers, the company's union, the division in which one works, one's profession, or the service

---

4   Laura Lane, "Workers believed jobs were secure," *The Herald Times*, Bloomington, Indiana, January 28, 1998, p. A5. This account is drawn from Laura Lane, "Workers believed jobs were secure" and "Employees feel betrayed," *The Herald Times*, Bloomington, Indiana, January 28, 1998, pp. A1–A5 and C1–C3.
5   Stroh and Reilly, "Rekindling Organizational Loyalty," pp. 42–45.
6   John Ladd, "Loyalty," in *Encyclopedia of Philosophy*, Vol. 5, ed. Paul Edwards (London: Macmillan Publishing Co. and The Free Press, 1987), p. 97.

or product delivered by the firm.[7] There can be multiple objects of loyalty within an organization, and, indeed, an employee might be simultaneously involved in a complex of loyalties within an organization. Nelda and Janice clearly had loyalties not only to coworkers and supervisors but to RCA/Thomson SA, itself. Multiple objects of loyalty within the same organization can produce conflicting loyalties for the employee. For example, there has been much discussion of the intense loyalties generated among peers in a police force and between police officers and their immediate superiors, and of the tension between such loyalties and loyalty to the force's mission of public service.[8]

It makes sense to talk of loyalty to an organization and not just to persons in it.[9] We may have loyalty to particular persons at a particular college; for example, at Hampden-Sydney College one might have loyalty to fellow students or to faculty or to administrators. However, students, faculty, administrators, and staff come and go, but our loyalty to the institution can remain. During their thirty-plus years of employment at RCA, coworkers, supervisors, managers, presidents, and even owners had come and gone, but Nelda and Janice still maintained a loyalty to the organization. Trustees of a college may have a personal loyalty to the president who appointed them to the board, but presumably, when the president leaves, the trustees still remain loyal to the college. In fact, we do attach loyalty to an institution independently of persons in it, and our common moral language reflects that. Consequently, an employee's loyalty to an organization is not necessarily reducible to loyalties to specifiable people in the organization. The object of loyalty can be the organization itself. I will return to this point in more detail.

Loyalty as a Relational Connection

Loyalty is not simply grounded in an object's characteristics but in some *relational* connection. I am loyal to X because he is *my* friend, not just because of his characteristics. Many people could have the same characteristics, but I might not feel any loyalty to them.[10] I am loyal to Hampden-Sydney College because it is *my* college, even though there may be other colleges with quite similar profiles.

---

7   John C. Haughey, "Does Loyalty in the Workplace Have a Future?" *Business Ethics Quarterly* 3 (1993): 5.
8   See, for example, Neil Richards, "A Question of Loyalty," *Criminal Justice Ethics* 12 (1993): 48–56; John Kleinig, "Police Loyalties. A Refuge for Scoundrels?" *Professional Ethics* 5 (1996): 29–42; Sam S. Souryal and Brian McKay, "Personal Loyalty to Superiors in Public Service," *Criminal Justice Ethics* 15 (1996): 44–62.
9   Here I take issue with Ladd, who thinks that "loyalty" is always "in our common moral language, as well as historically ... taken to refer to a relationship between persons." See Ladd, "Loyalty," p. 97.
10   Ibid. See also George P. Fletcher, *Loyalty: An Essay on the Morality of Relationships* (New York: Oxford University Press, 1993), pp. 6–18, 38–39; and Andrew Oldenquist, "The Ethics of Parts and Wholes," *Criminal Justice Ethics* 12 (1993): 43–44.

The causal ground of that connection of loyalty may be, in part, an accident of history or geography. Loyalties develop over time because of a continuity of overlapping, shared experiences of the same place or persons or events.[11] The loyalty of students and alumni to Hampden-Sydney College is partly due to association with a particular place; a particular set of social and educational experiences; a particular set of faculty, administrators, and staff; and relations to them. The loyalty of workers at Thomson is also partly a function of such particularities. To say that is not to confuse the process by which loyalties are developed with the nature of loyalty.[12] Nevertheless, for this reason it seems that, in general, there is no such thing as "instant loyalty." Loyalty cannot be turned on like a spigot but grows out of a relationship.[13]

Some may assert otherwise because they identify the loyalty relation with a set of duties, particularly when referring to employee loyalty. But relations of loyalty are much richer and not simply or even primarily reducible to duties. We may acquire duties instantaneously, for example, by saying "I promise" in a certain context, or by signing an employment contract, but not so for loyalties. I do want to acknowledge that, strictly speaking, there is a "minimalist" sense of loyalty, which simply involves fidelity to duty. The loyal employee in this minimalist sense is one who can be counted on to do her duty, to meet her contractual obligations. However, in this paper I will focus on a notion of loyalty with a richer set of elements that are not reducible to duties. "Loyalty" will not refer to the minimalist sense unless indicated.

Well-wishing

What are these richer elements? Consider for a moment the characterization of loyalty as "devotion to an object." A bond of loyalty contains an element of my well-wishing, a concern for the interests and welfare of the object of my loyalty. I want what is best for my wife, my family, my church, my organization. That concern draws me out of myself to something larger than myself. That is a central point in Josiah Royce's conception of loyalty.[14]

Identification

One's identification with the object of one's loyalty generates loyalty to the object. If one is loyal to one's teammates at Hampden-Sydney or one's unit in the military, one identifies with them rather than with their competitors or enemies. We invest

---

11   Ladd, "Loyalty." See also Fletcher, *Loyalty*, p. 7.
12   Neil Richards thinks George Fletcher is guilty of this confusion. See Richards, "A Question of Loyalty," p. 50.
13   Here I differ from Richards. See his view in "A Question of Loyalty," pp. 50, 52, 54.
14   Josiah Royce, *The Philosophy of Loyalty* (New York: The MacMillan Company, 1908).

ourselves in the objects of our loyalties. I can identify with a firm's mission, activity, or product. I invest myself in the corporation and take pride in it. Loyalty in this sense also allows us to sink roots and to draw boundaries between our group and others. (I am a loyal Hampden-Sydney alum rather than one from Washington and Lee. I am an employee of RCA rather than of Zenith.) One would anticipate that the capacity for identification with an organization and the degree of identification would tend to increase with the employee's knowledge of the organization, understanding of its mission, and degree of power in the organization. One would expect greater employee identification as one moves higher in the organizational structure.

Sacrifice

That identification can lead to putting the object's welfare above one's own interests, at least to some degree and some of the time. I am willing to sacrifice some of my own interests for the long-term welfare of the object of my loyalty: I may sacrifice convenience or immediate advantage for the sake of the person or group or organization to whom I am loyal. As a loyal employee, I may stay late or work extra hours to get the job done, even if I am not required to do so by contract. Nelda took risks beyond the call of duty to get to work in bad weather. A loyal employee may avoid looking for better positions or decline better offers. Sacrifice may also take the form of placing loyalty to the organization over conflicting loyalties, such as loyalty to family.

Notice that these features of well-wishing, identification, and sacrifice do presuppose a certain view of human nature, viz., that humans have a capacity for loyalty, including a capacity to act for other than self-interested reasons and to identify with the object of loyalty. It is the view of Adam Smith and David Hume, for example, that humans have a capacity for empathy and a capacity to sympathize and identify with the interests of others.[15] If, on the other hand, one holds a strictly egoistic view of human nature, one gets a much narrower conception of loyalty.

Reciprocity

There is an expectation of reciprocity of the well-wishing—a mutual well-wishing between me and my object and an actual reciprocity. The relation is somewhat akin to that mutual fellow feeling between citizens in Aristotle's notion of civic friendship.[16]

---

15   Adam Smith, *Theory of the Moral Sentiments* (Indianapolis Liberty Classics, 1976); David Hume, *A Treatise of Human Nature*, ed. Selby Bigge (Oxford: Clarendon Press, 1967).

16   See Aristotle, *Rhetoric*, Book II: Chapter 4; *Nicomachean Ethics*, Book VIII: Chapters 1–13 in R. McKeon, ed., *The Basic Works of Aristotle* (New York: Random House, 1941).

Not only do I wish the firm well, I expect that the firm reciprocates my well-wishing. A firm's expression of well-wishing toward an employee may simply take the form of some acknowledgment or expression of appreciation for the employee's loyalty and investment in the firm, or perhaps an award for the employee, such as Nelda's quality leadership award. Management theorists are conscious of the connection of loyalty to its recognition and reward.[17] If the object of my loyalty does not return a concern for my interests and welfare, if there is no reciprocity, my loyalty is not likely to be sustained. I come to realize that the fact that I have built the firm into *my* life plans means nothing to them, and I am reduced to a mere instrument of their purposes. Without reciprocity, I may lose my sense of loyalty and well-wishing for the corporation, as Janice and Nelda did in our narrative. This sense of reciprocity may not be a necessary condition of the notion of loyalty but a limiting condition on its continuance. Once one realizes that it is not reciprocated, loyalty may wither.

A natural outcome of the presence of these four elements of loyalty is the employee's increasing reluctance to leave the organization. The loyal employee will have less inclination to switch jobs at the least possible inducement, when the organization is in trouble or when a very attractive opportunity presents itself. We will return to this point later.

Loyalty and Duty

These elements of loyalty—well-wishing, identification, reciprocity, and sacrifice—involve a kind of commitment that can be offered by the employee but cannot be demanded or claimed as a duty by the organization. John Fielder argues that an employee's identification with a work group can generate additional duties of loyalty to the group that go beyond minimalist contractual obligations. Thus, in some circumstances, a request to an employee with sufficiently high identification with a work group to work overtime for the sake of the group or project may appropriately be regarded as a shift from being morally permissible to being morally obligatory.[18] While I grant there may be such circumstances, I deny that it is automatically or necessarily so when these four elements are present. An employee's loyalty can be an optional response. It is a gift to the organization, not a duty. Loyalty can motivate the employee to act for the organization above and beyond the call of duty, but there cannot be a duty to act above and beyond the call of duty.

Sometimes employers mean by "employee loyalty" a moral duty of employees to fulfill the terms of their contract, the responsibilities agreed to at the point of

17   See Raymond S. Pfeiffer, "Owing Loyalty to One's Employer," *Journal of Business Ethics* 11 (1992): 536.
18   Fielder, "Organizational Loyalty," pp. 81–84. For an extended argument against many of the grounds raised for an employee's moral or ethical duty of loyalty to an employer, see Pfeiffer, "Owing Loyalty."

employment, or specified in the job contract. This is what I have called a "minimalist" sense of loyalty. Employees certainly incur such employment obligations, but they can meet them without being loyal in the richer sense.

By employee loyalty, employers sometimes mean an employee's obligation not to betray the trust of the organization. Much of the worry about loyalty and what employees owe employers has come from reflection about whistle blowing as a kind of disloyalty. One can distinguish two senses of an obligation not to betray organizational trust. On the one hand, as a condition of employment, one may agree to keep trade secrets or not otherwise divulge confidences of the organization to those outside the organization, including competitors. It may make perfect sense to have such obligations. But again, these are employment obligations that can be understood perfectly well without an appeal to a notion of loyalty beyond the minimalist sense, and thus it seems to me that they are not a core element in the notion of loyalty.

On the other hand, an employer might mean by loyalty that employees have an obligation to do whatever the organization asks or else betray the organizational trust, an appeal to the wholehearted devotion of the employee.[19] If this usage includes a duty to engage in unethical or illegal behavior on behalf of the corporation or keep such behavior secret or to neglect other, nonemployment moral duties, then such duties cannot be part of a richer notion of loyalty. Devotion, even wholehearted devotion, does not imply all-consuming, blind loyalty or commitment. Employees cannot have a blanket moral duty to ignore other moral considerations in acting for the organization.

Some want to deny that there can be loyalties to corporations because they want to deny that one can have moral duties to formal organizations. Thus, one might argue that one can have moral duties only to persons, loyalties are a species of duty, and hence one can have loyalties only to persons, not to formal organizations. I have tried to argue that the notion of loyalty is not essentially a notion of duty, although there may be duties associated with loyal employees.

Loyalty, Nonloyalty, and Disloyalty

One can distinguish among loyalty, nonloyalty, and disloyalty. The four elements of loyalty I have identified are central to employee loyalty. Meeting one's basic employee obligations may be a necessary but certainly not sufficient condition

---

19   Marcia Baron cites a striking but extreme notion of employee loyalty, perhaps common in an earlier corporate era. A Phillips Petroleum chief executive in 1973 declares that a loyal employee would make all career decisions, spousal career decisions, consumer choices, and political activity, based on what would be in the best interest of Phillips. Marcia Baron, *The Moral Status of Loyalty*, p. 1.

for employee loyalty in the richer sense. An employee who failed to meet basic work obligations could hardly be called loyal in that richer sense.

However, an employee could lack these four elements of loyalty but meet all of her basic job responsibilities. Lacking these elements of loyalty, she may also have no reluctance to leave the organization and would do so at the drop of a hat. Such employees are not loyal, but neither are they disloyal. They are simply not loyal. "Nonloyal" does not imply "disloyal."

Disloyal employees certainly lack the four features of loyalty. However, disloyalty, it seems to me, is not merely an absence of the four elements of loyalty, not merely the absence of loyalty, but something beyond that. Disloyalty involves leading others to expect they can count on your loyalty and then betraying that expectation. Disloyal agents, as Raymond Pfeiffer puts it, "confirm their loyalty openly while they betray it clandestinely."[20] In that context, disloyal acts can include failure to meet basic employee responsibilities as well as violating reasonable expectations of trust and may particularly involve deliberately undermining the welfare of the organization. Not all instances of alleged disloyalty are, in fact, disloyalty. Sometimes employees are labeled as disloyal for a failure to completely identify with the organization and subordinate all their interests to those of the organization. Sometimes employees are held to be disloyal if they do anything whatever that appears to harm the organization. Disloyalty is often the charge brought against whistle blowers or those who take information outside the organization for any reason. If a key element of loyalty is acting in the best interests of the object of loyalty, then it is not obvious that such actions are always against the best interests of the organization and hence disloyal. There may be instances in which such action is in the best interest of the organization and in those cases one may well argue that they are acts of loyalty, not disloyalty. Sometimes the disloyalty is not to the organization but a violation of trust of a supervisor or another in the organization who is not acting in the best interests of the organization. In such instances, disloyalty to a person within the organization may well be an act of loyalty to the organization itself.

The disloyal employee, like the nonloyal employee, may have no reluctance to leave the organization. Merely leaving, as such, is not an act of disloyalty, but depends on the context. Thus, if the employee has been the recipient of benefits from the organization with the understanding that the organization can count on the employee's long-term commitment, then leaving could legitimately count as an act of disloyalty in some instances.

---

20   Pfeiffer, "Owning Loyalty," p. 539.

Firms as Objects of Loyalty

Some would argue that, given this analysis of loyalty, there can be no such thing as loyalty to an organization and, in particular, loyalty to a business firm. Consider first the objections to the very possibility of loyalty to any organizations whatever. There could be three reasons for this position. One might argue that, as an empirical matter of fact, people attach loyalties only to other people, never to organizations. That, it seems to me, is simply mistaken. One can think of many instances in which the devotion or commitment is to an organization. One may be loyal to a college, to a church, or to a country, even though the membership of the group has changed over time. A Cubs fan's loyalty is not tied to the specific personnel of the team. Members of a college come and go, and the loyalty of an alum is not dependent on keeping up with those changes or making a conscious transfer of loyalty to new personnel.

Or one might argue that, whatever the empirical situation, in ordinary language we use the term "loyal" to refer only to devotion to specifiable persons or as shorthand for such references. To do otherwise is simply to misuse the word. That again seems to me to be mistaken. In ordinary English, we frequently refer to loyal alums, citizens, fans, where in fact there may be no specifiable persons who are the objects of devotion.

Finally, one might argue that whatever the ordinary usage, the only proper concept of loyalty is one limited to relations between specifiable persons. John Ladd refers to the social atomists as holding such a view of loyalty.

> Loyalty is conceived as interpersonal, and it is also specific; a man is loyal
> to *his* lord, *his* father, or *his* comrades.... [I]t is conceptually impossible to
> be loyal to people in general (to humanity) or to a general principle, such as
> justice or democracy.[21]

Ladd rightly criticizes the atomists for not recognizing that loyalty to persons in certain kinds of groups is institution presupposing.

> The social atomist fails to recognize the special character and significance of
> the ties that bind individuals together and provide a basis for loyalties.... the
> special ties involved arise from the twofold circumstance that persons so
> bound are co-members of a specific group (community) distinguished by a
> specific common background and sharing specific interests, and are related
> in terms of some role differentiation within that group.... Specialties of this

---

21   Ladd, "Loyalty," p. 97.

sort provide the necessary and sufficient conditions for a person to be a proper object of loyalty.[22]

Ladd does not admit that this gives certain kinds of groups a reality of their own, although it seems he should. As Ron Duska argues,

> There do seem to be groups in which their relationships and interactions create a new ... entity. A group takes on an identity and reality of its own that is determined by its purpose and this purpose defines the various relationships and roles set up within the group.... The membership is, then, not of individuals who are the same but of individuals who have specific relationships to one another determined by the aim of the group.[23]

Although Duska admits the possibility of loyalty to organizations, he does deny the possibility of loyalty to one particular kind of organization, namely, the corporation or business firm.

> Once I have admitted that we can have loyalty to a group, do I not open myself up to the criticism from the proponent of loyalty to the company? ... [C]ompanies are groups. Therefore, companies are proper objects of loyalty.

> The point seems well taken except for the fact that the kinds of relationships that loyalty requires are just the kind that one does not find in business. A business or a corporation does two things ... it produces a good or service and makes a profit. People are bound together in a business not for mutual fulfillment and support, but to divide labor or make a profit.

> Loyalty depends on ties that demand self-sacrifice with no expectation of reward. Business functions on the basis of enlightened self-interest.... I am not devoted to it at all, nor should I be. I work for it because it pays me.

> The cold, hard truth is that the goal of profit is what gives birth to a company and forms that particular group. Money is what ties the group together. But in such a commercial venture, with such a goal, there is no loyalty, or at least none need be expected. An employer will release an employee and an

---

22   Ibid.
23   Ronald Duska, "Whistle Blowing and Employee Loyalty," in *Ethical Theory and Business*, 5th ed., ed. Thomas L. Beauchamp and Norman Bowie (Upper Saddle River, NJ: Prentice Hall, 1997), p. 337.

employee will walk away from an employer when it is profitable for either one to do so.[24]

It seems to me that Duska is mistaken on three counts in distinguishing firms from other organizations. To begin with, as my vignette of Nelda and Janice illustrates, employees in fact often do have loyalties to companies. Duska may argue that is imprudent, but they have them nevertheless.

Secondly, as John Boatright points out, the mere fact that a commercial relationship is involved does not rule out the possibility of a loyalty relation. The physician-patient relationship or the lawyer-client relationship is certainly a commercial one, but that does not preclude loyalty relations.[25] Duska apparently allows nonprofits to count as groups that can be the object of employee loyalty. It is not clear that business firms are made relevantly different from such organizations simply by the presence of the profit motive.

If one allows communities to be objects of loyalty, as Duska does, then it seem to me that corporations have the essential elements of community relevant for this discussion of loyalty. Robert Solomon puts it well:

> In a corporation, relations between people, whether affection, friendship, loyalty, power, position, or expertise, define the organization. Social contract theory only muddles the picture because it suggests almost always falsely that the primary relationships involved are predominantly contractual. That is a sure way to misunderstand the notion that corporations are communities.[26]

> A corporation is about as well defined and tangible as a community can be. The particular individuals may come and go.... But the relationships are always forming, being reinforced and reforming even in the midst of restructuring.... communities and the spirit of community are fundamentally concerned with complementarity and differences, out of which emerge relationships of reciprocity and cooperation. The corporate budget and, for that matter, even the organizational chart are entirely secondary to the flesh and blood exchanges that take place in the halls, offices, and lunchrooms of the corporation. These relationships consist first of all in a shared sense

---

24   Ibid., pp. 337–38.
25   John Boatright, *Ethics and the Conduct of Business* (Englewood Cliffs, NJ: Prentice Hall, 1993), p. 141.
26   Robert C. Solomon, "The Corporation as Community. A Reply to Ed Hartman," *Business Ethics Quarterly* 4 (1994): 274.

of belonging, a shared sense of mission, or at least a shared sense of mutual interest.[27]

Consider then the organization as the object of loyalty. It is possible to be loyal to the organization itself, with its structure, current values, and practices, or only to its mission, or to both. Thus, one might be loyal to a particular religious congregation with its very specific mix of organizational activity and values, or one might be loyal only to its historic mission, even if the current congregation falls short of that. Employee loyalty can be directed to the kind of organization it actually is. Janice and Nelda were loyal to an RCA that treated its employees fairly and stood for excellence in electronic manufacturing. In public service organizations, such as police departments or city governments or the military, the employee might not be loyal to a current corrupt organization but to the organization insofar as it is, in principle, a servant of the public interest. Here loyalty to the organization is closely tied to the performance of its mission. (In public service organizations, unlike many for-profits, the mission of the organization routinely reaches beyond its own welfare.) Loyalty, on the analysis I have given, can be toward the organization's "best" interests or mission, even if the interests or mission are morally indefensible. That is to say, one can have loyalty to evil organizations such as the Nazi party.

In certain kinds of institutions, the mission of the organization is closely identified with the employee's own professional loyalties. Thus, professors at a small college may identify closely with the educational mission of the college, or physicians and nurses at a nonprofit hospital may identify with the mission of the hospital. In certain nonprofit organizations, the organizational mission is more likely to be one that merges with the professional aims of the professional employees and, for these employees, the distinction between loyalty to their profession and loyalty to the organization may blur. In the case of for-profit institutions, the mission of the organization is not so likely to aim beyond itself and its profits to a higher calling or professional objective. Consequently, an employee's loyalty to a for-profit organization is not likely to merge with loyalty to a higher public service or professional objective. Hence, in a business, one may have only the mission of the organization itself as an object of loyalty and not some higher purpose.

It is possible that one is loyal to an organization only because it is good or does good things. In that instance, the employee's loyalty may attach to the organization only while it is good or because it does good things rather than attaching to the institution as such. But institutions may be morally neutral, not particularly good or bad. I want to say that it is still possible for employees to be loyal to such an institution.

---

27 Ibid., p. 277.

It does seem to me that loyalty to a firm differs from that of loyalty to a family or college in that loyalty to a firm usually begins and ends, however gradually, with employment. It is more conditional than loyalty to a family or to an organization such as a college, which tends to continue even after separation.[28]

Loyalty's Moral Significance for Employees

The moral significance of loyalty partly depends upon one's conception of human nature. We are social creatures, and the development of ties of loyalty is a natural human phenomenon.[29] The development of a loyalty involves identification with others and their interests. As Adam Smith and David Hume have argued, we are "hard-wired" with a capacity for empathy, benevolence, and identification with others.[30] As such, we have a capacity for loyalty.

We not only have a capacity for loyalty, we have, in several senses, a *need* for loyalty. Social atomists hold that we have an identity that is completely self-contained and prior to and independent of relations or attachments with other persons, organizations, or causes. I think that is mistaken. As a person, my relations to others, in part, define me by what I do and with whom I do it. We create our own identities in part by the loyalties we develop. The objects of our loyalties help define us as persons. As Royce puts it, "Loyalty ... tends to unify life, to give it centre, fixity, stability."[31] The fact that I am affiliated with this particular corporation and not another—say its competitor—partly defines who I am. At a personal level, we need loyalties, and indeed, we cannot help forming them.

Humans also have a need for social institutions, and loyalty is of one of the features that allows for the development and functioning of such institutions. John Kleinig observes that loyalty "enables us to persevere in our relational, communal and collective commitments even when it would be in our self-interest to withdraw.... [A] loyal colleague will provide help even though great inconvenience is involved.... [It] protects our valued personal, communal and collective relationships from the ravages of self-interest and rugged individualism."[32] Given these considerations, humans have a very deep need for loyalties.

Most of us now spend much of our waking life in the workplace, and it is natural for us to look for some of our loyalties there, as the stories of Janice and Nelda

---

28   See Pfeiffer, "Owing Loyalty," p. 536.
29   R.E. Ewin, "Loyalties and Why Loyalty Should Be Ignored," *Criminal Justice Ethics* 12 (1993): 40–41.
30   Adam Smith, *Theory of the Moral Sentiments*, Part I, Section I, Chapter 1: Part VII, Section III, Chapter 1; David Hume, *A Treatise of Human Nature* Book II, Part I, Section 1x: Book III, Part I, Sections, 111, 1v.
31   Royce, *The Philosophy of Loyalty*, p. 22. See also Fletcher, *Loyalty*, p. 8.
32   Kleinig, "Police Loyalties."

illustrate. If we do not find loyalties in the workplace, we will look for them else-where.[33] Because of our capacity and need for loyalty, most of us are "susceptible to loyalty," to the tug to develop loyalties to the organization. That fact does make employees vulnerable to the exploitation of their loyalties by the firm.

Is Loyalty to the Organization Good for Employees?

I have argued that employees can be loyal to an organization as such, above and beyond loyalties to particular persons within the organization. Of course, employees may not feel such a distinction when supervisors or managers insist that the employ-ees' personal loyalty to them is identical with loyalty to the organization. Loyalty to an organization could be good for an employee even if loyalty to a particular person in the organization is not and vice versa. Most of what I have said and will say applies to both nonprofit organizations and for-profit firms and to employees at all levels. However, in what follows, I will frequently speak from the perspective of "managers" and "executives" to remind ourselves that loyalty to the organization is not simply a blue-collar labor issue.

An executive's loyalty to an organization, that is, her wholehearted devotion to it, can give that executive part of her identity. We are, in part, our relations with others, and our work environment partially shapes our identity and our sense of who we are. As John Haughey argues, loyalty to an organization allows us to sink roots and provide boundaries that "mark off what the self counts as included in the ambit of its well-being and what lies beyond these."[34] Part of that identity is the result of being a member of a group. At some point, as John Fletcher notes, that membership may "crystallize" into a sense of one's personal identity as fused with the group identity.[35] At that point one thinks of oneself essentially as a member of, for example, RCA or Indiana University. Of course, whether that identity is a good thing may depend on the organization. It does make a difference to the value of our identity whether we are executives at a tobacco company or a cancer society.

We are not only defined by our relations with others; we are also what we do. Particularly at the professional level, our identity is shaped by our preparation for a career but also by practice. The skills an executive develops in an MBA program may partially define her identity, but in many instances those skills can be put to use only in an organizational context. The work organization provides the occasion to practice and develop her skills and hence to develop her identity. In that sense, she would not be who she is without that specific organization.

---

33 John Haughey makes a similar point. See Haughey, "Does Loyalty in the Workplace Have a Future?" p. 3.
34 Ibid., p. 4.
35 Fletcher, *Loyalty*, pp. 33–34.

Loyalty can not only provide us with a sense of identity, but can also give meaning to our work. John Haughey argues that we have a "universal thirst for meaningful work.... [W]e voraciously seek to do what is meaningful—work that has some significance to me or others" and "will do what is meaningless only grudgingly and only if forced to."[36] Loyalty to the organization allows the executive an opportunity to reach beyond herself, to live for something larger than herself. John Fletcher observes:

> The cause, the idea ... brings meaning to their lives. In the grip of a cause, one lives not for consumption and pleasure but for the victory of ... the company.... Enormous personal gratifications accrue to those who are part of the struggle. When it is all for one and one for all, a larger life pulsates in every individual.[37]

An employee may begin by exhibiting that minimal loyalty signaling her fidelity to duty. She can be counted on to execute her duties faithfully, to meet her contractual obligations. Such loyalty can win the trust of her firm and open for her greater opportunities for growth, freedom to take initiative and display creativity in serving the organization. As her expertise and authority increase, so does her capacity to identify with the organization and its mission. Increasing wholehearted devotion will also signal her willingness to sacrifice and go above and beyond the call of duty for the welfare of the company. She may subordinate some of her private interests to the firm's interests, work longer hours, give up some weekends. Josiah Royce argues in *The Philosophy of Loyalty* that this sort of loyalty enables people to live for more than themselves and that is important for their spiritual well-being. It enlarges the soul. Whether we invest ourselves in work because it is meaningful or it is meaningful because we invest ourselves in it, the self-investment elicits loyalty. As our vignette illustrates, Janice and Nelda did develop a sense of fellow feeling, pride in the company, and loyalty to RCA in their working relationship with the corporation.

Given all these considerations, one might say that loyalty to the firm is good for employees. Nevertheless, employee loyalty to the workplace is not necessarily always good for the employee. As John Kleinig notes, loyalty has a Janus-like quality.[38] There can be problems with wholehearted devotion to even the best of organizations. Some executives get their entire identity from their work. It is not so much that their loyalty to the firm helps shape their identity, it *is* their identity. Perhaps we can all think of colleagues or acquaintances whose life ends on their last day on

---

36 Haughey, "Does Loyalty in the Workplace Have a Future?" p. 3.
37 Fletcher, *Loyalty*, p. 33.
38 Kleinig, "Police Loyalties," p. 29.

the job.[39] An extreme loyalty may lead one to perceive one's worth solely in terms of one's contribution to the firm and hence distorts one's perception of self-worth.

Even if the executive's whole identity is not tied to the firm, loyalty can still be all-consuming. She may even ignore other legitimate interests, of family and church for example, for the corporation. It can lead the executive to become a workaholic, to the neglect of spouse, family, the cultivation of friends, community, and her own health.

The issue is compounded if the organization's values or mission are not worthy of the employee's loyalty. Socialization into an organization in order to fit in, identify, and be loyal can shape one's second-order desires. If, for example, the organization encourages ruthlessness or single-minded selfishness on the part of employees, or believes that unbridled competition between employees best serves the corporation, then the loyal employee may not be a better person for working at the organization.[40]

One of the difficulties with loyalty is that it may tempt one to suspend moral judgment about the object of one's loyalty. That can be encouraged by confusion over the nature of loyalty. Some have argued that the very nature of loyalty requires the employee to have blind allegiance to the organization. This confusion over the moral concept of loyalty has sometimes been fostered by the importation of the legal concept of loyalty embedded in the law of agency. The law of agency defines a fiduciary relation between employer and employee. The employee acts as agent for the employer, as an extension of the employer who controls the employee. As such, the employee owes the employer "undivided loyalty" and must "obey all lawful instruction given him no matter how arbitrary or capricious."[41]

There is a sense here of blind obedience. The so-called loyal agent argument asserts that the employee, in virtue of her employment, agrees to act solely as an agent of the organization's interests, to work as directed, and to be loyal. That would suggest that the employee has a moral obligation of loyalty to do what the corporation asks even if it asks the employee to act unethically. That concern is what prompts a great deal of the discussion in the literature regarding employee loyalty and whistle blowing, a problem that can be particularly acute in public service organizations.[42]

But even in law there are qualifications to this obedience. The agent has an obligation to obey all "reasonable" directives. The employee may refuse if asked to do something unethical or illegal, including suppressing evidence of a crime. The loyal agent's legal obligations are confirmed to the "needs of the relation." "Reasonable

---

39   Haughey, "Does Loyalty in the Workplace Have a Future?" p. 6.
40   For a discussion of this issue, see Edwin M. Hartman, "The Commons and the Moral Organization," *Business Ethics Quarterly* 4 (1994): 256–59; and Solomon, "Corporation as Community," pp. 282–84.
41   See Fiedler, "Organizational Loyalty," p. 72.
42   See Kleinig, "Police Loyalties"; Souryal and McKay, "Personal Loyalty"; and Haughey, "Does Loyalty in the Workplace Have a Future?"

directives" is construed to mean directives limited to the purposes for which the agent was hired.[43]

There is no reason to assume that one ought to simply allow the legal concept of a loyal agent to define the moral concept of employee loyalty. Suppose, however, we allow that when an employee signs an employment contract with an organization, she agrees to be a loyal agent in the execution of her role responsibilities. That is certainly not an agreement to carry out activities beyond the scope of her role responsibilities or to suspend her moral judgment in carrying out her duties. That is not an agreement that all employer directives override all the employee's other moral considerations or commitments outside the organization. There can be no moral ground of loyalty to act immorally for the organization.

It is not the case that loyalty requires the suspension of moral judgment. Having a wholehearted devotion to the organization does not require that devotion to be uncritical, any more than loyalty to a child or a friend requires uncritical devotion. Loyalty does not require blind devotion to the organization, although the temptation may be there.[44] One can be loyal to the best interests of the organization, or its true mission, even when individuals in the corporation are urging you to do otherwise in the name of loyalty. The appeal to "best interests" of the organization can provide one criterion for resisting urging to the contrary by members of the organization.[45]

Even if loyalty does not require us to suspend judgment, it may lead to a corruption of our judgment. If a firm to which we are loyal is not worthy of our loyalty and our investment in it, say because the firm is corrupt, we can be deformed by that relationship. A lawyer in a large law firm in a Midwestern city confided that he had been a loyal employee of the firm for 20 years. Because of the things he had been asked to do over the years for that firm, he could no longer look himself in the eye in the morning. He had become someone he never intended to become. He was now getting out, but he had paid a high price for his loyalty.

It is realistic to recognize that there are such deforming pressures in organizations. In a recent business ethics survey conducted by the Ethics Resource Center, nearly half of the human resources professionals surveyed said they feel pressured by other employees or managers to compromise their organization's standards of ethical business conduct in order to achieve business objectives. The pressures included: 1) meeting overly aggressive financial objectives, 2) meeting schedule pressures, 3) helping the organization survive, 4) advancing the boss's career interests.

---

43   See Boatright, *Ethics and the Conduct of Business*, pp. 135–37.
44   See Stephen Nathanson, "Fletcher on Loyalty and Universal Morality," *Criminal Justice Ethics* 12 (1993): 59.
45   Boatright, *Ethics and the Conduct of Business*, p. 137.

If an executive is blindly loyal to the company's interests without regard to whether they are legitimate, then loyalty may corrupt his judgment and lead him, for example, to falsify reports to the EPA regarding pollution violations by the firm. If loyalty is blind, the executive may inappropriately subordinate his interests to those of the company, and do things he once knew he should not do, for example, lie or break the law for the corporation. Witness the tobacco company executives who recently perjured themselves before Congress.

Blind loyalty also can make one vulnerable to being treated purely as an instrument for corporate manipulation, or lead one to decline considering exiting the company when it is prudent to do so, as the cases of Janice and Nelda may illustrate. Loyalty to the right kind of organization can be good for the employee, but not an unmitigated good.

Is Employee Loyalty Good for the Corporation?

At a general level, one might argue that it is. To the extent that the loyal employee identifies with the firm, identification changes what the employee recognizes as her interests. Hence, the loyal employee will subordinate her interests to some extent for the sake of the organization. That may mean that she will be motivated to do her duty and ensures her work performance and reliability. She will not just be a clock-watcher; she will require less supervision. Loyalty may motivate the employee to go above and beyond the call of duty: She will put in longer hours, will take extra care in her work, will go an extra mile to satisfy the customer, will take some risks for the corporation, and may even take pay cuts in a crisis.[46]

As we have already argued, one can have employees who do their jobs well but have absolutely no allegiance to the firm, or employees who do only what is required. These employees may be said to lack loyalty without being disloyal. The *disloyal* employee, on the other hand, may well deliberately *undermine* the welfare of the firm. Both can be a liability to the firm.

It is reasonable to think that productivity in the firm is tied to employee morale, which in turn depends on having at least a critical mass of loyal employees.[47] As Haughey argues, "High absenteeism, high turnover, low productivity, poor product quality and alarming increases in employee theft" are at least partly a function of low percentages of loyal employees in the organization.[48] Some have estimated that these costs to U.S. firms may be $60 to 70 billion annually.[49] The greatest of these

---

46   R.E. Ewin, "Corporate Loyalty and Its Grounds," *Journal of Business Ethics* 12 (1993): 390.

47   Haughey, "Does Loyalty in the Workplace Have A Future?" p. 1.

48   Ibid., p. 4.

49   Carol K. Goman, *The Loyalty Factor* (Berkeley: KCS Publishing, 1990), pp. 10–11.

costs is the cost of replacing employees. The free market system teaches us that if we do not like a firm's products or services we ought to consider the competition. Leaving is a virtue.[50] Presumably the virtue of leaving applies to jobs in the firm as well as products and services provided by the firm.

How would companies fare if there were no such thing as employee loyalty? Imagine for a moment a world in which most of the employees in the United States switched firms every year, or every six months or weekly. I mean, of course, everyone from the CEO down. The entire firm would become staffed with temps. We may be closer to this scenario than one might think. According to Frederick Reichheld, on the average, U.S. corporations lose half their employees every four years, and annual turnover rates of 25 percent are common.[51] At some point, firms would be completely paralyzed. All they would get done is hiring and training new employees. They would lack the institutional memory and the trust needed to develop leadership, communication, team projects, management by objective, or implementation of decisions to carry on the firm's business.

Employee loyalty tends to check an inclination to exit the company, to check employee flight. In our imagined scenario, the conditions for creating employee loyalty would never exist because there is no possibility of establishing a long-term relationship between the employee and the company. It also reminds us that, ultimately, one cannot buy employee loyalty. If only the salary holds employees, they will be gone with a better offer. Corporations deny this fact when they view and treat employees as interchangeable parts to be kept or dropped as downsizing is used to maximize the bottom line. They hold the short-term bottom line as more important than a loyal work force. I suspect some firms have taken this approach only because they seriously underestimate the significance of a loyal work force in the trade-off with the bottom line.

Frederich Reichheld argues that profits follow customer loyalty since it is customer loyalty that produces sustainable growth. But customer loyalty is very tightly linked to employee loyalty; customers prefer to deal with employees they know and trust. Without employee loyalty, business is conducted among strangers. Building personal relationships with customers takes time. Only if the firm has good, long-term, loyal employees can they establish such relations with customers.[52] One might argue that employee loyalty increases productivity in a manner that is certainly cheaper than a bonus system; hence it is good for the corporation.[53]

---

50   Fletcher, *Loyalty*, p. 3.
51   Frederick Reichheld, *The Loyalty Effect. The Hidden Force behind Growth, Profits and Lasting Value* (Boston: Bain and Co., Harvard Business School Press, 1996), p. 1.
52   Ibid., pp. 21–23.
53   On the other hand, Cowie argues that RCA clearly chose to encourage high employee turnover and the expenses associated with new hiring and training rather than have workers develop levels of commitment (cont'd)

However, loyalty can be a two-edged sword for a firm. Its value will depend in part on the kind of loyalty under consideration.[54] If an executive's loyalty is personal loyalty to a person in the corporation (for example, a higher-level manager), then it may lead the employee to act for the benefit of the person, which may not be for the good of the firm. For example, it may lead the executive to help cover up the manager's mistakes or even worse, it may involve covering up corruption. The executive then provides no check on the manager's activities either for the manager's benefit or for the benefit of the company. That does not serve the company's interests.

If the loyalty is merely to the status, prestige, and benefits of the executive's position in the firm and not to any characteristics peculiar to the firm, then the executive's loyalty does not provide any particular motivation to work hard to make the firm's products the very best ones possible or to seek out and correct the products' faults. Rather, the executive may be motivated to do whatever preserves his personal benefits, and that may mean taking no risks for the company, avoiding rocking the boat, or downplaying any difficulties the company needs to address.

It is possible for loyalty to a company to be based on the company's high ethical standards and high standards of excellence for its service or product. In such a situation, the executive may well be motivated to do her best and to take pride in her work and her association with the company. In this context, loyalty may lead the executive to help find and correct the firm's mistakes, jealously guard the company's integrity, and blow the whistle on any employee who harms the company's standards. In the long run, such loyalty could be very beneficial to the firm.

Conditions for Employee Loyalty

I have argued that humans are so built that there is an inclination, a want, and a need for employees to give the right sort of loyalty to the organization and that it is in the interest of the corporation to have that sort of loyalty. It would be wrong for employers to exploit that tendency of human nature and the fruits of employee loyalty without reciprocating that loyalty. But the issue is deeper than that.

There can be organizational and corporate environments where it is not even possible to exploit employee loyalty because loyalty cannot develop or endure for a significant fraction of employees. Certainly loyalty will not develop if employees perceive the organization as unworthy of sacrifice or identification, perhaps because it has a morally unjustified mission, is badly managed, or is unjust or corrupt. As one professional remarked after family relocation forced a switch from one corporation

---

to their jobs that could lead to demands for better working conditions and higher wages. See Cowie, p. 161.
54   See Ewin, "Corporate Loyalty and Its Grounds," pp. 391ff.

to a competitor in the industry, "This is not a company I respect. I was loyal to my previous company. Here I am just drawing a paycheck."

To enable employees to invest in the firm, the firm must ensure that employees understand how their work fits in and contributes to the mission of the firm. This recognition allows all employees to view themselves as part of the enterprise and not merely as instruments of the corporation. There should be clear articulation and adherence to devotion to excellence in the firm so that employees can take pride in the firm and attach their loyalty to the company's excellence.[55]

However, in order for employees to be able to identify with an organization, to be prepared to sacrifice for the organization, or to reasonably expect reciprocity from the organization (in short, to be loyal to the organization), a minimal condition is that the employee must be able to envision a future in common with the organization. At a practical level, that means reasonable job security. Edwin Hartman argues:

> It is loyal employees and employers who make efficient joint investments, for example in job-specific training. Loyal employees will do things that benefit the organization in the long term at the expenses of lesser short-term benefits and generally will be motivated by the interests of others in the organization.... They expect their loyalty to be reciprocated in the form of employment that lasts long enough for them to share in the long-term benefits.[56]

Can employee loyalty to an organization make any sense in an organizational environment in which there is no job security at any position? I think not. If employees get the sense that they are viewed as dispensable and interchangeable parts in downsizing whenever it suits the objective of maximization of the bottom line, then that organization will not have the option of loyalty from employees. Employees simply cannot imagine a shared future and, hence, conditions for employee loyalty simply do not exist in that environment. Patricia Werhane argues that employer reciprocity is not only a matter of necessity but also a matter of justice.

> If a manager has hired someone and that person is loyal to the company and performs well, there is a build up of an implicit employment contract—a reciprocal managerial commitment of loyalty to the employee which consists, at minimum, that the employee will keep her job ... [O]ne cannot

55   Ibid., pp. 394–95.
56   Hartman, "The Commons and the Moral Organization," p. 262.

expect loyalty and sacrifice from employees without having reciprocal implicit contracts.[57]

Unfortunately, it is no longer only a matter of creating a climate suitable for employee loyalty in a single organization. We are now in an environment in which "in virtually every industry, at virtually every level, no job is secure."[58] That can generate an employee disposition to resist giving loyalty, even to organizations that may merit it.

In the current global economic environment, many firms find it hard to hold out the promise of job security. There may be corporations or even industries where external forces make it impossible to ensure job security. Perhaps that was the case with RCA. There are, I gather, also management perspectives that make job security problematic, e.g., the practice of dumping more senior, higher-paid managers to enhance the bottom line. I suspect we have come to this situation not so much because of inexorable economic forces of nature but because corporate heads and managers have been blind to the significance of the notion of community in organizations and have discounted its supporting features such as employee loyalty.

Job security may be a necessary condition of loyalty, but that does not necessarily ensure employee loyalty. Academic institutions, for example, are organizations that provide job security at least for faculty in the form of tenure. Although many faculty at many institutions are loyal to their institutions, that is not universally so. Many do not identify with the best interests or mission of their institutions but rather have overriding loyalties to a department or discipline.

This is a cautionary tale. Employee loyalty is not an unqualified good for either the employee or the employer. Employee loyalty to a firm, of the right sort, can be uplifting and enriching to the employee; the wrong sort can be destructive for the employee. Employees ought not be naive about the kind of loyalty they extend to an employer. Employee loyalty of the right sort can enhance the strength of a firm. I also have tried to suggest why the wrong sort is harmful to the firm; employers need to take care regarding the sort of loyalty they encourage in employees. I have tried to suggest that there are, nevertheless, some reasons why both employees and firms ought to value at least certain kinds of employee loyalty. Given human nature, employees are susceptible to the tug of forming loyalties to their workplace organization, although that may make them especially vulnerable, given current management practices. In an era in which the survival of many organizations may depend on a loyal work force, many for-profit firms are sacrificing conditions for having loyal employees.

---

57   Patricia Werhane, "Justice, Impartiality and Reciprocity: A Response to Edwin Hartman," *Business Ethics Quarterly* 4 (1994): 289.
58   Solomon, "Corporation as Community," p. 273.

Employer Loyalty

Our focus has been on employee loyalty. The vignette with which we began does cry out for an answer to the question, "What did RCA 'owe' their loyal employees in terms of loyalty?"[59]

I have argued that employees are "susceptible to loyalty," that is, given human nature we are prone to offer our loyalty to employers and furthermore that, in general, organizations benefit from loyal employees. For these reasons it seems to me that, morally speaking, organizational indifference to employee loyalty is unacceptable.[60]

It is morally unacceptable for an organization to take advantage of a long-term employee's loyalty without reciprocation. As we have argued, one outcome of employee loyalty is a stable work force. Throughout their careers at a company, workers may risk job security by passing up other employment opportunities in order to stay with the organization. Consequently, it is reasonable to consider job security as one element in the reciprocal behavior of the organization. But ought implies can. There may be good reasons why an organization cannot always offer extended job security. Colleges fail, organizations go bankrupt, corporations move, are sold, or undergo hostile takeovers.

The RCA case is complicated by decisions to move and by transfer of ownership. That raises issues of identity and transfer of loyalty that are beyond the scope of this paper. I will simply observe that when a corporation changes ownership, employees are certainly capable of transferring loyalty, as Janice and Nelda demonstrate. New owners of a corporation not only acquire tangible assets and liabilities but may also inherit a loyal work force and instantly benefit from that loyalty (a loyalty that is, presumably, theirs to lose). Why should not organizations in that situation also acquire some obligation of reciprocity?

Consider, however, a simpler case, that of a long-term organization that does not undergo change of ownership or location. What is it reasonable to expect of organizations in that circumstance? If indifference to employee loyalty is unacceptable, why should not organizations at least owe the truth to employees? Why should it not be the case that when an organization hires an employee, the organization has three alternatives? 1) The organization explicitly tells the employee that his/her loyalty is not valued or desired and will not be reciprocated, and the organization does not care whether the employee stays or leaves. 2) The organization explicitly tells the employee that his/her loyalty—if that involves something beyond fulfilling

59   For a recent discussion of the broader question of the moral grounds of duties of managers to employees in decisions regarding corporate downsizing, see John Orlando, "The Fourth Wave: The Ethics of Corporate Downsizing," *Business Ethics Quarterly* 9 (1999): 295–314.
60   I would like to acknowledge Michael Pritchard for this way of putting it.

agreed-upon responsibilities—is not expected, organizational reciprocity should not be expected, and the organization does not oppose the employee leaving when a better opportunity arises.[61] 3) The organization explicitly states that the employee may legitimately assume his/her loyalty is valued and will be reciprocated.

In the first alternative, employees would know at the outset that this job is nothing more than a day's pay for a day's work. I suspect that almost no organization would choose the first alternative, because it would put them at a competitive disadvantage in hiring and because of the obvious benefits of employee loyalty. Engaging in the practice described in the first alternative while refusing to admit it amounts to tacit admission of parasitic behavior by the organization. Such organizations are milking employees of the benefits of their loyal behavior without reciprocating or letting them know in advance that their loyalty will not be valued or reciprocated.[62]

The second alternative is the kind one might use for employees who are temporary hires (for example, faculty who receive a term appointment). The point would be to reinforce the fact that, from the employer's perspective, this is not a long-term commitment and that any developing loyalty by the employee, though appreciated, will not necessarily be reciprocated. If a shift from a temporary to a permanent position occurs, then there should be at that point an explicit acknowledgment in terms of expectations of reciprocal loyalty. It would be possible to use this notification process to differentiate between employees. Some would be advised that their loyalty would be valued and others that it would not.

Presumably the same kinds of notification should go to all employees whenever there is a change of leadership in the organization, to ensure there is no misunderstanding of the new leadership's position. However, if the company had already promised to reciprocate loyalty to at least some employees, new leadership would be bound by that commitment.

In the third alternative, if organizations accept the employee's loyalty, that requires some sort of reciprocal loyalty. What sort of reciprocity is appropriate? I have argued that some sort of job security is a necessary condition for the development of employee loyalty. It is possible that some organizations can reasonably offer a job for life: tenure in an academic community may approximate that. But in other nonprofit and for-profit firms, that may not be realistic. Firms go out of business for all sorts of reasons. If a business simply cannot be maintained, then maintaining job security may be impossible. But there is a difference between letting go employees

---

61   I am grateful to Michael Pritchard for suggesting this alternative.

62   However, something approximating this is perhaps already at work. Apparently it is now becoming standard practice at many large companies to include a prominent statement of an "Employment-at-Will" clause in all employee contracts. I am grateful to Terry Dworkin for pointing out this practice to me.

as a last resort and routinely downsizing loyal employees to tweak the bottom line. There is a difference, that is, if one recognizes the value of employee loyalty and the value of keeping commitments.

Note

Earlier versions of this paper were delivered at a symposium on Corporate Responsibility and the Community, Hampden-Sydney College, Virginia, February 18–19, 1998, and at a conference on Ethics in the Professions and Practice, University of Montana, August 2–6, 1998. I also wish to express my appreciation to Michael Pritchard and Terry Dworkin for comments on an earlier draft.

References

Aristotle. *Nicomachean Ethics*. Book VIII: Chapters 1–13. R. McKeon, ed., *The Basic Works of Aristotle*. New York: Random House, 1941.

Aristotle. *Rhetoric*. Book II, Chapter 4. R. McKeon, ed., *The Basic Works of Aristotle*. New York: Random House, 1941.

Baron, Marcia. *The Moral Status of Loyalty*. Module Series in Applied Ethics, Center for the Study of Ethics in the Professions, Illinois Institute of Technology, Vivian Weil, series ed. Chicago: Kendall/Hunt, 1984.

Boatright, John. *Ethics and the Conduct of Business*. Englewood Cliffs, N.J.: Prentice Hall, 1993.

Cowie, Jefferson. *Capital Moves: RCA's Seventy-Year Quest for Cheap Labor*. Ithaca, N.Y.: Cornell University Press, 1999.

Duska, Ronald. "Whistle Blowing and Employee Loyalty." In *Ethical Theory and Business*, 5th edition, ed. Thomas Beauchamp and Norman Bowie. Upper Saddle River, N.J.: Prentice Hall, 1997.

Ewin, R.E. "Corporate Loyalty: Its Objects and Its Grounds." *Journal of Business Ethics* 12 (1993): 387–96.

——. "Loyalties, and Why Loyalty Should Be Ignored." *Criminal Justice Ethics* 12 (1993): 36–42.

Fielder, John H. "Organizational Loyalty." *Business and Professional Ethics Journal* II (1992): 71–90.

Fletcher, George P. *Loyalty: An Essay on the Morality of Relationships*. New York: Oxford University Press, 1993.

Hall, D. and J. Moss. "The New Protean Career Contract: Helping Organizations and Employees Adapt." *Organizational Dynamics*, Winter 1998, pp. 22–37.

Hanson, Karen. "The Demands of Loyalty," *Idealistic Studies* 16 (1986): 195–204.

Hartman, Edwin M. "The Commons and the Moral Organization." *Business Ethics Quarterly* 4 (1994): 253–69.

Haughey, John C. "Does Loyalty in the Workplace Have a Future?" *Business Ethics Quarterly* 4 (1993): 1–16.

Hume, David. *A Treatise of Human Nature.* Ed. Selby Bigge. Oxford: Clarendon Press, 1967.

Kleinig, John. "Police Loyalties: A Refuge for Scoundrels?" *Professional Ethics* 5 (1996): 29–42.

——. "Loyalty and Public Service." *Public Interest* (Royal Institute of Public Administration, Queensland) 1, no. 3 (1994): 10–11.

——. "Loyalty: Editor's Introduction." *Criminal Justice Ethics* 12, no. 1 (1993): 34–35.

Ladd, John. "Loyalty." In *Encyclopedia of Philosophy*, Vol. 5, ed. Paul Edwards. London: Macmillan Publishing Co. and The Free Press, 1987.

Lane, Laura. "Workers believed jobs were secure," *Herald Times*, Bloomington, Indiana, January 28, 1998, pp. A1–5.

——. "Employees feel betrayed." *Herald Times*, Bloomington, Indiana, January 28, 1998, pp. C1–3.

Nathanson, S. "Fletcher on Loyalty and Universal Morality," *Criminal Justice Ethics* 12, no. I (1993): 56–62.

Oldenquist, Andrew. "The Ethics of Parts and Wholes," *Criminal Justice Ethics* 12, no. 1 (1993): 43–47.

Orlando, John. "The Fourth Wave: The Ethics of Corporate Downsizing." *Business Ethics Quarterly* 9 (1999): 295–314.

Pfeiffer, Raymond S. "Owing Loyalty to One's Employer." *Journal of Business Ethics* 11 (1992): 535–43.

Reichheld, Frederick F. *The Loyalty Effect: The Hidden Force behind Growth, Profits and Lasting Value.* Boston: Bain and Co., Harvard Business School Press, 1996.

Richards, Neil. "A Question of Loyalty." *Criminal Justice Ethics* 12, no.1 (1993): 48–56.

Royce, Josiah. *The Philosophy of Loyalty.* New York: The MacMillan Company, 1908.

Smith, Adam. *Theory of the Moral Sentiments.* Indianapolis: Liberty Classics, 1976.

Solomon, Robert C. "The Corporation as Community: A Reply to Ed Hartman." *Business Ethics Quarterly* 4 (1994): 271–85.

Souryal, Sam S. and Brian McKay. "Personal Loyalty to Superiors in Public Service." *Criminal Justice Ethics* 15, no. 2 (1996): 44–62.

Stroh, Linda and A. Reilly "Rekindling Organizational Loyalty: The Role of Career Mobility." *Journal of Career Development* 24, no. 1 (1997): 39–54.

Werhane, Patricia. "Justice, Impartiality and Reciprocity: A Response to Edwin Hartman." *Business Ethics Quarterly* 4 (1994): 287–90.

Questions

1. What are the elements of the richer sense of loyalty that Schrag identifies?

2. Who does Schrag look at as an object of loyalty?

3. What is the "minimalist" sense of loyalty?

4. How do loyalty, nonloyalty, and disloyalty differ from one another?

5. What is social atomism?

6. In what ways might loyalty to a company be bad for an employee?

7. What problems can result from not having loyal employees?

8. What are the alternatives Schrag identifies for how employers should respond to employee loyalty?

Further Reading

Hajdin, Mane. "Employee Loyalty: An Examination." *Journal of Business Ethics*, vol. 59, no. 3, 2005, pp. 259–80.

Larmer, Robert. "Whistleblowing and Employee Loyalty." *Journal of Business Ethics*, vol. 11, no. 2, 1992, pp. 125–28.

Ogunyemi, Kemi. "Employer Loyalty: The Need for Reciprocity." *Philosophy of Management*, vol. 13, no. 3, 2014, pp. 21–32.

20.

"BEER AND FREE LUNCHES

WHAT IS BEHAVIORAL ECONOMICS, AND

WHERE ARE THE FREE LUNCHES?"

DAN ARIELY

About This Reading

In his book, *Predictably Irrational*, Dan Ariely challenges the idea found in standard economics that people are rational, fully informed, and choose those things that benefit them the most. This underlying assumption is used to "draw far-reaching conclusions about everything from shopping trends to law to public policy." For many in business, these assumptions, along with the invisible hand of the market, are all we need to make business decisions.

But what if we are not the rational beings posited by standard economics? According to Ariely, it is the emerging field of behavioral economics that better reflects the ways in which we actually make decisions. Human beings make irrational decisions. These decisions are influenced in ways people do not realize. But, as Ariely notes, the upside is that there is a certain amount of predictability in this irrationality. Knowing how our mind operates may help us make better, more informed decisions.

The Carolina Brewery is a hip bar on Franklin Street, the main street outside the University of North Carolina at Chapel Hill. A beautiful street with brick buildings and old trees, it has many restaurants, bars, and coffee shops—more than one would expect to find in a small town.

As you open the doors to the Carolina Brewery, you see an old building with high ceilings and exposed beams, and a few large stainless steel beer containers that promise a good time. There are semiprivate tables scattered around. This is a favorite place for students as well as an older crowd to enjoy good beer and food.

Soon after I joined MIT, Jonathan Levav (a professor at Columbia) and I were mulling over the kinds of questions one might conjure up in such a pleasant pub. First, does the sequential process of taking orders (asking each person in turn to state his or her order) influence the choices that the people sitting around the table ultimately make? In other words, are the patrons influenced by the selections of the others around them? Second, if this is the case, does it encourage conformity or nonconformity? In other words, would the patrons sitting around a table intentionally choose beers that were different from or the same as the choices of those ordering before them? Finally, we wanted to know whether being influenced by others' choices would make people better or worse off, in terms of how much they enjoyed their beer....

To get to the bottom of the sudsy barrel of questions that we thought of at the Carolina Brewery, Jonathan and I decided to plunge in—metaphorically, of course. We started by asking the manager of the Carolina Brewery to let us serve free samples of beer to the customers—as long as we paid for the beer ourselves. (Imagine how difficult it was, later, to convince the MIT accountants that a $1,400 bill for beer is a legitimate research expense.) The manager of the bar was happy to comply. After all, he would sell us the beer and his customers would receive a free sample, which would presumably increase their desire to return to the brewery.

Handing us our aprons, he established his one and only condition: that we approach the people and get their orders for samples within one minute of the time they sat down. If we couldn't make it in time, we would indicate this to the regular waiters and they would approach the table and take the orders. This was reasonable. The manager didn't know how efficient we could be as waiters, and he didn't want to delay the service by too much. We started working.

I approached a group as soon as they sat down. They seemed to be undergraduate couples on a double date. Both guys were wearing what looked like their best slacks, and the girls had on enough makeup to make Elizabeth Taylor look unadorned in comparison. I greeted them, announced that the brewery was offering free beer samples, and then proceeded to describe the four beers:

1. Copperline Amber Ale: A medium-bodied red ale with a well-balanced hop and malt character and a traditional ale fruitiness.

2. Franklin Street Lager: A Bohemian pilsner-style golden lager brewed with a soft maltiness and a crisp hoppy finish.

327

3. India Pale Ale: A well-hopped robust ale originally brewed to withstand the long ocean journey from England around the cape of Africa to India. It is dry-hopped with cascade hops for a fragrant floral finish.

4. Summer Wheat Ale: Bavarian-style ale, brewed with 50 percent wheat as a light, spritzy, refreshing summer drink. It is gently hopped and has a unique aroma reminiscent of banana and clove from an authentic German yeast strain.

Which would you choose?

- Copperline Amber Ale
- Franklin Street Lager
- India Pale Ale
- Summer Wheat Ale

After describing the beers, I nodded at one of the guys—the blond-haired guy—and asked for his selection; he chose the India Pale Ale. The girl with the more elaborate hairdo was next; she chose the Franklin Street Lager. Then I turned to the other girl. She opted for the Copperline Amber Ale. Her boyfriend, who was last, selected the Summer Wheat Ale. With their orders in hand, I rushed to the bar, where Bob—the tall, handsome bartender, a senior in computer science—stood smiling. Aware that we were in a hurry, he filled my order before any of the others. I then took the tray with the four two-ounce samples back to the double-daters' table and placed their beers in front of them.

Along with their samples, I handed each of them a short survey, printed on the brewery's stationery. In this survey we asked the respondents how much they liked their beer and whether they had regretted choosing that particular brew. After I collected their surveys, I continued to observe the four people from a distance to see whether any of them took a sip of anyone else's beer. As it turned out, none of them shared a sample.

Jonathan and I repeated this procedure with 49 more tables. Then we continued, but for the next 50 tables we changed the procedure. This time, after we read the descriptions of the beers, we handed the participants a small menu with the names of the four beers and asked each of them to write down their preferred beer, rather than simply say it out loud. In so doing, we transformed ordering from a public event into a private one. This meant that each participant would not hear what the others—including, perhaps, someone they were trying hard to impress—ordered and so could not be influenced by it.

What happened? We found that when people order out loud in sequence, they choose differently from when they order in private. When ordering sequentially (publicly), they order more types of beer per table—in essence opting for variety. A basic way to understand this is by thinking about the Summer Wheat Ale. This brew was not very attractive to most people. But when the other beers were "taken," our participants felt that they had to choose something different—perhaps to show that they had a mind of their own and weren't trying to copy the others—and so they chose a different beer, one that they may not have initially wanted, but one that conveyed their individuality.

What about their enjoyment of the beer? It stands to reason that if people choose beer that nobody has chosen just to convey uniqueness, they will probably end up with a beer that they don't really want or like. And indeed this was the case. Overall, those who made their choices out loud, in the standard way that food is ordered at restaurants, were not as happy with their selections as those who made their choices privately, without taking others' opinions into consideration. There was, however, one very important exception: the first person to order beer in the group that made its decisions out loud was de facto in the same condition as the people who expressed their opinion privately, since he or she was unencumbered, in choosing, by other people's choices. Accordingly, we found that the first person to order beer in the sequential group was the happiest of his or her group and just as happy as those who chose their beers in private.

By the way, a funny thing happened when we ran the experiment in the Carolina Brewery: Dressed in my waiter's outfit, I approached one of the tables and began to read the menu to the couple there. Suddenly, I realized that the man was Rich, a graduate student in computer science, someone with whom I had worked on a project related to computational vision three or four years earlier. Because the experiment had to be conducted in the same way each time, this was not a good time for me to chat with him, so I put on a poker face and launched into a matter-of-fact description of the beers. After I finished, I nodded to Rich and asked, "What can I get you?" Instead of giving me his order, he asked how I was doing.

"Very well, thank you," I said. "Which of the beers can I get you?"

He and his companion both selected beers, and then Rich took another stab at conversation: "Dan, did you ever finish your PhD?"

"Yes," I said, "I finished about a year ago. Excuse me; I will be right back with your beers." As I walked to the bar to fill their order, I realized that Rich must have thought that this was my profession and that a degree in social science would only get someone a job as a beer server. When I got back to the table with the samples, Rich and his companion—who was his wife—tasted the beers and answered the short questionnaire. Then Rich tried again. He told me that he had recently read one of my papers and liked it a lot. It was a good paper, and I liked it, too, but I think he was just trying to make me feel better about my job as a beer server.

Another study, conducted later at Duke with wine samples and MBA students, allowed us to measure some of the participants' personality traits—something the manager of the Carolina Brewery had not been thrilled about. That opened the door for us to find out what might be contributing to this interesting phenomenon. What we found was a correlation between the tendency to order alcoholic beverages that were different from what other people at the table had chosen and a personality trait called "need for uniqueness." In essence, individuals more concerned with portraying their own uniqueness were more likely to select an alcoholic beverage not yet ordered at their table in an effort to demonstrate that they were in fact one of a kind.

What these results show is that people are sometimes willing to sacrifice the pleasure they get from a particular consumption experience in order to project a certain image to others. When people order food and drinks, they seem to have two goals: to order what they will enjoy most and to portray themselves in a positive light in the eyes of their friends. The problem is that once they order, say, the food, they may be stuck with a dish they don't like—a situation they often regret. In essence, people, particularly those with a high need for uniqueness, may sacrifice personal utility in order to gain reputational utility.

Although these results were clear, we suspected that in other cultures—where the need for uniqueness is not considered a positive trait—people who ordered aloud in public would try to portray a sense of belonging to the group and express more conformity in their choices. In a study we conducted in Hong Kong, we found that this was indeed the case. In Hong Kong, individuals also selected food that they did not like as much when they selected it in public rather than in private, but these participants were more likely to select the same item as the people ordering before them—again making a regrettable mistake, though a different type of mistake, when ordering food.

From what I have told you so far about this experiment, you can see that a bit of simple life advice—a free lunch—comes out of this research. First, when you go to a restaurant, it's a good idea to plan your order before the waiter approaches you, and stick to it. Being swayed by what other people choose might lead you to choose a worse alternative. If you're afraid that you might be swayed anyway, a useful strategy is to announce your order to the table before the waiter comes. This way, you have staked a claim to your order, and it's less likely that the other people around the table will think you are not unique, even if someone else orders the same dish before you get your chance. But of course the best option is to order first.

Perhaps restaurant owners should ask their customers to write out orders privately (or quietly give their orders to the waiters), so that no customer will be influenced by the orders of his or her companions. We pay a lot of money for the pleasure of dining out. Getting people to order anonymously is most likely the cheapest and simplest way to increase the enjoyment derived from these experiences.

But there's a bigger lesson that I would like to draw from this experiment—and in fact from all that I have said in the preceding chapters. Standard economics assumes that we are rational—that we know all the pertinent information about our decisions, that we can calculate the value of the different options we face, and that we are cognitively unhindered in weighing the ramifications of each potential choice.

The result is that we are presumed to be making logical and sensible decisions. And even if we make a wrong decision from time to time, the standard economics perspective suggests that we will quickly learn from our mistakes either on our own or with the help of "market forces." On the basis of these assumptions, economists draw far-reaching conclusions about everything from shopping trends to law to public policy.

[...] We are all far less rational in our decision making than standard economic theory assumes. Our irrational behaviors are neither random nor senseless—they are systematic and predictable. We all make the same types of mistakes over and over, because of the basic wiring of our brains. So wouldn't it make sense to modify standard economics and move away from naive psychology, which often fails the tests of reason, introspection, and—most important—empirical scrutiny?

Wouldn't economics make a lot more sense if it were based on how people actually behave, instead of how they should behave? [...] That simple idea is the basis of behavioral economics, an emerging field focused on the (quite intuitive) idea that people do not always behave rationally and that they often make mistakes in their decisions.

In many ways, the standard economic and Shakespearean views are more optimistic about human nature, since they assume that our capacity for reasoning is limitless. By the same token the behavioral economics view, which acknowledges human deficiencies, is more depressing, because it demonstrates the many ways in which we fall short of our ideals. Indeed, it can be rather depressing to realize that we all continually make irrational decisions in our personal, professional, and social lives. But there is a silver lining: the fact that we make mistakes also means that there are ways to improve our decisions—and therefore that there are opportunities for "free lunches."

One of the main differences between standard and behavioral economics involves this concept of "free lunches." According to the assumptions of standard economics, all human decisions are rational and informed, motivated by an accurate concept of the worth of all goods and services and the amount of happiness (utility) all decisions are likely to produce. Under this set of assumptions, everyone in the marketplace is trying to maximize profit and striving to optimize his experiences. As a consequence, economic theory asserts that there are no free lunches—if there were any, someone would have already found them and extracted all their value.

Behavioral economists, on the other hand, believe that people are susceptible to irrelevant influences from their immediate environment (which we call context effects), irrelevant emotions, short-sightedness, and other forms of irrationality [...]. What good news can accompany this realization? The good news is that these mistakes also provide opportunities for improvement. If we all make systematic mistakes in our decisions, then why not develop new strategies, tools, and methods to help us make better decisions and improve our overall well-being? That's exactly the meaning of free lunches from the perspective of behavioral economics—the idea that there are tools, methods, and policies that can help all of us make better decisions and as a consequence achieve what we desire.

For example, the question as to why Americans are not saving enough for retirement is meaningless from the perspective of standard economics. If we are all making good, informed decisions in every aspect of our lives, then we are also saving the exact amount that we want to save. We might not save much because we don't care about the future, because we are looking forward to experiencing poverty at retirement, because we expect our kids to take care of us, or because we are hoping to win the lottery—there are many possible reasons. The main point is that from the standard economic perspective, we are saving exactly the right amount in accordance with our preferences.

But from the perspective of behavioral economics, which does not assume that people are rational, the idea that we are not saving enough is perfectly reasonable. In fact, research in behavioral economics points to many possible reasons why people are not saving enough for retirement. People procrastinate. People have a hard time understanding the real cost of not saving as well as the benefits of saving. (By how much would your life better in the future if you were to deposit an additional $1,000 in your retirement account every month for the next 20 years?) Being "house rich" helps people believe that they are indeed rich. It is easy to create consumption habits and hard to give them up. And there are many, many more reasons.

The potential for free lunches from the perspective of behavioral economics lies in new methods, mechanisms, and other interventions that would help people achieve more of what they truly want. [An] example [...] on self-control [...] is a mechanism called "save more tomorrow," which Dick Thaler and Shlomo Benartzi proposed and tested a few years ago.

Here's how "save more tomorrow" works. When new employees join a company, in addition to the regular decisions they are asked to make about what percentage of their paycheck to invest in their company's retirement plan, they are also asked what percentage of their future salary raises they would be willing to invest in the retirement plan. It is difficult to sacrifice consumption today for saving in the distant future, but it is psychologically easier to sacrifice consumption in the future, and even easier to give up a percentage of a salary increase that one does not yet have.

When the plan was implemented in Thaler and Benartzi's test, the employees joined and agreed to have their contribution, as a percentage, increase with their future salary raises. What was the outcome? Over the next few years, as the employees received raises, the saving rates increased from about 3.5 percent to around 13.5 percent—a gain for the employees, their families, and the company, which by now had more satisfied and less worried employees.

This is the basic idea of free lunches—providing benefits for all the parties involved. Note that these free lunches don't have to be without cost (implementing the self-control credit card or "save more tomorrow" inevitably involves a cost). As long as these mechanisms provide more benefits than costs, we should consider them to be free lunches—mechanisms that provide net benefits to all parties.

If I were to distill one main lesson from the research described in this book, it is that we are pawns in a game whose forces we largely fail to comprehend. We usually think of ourselves as sitting in the driver's seat, with ultimate control over the decisions we make and the direction our life takes; but, alas, this perception has more to do with our desires—with how we want to view ourselves—than with reality.

Each of the chapters in *Predicably Irrational* describes a force (emotions, relativity, social norms, etc.) that influences our behavior. And while these influences exert a lot of power over our behavior, our natural tendency is to vastly underestimate or completely ignore this power. These influences have an effect on us not because we lack knowledge, lack practice, or are weak-minded. On the contrary, they repeatedly affect experts as well as novices in systematic and predictable ways. The resulting mistakes are simply how we go about our lives, how we "do business." They are a part of us.

Visual illusions are also illustrative here. Just as we can't help being fooled by visual illusions, we fall for the "decision illusions" our minds show us. The point is that our visual and decision environments are filtered to us courtesy of our eyes, our ears, our senses of smell and touch, and the master of it all, our brain. By the time we comprehend and digest information, it is not necessarily a true reflection of reality. Instead, it is our representation of reality, and this is the input we base our decisions on. In essence we are limited to the tools nature has given us, and the natural way in which we make decisions is limited by the quality and accuracy of these tools.

A second main lesson is that although irrationality is commonplace, it does not necessarily mean that we are helpless. Once we understand when and where we may make erroneous decisions, we can try to be more vigilant, force ourselves to think differently about these decisions, or use technology to overcome our inherent shortcomings. This is also where businesses and policy makers could revise their thinking and consider how to design their policies and products so as to provide free lunches.

Questions

1. How does Ariely's research affect how we think about business transactions?

2. Many libertarians hold that people should be free to exchange goods or not exchange goods with others regardless of the reason. If someone doesn't like minorities, women, or homosexuals, they should be free to not do business with them. This position is often defended by claiming that most people will not engage in discriminatory practices because it would not be in their rational self interest to do so. How might Ariely respond to this view.

3. Does Ariely hold that people can't act rationally, or that they generally don't?

4. What does Ariely believe we can do about our predictable irrationality?

Further Reading

Ariely, Dan. "The End of Rational Economics." *Harvard Business Review*, vol. 87, nos. 7–8, 2009, pp. 78–84.
Ariely, Dan. *Predictably Irrational,* Revised and Expanded Edition. London: HarperCollins, 2009.

21.

"MANAGING FOR STAKEHOLDERS"

R. EDWARD FREEMAN[1]

About This Reading

It is common to assume a simplistic view of a business whereby the only people that matter are its shareholders. This is what Freeman calls the "dominant view" of business activity. This particular dominant view has numerous problems. Freeman identifies these problems and rejects the dominant view in favor of what he calls the "stakeholder view." This is a much broader take on who matters in business. The stakeholder is defended by arguments from each of the three traditional ethical theories, but Freeman offers what he takes to be a stronger argument: the argument from pragmatism.

I. Introduction

The purpose of this essay is to outline an emerging view of business that we shall call "managing for stakeholders."[2] This view has emerged over the past thirty years from a group of scholars in a diverse set of disciplines, from finance to philosophy.[3] The

---

1   The ideas in this paper have had a long gestation and have been reworked from the following sources: R. Edward Freeman, *Strategic Management: A Stakeholder Approach* (Boston: Pitman, 1984); R. Edward Freeman, "A Stakeholder Theory of the Modern Corporation," in T. Beauchamp and N. Bowie (eds.), *Ethical Theory and Business* (Englewood Cliffs: Prentice Hall, 7th ed., 2005), also in earlier editions coauthored with William Evan; Andrew Wicks, R. Edward Freeman, Patricia Werhane, Kirsten Martin, *Business Ethics: A Managerial Approach* (Englewood Cliffs: Prentice Hall, 2010); and, R. Edward Freeman, Jeffrey Harrison, and Andrew Wicks, *Managing for Stakeholders* (New Haven: Yale University Press, 2007). I am grateful to editors and coauthors for permission to rework these ideas here.
2   It has been called a variety of things, from "stakeholder management," "stakeholder capitalism," "a stakeholder theory of the modern corporation," etc. Our reasons for choosing "managing for stakeholders" will become clearer as we proceed. Many others have worked on these ideas, and should not be held accountable for the rather idiosyncratic view outlined here.
3   For a stylized history of the idea, see R. Edward Freeman, "The Development of Stakeholder Theory: An Idiosyncratic Approach," in K. Smith and M. Hitt (eds.), *Great Minds in Management* (Oxford: Oxford (cont'd)

basic idea is that businesses, and the executives who manage them, actually do and should create value for customers, suppliers, employees, communities, and financiers (or shareholders). And that we need to pay careful attention to how these relationships are managed and how value gets created for these stakeholders. We contrast this idea with the dominant model of business activity; namely, that businesses are to be managed solely for the benefit of shareholders. Any other benefits (or harms) that are created are incidental.[4]

Simple ideas create complex questions, and we proceed as follows. In the next section we examine why the dominant story or model of business that is deeply embedded in our culture is no longer workable. It is resistant to change, not consistent with the law, and for the most part, simply ignores matters of ethics. Each of these flaws is fatal in the business world of the 21st Century.

We then proceed to define the basic ideas of "managing for stakeholders" and why it solves some of the problems of the dominant model. In particular we pay attention to how using "stakeholder" as a basic unit of analysis makes it more difficult to ignore matters of ethics. We argue that the primary responsibility of the executive is to create as much value for stakeholders as possible, and that no stakeholder interest is viable in isolation of the other stakeholders. We sketch three primary arguments from ethical theory for adopting "managing for stakeholders." We conclude by outlining a fourth "pragmatist argument" that suggests we see managing for stakeholders as a new narrative about business that lets us improve the way we currently create value for each other. Capitalism is on this view a system of social cooperation and collaboration, rather than primarily a system of competition.

II. The Dominant Story: Managerial Capitalism with Shareholders at the Center

The modern business corporation has emerged during the twentieth century as one of the most important innovations in human history. Yet the changes that we are now experiencing call for its reinvention. Before we suggest what this revision, "managing for stakeholders" or "stakeholder capitalism," is, first we need to understand how the dominant story came to be told.

Somewhere in the past, organizations were quite simple and "doing business" consisted of buying raw materials from suppliers, converting it to products, and selling it to customers. For the most part owner-entrepreneurs founded such simple businesses and worked at the business along with members of their families. The development of new production processes, such as the assembly line, meant that jobs could be specialized and more work could be accomplished. New technologies

---

University Press, 2005).
4   One doesn't manage "for" these benefits (and harms).

and sources of power became readily available. These and other social and political forces combined to require larger amounts of capital, well beyond the scope of most individual owner-manager-employees. Additionally, "workers" or non-family members began to dominate the firm and were the rule rather than the exception.

Ownership of the business became more dispersed, as capital was raised from banks, stockholders, and other institutions. Indeed, the management of the firm became separated from the ownership of the firm. And, in order to be successful, the top managers of the business had to simultaneously satisfy the owners, the employees and their unions, suppliers and customers. This system of organization of businesses along the lines set forth here was known as managerial capitalism or laissez faire capitalism, or more recently, shareholder capitalism.[5]

As businesses grew, managers developed a means of control via the divisionalized firm. Led by Alfred Sloan at General Motors, the divisionalized firm with a central headquarters staff was widely adapted.[6] The dominant model for managerial authority was the military and civil service bureaucracy. By creating rational structures and processes, the orderly progress of business growth could be well-managed.

Thus, managerialism, hierarchy, stability, and predictability all evolved together, in the United States and Europe, to form the most powerful economic system in the history of humanity. The rise of bureaucracy and managerialism was so strong, that the economist Joseph Schumpeter predicted that it would wipe out the creative force of capitalism, stifling innovation in its drive for predictability and stability.

During the last 50 years this "Managerial Model" has put "shareholders" at the center of the firm as the most important group for managers to worry about. This mindset has dealt with the increasing complexity of the business world by focusing more intensely on "shareholders" and "creating value for shareholders." It has become common wisdom to "increase shareholder value," and many companies have instituted complex incentive compensation plans aimed at aligning the interests of executives with the interests of shareholders. These incentive plans are often tied to the price of a company's stock which is affected by many factors not the least of which is the expectations of Wall Street analysts about earnings per share each quarter. Meeting Wall Street targets and forming a stable and predictable base of quarter over quarter increases in earnings per share has become the standard

---

5   The difference between managerial and shareholder capitalism is large. However, the existence of agency theory lets us treat the two identically for our purposes here. Both agree on the view that the modern firm is characterized by the separation of decision making and residual risk bearing. The resulting agency problem is the subject of a vast literature.

6   Alfred Chandler's brilliant book, *Strategy and Structure* (Boston: MIT Press, 1970), chronicles the rise of the divisionalized corporation. For a not so flattering account of General Motors during the same time period, see Peter Drucker's classic work, *The Concept of the Corporation* (New York: Transaction Publishers, Reprint Edition, 1993).

for measuring company performance. Indeed all of the recent scandals at Enron, Worldcom, Tyco, Arthur Anderson and others are in part due to executives trying to increase shareholder value, sometimes in opposition to accounting rules and law. Unfortunately, the world has changed so that the stability and predictability required by the shareholder approach can no longer be assured.

The Dominant Model Is Resistant to Change

The Managerial View of business with shareholders at the center is inherently resistant to change. It puts shareholders' interests over and above the interests of customers, suppliers, employees, and others, as if these interests must conflict with each other. It understands a business as an essentially hierarchical organization fastened together with authority to act in the shareholders' interests. Executives often speak in the language of hierarchy as "working for shareholders," "shareholders are the boss," and "you have to do what the shareholders want." On this interpretation, change should occur only when the shareholders are unhappy, and as long as executives can produce a series of incrementally better financial results there is no problem. According to this view the only change that counts is change oriented toward shareholder value. If customers are unhappy, if accounting rules have been compromised, if product quality is bad, if environmental disaster looms, even if competitive forces threaten, the only interesting questions are whether and how these forces for change affect shareholder value, measured by the price of the stock every day. Unfortunately in today's world there is just too much uncertainty and complexity to rely on such a single criterion. Business in the twenty-first century is global and multi-faceted, and shareholder value may not capture that dynamism. Or, if it does, as the theory suggests it must eventually, it will be too late for executives to do anything about it. The dominant story may work for how things turn out in the long run on Wall Street, but managers have to act with an eye to Main Street as well, to anticipate change to try and take advantage of the dynamism of business.[7]

---

7   Executives can take little comfort in the nostrum that in the long run things work out and the most efficient companies survive. Some market theorists suggest that finance theory acts like "universal acid" cutting through every possible management decision, whether or not actual managers are aware of it. Perhaps the real difference between the dominant model and the "managing for stakeholders" model proposed here is that they are simply "about" different things. The dominant model is about the strict and narrow economic logic of markets, and the "managing for stakeholders" model is about how human beings create value for each other.

The Dominant Model Is Not Consistent with the Law

In actual fact the clarity of putting shareholders' interests first, above that of customers, suppliers, employees, and communities, flies in the face of the reality of the law. The law has evolved to put constraints on the kinds of tradeoffs that can be made. In fact the law of corporations gives a less clear answer to the question of in whose interest and for whose benefit the corporation should be governed. The law has evolved over the years to give *de facto* standing to the claims of groups other than stockholders. It has in effect required that the claims of customers, suppliers, local communities, and employees be taken into consideration.

For instance, the doctrine of "privity of contract," as articulated in *Winterbottom v. Wright* in 1842, has been eroded by recent developments in products liability law. *Greenman v. Yuba Power* gives the manufacturer strict liability for damage caused by its products, even though the seller has exercised all possible care in the preparation and sale of the product and the consumer has not bought the product from nor entered into any contractual arrangement with the manufacturer. *Caveat emptor* has been replaced in large part with *caveat venditor*. The Consumer Product Safety Commission has the power to enact product recalls, essentially leading to an increase in the number of voluntary product recalls by companies seeking to mitigate legal damage awards. Some industries are required to provide information to customers about a product's ingredients, whether or not the customers want and are willing to pay for this information. Thus, companies must take the interests of customers into account, by law.

A similar story can be told about the evolution of the law forcing management to take the interests of employees into account. The National Labor Relations Act gave employees the right to unionize and to bargain in good faith. It set up the National Labor Relations Board to enforce these rights with management. The Equal pay Act of 1963 and Title VII of the Civil Rights Act of 1964 constrain management from discrimination in hiring practices; these have been followed with the Age Discrimination in Employment Act of 1967 and recent extensions affecting people with disabilities. The emergence of a body of administrative case law arising from labor-management disputes and the historic settling of discrimination claims with large employers have caused the emergence of a body of management practice that is consistent with the legal guarantee of the rights of employees.

The law has also evolved to try and protect the interests of local communities. The Clean Air Act and Clean Water Act, and various amendments to these classic pieces of legislation, have constrained management from "spoiling the commons." In an historic case, *Marsh v. Alabama*, the Supreme Court ruled that a company-owned town was subject to the provisions of the U.S. Constitution, thereby guaranteeing the rights of local citizens and negating the "property rights" of the firm. Current issues center around protecting local businesses, forcing companies to pay the health care costs of their employees, increases in minimum wages, environmental standards, and the effects of business development on the lives of local community members. These issues fill the local political landscapes and executives and their companies must take account of them.

Some may argue that the constraints of the law, at least in the U.S., have become increasingly irrelevant in a world where business is global in nature. However, globalization simply makes this argument stronger. The laws that are relevant to business have evolved differently around the world, but they have evolved nonetheless to take into account the interests of groups other than just shareholders. Each state in India has a different set of regulations that affect how a company can do business. In China the law has evolved to give business some property rights but it is far from exclusive. And, in most of the European Union, laws around "civil society" and the role of "employees" are much more complex than even U.S. law.

"Laissez faire capitalism" is simply a myth. The idea that business is about "maximizing value for stockholders regardless of the consequences to others" is one that has outlived its usefulness. The dominant model simply does not describe how business operates. Another way to see this is that if executives always have to qualify "maximize shareholder value" with exceptions of law, or even good practice, then the dominant story isn't very useful anymore. There are just too many exceptions. The dominant story could be saved by arguing that it describes a normative view about how business should operate, despite how actual businesses have evolved.[8] So, we need to look more closely at some of the conceptual and normative problems that the dominant model raises.

The Dominant Model Is Not Consistent with Basic Ethics

Previously we have argued that most theories of business rely on separating "business" decisions from "ethical" decisions.[9] This is seen most clearly in the popular joke about "business ethics as an oxymoron." More formally we might suggest that we define:

---

8   Often the flavor of the response of finance theorists sounds like this. The world would be better off if, despite all of the imperfections, executives tried to maximize shareholder value. It is difficult to see how any rational being could accept such a view in the face of the recent scandals, where it could be argued that the worst offenders were the most ideologically pure, and the result was the actual destruction of shareholder value; see *Breaking the Short Term Cycle* (Charlottesville, VA: Business Roundtable Institute for Corporate Ethics/CFA Center for Financial Market Integrity, 2006). Perhaps we have a version of Aristotle's idea that happiness is not a result of trying to be happy, or Mill's idea that it does not maximize utility to try and maximize utility. Collins and Porras have suggested that even if executives want to maximize shareholder value, they should focus on purpose instead, that trying to maximize shareholder value does not lead to maximum value; see J. Collins and J. Porras, *Built to Last* (New York: HarperCollins, 2002).

9   See R. Edward Freeman, "The Politics of Stakeholder Theory: Some Future Directions," *Business Ethics Quarterly*, vol. 4, 409–22.

The Separation Fallacy

It is useful to believe that sentences like "x is a business decision" have no ethical content or any implicit ethical point of view. And it is useful to believe that sentences like "x is an ethical decision, the best thing to do all things considered" have no content or implicit view about value creation and trade (business).

This fallacy underlies much of the dominant story about business, as well as in other areas in society. There are two implications of rejecting the Separation Fallacy. The first is that almost any business decision has some ethical content. To see that this is true one need only ask whether the following questions make sense for virtually any business decision:

The Open Question Argument

(1) If this decision is made, for whom is value created and destroyed?

(2) Who is harmed and/or benefited by this decision?

(3) Whose rights are enabled and whose values are realized by this decision (and whose are not)?

(4) What kind of person will I (we) become if we make this decision?

Since these questions are always open for most business decisions, it is reasonable to give up the Separation Fallacy, which would have us believe that these questions aren't relevant for making business decisions, or that they could never be answered. We need a theory about business that builds in answers to the "Open Question Argument" above. One such answer would be "Only value to shareholders counts," but such an answer would have to be enmeshed in the language of ethics as well as business. Milton Friedman, unlike most of his expositors, may actually give such a morally rich answer. He claims that the responsibility of the executive is to make profits subject to law and ethical custom. Depending on how "law and ethical custom" is interpreted, the key difference with the stakeholder approach may well be that we disagree about how the world works. In order to create value we believe that it is better to focus on integrating business and ethics within a complex set of stakeholder relationships rather than treating ethics as a side constraint on making profits. In short we need a theory that has as its basis what we might call:

The Integration Thesis

Most business decisions, or sentences about business, have some ethical content, or implicit ethical view. Most ethical decisions, or sentences about ethics, have some business content or implicit view about business.[10]

One of the most pressing challenges facing business scholars is to tell compelling narratives that have the Integration Thesis at its heart. This is essentially the task that a group of scholars, "business ethicists" and "stakeholder theorists," have begun over the last 30 years. We need to go back to the very basics of ethics. Ethics is about the rules, principles, consequences, matters of character, etc. that we use to live together. These ideas give us a set of open questions that we are constantly searching for better ways to answer in reasonable complete ways.[11] One might define "ethics" as a conversation about how we can reason together and solve our differences, recognize where our interests are joined and need development, so that we can all flourish without resorting to coercion and violence. Some may disagree with such a definition, and we do not intend to privilege definitions, but such a pragmatist approach to ethics entails that we reason and talk together to try and create a better world for all of us.

If our critiques of the dominant model are correct, then we need to start over by re-conceptualizing the very language that we use to understand how business operates. We want to suggest that something like the following principle is implicit in most reasonably comprehensive views about ethics.

The Responsibility Principle[12]

Most people, most of the time, want to, actually do, and should accept responsibility for the effects of their actions on others.

---

10 The second part of the integration thesis is left for another occasion. Philosophers who read this essay may note the radical departure from standard accounts of political philosophy. Suppose we began the inquiry into political philosophy with the question of "how is value creation and trade sustainable over time" and suppose that the traditional beginning question, "how is the state justified," was a subsidiary one. We might discover or create some very different answers from the standard accounts of most political theory. See R. Edward Freeman and Robert Phillips, "Stakeholder Theory: A Libertarian Defense," *Business Ethics Quarterly*, Vol. 12, No. 3, 2002, pp. 331ff.

11 Here we roughly follow the logic of John Rawls in *Political Liberalism* (New York: Columbia University Press, 1995).

12 There are many statements of this principle. Our argument is that whatever the particular conception of responsibility there is some underlying concept that is captured, like our willingness or our need, to justify our lives to others. Note the answer that the dominant view of business must give to questions about responsibility. "Executives are responsible only for the effects of their actions on shareholders, or only in so far as their actions create or destroy shareholder value."

Clearly the Responsibility Principle is incompatible with the Separation Fallacy. If business is separated from ethics, there is no question of moral responsibility for business decisions; hence, the joke is that "business ethics" is an oxymoron. More clearly still, without something like the Responsibility Principle it is difficult to see how ethics gets off the ground. "Responsibility" may well be a difficult and multi-faceted idea. There are surely many different ways to understand it. But, if we are not willing to accept the responsibility for our own actions (as limited as that may be due to complicated issues of causality and the like), then ethics, understood as how we reason together so we can all flourish, is likely an exercise in bad faith.

If we want to give up the separation fallacy and adopt the integration thesis, if the open question argument makes sense, and if something like the responsibility thesis is necessary, then we need a new model for business. And, this new story must be able to explain how value creation at once deals with economics and ethics, and how it takes account of all of the effects of business action on others. Such a model exists, and has been developing over the last 30 years by management researchers and ethics scholars, and there are many businesses which have adopted this "stakeholder framework" for their businesses.

III. Managing for Stakeholders

The basic idea of "managing for stakeholders" is quite simple. Business can be understood as a set of relationships among groups which have a stake in the activities that make up the business. Business is about how customers, suppliers, employees, financiers (stockholders, bondholders, banks, etc.), communities and managers interact and create value. To understand a business is to know how these relationships work. And the executive's or entrepreneur's job is to manage and shape these relationships; hence the title "managing for stakeholders."

Figure 1 depicts the idea of "managing for stakeholders" in a variation of the classic "wheel and spoke" diagram.[13] However, it is important to note that the stakeholder idea is perfectly general. Corporations are not the center of the universe, and there are many possible pictures. One might put customers in the center to signal that a company puts customers as the key priority. Another might put employees in the center and link them to customers and shareholders. We prefer the generic diagram because it suggests, pictorially, that "managing for stakeholders" is a theory about management and business; hence, managers and companies in the center. But there is no larger metaphysical claim here.

---

13   The spirit of this diagram is from R. Phillips, *Stakeholder Theory and Organizational Ethics* (San Francisco: Berret-Koehler Publishers, 2003).

FIGURE 1

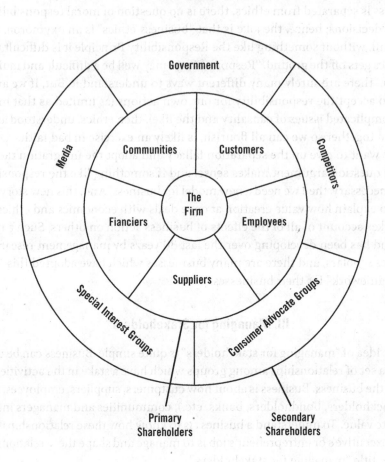

Stakeholders and Stakes

Owners or financiers (a better term) clearly have a financial stake in the business in the form of stocks, bonds, and so on, and they expect some kind of financial return from them. Of course, the stakes of financiers will differ by type of owner, preferences for money, moral preferences, and so on, as well as by type of firm. The shareholders of Google may well want returns as well as be supportive of Google's articulated purpose of "Do No Evil." To the extent that it makes sense to talk about the financiers "owning the firm," they have a concomitant responsibility for the uses of their property.

Employees have their jobs and usually their livelihood at stake; they often have specialized skills for which there is usually no perfectly elastic market. In return for their labor, they expect security, wages, benefits and meaningful work. Often, employees are expected to participate in the decision making of the organization, and if the employees are management or senior executives we see them as shouldering a great deal of responsibility for the conduct of the organization as a whole. And employees are sometimes financiers as well, since many companies have stock ownership plans, and loyal employees who believe in the future of their companies often voluntarily invest. One way to think about the employee relationship is in terms of contracts. Customers and suppliers exchange resources for the products and services of the firm and in return receive the benefits of the products and services. As with financiers and employees, the customer and supplier relationships are enmeshed in ethics. Companies make promises to customers via their advertising, and when products or services don't deliver on these promises then management has a responsibility to rectify the situation. It is also important to have suppliers who are committed to making a company better. If suppliers find a better, faster, and cheaper way of making critical parts or services, then both supplier and company can win. Of course, some suppliers simply compete on price, but even so, there is a moral element of fairness and transparency to the supplier relationship.

Finally, the local community grants the firm the right to build facilities, and in turn, it benefits from the tax base and economic and social contributions of the firm. Companies have a real impact on communities, and being located in a welcoming community helps a company create value for its other stakeholders. In return for the provision of local services, companies are expected to be good citizens, as is any individual person. It should not expose the community to unreasonable hazards in the form of pollution, toxic waste, etc. It should keep whatever commitments it makes to the community, and operate in a transparent manner as far as possible. Of course, companies don't have perfect knowledge, but when management discovers some danger or runs afoul of new competition, it is expected to inform and work with local communities to mitigate any negative effects, as far as possible.

While any business must consist of financiers, customers, suppliers, employees, and communities, it is possible to think about other stakeholders as well. We can define "stakeholder" in a number of ways. First of all we could define the term fairly narrowly to capture the idea that any business, large or small, is about creating value for "those groups without whose support, the business would cease to be viable." The inner circle of Figure 1 depicts this view. Almost every business is concerned at some level with relationships among financiers, customers, suppliers, employees, and communities. We might call these groups "primary" or "definitional." However, it should be noted that as a business starts up, sometimes one particular stakeholder is more important than another. In a new business start up, sometimes there are no suppliers, and paying lots of attention to one or two key customers, as well as to the venture capitalist (financier) is the right approach.

There is also a somewhat broader definition that captures the idea that if a group or individual can affect a business, then the executives must take that group into consideration in thinking about how to create value. Or, a stakeholder is any group or individual that can affect or be affected by the realization of an organization's purpose. At a minimum some groups affect primary stakeholders and we might see these as stakeholders in the outer ring of Figure 1 and call them "secondary" or "instrumental."

There are other definitions that have emerged during the last 30 years, some based on risks and rewards, some based on mutuality of interests. And, the debate over finding the one "true definition" of 'stakeholder' is not likely to end. We prefer a more pragmatist approach of being clear of the purpose of using any of the proposed definitions. Business is a fascinating field of study. There are very few principles and definitions that apply to all businesses all over the world. Furthermore, there are many different ways to run a successful business, or if you like, many different flavors of "managing for stakeholders." We see limited usefulness in trying to define one model of business, either based on the shareholder or stakeholder view, which works for all businesses everywhere. We see much value to be gained in examining how the stakes work in the value creation process, and the role of the executive.

IV. The Responsibility of the Executive in Managing for Stakeholders

Executives play a special role in the activity of the business enterprise. On the one hand, they have a stake like every other employee in terms of an actual or implied employment contract. And that stake is linked to the stakes of financiers, customers, suppliers, communities, and other employees. In addition, executives are expected to look after the health of the overall enterprise, to keep the varied stakes moving in roughly the same direction and to keep them in balance.[14]

No stakeholder stands alone in the process of value creation. The stakes of each stakeholder group are multi-faceted, and inherently connected to each other. How could a bondholder recognize any returns without management paying attention to the stakes of customers or employees? How could customers get the products and services they need without employees and suppliers? How could employees have a decent place to live without communities? Many thinkers see the dominant problem of "managing for stakeholders" as how to solve the priority problem, or "which

---

14   In earlier versions of this essay [...] we suggested that the notion of a fiduciary duty to stockholders be extended to "fiduciary duty to stakeholders." We believe that such a move cannot be defended without doing damage to the notion of "fiduciary." The idea of having a special duty to either one or a few stakeholders is not helpful.

stakeholders are more important," or "how do we make tradeoffs among stakeholders." We see this as a secondary issue.

First and foremost, we need to see stakeholder interests as joint, as inherently tied together. Seeing stakeholder interests as "joint" rather than opposed is difficult. It is not always easy to find a way to accommodate all stakeholder interests. It is easier to trade off one versus another. Why not delay spending on new products for customers in order to keep earnings a bit higher? Why not cut employee medical benefits in order to invest in a new inventory control system?

Managing for stakeholders suggests that executives try to reframe the questions. How can we invest in new products and create higher earnings? How can we be sure our employees are healthy and happy and are able to work creatively so that we can capture the benefits of new information technology such as inventory control systems? In a recent book reflecting on his experience as CEO of Medtronic, Bill George summarized the managing for stakeholders mindset:[15]

> Serving all your stakeholders is the best way to produce long-term results and create a growing, prosperous company.... Let me be very clear about this: there is no conflict between serving all your stakeholders and providing excellent returns for shareholders. In the long term it is impossible to have one without the other. However, serving all these stakeholder groups requires discipline, vision, and committed leadership.

The primary responsibility of the executive is to create as much value as possible for stakeholders.[16] Where stakeholder interests conflict, the executive must find a way to rethink the problems so that these interests can go together, so that even more value can be created for each. If tradeoffs have to be made, as often happens in the real world, then the executive must figure out how to make the tradeoffs, and immediately begin improving the tradeoffs for all sides. *Managing for stakeholders is about creating as much value as possible for stakeholders, without resorting to tradeoffs.*

We believe that this task is more easily accomplished when a business has a sense of purpose. Furthermore, there are few limits on the kinds of purpose that can drive a business. Wal-Mart may stand for "everyday low prices." Merck can stand for "alleviating human suffering." The point is that if an entrepreneur or an executive can find a purpose that speaks to the hearts and minds of key stakeholders, it is more likely that there will be sustained success.

---

15   Bill George, *Authentic Leadership* (San Francisco: Jossey Bass, Inc., 2004).

16   This is at least as clear as the directive given by the dominant model: Create as much value as possible for shareholders.

Purpose is complex and inspirational. The Grameen Bank wants to eliminate poverty. Fannie Mae wants to make housing affordable to every income level in society. Tastings (a local restaurant) wants to bring the taste of really good food and wine to lots of people in the community. And all of these organizations have to generate profits, or else they cannot pursue their purposes. Capitalism works because we can pursue our purpose with others. When we coalesce around a big idea, or a joint purpose evolves from our day-to-day activities with each other, then great things can happen.

To create value for stakeholders, executives must understand that business is fully situated in the realm of humanity. Businesses are human institutions populated by real live complex human beings. Stakeholders have names and faces and children. They are not mere placeholders for social roles. As such, matters of ethics are routine when one takes a managing for stakeholders approach. Of course this should go without saying, but a part of the dominant story about business is that business people are only in it for their own narrowly defined self-interest. One main assumption of the managerial view with shareholders at the center is that shareholders only care about returns, and therefore their agents, managers, should only care about returns. However, this does not fit either our experiences or our aspirations. In the words of one CEO, "The only assets I manage go up and down the elevators every day."

Most human beings are complicated. Most of us do what we do because we are self-interested and interested in others. Business works in part because of our urge to create things with others and for others. Working on a team, or creating a new product or delivery mechanism that makes customers lives better or happier or more pleasurable all can be contributing factors to why we go to work each day. And, this is not to deny the economic incentive of getting a pay check. The assumption of narrow self-interest is extremely limiting, and can be self-reinforcing—people can begin to act in a narrow self-interested way if they believe that is what is expected of them, as some of the scandals such as Enron, have shown. We need to be open to a more complex psychology—one any parent finds familiar, as they have shepherded the growth and development of their children.

V. Some Arguments for Managing for Stakeholders

Once you say stakeholders are persons, then the ideas of ethics are automatically applicable. However you interpret the idea of "stakeholders," you must pay attention to the effects of your actions on others. And, something like the Responsibility Principle suggests that this is a cornerstone of any adequate ethical theory. There are at least three main arguments for adopting a managing for stakeholders approach. Philosophers will see these as connected to the three main approaches to ethical theory that have developed historically. We shall briefly set forth sketches of these arguments, and then suggest that there is a more powerful fourth argument.[17]

The Argument from Consequences

A number of theorists have argued that the main reason that the dominant model of managing for shareholders is a good idea is that it leads to the best consequences for all. Typically these arguments invoke Adam Smith's idea of the invisible hand, whereby each business actor pursues her own self-interest and the greatest good of all actually emerges. The problem with this argument is that we now know with modern general equilibrium economics that the argument only works under very specialized conditions that seldom describe the real world. And further, we know that if the economic conditions get very close to those needed to produce the greatest good, there is no guarantee that the greatest good will actually result.

Managing for stakeholders may actually produce better consequences for all stakeholders because it recognizes that stakeholder interests are joint. If one stakeholder pursues its interests at the expense of all the others, then the others will either withdraw their support, or look to create another network of stakeholder value creation. This is not to say that there are not times when one stakeholder will benefit at the expense of others, but if this happens continuously over time, then in a relatively free society, stakeholders will either (1) exit to form a new stakeholder network that satisfies their needs; (2) use the political process to constrain the offending stakeholder; or (3) invent some other form of activity to satisfy their particular needs.[18]

Alternatively, if we think about stakeholders engaged in a series of bargains among themselves, then we would expect that as individual stakeholders recognized their

---

17   Some philosophers have argued that the stakeholder approach is in need of a "normative justification." To the extent that this phrase has any meaning, we take it as a call to connect the logic of managing for stakeholders with more traditional ethical theory. As pragmatists we eschew the "descriptive vs. normative vs. instrumental" distinction that so many business thinkers (and stakeholder theorists) have adopted. Managing for stakeholders is inherently a narrative or story that is at once *descriptive* of how some businesses do act, *aspirational* and *normative* about how they could and should act, *instrumental* in terms of what means lead to what ends, and *managerial* in that it must be coherent on all of these dimensions and actually guide executive action.

18   See S. Venkataraman, "Stakeholder Value Equilibration and the Entrepreneurial Process," *Ethics and Entrepreneurship*, The Ruffin Series, 3: 45–57, 2002; S.R. Velamuri, "Entrepreneurship, Altruism, and the Good Society," *Ethics and Entrepreneurship*, The Ruffin Series, 3: 125–43, 2002; and, T. Harting, S. Harmeling, and S. Venkataraman, "Innovative Stakeholder Relations: When 'Ethics pays' (and When It Doesn't)," *Business Ethics Quarterly*, 16: 43–68, 2006.

joint interests, and made good decisions based on these interests, better consequences would result, than if they each narrowly pursued their individual self interests.[19]

Now it may be objected that such an approach ignores "social consequences" or "consequences to society," and hence, that we need a concept of "corporate social responsibility" to mitigate these effects. This objection is a vestigial limb of the dominant model. Since the only effects, on that view, were economic effects, then we need to think about "social consequences" or "corporate social responsibility." However, if stakeholder relationships are understood to be fully embedded in morality, then there is no need for an idea like corporate social responsibility. We can replace it with "corporate stakeholder responsibility," which is a dominant feature of managing for stakeholders.

The Argument from Rights

The dominant story gives property rights in the corporation exclusively to shareholders, and the natural question arises about the rights of other stakeholders who are affected. One way to understand managing for stakeholders is that it takes this question of rights seriously. If you believe that rights make sense, and further that if one person has a right to X then all persons have a right to X, it is just much easier to think about these issues using a stakeholder approach. For instance, while shareholders may well have property rights, these rights are not absolute, and should not be seen as such. Shareholders may not use their property to abridge the rights of others. For instance, shareholders and their agents, managers, may not use corporate property to violate the right to life of others. One way to understand managing for stakeholders is that it assumes that stakeholders have some rights. Now it is notoriously difficult to parse the idea of "rights." But, if executives take managing for stakeholders seriously, they will automatically think about what is owed to customers, suppliers, employees, financiers and communities, in virtue of their stake, and in virtue of their basic humanity.

The Argument from Character

One of the strongest arguments for managing for stakeholders is that it asks executives and entrepreneurs to consider the question of what kind of company they want to create and build. The answer to this question will be in large part an issue of character. Aspiration matters. The business virtues of efficiency, fairness, respect, integrity, keeping commitments, and others are all critical in being successful at creating value

---

19 Sometimes there are tradeoffs and situations that economists would call a "prisoner's dilemma," but these are not the paradigmatic cases, or if they are, we seem to solve them routinely, as Russell Hardin has suggested in *Morality within the Limits of Reason* (Chicago: University of Chicago Press, 1998).

for stakeholders. These virtues are simply absent when we think only about the dominant model and its sole reliance on a narrow economic logic.

If we frame the central question of management as "how do we create value for shareholders," then the only virtue that emerges is one of loyalty to the interests of shareholders. However if we frame the central question more broadly as "how do we create and sustain the creation of value for stakeholders" or "how do we get stakeholder interests all going in the same direction," then it is easy to see how many of the other virtues are relevant. Taking a stakeholder approach helps people decide how companies can contribute to their well-being and the kinds of lives they want to lead. By making ethics explicit and building it into the basic way we think about business, we avoid a situation of bad faith and self-deception.

The Pragmatist's Argument

The previous three arguments point out important reasons for adopting a new story about business. Pragmatists want to know how we can live better, how we can create both ourselves and our communities in ways where values such as freedom and solidarity are present in our everyday lives to the maximal extent. While it is sometimes useful to think about consequences, rights, and character in isolation, in reality our lives are richer if we can have a conversation about how to live together better. There is a long tradition of pragmatist ethics dating to philosophers such as William James and John Dewey. More recently philosopher Richard Rorty has expressed the pragmatist ideal.[20]

> ... pragmatists ... hope instead that human beings will come to enjoy more money, more free time, and greater social equality, and also that they will develop more empathy, more ability to put themselves in the shoes of others. We hope that human beings will behave more decently toward one another as their standard of living improves.

By building into the very conceptual framework we use to think about business a concern with freedom, equality, consequences, decency, shared purpose, and paying attention to all of the effects of how we create value for each other, we can make business a human institution, and perhaps remake it in a way that sustains us.

For the pragmatist, business (and capitalism) has evolved as a social practice, an important one that we use to create value and trade with each other. On this view, first and foremost, business is about collaboration. Of course, in a free society,

---

20 E. Mendieta (ed.), *Take Care of Freedom and Truth Will Take Care of Itself: Interviews with Richard Rorty* (Stanford: Stanford University Press, 2006), p. 68.

stakeholders are free to form competing networks. But, the fuel for capitalism is our desire to create something of value, and to create it for ourselves and others. The spirit of capitalism is the spirit of individual achievement together with the spirit of accomplishing great tasks in collaboration with others. Managing for stakeholders makes this plain so that we can get about the business of creating better selves and better communities.

Questions

1. What is the dominant view of business activity?

2. What problems with the dominant view does Freeman identify?

3. What is the "separation fallacy" as described by Freeman?

4. What is Freeman's argument against the "separation fallacy"?

5. What alternative to the dominant model does Freeman suggest and how does he argue for it?

Further Reading

Freeman, R. Edward, Bidhan Parmar, and Kirsten Martin. "Stakeholder Capitalism." *Journal of Business Ethics*, vol. 74, no. 4, 2007, pp. 303–14.

Richter, Ulf Henning, and Kevin E. Dow. "Stakeholder Theory: A Deliberative Perspective." *Business Ethics: A European Review*, vol. 26, no. 4, 2017, pp. 428–42.

Rönnegard, David, and N. Craig Smith. "Shareholders vs. Stakeholders: How Liberal and Libertarian Political Philosophy Frames the Basic Debate in Business Ethics." *Business and Professional Ethics Journal*, vol. 32, nos. 3–4, 2013, pp. 183–220.

22.

"SOCIAL RESPONSIBILITY AND ECONOMIC EFFICIENCY"[1]

KENNETH J. ARROW

About This Reading

The question of how much governmental interference there should be in the practice of business is an ongoing one. This covers questions about environmental regulations, work-safety standards, and wage and vacation mandates. Most limits on businesses in this vein interfere with or cut into profits for the company so regulated. Insofar as this is the case, such regulations interfere with a goal of maximizing profits.

Economist Kenneth Arrow points out that companies ought to maximize profits, and that there are many benefits from allowing the free exchange of goods and services. Primarily, these benefits stem from the efficiency of such a system. However, there are also several places where this efficiency breaks down. Such cases require some kind of government intervention to correct. One of the issues that Arrow raises deals with externalities, which is an issue that can actually be found in many other articles in this book.

This paper makes some observations on the widespread notion that the individual has some responsibility to others in the conduct of his economic affairs. It is held that there are a number of circumstances under which the economic agent should forgo profit or other benefits to himself in order to achieve some social goal, especially to avoid a disservice to other individuals. For the purpose of keeping the discussion within bounds, I shall confine my attention to the obligations that might be imposed on business firms. Under what circumstances is it reasonable to expect a business

1   This is a revised version of the Carl Snyder Memorial Lecture delivered at the University of California, Santa Barbara, in April 1972.

firm to refrain from maximizing its profits because it will hurt others by doing so? What institutions can we expect to serve the function not merely of limiting profits but of limiting them in just those ways that will avoid harm to others? Is it reasonable to expect that ethical codes will arise or be created? My purpose in discussing these questions is not so much to achieve definitive answers as to analyze the kinds of consideration that enter into discussing them.

First of all, it may be well to review what possible ways there are by which the economic activity of one firm may affect other members of the economy. A substantial list comes to mind; a few illustrations will serve. A firm affects others by competing with them in the product markets and in the factory markets, in the buying of labor, buying of other goods for its use, and in the selling of its products. It pays wages to others. It buys goods from others. It sets prices to its customers, and so enters into an economic relation with them. The firm typically sets working conditions, including—of greatest importance—conditions that affect the health and possibility for accident within the plant. We are reminded in recent years that the firm, as well as the private individual, is a contributor to pollution. Pollution has a direct effect on the welfare of other members of the economy. Less mentioned, but of the same type, are the effects of economic activity on congestion. Bringing a new plant into an already crowded area is bound to create costs, disservices, and disutilities to others in the area if by nothing else than by crowding the streets and the sidewalks and imposing additional burdens on the public facilities of the area. Indeed, although congestion has not been discussed as much as has pollution, it may have greater economic impact and probably even greater health costs. Certainly the number of automobile deaths arising from accidents far exceeds the health hazards arising from automobile pollution. The firm affects others through determining the quality of its products, and again, among the many aspects of product quality we may especially single out the qualities of the product with respect to its pollution-creating ability, as in the case of automobiles, and with respect to its safety, the hazards it poses to its user. The question of social responsibility takes very different forms with regard to the different items on this varied list. It is not a uniform characteristic at all.

Let us first consider the case against social responsibility: the assumption that the firms should aim simply to maximize their profits. One strand of that argument is empirical rather than ethical or normative. It simply states that firms *will* maximize their profits. The impulse to gain, it is argued, is very strong and the incentives for selfish behavior are so great that any kind of control is likely to be utterly ineffectual. This argument has some force but is by no means conclusive. Any mechanism for enforcing or urging social responsibility upon firms must of course reckon with a profit motive, with a desire to evade whatever response of controls are imposed. But it does not mean that we cannot expect any degree of responsibility at all.

One finds a rather different argument, frequently stated by some economists. It will probably strike the noneconomist as rather strange, at least at first hearing. The assertion is that firms *ought* to maximize profits; not merely do they like to do so but there is practically a social obligation to do so. Let me briefly sketch the argument:

Firms buy the goods and services they need for production. What they buy they pay for and therefore they are paying for whatever costs they impose upon others. What they receive in payment by selling their goods, they receive because the purchaser considers it worthwhile. This is a world of voluntary contracts; nobody *has* to buy the goods. If he chooses to buy it, it must be that he is getting a benefit measured by the price he pays. Hence, it is argued, profit really represents the net contribution that the firm makes to the social good, and the profits should therefore be made as large as possible. When firms compete with each other, in selling their goods or in buying labor or other services, they may have to lower their selling prices in order to get more of the market for themselves or raise their wages; in either case the benefits which the firm is deriving are in some respects shared with the population at large. The forces of competition prevent the firms from engrossing too large a share of the social benefit. For example, if a firm tries to reduce the quality of its goods, it will sooner or later have to lower the price which it charges because the purchaser will no longer find it worthwhile to pay the high price. Hence, the consumers will gain from price reduction at the same time as they are losing through quality deterioration. On detailed analysis it appears the firm will find it privately profitable to reduce quality under these circumstances only if, in fact, quality reduction is a net social benefit, that is, if the saving in cost is worth more to the consumer than the quality reduction. Now, as far as it goes this argument is sound. The problem is that it may not go far enough.

Under the proper assumptions profit maximization is indeed efficient in the sense that it can achieve as high a level of satisfaction as possible for any one consumer without reducing the levels of satisfaction of other consumers or using more resources than society is endowed with. But the limits of the argument must be stressed. I want to mention two well-known points in passing without making them the principal focus of discussion. First of all, the argument assumes that the forces of competition are sufficiently vigorous. But there is no social justification for profit maximization by monopolies. This is an important and well-known qualification. Second, the distribution of income that results from unrestrained profit maximization is very unequal. The competitive maximizing economy is indeed efficient—this shows up in high average incomes—but the high average is accompanied by widespread poverty on the one hand and vast riches, at least for a few, on the other. To many of us this is a very undesirable consequence.

Profit maximization has yet another effect on society. It tends to point away from the expression of altruistic motives. Altruistic motives are motives whose gratification is just as legitimate as selfish motives, and the expression of those motives is something we probably wish to encourage. A profit-maximizing, self-centered form of economic behavior does not provide any room for the expression of such motives.

If the three problems above were set aside, many of the ways by which firms affect others should not be tampered with. Making profits by competition is, if anything, to be encouraged rather than discouraged. Wage and price bargains between the firm and uncoerced workers and customers represent mutually beneficial exchanges. There is, therefore, no reason within the framework of the discussion to interfere with them. But these examples far from exhaust the list of interactions with which we started. The social desirability of profit maximization does not extend to all the interactions on the list. There are two categories of effects where the arguments for profit maximization break down: The first is illustrated by pollution or congestion. Here it is no longer true (and this is the key to these issues) that the firm in fact does pay for the harm it imposes on others. When it takes a person's time and uses it at work, the firm is paying for this, and therefore the transaction can be regarded as a beneficial exchange from the point of view of both parties. We have no similar mechanism by which the pollution which a firm imposes upon its neighborhood is paid for. Therefore the firm will have a tendency to pollute more than is desirable. That is, the benefit to it or to its customers from the expanded activity is really not as great, or may not be as great, as the cost it is imposing upon the neighborhood. But since it does not pay that cost, there is no profit incentive to refrain.

The same argument applies to traffic congestion when no change is made for the addition of cars or trucks on the highway. It makes everybody less comfortable. It delays others and increases the probability of accidents; in short, it imposes a cost upon a large number of members of the society, a cost which is not paid for by the imposer of the cost, at least not in full. The person congesting is also congested, but the costs he is imposing on others are much greater than those he suffers himself: Therefore there will be a tendency to over-utilize those goods for which no price is charged, particularly scarce highway space.

There are many other examples of this kind, but these two will serve to illustrate the point in question: some effort must be made to alter the profit-maximizing behavior of firms in those cases where it is imposing costs on others which are not easily compensated through an appropriate set of prices.

The second category of effects where profit maximization is not socially desirable is that in which there are quality effects about which the firm knows more than the buyer. In my examples I will cite primarily the case of quality in the product sold, but actually very much the same considerations apply to the quality of working conditions. The firm is frequently in a better position to know the consequences (the health hazards, for example) involved in working conditions than the worker is, and the considerations I am about to discuss in the case of sale of goods have a direct parallel in the analysis of working conditions in the relation of a firm to its workers. Let me illustrate by considering the sale of a used car. (Similar considerations apply to the sale of new cars.) A used car has potential defects and typically the seller knows more about the defects than the buyer. The buyer is not in a position to distinguish among used cars, and therefore he will be willing to pay the same amount for two used cars of differing quality because he cannot tell the difference between them. As a result, there is an inefficiency in the sale of used cars. If somehow or other the cars were distinguished as to their quality, there would be some buyers who would prefer a cheaper car with more defects because they intend to use it very little or they only want it for a short period, while others will want a better car at a higher price. In fact, however, the two kinds of car are sold indiscriminately to the two groups of buyers at the same price, so that we can argue that there is a distinct loss of consumer satisfaction imposed by the failure to convey information that is available to the seller. The buyers are not necessarily being cheated. They may be, but the problem of inefficiency would remain if they weren't. One can imagine a situation where, from past experience, buyers of used cars are aware that cars that look alike may turn out to be quite different. Without knowing whether a particular car is good or bad, they do know that there are good and bad cars, and of course their willingness to pay for the cars is influenced accordingly. The main loser from a monetary viewpoint may not be the customer, but rather the seller of the good car. The buyer will pay a price which is only appropriate to a lottery that gives him a good car or a bad car with varying probabilities, and therefore the seller of the good car gets less than the value of the car. The seller of the bad car is, of course, the beneficiary. Clearly then, if one could arrange to transmit the truth from the sellers to the buyers, the efficiency of the market would be greatly improved. The used-car illustration is an example of a very general phenomenon.

Consider now any newly produced complex product, such as a new automobile. The seller is bound to know considerably more about its properties than all but a very few of its buyers. In order to develop the car, the producer has had to perform tests of one kind or another. He knows the outcome of the tests. Failure to reveal this knowledge works against the efficiency of satisfying consumers' tastes. The argument of course applies to any aspect of the quality of a product, durability or the ability to perform under trying circumstances or differing climatic conditions. Perhaps we are most concerned about the safety features of the automobile. The risks involved in the use of automobiles are not trivial, and the kind of withholding of safety information which has been revealed to exist in a number of cases certainly cannot be defended as a socially useful implication of profit maximization. The classical efficiency arguments for profit maximization do not apply here, and it is wrong to obfuscate the issue by invoking them.

Perhaps even more dramatic, though on a smaller scale, are the repeated examples of misleading information about the risks and use of prescription drugs and other chemicals. These again manifest the same point. Profit maximization can lead to consequences which are clearly socially injurious. This is the case if the buyers are on the average deceived—if, for example, they have higher expectations than are in fact warranted. They are also injured when on the average they are not deceived but merely uncertain, although here the argument is more subtle. One consequence may be the excessively limited use of some new drugs, for example. If the users of the drugs become fully aware of the risks involved but are not able to assess the risk with respect to any particular drug, the result may be an indiscriminate rejection of new treatments which is rational from the point of view of the user; this, in the long run, may be just as serious an error as the opposite.

Defenders of unrestricted profit maximization usually assume that the consumer is well informed or at least that he becomes so by his own experience, in repeated purchases, or by information about what has happened to other people like him. This argument is empirically shaky; even the ability of individuals to analyze the effects of their own past purchases may be limited, particularly with respect to complicated mechanisms. But there are two further defects. The risks, including death, may be so great that even one misleading experience is bad enough, and the opportunity to learn from repeated trials is not of much use. Also, in a world where the products are continually changing, the possibility of learning from experience is greatly reduced. Automobile companies are continually introducing new models which at least purport to differ from what they were in the past, though doubtless the change is more external than internal. New drugs are being introduced all the time; the fact that one has had bad experiences with one drug may provide very little information about the next one.

Thus there are two types of situation in which the simple rule of maximizing profits is socially inefficient: the case in which costs are not paid for, as in pollution, and the case in which the seller has considerably more knowledge about his product than the buyer, particularly with regard to safety. In these situations it is clearly desirable to have some idea of social responsibility, that is, to experience an obligation, whether ethical, moral, or legal. Now we cannot expect such an obligation to be created out of thin air. To be meaningful, any obligation of this kind, any feeling or rule of behavior has to be embodied in some definite social institution. I use that term broadly: a legal code is a social institution in a sense. Exhortation to do good must be made specific in some external form, a steady reminder and perhaps enforcer of desirable values. Part of the need is simply for factual information as a guide to individual behavior. A firm may need to be told what is right and what is wrong when in fact it is polluting, or which safety requirements are reasonable and which are too extreme or too costly to be worth consideration. Institutionalization of the social responsibility of firms also serves another very important function. It provides some assurance to any one firm that the firms with which it is in competition will also accept the same responsibility. If a firm has some code imposed from the outside, there is some expectation that other firms will obey it too, and therefore there is some assurance that it need not fear any excessive cost to its good behavior.

Let me then turn to some alternative kinds of institutions that can be considered as embodying the possible social responsibilities of firms. First, we have legal regulation, as in the case of pollution where laws are passed about the kind of burning that may take place, and about setting maximum standards for emissions. A second category is that of taxes. Economists, with good reason, like to preach taxation as opposed to regulation. The movement to tax polluting emissions is getting under way and there is a fairly widely backed proposal in Congress to tax sulfur dioxide emissions from industrial smokestacks.[2] That is an example of the second kind of institutionalization of social responsibility. The responsibility is made very clear: the violator pays for violations.

A third very old remedy or institution is that of legal liability, the liability of the civil law. One can be sued for damages. Such cases apparently go back to the Middle Ages. Regulation also extends back very far. There was an ordinance in London about the year 1300 prohibiting the burning of coal, because of the smoke nuisance.

The fourth class of institutions is represented by ethical codes. Restraint is achieved not by appealing to each individual's conscience but rather by having some generally understood definition of appropriate behavior. Let me discuss the advantages and disadvantages of these four institutions.

In regard to the first two, regulation and taxes, I shall be rather brief because these are the more familiar. We can have regulations governing pollution. We can also regulate product safety. We may even have standards to insure quality in dimensions other than safety. The chief drawback of direct regulation is associated with the fact that it is hard to make regulations flexible enough to meet a wide variety of situations and yet simple enough to be enforceable. In addition, there is a slowness in response to new situations. For example, if a new chemical, such as a pesticide, comes on the market and after a period of time is recognized as a danger, it requires a long and complicated process to get this awareness translated into legal action. One problem is that legislative time is a very scarce factor; a proposal to examine the problems involved in some pesticide may at any given time be competing with totally different considerations for the attention of the legislature or regulatory body. In short, there is considerable rigidity in most regulatory structures. For certain purposes it is clear that regulation is best, but it is equally clear that it is not useful as a

---

2   Editor's note: This idea continues to struggle. It is often referred to as a "carbon tax." There are only a few communities in the United States that currently have such a tax, and there is no federal carbon tax.

universal device. In the case of taxes on the effects, rather than on the causes, there is a little more built-in flexibility. To combat pollution, taxation is probably the most appropriate device; a tax is imposed on the emission by the plant, whether in water or in air. Now this means the plant is free to find its own way of minimizing the tax burden. It is not told it must do one thing, such as raising smokestacks to a certain height. It is free to try to find the cheapest way of meeting the pollution problem. It may well decide that the profitability situation is such that it will continue to pollute and sell the product presumably at a somewhat higher price. This decision is not necessarily bad; it implies that the product is in fact much desired and it provides an automatic test of the market to see whether it is worth polluting or not, because in effect the consumer is ultimately paying for the pollution he induces. However, it is difficult to see how this method, useful though it is in the case of pollution, would have any relevance to safety, to see how one could frame a tax which would make very much sense. Taxation appears to be a rather blunt instrument for controlling product safety.

Legal liability can be and has been applied; i.e., courts have allowed damages in cases arising out of pollution or out of injury or death due to unsafe products. The nature of the law in this area is still evolving; under our system this means that it is being developed by a sequence of court decisions. Just exactly what the company or its officers have to know before they can be regarded as liable for damages due to unsafe products is not yet clear. No doubt it would certainly be held even today that if officers of a company were aware that a product had a significant probability of a dangerous defect and they sold it anyway without saying so, and if the defect occurred, legal liability would be clear. But it is frequently hard to establish such knowledge. No doubt if society wants to use the route of legal liability as a way of imposing social responsibility, then it can change the principles on which the decision is based. For example, one might throw the burden of proof on the company, so that in the case of any new product they have to run tests to show positively that it is safe. Their failure to make such tests would be an indication of their liability. One could imagine changes of this kind which would bring the law more into line with what is desirable. But there are some intrinsic defects in the liability route which, in my opinion, make it unsuitable in its present form as a serious method of achieving social control or of imposing responsibility on profit-making firms. First, litigation is costly. In many cases there are social wrongs or social inefficiencies which are quite significant in the aggregate and are perceived by a large number of people, each of whom bears a small part of the cost. This is characteristic of pollution and may be the case with certain kinds of quality standards. It really does not pay any particular person to sue, and if a few people do sue it does not really do the company much harm.

Another problem is that the notion of liability in law is really too simple a concept. Legal liability tends to be an all-or-none proposition. Consider a product such as plastic bags. They are perfectly all right for storing clothes or food but there is a risk that small children will misuse them, with serious consequences. One would hardly want to say that there is any legal liability ascribable to the plastic-bag makers, for even the safest product can be misused. On the other hand, one might argue that a product that can be misused ought to be somewhat discouraged and perhaps some small degree of responsibility should be imposed, particularly if no adequate warning is issued. The law does not permit any such distinctions. Thus, in an automobile case, one party or the other must be found wrong, even though in fact a crash may clearly be due to the fact that both drivers were behaving erratically, and it would be reasonable to have some splitting of responsibility. At present, with some minor exceptions, the law does not permit this, and I suppose it would confuse legal proceedings irreparably to start introducing partial causation. Economists are accustomed to the idea that almost nothing happens without the cooperation of a number of factors, and we have large bodies of doctrine devoted to imputing in some appropriate way the consequences of an action to all of its causes. It is for these reasons that this kind of crude liability doctrine seems to be unsuitable in many cases.

A number of other problems with litigation could be mentioned. Consider very high-risk situations that involve a very low probability of death or other serious adverse consequence, as in the case of drugs, or possible radiation from nuclear power plants. The insurance companies are willing to insure because the probability is low. But once insurance is introduced the incentive to refrain from incurring the risk is dulled. If you are insured against a loss you have less of an incentive to prevent it. In the field of automobile liability, it has become clear that the whole system of liability has to a very great extent broken down. The result is a widespread movement toward no-fault insurance, which in effect means people are compensated for their losses but no attempt is made to charge damages to the persons responsible. Responsibility is left undecided.

Finally, litigation does not seem suitable for continuing problems. Pollution will be reduced but not eliminated; indeed it is essentially impossible to eliminate it. There remain continuous steady damages to individuals. These should still be charged to firms in order to prevent them from polluting more. But enforcement by continuous court action is a very expensive way of handling a repetitious situation. It is silly to keep on going to court to establish the same set of facts over and over again. For these reasons taxes which have the same incentive effects are superior.

Let me turn to the fourth possibility, ethical codes. This may seem to be a strange possibility for an economist to raise. But when there is a wide difference in knowledge between the two sides of the market, recognized ethical codes can be, as has already been suggested, a great contribution to economic efficiency. Actually we do have examples of this in our everyday lives, but in very limited areas. The case of medical ethics is the most striking. By its very nature there is a very large difference in knowledge between the buyer and the seller. One is, in fact, buying precisely the service of someone with much more knowledge than you have. To make this relationship a viable one, ethical codes have grown up over the centuries, both to avoid the possibility of exploitation by the physician and to assure the buyer of medical services that he is not being exploited. I am not suggesting that these are universally obeyed, but there is a strong presumption that the doctor is going to perform to a large extent with your welfare in mind. Unnecessary medical expenses or other abuses are perceived as violations of ethics. There is a powerful ethical background against which we make this judgment. Behavior that we would regard as highly reprehensible in a physician is judged less harshly when found among businessmen. The medical profession is typical of professions in general. All professions involve a situation in which knowledge is unequal on two sides of the market by the very definition of the profession, and therefore there have grown up ethical principles that afford some protection to the client. Notice there is a mutual benefit in this. The fact is that if you had sufficient distrust of a doctor's services, you wouldn't buy them. Therefore the physician wants an ethical code to act as assurance to the buyer, and he certainly wants his competitors to obey this same code, partly because any violation may put him at a disadvantage but more especially because the violation will reflect on him, since the buyer of the medical services may not be able to distinguish one doctor from another. A close look reveals that a great deal of economic life depends for its viability on a certain limited degree of ethical commitment. Purely selfish behavior of individuals is really incompatible with any kind of settled economic life. There is almost invariably some element of trust and confidence. Much business is done on the basis of verbal assurance. It would be too elaborate to try to get written commitments on every possible point. Every contract depends for its observance on a mass of unspecified conditions which suggest that the performance will be carried out in good faith without insistence on sticking literally to its wording. To put the matter in its simplest form, in almost every economic transaction, in any exchange of goods for money, somebody gives up his valuable asset before he gets the other's: either the goods are given before the money or the money is given before the goods. Moreover there is a general confidence that there won't be any violation of the implicit agreement. Another example in daily life of this kind of ethics is the observance of queue discipline. People line up; there are people who try to break in ahead of you, but there is an ethic which holds that this is bad. It is clearly an ethic which is in everybody's interest to preserve; one waits at the end of the line this time, and one is protected against somebody's coming in ahead of him.

In the context of product safety, efficiency would be greatly enhanced by accepted ethical rules. Sometimes it may be enough to have an ethical compulsion to reveal all the information available and let the buyer choose. This is not necessarily always the best. It can be argued that under some circumstances setting minimum safety standards and simply not putting out products that do not meet them would be desirable and should be felt by the businessman to be an obligation.

Now I've said that ethical codes are desirable. It doesn't follow from that that they will come about. An ethical code is useful only if it is widely accepted. Its implications for specific behavior must be moderately clear, and above all it must be clearly perceived that the acceptance of these ethical obligations by everybody does involve mutual gain. Ethical codes that lack the latter property are unlikely to be viable. How do such codes develop? They may develop as a consensus out of lengthy public discussion of obligations, discussion which will take place in legislatures, lecture halls, business journals, and other public forums. The codes are communicated by the very process of coming to an agreement. A more formal alternative would be to have some highly prestigious group discuss ethical codes for safety standards. In either case to become and to remain a part of the economic environment, the codes have to be accepted by the significant operating institutions and transmitted from one generation of executives to the next through standard operating procedures, through education in business schools, and through indoctrination of one kind or another. If we seriously expect such codes to develop and to be maintained, we might ask how the agreements develop and above all, how the codes remain stable. After all, an ethical code, however much it may be in the interest of all, is, as we remarked earlier, not in the interest of any one firm. The code may be of value to the running of the system as a whole, it may be of value to all firms if all firms maintain it, and yet it will be to the advantage of any one firm to cheat—in fact the more so, the more other firms are sticking to it. But there are some reasons for thinking that ethical codes can develop and be stable. These codes will not develop completely without institutional support. That is to say, there will be need for focal organizations, such as government agencies, trade associations, and consumer defense groups, or all combined to make the codes explicit, to iterate their doctrine and to make their presence felt. Given that help, I think the emergence of ethical codes, on matters such as safety at least, is possible. One positive factor here is something that is a negative factor in other contexts, namely that our economic organization is to such a large extent composed of large firms. The corporation is no longer a single individual; it is a social organization with internal social ties and internal pressures for acceptability and esteem. The individual members of the corporation are not only parts of the corporation but also members of a larger society whose esteem is desired. Power in a large corporation is necessarily diffused; not many individuals in such organizations feel so thoroughly identified with the corporation that other kinds of social pressures become irrelevant. Furthermore, in a large, complex firm where many people have to participate in any decision, there are likely to be some who are motivated to call attention to violations of the code. This kind of check has been conspicuous in government in recent years. The Pentagon Papers are an outstanding illustration of the fact that within the organization there are those who recognize moral guilt and take occasion to blow the whistle. I expect the same sort of behavior to occur in any large organization when there are well-defined ethical rules whose violation can be observed.

One can still ask if the codes are likely to be stable. Since it may well be possible and profitable for a minority to cheat, will it not be true that the whole system may break down? In fact, however, some of the pressures work in the other direction. It is clearly in the interest of those who are obeying the codes to enforce them, to call attention to violations, to use the ethical and social pressures of the society at large against their less scrupulous rivals. At the same time the value of maintaining the system may well be apparent to all, and no doubt ways will be found to use the assurance of quality generated by the system as a positive asset in attracting consumers and workers.

One must not expect miraculous transformations in human behavior. Ethical codes, if they are to be viable, should be limited in their scope. They are not a universal substitute for the weapons mentioned earlier, the institutions, taxes, regulations, and legal remedies. Further, we should expect the codes to apply only in situations where the firm has superior knowledge of the situation. I would not want the firm to act in accordance with some ethical principles in regard to matters of which it has little knowledge. For example, with quality standards which consumers can observe, it may not be desirable that the firm decide for itself, at least on ethical grounds, because it is depriving the consumer of the freedom of choice between high-quality, high-cost and low-quality, low-cost products. It is in areas where someone is typically misinformed or imperfectly informed that ethical codes can contribute to economic efficiency.

Questions

1. What is the argument for the conclusion that firms ought to maximize profits?

2. What are the qualifiers for the argument that firms ought to maximize profits?

3. In what ways does the argument break down?

4. What are externalities?

Further Reading

Arrow, Kenneth J. "What Has Economics to Say about Racial Discrimination?" *Journal of Economic Perspectives*, vol. 12, no. 2, 1998, pp. 91–100.

Arrow, Kenneth J. "The Organization of Economic Activity: Issues Pertinent to the Choice of Market versus Nonmarket Allocation." *The Analysis and Evaluation of Public Expenditure: The PPB System*, vol. 1, 1969, pp. 59–73.

Demsetz, Harold. "Information and Efficiency: Another Viewpoint." *The Journal of Law and Economics*, vol. 12, no. 1, 1969, pp. 1–22.

Feiwel, George R. *Arrow and the Ascent of Modern Economic Theory*. New York: Springer, 2016.

Laffont, Jean-Jacques. "Macroeconomic Constraints, Economic Efficiency and Ethics: An Introduction to Kantian Economics." *Economica*, vol. 42, no. 168, 1975, pp. 430–37.

23.
"BUSINESS AND ENVIRONMENTAL ETHICS"

W. MICHAEL HOFFMAN[1]

About This Reading

It is a standard refrain in business ethics circles and classes to suggest that "ethical business is good business." The same kind of refrain can be, and is, offered regarding good environmental practices. Thus, it is argued that it is good for the bottom line to engage in both ethical business practices and environmentally friendly business practices. Hoffman takes this way of thinking about business ethics and environmental sustainability to task as being problematic in both cases. The examples he considers are a bit old, but newer examples abound. There is the 2010 BP oil spill in the Gulf of Mexico, for example. Hoffman argues for a view that locates the value of the environment and ethical practice in a more central place in the decision-making process. Maintaining ethical practice should not occur because it is good for the bottom line, but because, morally speaking, unethical practices are simply not allowed. The same goes for environmentally appropriate practices. Moreover, Hoffman argues that the environment should be valued not simply because of the value to humans, but because of the value of the environment. If the only reason for engaging in ethical practice or protecting the environment is that it is good for the bottom line, what happens when the bottom line changes and, instead of paying, such practices cost?

ABSTRACT This paper explores some interconnections between the business and environmental ethics movements. The first section argues that business has obligations to protect the environment over and above what is required by environmental law

---

1   *Center for Business Ethics*, Bentley College.

and that it should cooperate and interact with government in establishing environmental regulation. Business must develop and demonstrate environmental moral leadership. The second section exposes the danger of using the rationale of "good ethics is good business" as a basis for such business moral leadership in both the business and environmental ethics movements. The third section cautions against the moral shallowness inherent in the position or in the promotional strategy of ecological homocentrism which claims that society, including business, ought to protect the environment solely because of harm done to human beings and human interests. This paper urges business and environmental ethicists to promote broader and deeper moral perspectives than ones based on mere self-interest or human interest. Otherwise both movements will come up ethically short.

The business ethics movement, from my perspective, is still on the march. And the environmental movement, after being somewhat silent for the past twenty years, has once again captured our attention—promising to be a major social force in the 1990s. Much will be written in the next few years trying to tie together these two movements. This is one such effort.

Concern over the environment is not new. Warnings came out of the 1960s in the form of burning rivers, dying lakes, and oil-fouled oceans. Radioactivity was found in our food, DDT in mother's milk, lead and mercury in our water. Every breath of air in the North American hemisphere was reported as contaminated. Some said these were truly warnings from Planet Earth of eco-catastrophe, unless we could find limits to our growth and changes in our lifestyle.

Over the past few years Planet Earth began to speak to us even more loudly than before, and we began to listen more than before. The message was ominous, somewhat akin to God warning Noah. It spoke through droughts, heat waves, and forest fires, raising fears of global warming due to the buildup of carbon dioxide and other gases in the atmosphere. It warned us by raw sewage and medical wastes washing up on our beaches, and by devastating oil spills—one despoiling Prince William Sound and its wildlife to such an extent that it made us weep. It spoke to us through increased skin cancers and discoveries of holes in the ozone layer caused by our use of chlorofluorocarbons. It drove its message home through the rapid and dangerous cutting and burning of our primitive forests at the rate of one football field a second, leaving us even more vulnerable to greenhouse gases like carbon dioxide and eliminating scores of irreplaceable species daily. It rained down on us in the form of acid, defoliating our forests and poisoning our lakes and streams. Its warnings were found on barges roaming the seas for places to dump tons of toxic incinerator ash. And its message exploded in our faces at Chernobyl and Bhopal, reminding us of past warnings at Three Mile Island and Love Canal.

Senator Albert Gore said in 1988: "The fact that we face an ecological crisis without any precedent in historic times is no longer a matter of any dispute worthy of recognition."[2] The question, he continued, is not whether there is a problem, but how we will address it. This will be the focal point for a public policy debate which requires the full participation of two of its major players—business and government. The debate must clarify such fundamental questions as (1) What obligation does business have to help with our environmental crisis? (2) What is the proper relationship between business and government, especially when faced with a social problem of the magnitude of the environment crisis? And (3) what rationale should be used for making and justifying decisions to protect the environment? Corporations, and society in general for that matter, have yet to answer these questions satisfactorily. In the first section of this paper I will briefly address the first two questions. In the final two sections I will say a few things about the third question.

I.

In a 1989 keynote address before the "Business, Ethics and the Environment" conference at the Center for Business Ethics, Norman Bowie offered some answers to the first two questions.

> Business does not have an obligation to protect the environment over and above what is required by law; however, it does have a moral obligation to avoid intervening in the political arena in order to defeat or weaken environmental legislation.[3]

I disagree with Bowie on both counts.

Bowie's first point is very Friedmanesque.[4] The social responsibility of business is to produce goods and services and to make profit for its shareholders, while playing within the rules of the market game. These rules, including those to protect the environment, are set by the government and the courts. To do more than is required by these rules is, according to this position, unfair to business. In order to perform its proper function, every business must respond to the market and operate in the same arena as its competitors. As Bowie puts this:

---

2   Albert Gore, "What Is Wrong With Us?" *Time* (January 2, 1989), 66.
3   Norman Bowie, "Morality, Money, and Motor Cars," *Business, Ethics, and the Environment: The Public Policy Debate*, edited by W. Michael Hoffman, Robert Frederick, and Edward S. Petry, Jr. (New York: Quorum Books, 1990), p. 89.
4   See Milton Friedman, "The Social Responsibility of Business Is to Increase Its Profits," *The New York Times Magazine* (September 13, 1970).

> An injunction to assist in solving societal problems [including depletion of natural resources and pollution] makes impossible demands on a corporation because, at the practical level, it ignores the impact that such activities have on profit.[5]

If, as Bowie claims, consumers are not willing to respond to the cost and use of environmentally friendly products and actions, then it is not the responsibility of business to respond or correct such market failure.

Bowie's second point is a radical departure from this classical position in contending that business should not lobby against the government's process to set environmental regulations. To quote Bowie:

> Far too many corporations try to have their cake and eat it too. They argue that it is the job of government to correct for market failure and then they use their influence and money to defeat or water down regulations designed to conserve and protect the environment.[6]

Bowie only recommends this abstinence of corporate lobbying in the case of environmental regulations. He is particularly concerned that politicians, ever mindful of their reelection status, are already reluctant to pass environmental legislation which has huge immediate costs and in most cases very long-term benefits. This makes the obligations of business to refrain from opposing such legislation a justified special case.

I can understand why Bowie argues these points. He seems to be responding to two extreme approaches, both of which are inappropriate. Let me illustrate these extremes by the following two stories.

At the Center's First National Conference on Business Ethics, Harvard Business School Professor George Cabot Lodge told of a friend who owned a paper company on the banks of a New England stream. On the first Earth Day in 1970, his friend was converted to the cause of environmental protection. He became determined to stop his company's pollution of the stream, and marched off to put his new-found religion into action. Later, Lodge learned his friend went broke, so he went to investigate. Radiating a kind of ethical purity, the friend told Lodge that he spent millions to stop the pollution and thus could no longer compete with other firms that did not follow his example. So the company went under, 500 people lost their jobs, and the stream remained polluted.

---

5   Bowie, p. 91.
6   Bowie, p. 94.

When Lodge asked why his friend hadn't sought help from the state or federal government for stricter standards for everyone, the man replied that was not the American way, that government should not interfere with business activity, and that private enterprise could do the job alone. In fact, he felt it was the social responsibility of business to solve environmental problems, so he was proud that he had set an example for others to follow.

The second story portrays another extreme. A few years ago "Sixty Minutes" interviewed a manager of a chemical company that was discharging effluent into a river in upstate New York. At the time, the dumping was legal, though a bill to prevent it was pending in Congress. The manager remarked that he hoped the bill would pass, and that he certainly would support it as a responsible citizen. However, he also said he approved of his company's efforts to defeat the bill and of the firm's policy of dumping wastes in the meantime. After all, isn't the proper role of business to make as much profit as possible within the bounds of law? Making the laws—setting the rules of the game—is the role of government, not business. While wearing his business hat the manager had a job to do, even if it meant doing something that he strongly opposed as a private citizen.

Both stories reveal incorrect answers to the questions posed earlier, the proof of which is found in the fact that neither the New England stream nor the New York river was made any cleaner. Bowie's points are intended to block these two extremes. But to avoid these extremes, as Bowie does, misses the real managerial and ethical failure of the stories. Although the paper company owner and the chemical company manager had radically different views of the ethical responsibilities of business, both saw business and government performing separate roles, and neither felt that business ought to cooperate with government to solve environmental problems.[7]

If the business ethics movement has led us anywhere in the past fifteen years, it is to the position that business has an ethical responsibility to become a more active partner in dealing with social concerns. Business must creatively find ways to become a part of solutions, rather than being a part of problems. Corporations can and must develop a conscience, as Ken Goodpaster and others have argued—and this includes an environmental conscience.[8] Corporations should not isolate themselves from participation in solving our environmental problems, leaving it up to others to find the answers and to tell them what not to do.

Corporations have special knowledge, expertise, and resources which are invaluable in dealing with the environmental crisis. Society needs the ethical vision and

---

7   Robert Frederick, Assistant Director of the Center for Business Ethics, and I have developed and written these points together. Frederick has also provided me with invaluable assistance on other points in this paper.

8   Kenneth E. Goodpaster, "Can a Corporation Have an Environmental Conscience?" *The Corporation, Ethics, and the Environment,* edited by W. Michael Hoffman, Robert Frederick, and Edward S. Petry, Jr. (New York: Quorum Books, 1990).

cooperation of all its players to solve its most urgent problems, especially one that involves the very survival of the planet itself. Business must work with government to find appropriate solutions. It should lobby for good environmental legislation and lobby against bad legislation, rather than isolating itself from the legislative process as Bowie suggests. It should not be ethically quixotic and try to go it alone, as our paper company owner tried to do, nor should it be ethically inauthentic and fight against what it believes to be environmentally sound policy, as our chemical company manager tried to do. Instead business must develop and demonstrate moral leadership.

There are examples of corporations demonstrating such leadership, even when this has been a risk to their self-interest. In the area of environmental moral leadership one might cite DuPont's discontinuing its Freon products, a $750-million-a-year-business, because of their possible negative effects on the ozone layer, and Proctor and Gamble's manufacture of concentrated fabric softener and detergents which require less packaging. But some might argue, as Bowie does, that the real burden for environmental change lies with consumers, not with corporations. If we as consumers are willing to accept the harm done to the environment by favoring environmentally unfriendly products, corporations have no moral obligation to change so long as they obey environmental law. This is even more the case, so the argument goes, if corporations must take risks or sacrifice profits to do so.

This argument fails to recognize that we quite often act differently when we think of ourselves as *consumers* than when we think of ourselves as *citizens*. Mark Sagoff, concerned about our over-reliance on economic solutions, clearly characterizes this dual nature of our decision making.[9] As consumers, we act more often than not for ourselves; as citizens, we take on a broader vision and do what is in the best interests of the community. I often shop for things I don't vote for. I might support recycling referendums, but buy products in nonreturnable bottles. I am not proud of this, but I suspect this is more true of most of us than not. To stake our environmental future on our consumer willingness to pay is surely shortsighted, perhaps even disastrous.

I am not saying that we should not work to be ethically committed citizen consumers, and investors for that matter. I agree with Bowie that "consumers bear a far greater responsibility for preserving and protecting the environment than they have actually exercised,"[10] but activities which affect the environment should not be left up to what we, acting as consumers, are willing to tolerate or accept. To do this would be to use a market-based method of reasoning to decide on an issue

---

9   Mark Sagoff, "At the Shrine of Our Lady of Fatima, or Why Political Questions Are Not All Economic," found in *Business Ethics: Readings and Cases in Corporate Morality*, 2nd edition, edited by W. Michael Hoffman and Jennifer Mills Moore (New York: McGraw-Hill, 1990), pp. 494–503.
10   Bowie, p. 94.

which should be determined instead on the basis of our ethical responsibilities as a member of a social community.

Furthermore, consumers don't make the products, provide the services, or enact the legislation which can be either environmentally friendly or unfriendly. Grass roots boycotts and lobbying efforts are important, but we also need leadership and mutual cooperation from business and government in setting forth ethical environmental policy. Even Bowie admits that perhaps business has a responsibility to educate the public and promote environmentally responsible behavior. But I am suggesting that corporate moral leadership goes far beyond public educational campaigns. It requires moral vision, commitment, and courage, and involves risk and sacrifice. I think business is capable of such a challenge. Some are even engaging in such a challenge. Certainly the business ethics movement should do nothing short of encouraging such leadership. I feel morality demands such leadership.

II.

If business has an ethical responsibility to the environment which goes beyond obeying environmental law, what criterion should be used to guide and justify such action? Many corporations are making environmentally friendly decisions where they see there are profits to be made by doing so. They are wrapping themselves in green where they see a green bottom line as a consequence. This rationale is also being used as a strategy by environmentalists to encourage more businesses to become environmentally conscientious. In December 1989 the highly respected Worldwatch Institute published an article by one of its senior researchers entitled "Doing Well by Doing Good" which gives numerous examples of corporations improving their pocket-books by improving the environment. It concludes by saying that "fortunately, businesses that work to preserve the environment can also make a buck."[11]

In a recent Public Broadcast Corporation documentary entitled "Profit the Earth," several efforts are depicted of what is called the "new environmentalism" which induces corporations to do things for the environment by appealing to their self-interest. The Environmental Defense Fund is shown encouraging agribusiness in Southern California to irrigate more efficiently and profit by selling the water saved to the city of Los Angeles. This in turn will help save Mono Lake. EDF is also shown lobbying for emissions trading that would allow utility companies which are under their emission allotments to sell their "pollution rights" to those companies which are over their allotments. This is for the purpose of reducing acid rain. Thus the frequent strategy of the new environmentalists is to get business to help solve

---

11 Cynthia Pollock Shea, "Doing Well by Doing Good," *World-Watch* (November/December 1989), p. 30.

environmental problems by finding profitable or virtually costless ways for them to participate. They feel that compromise, not confrontation, is the only way to save the earth. By using the tools of the free enterprise system, they are in search of win-win solutions, believing that such solutions are necessary to take us beyond what we have so far been able to achieve.

I am not opposed to these efforts; in most cases I think they should be encouraged. There is certainly nothing wrong with making money while protecting the environment, just as there is nothing wrong with feeling good about doing one's duty. But if business is adopting or being encouraged to adopt the view that good environmentalism is good business, then I think this poses a danger for the environmental ethics movement—a danger which has an analogy in the business ethics movement.

As we all know, the position that good ethics is good business is being used more and more by corporate executives to justify the building of ethics into their companies and by business ethics consultants to gain new clients. For example, the Business Roundtable's *Corporate Ethics* report states:

> The corporate community should continue to refine and renew efforts to improve performance and manage change effectively through programs in corporate ethics ... corporate ethics is a strategic key to survival and profitability in this era of fierce competitiveness in a global economy.[12]

And, for instance, the book *The Power of Ethical Management* by Kenneth Blanchard and Norman Vincent Peale states in big red letters on the cover jacket that "Integrity Pays! You Don't Have to Cheat to Win." The blurb on the inside cover promises that the book "gives hard-hitting, practical, *ethical* strategies that build profits, productivity, and long-term success."[13] Whoever would have guessed that business ethics could deliver all that! In such ways business ethics gets marketed as the newest cure for what ails corporate America.

Is the rationale that good ethics is good business a proper one for business ethics? I think not. One thing that the study of ethics has taught us over the past 2500 years is that being ethical may on occasion require that we place the interests of others ahead of or at least on par with our own interests. And this implies that the ethical thing to do, the morally right thing to do, may not be in our own self-interest. What happens when the right thing is not the best thing for the business?

---

12   *Corporate Ethics A Prime Business Asset*, a report by The Business Roundtable, February 1988, p. 4.
13   Kenneth Blanchard, and Norman Vincent Peale, *The Power of Ethical Management* (New York: William Morrow and Company, Inc., 1988).

Although in most cases good ethics may be good business, it should not be advanced as the only or even the main reason for doing business ethically. When the crunch comes, when ethics conflicts with the firm's interests, any ethics program that has not already faced up to this possibility is doomed to fail because it will undercut the rationale of the program itself. We should promote business ethics, not because good ethics is good business, but because we are morally required to adopt the moral point of view in all our dealings—and business is no exception. In business, as in all other human endeavors, we must be prepared to pay the costs of ethical behavior.

There is a similar danger in the environmental movement with corporations choosing or being wooed to be environmentally friendly on the grounds that it will be in their self-interest. There is the risk of participating in the movement for the wrong reasons. But what does it matter if business cooperates for reasons other than the right reasons, as long as it cooperates? It matters if business believes or is led to believe that it only has a duty to be environmentally conscientious in those cases where such actions either require no sacrifice or actually make a profit. And I am afraid this is exactly what is happening. I suppose it wouldn't matter if the environmental cooperation of business was only needed in those cases where it was also in business' self-interest. But this is surely not the case, unless one begins to really reach and talk about that amorphous concept "long-term" self-interest. Moreover, long-term interests, I suspect, are not what corporations or the new environmentalists have in mind in using self-interest as a reason for environmental action.

I am not saying we should abandon attempts to entice corporations into being ethical, both environmentally and in other ways, by pointing out and providing opportunities where good ethics is good business. And there are many places where such attempts fit well in both the business and environmental ethics movements. But we must be careful not to cast this as the proper guideline for business' ethical responsibility. Because when it is discovered that many ethical actions are not necessarily good for business, at least in the short-run, then the rationale based on self-interest will come up morally short, and both ethical movements will *be* seen as deceptive and shallow.

III.

What is the proper rationale for responsible business action toward the environment? A minimalist principle is to refrain from causing or prevent the causing of unwarranted harm, because failure to do so would violate certain moral rights not to be harmed. There is, of course, much debate over what harms are indeed unwarranted due to conflict of rights and questions about whether some harms are offset by certain benefits. Norm Bowie, for example, uses the harm principle, but contends that business does not violate it as long as it obeys environmental law. Robert Frederick, on the other hand, convincingly argues that the harm principle morally requires business to find ways to prevent certain harm it causes even if such harm violates no environmental law.[14]

However, Frederick's analysis of the harm principle is largely cast in terms of harm caused to human beings and the violation of rights of human beings. Even when he hints at the possible moral obligation to protect the environment when no one is caused unwarranted harm, he does so by suggesting that we look to what we, as human beings, value.[15] This is very much in keeping with a humanistic position of environmental ethics which claims that only human beings have rights or moral standing because only human beings have intrinsic value. We may have duties with regard to nonhuman things (penguins, trees, islands, etc.) but only if such duties are derivative from duties we have toward human beings. Nonhuman things are valuable only if valued by human beings.

Such a position is in contrast to a naturalistic view of environmental ethics which holds that natural things other than human beings are intrinsically valuable and have, therefore, moral standing. Some naturalistic environmentalists only include other sentient animals in the framework of being deserving of moral consideration; others include all things which are alive or which are an integral part of an ecosystem. This latter view is sometimes called a biocentric environmental ethic as opposed to the homocentric view which sees all moral claims in terms of human beings and their interests. Some characterize these two views as deep *versus* shallow ecology.

The literature on these two positions is vast and the debate is ongoing. The conflict between them goes to the heart of environmental ethics and is crucial to our making of environmental policy and to our perception of moral duties to the environment, including business'. I strongly favor the biocentric view. And although this is not the place to try to adequately argue for it, let me unfurl its banner for just a moment.

A version of R. Routley's "last man" example[16] might go something like this: Suppose you were the last surviving human being and were soon to die from nuclear poisoning, as all other human and sentient animals have died before you. Suppose also that it is within your power to destroy all remaining life, or to make it simpler, the last tree which could continue to flourish and propagate if left alone. Furthermore you will not suffer if you do not destroy it. Would you do anything wrong by cutting

---

14   Robert Frederick, "Individual Rights and Environmental Protection," presented at the Annual Society for Business Ethics Conference in San Francisco, August 10 and 11, 1990.

15   Frederick.

16   Richard Routley and Val Routley, "Human Chauvinism and Environmental Ethics," *Environmental Philosophy*, Monograph Series, No. 2, edited by Don Mannison, Michael McRobbie, and Richard Routley (Australian National University, 1980), pp. 121ff.

it down? The deeper ecological view would say yes because you would be destroying something that has value in and of itself, thus making the world a poorer place.

It might be argued that the only reason we may find the tree valuable is because human beings generally find trees of value either practically or aesthetically, rather than the atoms or molecules they might turn into if changed from their present form. The issue is whether the tree has value only in its relation to human beings or whether it has a value deserving of moral consideration inherent in itself in its present form. The biocentric position holds that when we find something wrong with destroying the tree, as we should, we do so because we are responding to an intrinsic value in the natural object, not to a value we give to it. This is a view which argues against a humanistic environmental ethic and which urges us to channel our moral obligations accordingly.

Why should one believe that nonhuman living things or natural objects forming integral parts of ecosystems have intrinsic value? One can respond to this question by pointing out the serious weaknesses and problems of human chauvinism.[17] More complete responses lay out a framework of concepts and beliefs which provides a coherent picture of the biocentric view with human beings as a part of a more holistic value system. But the final answer to the question hinges on what criterion one decides to use for determining moral worth—rationality, sentience, or a deeper biocentric one. Why should we adopt the principle of attributing intrinsic value to all living beings, or even to all natural objects, rather than just to human beings? I suspect Arne Naess gives as good an answer as can be given.

> Faced with the ever returning question of 'Why?', we have to stop some-
> where. Here is a place where we well might stop. We shall admit that the
> value in itself is something shown in intuition. We attribute intrinsic value
> to ourselves and our nearest, and the validity of further identification can
> be contested, and *is* contested by many. The negation may, however, also be
> attacked through a series of 'whys?' Ultimately, we are in the same human
> predicament of having to start somewhere, at least for the moment. We
> must stop somewhere and treat where we then stand as a foundation.[18]

---

17   See Paul W. Taylor, "The Ethics of Respect for Nature," *People, Penguins, and Plastic Trees*, edited by Donald Van De Veer and Christine Pierce (Belmont, California: Wadsworth, 1986), pp. 178–83. Also see R. and V. Routley, "Against the Inevitability of Human Chauvinism," in *Ethics and the Problems of the 21st Century*, edited by K.E. Goodpaster and K.M. Sayre (Notre Dame: University of Notre Dame Press, 1979), pp. 36–59.
18   Arne Naess, "Identification as a Source of Deep Ecological Attitudes," *Deep Ecology*, edited by Michael Tobias (San Marcos, California: Avant Books, 1988), p. 266.

In the final analysis, environmental biocentrism is adopted or not depending on whether it is seen to provide a deeper, richer, and more ethically compelling view of the nature of things.

If this deeper ecological position is correct, then it ought to be reflected in the environmental movement. Unfortunately, for the most part, I do not think this is being done, and there is a price to be paid for not doing so. Moreover, I fear that even those who are of the biocentric persuasion are using homocentric language and strategies to bring business and other major players into the movement because they do not think they will be successful otherwise. They are afraid, and undoubtedly for good reason, that the large part of society, including business, will not be moved by arguments regarding the intrinsic value and rights of natural things. It is difficult enough to get business to recognize and act on their responsibilities to human beings and things of human interest. Hence many environmentalists follow the counsel of Spinoza:

> ... it is necessary that while we are endeavoring to attain our purpose ... we are compelled ... to speak in a manner intelligible to the multitude ... For we can gain from the multitude no small advantages....[19]

I understand the temptation of environmentalists employing a homocentric strategy, just as I understand business ethicists using the rationale that good ethics is good business. Both want their important work to succeed. But just as with the good ethics is good business tack, there are dangers in being a closet ecocentrist. The ethicists in both cases fail to reveal the deeper moral base of their positions because it's a harder sell. Business ethics gets marketed in terms of self-interest, environmental ethics in terms of human interest.

A major concern in using the homocentric view to formulate policy and law is that nonhuman nature will not receive the moral consideration it deserves. It might be argued, however, that by appealing to the interests and rights of human beings, in most cases nature as a whole will be protected. That is, if we are concerned about a wilderness area, we can argue that its survival is important to future generations who will otherwise be deprived of contact with its unique wildlife. We can also argue that it is important to the aesthetic pleasure of certain individuals or that, if it is destroyed, other recreational areas will become overcrowded. In this way we stand a chance to save the wilderness area without having to refer to our moral obligations to respect the intrinsic value of the spotted owl or of the old-growth forest. This is simply being strategically savvy. To trot out our deeper ecological

---

19   Benedict de Spinoza, "On the Improvement of the Understanding," *Philosophy of Benedict de Spinoza*, translated by R.H.M. Elwes (New York: Tudor Publishing Co., 1936), p. 5.

moral convictions runs the risk of our efforts being ignored, even ridiculed, by business leaders and policy makers. It also runs head-on against a barrage of counter arguments that human interests take precedence over nonhuman interests. In any event it will not be in the best interest of the wilderness area we are trying to protect. Furthermore, all of the above homocentric arguments happen to be true—people will suffer if the wilderness area is destroyed.

In most cases, what is in the best interests of human beings may also be in the best interests of the rest of nature. After all, we are in our present environmental crisis in large part because we have not been ecologically intelligent about what is in our own interest—just as business has encountered much trouble because it has failed to see its interest in being ethically sensitive. But if the environmental movement relies only on arguments based on human interests, then it perpetuates the danger of making environmental policy and law on the basis of our strong inclination to fulfill our immediate self-interests, on the basis of our consumer viewpoints, on the basis of our willingness to pay. There will always be a tendency to allow our short-term interests to eclipse our long-term interests and the long-term interest of humanity itself. Without some grounding in a deeper environmental ethic with obligations to nonhuman natural things, then the temptation to view our own interests in disastrously short-term ways is that much more encouraged. The biocentric view helps to block this temptation.

Furthermore, there are many cases where what is in human interest is not in the interest of other natural things. Examples range from killing leopards for stylish coats to destroying a forest to build a golf course. I am not convinced that homocentric arguments, even those based on long-term human interests, have much force in protecting the interests of such natural things. Attempts to make these interests coincide might be made, but the point is that from a homocentric point of view the leopard and the forest have no morally relevant interests to consider. It is simply fortuitous if nonhuman natural interests coincide with human interests, and are thereby valued and protected. Let us take an example from the work of Christopher Stone. Suppose a stream has been polluted by a business. From a homocentric point of view, which serves as the basis for our legal system, we can only correct the problem through finding some harm done to human beings who use the stream. Reparation for such harm might involve cessation of the pollution and restoration of the stream, but it is also possible that the business might settle with the people by paying them for their damages and continue to pollute the stream. Homocentrism provides no way for the stream to be made whole again unless it is in the interests of human beings to do so. In short it is possible for human beings to sell out the stream.[20]

---

20   Christopher D. Stone, "Should Trees Have Standing?—Toward Legal Rights for Natural Objects," *People, Penguins, and Plastic Trees*, pp. 86–87.

I am not saying that human interests cannot take precedence over nonhuman interests when there are conflicts. For this we need to come up with criteria for deciding on interspecific conflicts of interests, just as we do for intraspecific conflicts of interest among human beings.[21] But this is a different problem from holding that nonhuman natural things have no interests or value deserving of moral consideration. There are times when causing harm to natural things is morally unjustifiable when there are no significant human interests involved and even when there are human interests involved. But only a deeper ecological ethic than homocentrism will allow us to defend this.

Finally, perhaps the greatest danger that biocentric environmentalists run in using homocentric strategies to further the movement is the loss of the very insight that grounded their ethical concern in the first place. This is nicely put by Lawrence Tribe:

> What the environmentalist may not perceive is that, by couching his claim in terms of human self-interest—by articulating environmental goals wholly in terms of human needs and preferences—he may be helping to legitimate a system of discourse which so structures human thought and feeling as to erode, over the long run, the very sense of obligation which provided the initial impetus for his own protective efforts.[22]

Business ethicists run a similar risk in couching their claims in terms of business self-interest.

The environmental movement must find ways to incorporate and protect the intrinsic value of animal and plant life and even other natural objects that are integral parts of ecosystems. This must be done without constantly reducing such values to human interests. This will, of course, be difficult, because our conceptual ideology and ethical persuasion is so dominantly homocentric; however, if we are committed to a deeper biocentric ethic, then it is vital that we try to find appropriate ways to promote it. Environmental impact statements should make explicit reference to nonhuman natural values. Legal rights for nonhuman natural things, along the lines of Christopher Stone's proposal, should be sought.[23] And naturalistic ethical guidelines, such as those suggested by Holmes Rolston, should be set forth for business to follow when its activities impact upon ecosystems.[24]

---

21   See Donald Van De Veer, "Interspecific Justice," *People, Penguins, and Plastic Trees*, pp. 51–66.

22   Lawrence H. Tribe, "Ways Not to Think about Plastic Trees: New Foundations for Environmental Law," *People, Penguins, and Plastic Trees*, p. 257.

23   Stone, pp. 83–96.

24   Holmes Rolston, III, *Environmental Ethics* (Philadelphia: Temple University Press, 1988), pp. 301–13.

At the heart of the business ethics movement is its reaction to the mistaken belief that business only has responsibilities to a narrow set of its stakeholders, namely its stockholders. Crucial to the environmental ethics movement is its reaction to the mistaken belief that only human beings and human interests are deserving of our moral consideration. I suspect that the beginnings of both movements can be traced to these respective moral insights. Certainly the significance of both movements lies in their search for a broader and deeper moral perspective. If business and environmental ethicists begin to rely solely on promotional strategies of self-interest, such as good ethics is good business, and of human interest, such as homocentrism, then they face the danger of cutting off the very roots of their ethical efforts.

Note

This paper was originally presented as the Presidential Address to the *Society for Business Ethics*, August 10, 1990, San Francisco, CA.

Questions

1. What is the problem, as argued by Hoffman, with the view that "good ethics is good business"?

2. What are the two approaches to environmental ethics identified by Hoffman?

3. Which view of environmental ethics does Hoffman advocate and what is his argument?

4. What is the problem with approaching the environment from the viewpoint Hoffman rejects?

Further Reading

Alexander, John. "Environmental Sustainability versus Profit Maximization: Overcoming Systemic Constraints on Implementing Normatively Preferable Alternatives." *Journal of Business Ethics*, vol. 76, no. 2, 2007, pp. 155–62.

Bowie, Norman. "Morality, Money, and Motor Cars." In *Business, Ethics, and the Environment: The Public Policy Debate*, edited by W. Michael Hoffman, Robert Frederick, and Edward S. Petry, Jr. New York: Quorum Books, 1990.

24.

"THE BUSINESS OF BOYCOTTING

HAVING YOUR CHICKEN AND EATING IT TOO"

ALAN TOMHAVE AND MARK C. VOPAT

About This Reading

In this article, Tomhave and Vopat examine business from another perspective, namely, that of the consumer. How should the consumer react to the actions and statements of business that they find offensive? Here the authors assume that there are certain causes that are morally wrong, and worth speaking out against and working to overcome, e.g., opposition to same-sex marriage. This seems to suggest that consumers should also be boycotting certain businesses, particularly those whose owners advocate such views. Ideally, for the boycotter, this will end up silencing certain views (political or otherwise), but this seems to cause two basic problems. First, it appears initially to be coercive, because it threatens the existence of the business. Second, it runs counter to the intuition that we should not force unpopular opinions out of the marketplace of ideas. Boycotting is by its very nature a coercive act, and thus we have to carefully consider what types of actions may warrant this type of coercive action. In this paper, Tomhave and Vopat argue that an organized boycott against a company is justified if and only if the actions taken by the company have negative consequences that outweigh the negative outcome of the boycott.

1. Introduction

In June of 2012, Dan Cathy, president of Chick-fil-A, appeared on the Ken Coleman radio show where he expressed his opposition to gay marriage. His comments on the radio program were actually a follow-up to those he had made to the *Baptist Press* stating that Chick-fil-A supported the "biblical definition of marriage"[1] (presumably not the polygamous one of the Hebrew Bible). This reference to Chick-fil-A's supporting a biblical definition of marriage is not metaphorical. As a privately held company, the views of Chick-fil-A represent Dan Cathy and those of his family.

As might be expected, Cathy's remarks elicited responses from across the political spectrum. The then Republican presidential hopeful Rick Santorum and former governor Mike Huckabee expressed their hunger for a chicken sandwich. On the other side of political isle, mayors in Boston and Chicago made public statements opposing Chick-fil-A opening restaurants in their cities, and the Jim Henson Company announced it would remove its toys from Chick-fil-A restaurants.[2] Additionally, several regional and national gay rights groups called for a boycott of Chick-fil-A restaurants.[3]

The call for a boycott of Chick-fil-A is not surprising, and it is not the first company to feel the pressure of a boycott because of its position on an issue, or its corporate actions. In the late 1990s Gap Inc., Nike, and even Disney were the targets of organized boycotts. In some of these cases, the boycott resulted in a change in corporate policy or corporate actions.[4]

Although corporations (or the public faces of corporations) are often the target of boycotts, larger entities have also been targets. In March of 2015, the Indiana legislature passed a "religious freedom" law that essentially legalized discrimination of LGBT people. The bill "would allow any individual or corporation to cite its

---

1   "'Guilty as charged,' Cathy says of Chick-fil-A's stand on biblical & family values" by K. Allan Blume/ Biblical Recorder, posted Monday, July 16, 2012 http://www.bpnews.net/BPnews.asp?ID=38271. Last accessed 2016-5-9.

2   "Mike Huckabee Calls for Chick-Fil-A Day," July 23, 2012. JILIAN FAMA http://abcnews.go.com/blogs/ politics/2012/07/mike-huckabee-calls-for-chick-fil-a-day/; Jim Henson, "Company breaks ties with Chick-fil-A over gay marriage stance," Eric Pfeiffer, July 23, 2012 www.yahoo.com/news/blogs/the-sideshow/ jim-henson-company-breaks-ties-chick-fil-over-193837209.html.

3   See for example "Colleges Rally to Kick Chick-fil-A Off Campus," 08/17/2012 05:45 pm ET | Updated Feb 02, 2016, www.huffingtonpost.com/shane-l-windmeyer/chick-fil-a-colleges_b_1790565.html; and "Gay rights advocate to boycott Chick-fil-A," Felicity Lawrence, 21 November 2002 20.48 EST. www.newsday.com/ long-island/towns/gay-rights-advocate-to-boycott-chick-fil-a-1.6512942. Updated November 28, 2013 7:38 PM. Both sites last accessed 2016-5-9.

4   In the cases of Gap and Nike, both companies responded to the negative press by changing its practices in its factories. Disney was boycotted by religious groups because of its provision of benefits for same-sex couples. Disney did not alter its policies as a result of the boycott. See "Sweatshop campaigners demand Gap boycott: Union appeals to shoppers as evidence from factory workers alleges exploitative conditions," www.theguardian.com/uk/2002/nov/22/clothes.globalisation; "How activism forced Nike to change its ethical game," Simon Birch, Friday 6 July 2012 11.04 EDT www.theguardian.com/environment/green-living-blog/2012/ jul/06/activism-nike; "Southern Baptists vote for Disney boycott," June 18, 1997 Web posted at: 5:50 p.m. EDT. (2150 GMT) www.cnn.com/US/9706/18/baptists.disney/index.html?_s=PM:US. All sites last accessed 2016-5-9.

religious beliefs as a defense when sued by a private party."[5] This legal protection seems to imply that a coffee shop owner could, on religious grounds, refuse to serve a same-sex couple without fear of being sued.

As with the cases of what was perceived as corporate wrongdoing, there was a nationwide call to boycott Indiana until the law was repealed. Companies such as Salesforce and Angie's List, the musical group Wilco and stand-up comedian Nick Offerman, and AFCSME Women's conference and others all formally announced that they would cease to do business in the state.

The typical response to the morality of boycotts is probably similar to the short remarks regarding the issue made by Murray Rothbard. Rothbard, in *The Ethics of Liberty*, argues that boycotts are "legitimate *per se*" (Rothbard, 1998, p. 131):

> Any action would be legal in the libertarian society, provided that it does not invade property rights (whether of self-ownership or of material objects), and this would include boycotts against such activities, or counter-boycotts against the boycotters. The point is that coercion is not the only action that can be taken against what some consider to be immoral persons or activities; there are also such voluntary and persuasive actions as the boycott. (Rothbard, 1998, pp. 131–32)

Rothbard holds boycotts to be legitimate because boycotts don't involve coercion. Nor is he blind to the potential effects of a boycott. What is more of a concern for him is how the target of a boycott may respond to being boycotted. Writing of a fictional case involving a person named Smith,

> Smith may lose considerable income, and they [the boycotters] may well be doing this for trivial or even immoral reasons; but the fact remains that organizing such a boycott is perfectly within their rights, and if Smith tried to use violence to break up such boycott activities he would be a criminal invader of their property. (Rothbard, 1998, p. 77)

It is the threat or actual use of physical force that is the issue for Rothbard.

Rothbard defines coercion "as the invasive use of physical violence or the threat thereof against someone else's person or (just) property" (Rothbard, 1998, p. 219). Because boycotts do not involve coercion, boycotts are, *per se*, morally legitimate. It is this view we seek to challenge in the present work. We hold that there are indeed

5   "Indiana Governor Signs Anti-Gay 'Religious Freedom' Bill at Private Ceremony," 03/26/2015 12:23 pm ET. Updated Mar 27, 2015 Amanda Terkel www.huffingtonpost.com/2015/03/26/indiana-governor-mike-pence-anti-gay-bill_n_6947472.html. Last accessed 2016-5-9.

morally illegitimate boycotts. The issue, as we shall see, is far more complex than is usually assumed.

Although boycotts are a fixture of social and political protest, there has been surprisingly little written on either the nature or morality of boycotts. On the one hand, writers such as Mary Lyn Stoll have written on how corporations or corporate leaders should respond to boycotts (Stoll, 2009). On the other hand, Claudia Mills and Monroe Friedman have debated the merits of boycotts in their effectiveness at producing the desired outcome (Mills, 1996; Friedman, 1999). Our project is similar to that of the latter writers in that it attempts to provide an argument for when a boycott may be justified. While both Mills and Friedman assume that there is some wrongdoing and then proceed to examine the extent to which boycotts may be an effective response, our concern is with determining exactly what types of beliefs or categories of acts on the part of individuals or corporations may be used to justify a boycott.[6] The category of acts with which we are concerned is specifically a distinction between expressive acts and consequential acts, which we will discuss later in the essay.

We assume that there are certain causes that are morally wrong, worth speaking out against, and working to overcome, e.g., opposition to same sex marriage. This seems to suggest that we should also be boycotting certain businesses, particularly those whose owners advocate such views. Ideally, for the boycotter, this will end up changing beliefs or silencing certain views (political or otherwise), but this seems to cause two basic problems. First, it appears initially to be coercive, because it threatens the existence of the business. Second, it runs counter to the intuition that we should not force unpopular opinions out of the marketplace of ideas. Boycotts by their very nature tend to be intentionally coercive, and thus we have to carefully consider what types of actions may warrant this type of coercive action.[7] In this essay, we will argue that an organized boycott is justified if and only if the actions taken by the company have negative consequences that outweigh the negative outcome of the boycott. At this stage we intentionally leave ambiguous the terms "actions," "consequences," and the method by which one should "weigh" one consequence against another.

In what follows we will attempt to keep the issues at play artificially discrete. One of the distinctions we will make is the one between expressive and consequential acts. Though we will clarify these concepts below, it should be clear from their names that expressive acts are those where an idea is expressed, while consequential acts

---

6   We recognize that the ontological status of corporations is philosophically up for debate. However, in law and standard practice we accept both beliefs and actions on the part of corporations.

7   While it is possible that some boycotts may not end up coercing, the intention to coerce is part of all *organized* boycotts. Individual boycotts may or may not be intentionally coercive.

are those that have a bigger impact on others.[8] Additionally, in what follows we will clarify how we understand coercion, and make distinctions between personal and organized boycotts, as well as integrity and strategic boycotts. Again, there is very little in philosophical analysis regarding the legitimacy of boycotts. This essay is an initial analysis that will raise numerous issues that may need clarification in future, potentially longer, treatments.

Before discussing our argument, we would like to clarify the first set of distinctions and offer a focus for what is to come. When we are discussing boycotting, a distinction needs to be drawn between an *individual* boycott and an *organized* boycott. An individual boycott is one in which a person may choose, for any number of reasons, to boycott a company. Although a boycott may not effect any measurable change, one may still engage in the action on deontological grounds or because they wish to maintain a consistent set of moral views. On the other hand, an organized boycott is one that calls on a number of individuals to exert some sort of coercive force on an individual or company. Throughout this essay, we will be addressing the morality of *organized* boycotts.

It is worth discussing why we are focused solely on organized boycotts instead of also considering personal boycotts. Though some might wish to argue for the illegitimacy of personal boycotts, we find it difficult to do so. The main reason for this is that there is no obligation that a person has to buy a particular product from a particular business. Engaging in a personal boycott is simply refraining from engaging in doing business with a particular organization. If there is no obligation to work with or do business with a particular operation, then there can be no charge of the boycotter having violated the rights of the business owner. In the case of an individual boycott, the intention may or may not be to coerce the business—a single individual is unlikely to be able to exert any real coercive force. It is more likely that he or she is exercising a right to freedom of association. On the other hand, an organized boycott is not a refraining from action; an organized boycott is taking positive action. It is not simply refraining from doing business with an organization; it is an organized attempt to get many others to refrain from doing business with that organization. It is the positive nature of an organized boycott that is potentially problematic.

The distinction between positive and negative actions is important, as in this instance it reflects the way deontological and teleological elements enter into the morality of boycotts. The argument we defend in this essay holds that organized boycotts, that is, the organized use of coercive force, may be justified in order to stop businesses engaging in harmful acts. For example, assume that hypothetical oil

---

8   It should be readily apparent that such a distinction is muddled at best. Many expressive acts have a consequential impact. We will return to the muddled nature of this distinction later in the essay.

company Petrol X is paying security forces in a third-world nation to force villagers to sell their oil-rich land. These actions become public, and an organized boycott ensues. The boycott continues until Petrol X ceases its morally bad behavior. Such positive action appears justified in order to stop the harm being done to others. The positive action is required in order to bring about a positive outcome.

Now imagine another hypothetical company, Beef-gril-r. The CEO of Beef-gril-r happens to be against equal rights for LGBT people. He regularly attends a mainstream church that officially opposes same-sex marriage, and has spoken to groups sympathetic to that position. Although the CEO of Beef-gril-r holds these views, neither he, nor his company, discriminates in any way in terms of who they hire or serve. Imagine that a regular customer of Beef-gril-r, Jane, has recently become aware of the CEO's views. Jane decides that she cannot in good conscience continue to patronize Beef-gril-r. Furthermore, let's suppose that Jane doesn't simply stop frequenting Beef-gril-r, but she also encourages others to stop as well until the CEO changes his views. Is there any difference between this case and the case involving Petrol X? We believe there is and the difference is a deontological one. In this latter case, Jane (and those she can convince to join her) is attempting to forcibly change an individual's *beliefs*. They are in fact attempting to coerce someone into believing as they do. Whether Jane and the other protesters like it or not, individuals have a right to believe whatever they want. I can no more force someone to adopt my political position than I can force him or her to accept my religious convictions. While I am free not to associate with those whose moral, religious, or political views I find offensive, I am not justified in coercing them to change their views. These deontological considerations may be said to constrain when positive actions may be employed to achieve a particular outcome. It is this positive nature that moves the organized boycott into a coercive action, which we will discuss in the next section.

2. The Morality of Organized Boycotts

Our argument regarding the morality of organized boycotts rests on answers to two questions. First, are boycotts coercive? We will argue that boycotts are coercive in nature. Second, are there instances of boycotting that would fall into an unjust use of coercion?[9] We think that the answer to this second question is also yes. This is

---

9   It is worth commenting on the language here. Strictly speaking, all *organized* boycotts are coercive, while not all *organized* boycotts result in coercion. This is because while all *organized* boycotts exert coercive pressure or force, not all are successful. The target of an organized boycott may resist the coercive pressure of the boycott, thereby preventing a case of coercion. In what follows we sometimes use the word "coercive," but at other times it is more natural to use the word "coercion." We could replace "coercion" with the clunkier "make use of coercive force." We have opted for the more elegant "coercion."

particularly the case in examples involving what is referred to as the marketplace of ideas. This forms the core of our basic argument, which could be stated as follows:

1. Boycotts are coercive.

2. Boycotts sometimes attempt to silence voices in the marketplace of ideas.

3. The use of coercion to silence voices in the marketplace of ideas is *pro tanto* morally wrong.

4. Therefore, some boycotts are *pro tanto* morally wrong.

After we have more carefully explained our basic argument, we will expand on the issue and consider boycotting over different kinds of actions and with different end-goals for boycotts. Let us now turn to the first step of our basic argument.

Although they are a ubiquitous element of protests, boycotts are at their core a form of coercion. This is not a controversial claim to make. Anthropologist Talal Asad, writing about Muslim boycotts of Danish and Norwegian products, states "If physical violence was sometimes used by some of those who advocated a boycott, this should not obscure the fact that a commercial boycott is always a form of violence, especially if it is infused with anger, because it attacks people's livelihood" (Asad, 2008, pp. 590–91). Though this quotation seems to suggest otherwise, we take coercion itself to be, conceptually, morally neutral. If I threaten someone to force some action against his or her will, that threat is either justified or unjustified. In either case, the threat is coercive regardless of its moral status. While this claim to the moral neutrality of coercion may strike some as odd, it is not out of place in the literature on coercion. Cheney Ryan, surveying definitions of coercion offered by Virginia Held, Christian Bay, and Robert Nozick, has noted that "These accounts and others that philosophers have given of coercion share one common feature: they make no reference to the rights and obligations of the parties involved. Judgments as to whether P's actions towards Q constitute coercion need not appeal, in this sense, to the normative context of the action" (Ryan, 1980, p. 483). Ryan then goes on to describe what seem to be outlandish examples that show the absurdity of the neutral view. For example, one of his cases involves a mugging where the victim's camera is stolen. The victim pulls out a gun and threatens the mugger and gets the camera back (Ryan, 1980, p. 484). On the morally neutral account of coercion, this is still coercion. We accept that this example and others that could be offered might initially sound odd; nevertheless, we accept them as cases of coercion. It is not the fact that the victim has a right to the stolen item or that the mugger has a duty to refrain from mugging that determine the coerciveness. These issues serve as an aid to the moral conclusion, the wrongness of the mugger's actions in this case and to the permissibility of the actions of the victim. The victim's actions are still a case of coercion. The call for an organized boycott is a call for the use of a kind of force, that is, using the threat of economic loss to compel an individual or company to change a belief or practice. This is, contra Rothbard, a standard analysis of coercion. If this view of coercion is accepted, then boycotts are indeed coercive by nature. However, at this point we cannot claim boycotts to be morally wrong. To make this further claim of any case of coercion we must further examine the instances of boycotting and the use to which the strategy is put.

2.1 Your Money or Your Life

We assume without argument that if a person had his or her life threatened because of a view that was held or expressed, that this would be morally problematic. For example, suppose that we threatened to shoot an individual simply for espousing and defending a libertarian political view. This type of coercion would be unjust, and obviously so. Just as wrong would be a threat to fire someone simply for espousing and defending a libertarian political view, or simply threatening to take the person's wallet for this reason.[10]

The question is, how is this different from threatening, or engaging in, an organized boycott of a company? At least some boycotts are an attempt to get a company to change a given policy or to stop espousing certain views. The threat occurs because the boycott is a threat to affect the bottom line of the company. The ultimate results of a boycott, ideally, are either that the company changes its policy, stops advocating the identified view, or goes out of business. Mary Lyn Stoll, writing of the problems that companies experience regarding boycotts, states that "the companies in question must balance the bottom line with the triple bottom line. If the company is harmed too greatly by any policy decision, then it risks its future as an institutional entity" (Stoll, 2009, p. 5). Thus, a boycott is a true threat to the existence of the company in question. The main problem is that such boycotts often come in the context of expressing ideas. Let us now turn to the Marketplace of Ideas.

---

10   We qualify this example as "simply" espousing or defending a libertarian view because there may be other examples where further details are relevant (e.g., a job with an agreement to defend only anti-libertarian views) and would cause a change in the analysis presented here. We thank an anonymous reviewer for pointing this out.

2.2 The Marketplace of Ideas

In addition to the morally problematic use of direct force—threatening to shoot someone over a libertarian political view—there is the perhaps fewer dire consequences of coercion on the marketplace of ideas. Boycotts do not always attempt to change or influence actions; they are often an attempt to change attitudes or views. In some cases, the intent is to silence views that one finds objectionable. But the silencing of objectionable views (even if those views are *morally* objectionable) is not without its problems. In *On Liberty*, John Stuart Mill presents a compelling case against the censorship of ideas.

Mill writes, "The time, it is to be hoped, is gone by, when any defense would be necessary of the 'liberty of the press' as one of the securities against corrupt or tyrannical government" (Mill, 1859, Chapter 2). Mill then proceeds to express the wrongness not simply of suppressing the press, but of the ideas of others in general. We would hope the time is gone by when any defense would be necessary of the value of the marketplace of ideas and of the wrongness of interfering with such a marketplace. Nonetheless, we will engage in that discussion, however briefly, as a way to set up the argument to come in the next section.

Mill's basic argument begins by pointing out that the government has the power to stop the expression of certain views. He then writes the following:

> Let us suppose, therefore, that the government is entirely at one with the people, and never thinks of exerting any power of coercion unless in agreement with what it conceives to be their voice. But I deny the right of the people to exercise such coercion, either by themselves or by the government. The power itself is illegitimate. The best government has no more title to it than the worst. It is as noxious, or more noxious, when exerted in accordance with public opinion, than when in opposition to it. If all mankind minus one were of one opinion, and only one person were of the contrary opinion, mankind would be no more justified in silencing that one person, than he, if he had the power, would be justified in silencing mankind.... But the peculiar evil of silencing the expression of an opinion is, that it is robbing the human race: posterity as well as the existing generation; those who dissent from the opinion, still more than those who hold it. If the opinion is right, they are deprived of the opportunity of exchanging error for truth; if wrong, they lose, what is almost as great a benefit, the clearer proportion and livelier impression of truth, produced by its collision with error. (Mill, 1859, Chapter 2)

The true value of the marketplace of ideas is found in the idea that the best or true ideas shall win out over the bad or false ideas. This requires, however, that the false ideas be allowed to compete. Otherwise the accepted truth is really tantamount to dogma that may not be challenged.

Galileo's experience with heliocentrism is often taken as a story of a victory of science over religious dogma. Galileo was, after all, correct, yet ultimately sentenced to house arrest for his views. This is a clear case where the ideals of the marketplace of ideas are violated. However, is this an example simply because in the end Galileo was correct? Would it not be an equally powerful example if it had turned out that Galileo was mistaken, and that geocentricism was the correct view? The obvious way to ensure that the truth is winning out is to allow for challenges to come from all sides. In cases where the arguments pull away from an idea, that is a good thing, as long as it is the argumentation that is doing the work. Coercion used to enforce certain ideas over others is a gross violation of the marketplace principles.

We see a similar idea in the work of John Rawls (among others), who argues that a free exchange of ideas—even unpopular ideas—is needed in determining fair terms of social cooperation. Though Rawls is concerned with a specific political context, his ideas are more widely applicable than the use to which he puts them. With regard to the selection of principles, he writes:

> The criterion of reciprocity requires that when those terms are proposed as the most reasonable terms of fair cooperation, those proposing them must also think it at least reasonable for others to accept them, as free and equal citizens, and not as dominated or manipulated, or under the pressure of an inferior political or social position. (Rawls, 1990, p. 137)

Thus, the acceptance of views should not be based simply on pressure due to one's inferior position in terms of social standing or popularity, but on reasonable discourse. Rawls writes elsewhere that candidates for public office must follow ideals of public reason. He writes that such candidates should "act from and follow the idea of public reason and explain to other citizens their reasons for supporting fundamental political questions in terms of the political conception of justice that they regard as the most reasonable. In this way they fulfill what I shall call their duty of civility to one another and to other citizens" (Rawls, 1990, p. 56). Though Rawls is concerned with political operations, this is easily applied to the broader context of the marketplace of ideas. Ideas should be accepted or rejected not simply because they are advocated by particular persons or groups, but because the argumentation and reason points to them as the correct views.

We should all recognize the possibility that whatever view we hold dear is possibly false. The only way to help prevent this is to engage in discussion of all possibilities that are put forth. If coercion is used to prevent this free exchange in the marketplace of ideas, then this is an unjustified use of coercion. It seems clear that in some cases the calls for organized boycotts are over ideas that rightfully belong to exchanges in the marketplace of ideas. These would be cases where coercion is used in an attempt to silence the voices of those that hold unpopular views. Such coercion is *pro tanto* morally wrong. Thus, in at least some cases, boycotting is *pro tanto* morally wrong. We take our basic argument to be established. However, things are more complicated than this basic argument, so more considerations are in order.

3. Justified Boycotts

3.1 Expressive vs. Consequential Acts

The value of supporting a marketplace of ideas has implications for how we approach the issue of boycotting. If we value the free expression of ideas and the submission of even unpopular views to the scrutiny of public reason, then we need to distinguish between two types of acts: expressive acts and consequential acts. Our view is that only the latter types of acts may constitute justifiable grounds for a boycott, whereas expressive acts do not.

EXPRESSIVE ACTS

Expressive acts—as the name implies—are acts that express a view on a particular issue. When an individual, company, or company representative publicly supports a particular social or political position, they are contributing to the marketplace of ideas. In our view, while we may think these views or expressions are wrong-headed, mistaken, ill-informed, etc., we believe they ought not be silenced, apart from through the use of proper argumentation.

As was mentioned in the previous section, opinion (including false opinions) ought to be held up for public scrutiny in the marketplace of ideas. If the opinion lacks merit, then (ideally) the scrutiny it receives will make its falsity known to all. Additionally, in defending the truth against this falsity one is forced to clearly define one's own position. If the expression contains a partial truth, then we all benefit by exposure to that truth. Finally, if it is true, then as Mill noted, we gain the benefits of that truth. If the benefits of public reason and the marketplace of ideas are to carry any moral force, then it would seem that boycotts that attempt to curtail expression are themselves morally problematic. A boycott to silence expression is analogous to censoring the speech of an individual with whom one disagrees. The price of a free society that respects the freedom of expression of its members is having to allow offensive speech.[11]

---

11   As the fictional President Andrew Shepard states in *The American President*: "America is advanced citizenship. You've gotta want it bad, 'cause it's gonna put up a fight. It's gonna say, 'You want free speech? (cont'd)

CONSEQUENTIAL ACTS

In contrast to expressive acts, consequential acts (for lack of a better term) are those actions taken by an individual, company, or company representative that are either illegal or unethical and can be said to be the proximate cause of harm to others. For example, a company that actively discriminates against women, gays, or other minorities is not engaging in a public debate but is engaging in discrimination. Supporting such a company may contribute to these types of injustice, and thus boycotts may be justified.

There is of course a fine line between expressive acts and consequential acts. In the previously mentioned case of Dan Cathy and Chick-fil-A, Cathy's statements in support of "traditional marriage" and opposition to same-sex marriage could be viewed in a variety of ways. On the one hand, Cathy was simply expressing an opinion held by a large minority of the U.S. population. While some may disagree with the view, it is one side of an ongoing social debate. On the other hand, the expression of such views (along with contributions to groups opposing same-sex marriage) might be viewed as creating a hostile climate for LGBTQ persons. They may find his views offensive. Worse yet, his expression may result in others engaging in discriminatory acts.

While making the distinction between the two types of acts may be difficult, it is not impossible. All speech has the potential to offend, and one does not have a right to be shielded from all offensive speech. If Dan Cathy's expression was coupled with a change in corporate policy regarding homosexual workers or customers, then his expressive act would then be viewed as a consequential act.

3.2 Moral Boycotts

We cannot emphasize enough the tentative nature of the justification for boycotts as a response to consequential acts. While the prohibition against boycotting expressive acts can be broadly construed as deontological, the possible justification for boycotting consequential acts is unabashedly teleological. An act of boycotting is justified if and only if the boycott produces, on balance, more good than harm. The question of whether a boycott is justified is thus an empirical question. The harm or good that may be produced by a boycott is the overall harm or good. To determine whether the boycott is justified it is necessary to consider all the stakeholders that may be affected. It is not enough that those in authority may be penalized; it must also be the case that greater harm isn't caused to the most vulnerable, for example, workers or the wider community. Of course, this is not to say that we must ignore an

---

Let's see you acknowledge a man whose words make your blood boil, who's standing center stage and advocating at the top of his lungs that which you would spend a lifetime opposing at the top of yours.'"

injustice if a boycott would prove to cause more harm than good. A boycott is a tactic for addressing an injustice and may not be the appropriate approach to every injustice.

3.3 Virtues of the Consequentialist Approach

Restricting justified boycotts to consequential acts that have an overall positive impact allows us to sidestep some of the problems Claudia Mills has identified in her discussion on the topic (Mills, 1996). Although Mills shares our view that boycotts ought to be conceived of as a way to change actions, the problems she identifies leads her to conclude that they are an unacceptable tactic.

BOYCOTTING BOYCOTTS

According to Mills, all boycotts are about changing actions. The point of a boycott is to exert economic pressure on a commercial entity, political body or a business or business person for extra-business activities that the boycotter finds objectionable. Although this account of boycotts appears straightforward enough, the difficulty lies with the type of justification given for the boycott. Mills contends that there are two types of justifications given for engaging in a boycott. The first is the strategic justification, and the second is the integrity justification. Mills believes both justifications are problematic.

A strategic justification for engaging in a boycott is one which has as its successful outcome a changing of the target's actions. In the case of a strategic justification, the boycotter is not concerned with the attitudes or beliefs of the target of the boycott. For example, assume that a boycott of Walmart has been called for because of the substandard working conditions and low pay of its employees. Imagine that the boycott is successful and that Walmart improves the working conditions in its stores and increases wages. If a strategic justification was employed, then all that matters to the boycotters is the aforementioned changes. They do not care whether Walmart owners or executives now believe it is right, just, or fair to pay workers better. All that matters is that the boycott resulted in a change in practice.

According to Mills, there are three problems with this type of justification. First, there is the question of whether boycotts are actually effective. Consider again the Chick-fil-A example. After receiving an abundance of negative publicity for Cathy's comments, people lined up outside stores in a show of support. Secondly, there is the objection that boycotts may be unfair. While the target of a boycott may be a corporation, it is possible that it is the workers who will suffer. If a boycott is successful and the bottom line of the business is harmed, then the result may be that those least responsible for the corporate wrongdoing will be harmed. If Walmart begins to lose business, it may respond by laying off workers. In the end, a boycott may end up unfairly punishing the very people it was intended to help. Finally, a boycott may be coercive in the ways we mention in the previous section, namely, it could be an attempt to silence an unpopular idea that belongs in the marketplace of ideas.

The second justification for boycotts, the integrity account, is equally problematic. An integrity justification is one that is concerned with changing the attitudes of the target of the boycott. When one engages in an integrity-based boycott the desire is not merely to change the individual or corporation's actions, but to change its attitude as well. An integrity account wants the decision-makers in Walmart and Chick-fil-A to recognize that they hold a mistaken position, and embrace the ideas, beliefs, or principles of the boycotters. They want, in a nutshell, a change of heart on the part of the target. But like the strategic boycott, this position also has its problems. First there is Mills's claim that integrity justifications leave themselves open to a certain level of hypocrisy. To engage in activities that are essentially a form of shunning, the boycotter is making an implicit claim of moral superiority. This leaves the individual open to an examination of all his or her beliefs and actions. For example, how can one boycott Walmart while still shopping at Sam's Club (even if Sam's pays its workers better)? Secondly, much like the objection to the strategic account, there is the question of whether the shunning involved in a boycott is indiscriminate. Painting Walmart as unjust may have the effect of its workers also being identified as contributors to injustice.

While each of the two types of boycotts has its own problems, Mills persuasively argues that combining the two justifications is even more problematic. For example, assume that the target of a boycott is a business that has been engaging in discriminatory hiring practices, say on the basis of race. An organized boycott is called to exert pressure on the business. After a couple of months the boycott results in a change of the hiring practices on the part of the business owner. From a strategic standpoint, the boycott has been a success and can be called off. But, from an integrity standpoint, it is not clear whether the boycott is over. While the business owner may have changed his or her actions, he or she may still hold racist attitudes. In fact we could imagine a situation in which the owner acknowledges the toll the boycott has taken, and decided to give in to "those people." Clearly, the attitude of the owner has not changed, and thus the integrity boycott has not achieved its goal. The integrity account makes it difficult to determine when to end a boycott. Even if a corporation changes its practices, there is still the possibility that it refuses to acknowledge its wrongdoing. If there is not a change in attitude, then presumably there cannot be an end to the boycott.

RESPONSE TO MILLS

The virtue of viewing boycotts in terms of the types of act they target is that it allows us to sidestep many of Mills's concerns. On our account all justified *organized* boycotts are strategic, and their objective is always to change the morally offensive practices or policies that cause harm. Also, as was previously stated, determining whether a boycott is justified necessarily entails considering all the individuals that may be affected by the boycott. Undoubtedly there will be situations in which the interests of those not responsible for the corporate act may be harmed. As with all consequentialist evaluations, the long-term versus short-term harms, severity of the harms, and the likelihood of the eventual effectiveness of the boycott must be considered before determining the moral acceptability of the organized action. It is also necessary to consider whether there are other ways to effect change without engaging in a boycott. Although we view organized boycotts as strategic, this should not be taken to imply that integrity justifications are unimportant. On our account, integrity justifications may play a role in a *personal* boycott.

Mills's concerns about integrity justifications are less problematic if we view such justifications as solely part of personal rather than organized boycotts. When we engage in a personal boycott we are in essence exercising something like our right to freedom of association. I don't have to shop at a certain store or buy certain products. I don't have to frequent restaurants operated by racists or misogynists—even if such establishments don't themselves act on their beliefs. An analogy can be made between integrity boycotts and one's personal relationships. I am not required to associate with people whose moral, religious, or political views I find offensive. But, it is also the case that I am not justified in forcing or coercing those individuals into changing their views.[12] As such, I may engage in a "never-ending" boycott. While this would be problematic if I were attempting to stop someone from engaging in morally offensive *actions* it is not problematic if I simply don't want to be exposed to morally offensive *ideas*. While a boycott that causes individuals to reflect on and eventually change their views is desirable, the ultimate justification needs to be, first and foremost, to change the policies or actions of the target of the boycott. Thus, Mills's concerns about when to end a boycott don't apply so long as we are clear about the type and objective of the boycott we are engaging in.

4. Muddying the Waters

We would like to acknowledge what might be offered as an objection to the view we have espoused. This objection comes from the practical difficulties of the distinctions that we are trying to defend above. In reality, things are far more muddled than we have allowed. In particular, it may be that the distinction between expressive and consequential acts is far harder to maintain than it might first appear. Simply allowing for certain comments to be made can wound in important ways. Chris Cuomo, in

---

12   I can of course attempt to change their views by some other means. I may attempt to engage in a dialogue, or write a letter to the editor. Such actions would respect the right of individuals to hold whatever views they want, so long as they do not act on views that harm others. See the Petrol X and Beef-gril-r examples earlier in the paper.

"Dignity and the Right to Be Lesbian or Gay," makes the point well when arguing that dignity can be profoundly affected by the view from others. Cuomo writes:

> There is clearly something like a "homophobic gaze" that is similar to the sexist or racist gaze, that creates a serious and persistent form of harm that is more subtle than outright violence, and that is not reducible to a denial of rights. It is the part of oppression that gets under the skin and into the psyche, that can undermine flourishing even for those with great material comfort and the full exercise of liberty. It may even be the part of oppression that makes oppressed folks with economic and other social privileges less likely to continue to struggle for justice, for the homophobic denial of our dignity is quite tiresome, and leaves many longing for zones of freedom and autonomy that approximate the freedoms enjoyed by those who are completely at ease in straight worlds. (Cuomo, 2007, p. 84)

The suggestion here is that there are harms that come simply from the expressive acts, or even just the "gaze" in which people engage with one another. These harms are real harms, and specifically in this case, Cuomo argues that they occur at the cost of one's dignity. However, as she points out, it can also lead to people refraining from struggles for justice. Cuomo puts the issue most directly a short time later, writing that "Harsh judgment can be harmful to one's sense of dignity, even for those who enjoy a terrific range of social freedoms, and so it is certainly important not to lose sight of the political importance and requirements of dignity" (Cuomo, 2007, p. 84).

There is no way to avoid this concern and we wish to bring it out into the open and to make it clear that we agree with the concern that someone might have over this issue. There are some expressive acts that will cross over into consequential acts, and it is not always easy to judge which have done so. Cases where a person's dignity is at issue are prime cases. On the other hand, there will also be cases where the distinction is very clear. There are cases where someone might have an entirely hypothetical discussion about ideas. Friends might have a discussion where they start with positions that they assume would be easily dismissed. Plato engages in such discussions in most of his dialogues; ideas are put forward and discussed, before being dismissed.

The only conclusion that we can draw regarding this objection is that it is true that the distinction between expressive and consequential acts is not always as clear as we would like it to be. If it were, then the discussion would be a much easier one to have. Our conclusion then should perhaps be that in cases where an entirely expressive act is at issue, then boycotts are unjustified; while cases where an act is entirely consequential, boycotts are justified. For cases where the act falls somewhere in the middle, or cases which are unclear, the justification is also unclear.

Our suggestion would be that there would need to be more analysis of what the impact of the act is and what the impact of a boycott might be. This would require a larger theoretical apparatus than we have the space to present. It might be that what is required is a kind of "Just Boycott Theory" analogous to Just War Theory. Nevertheless, we would argue that discussion is best carried out in the open where ideas can be explored. Cuomo seems to agree with us as well. Immediately after the second quotation, above she writes, "But where free expression and diversity are allowed to flourish, the sort of consciousness-raising and familiarity that promotes mutual respect for dignity across difference becomes more possible, and the harsh judgments of stereotypes and prejudices have less power" (Cuomo, 2007, p. 85). People have to feel free to express ideas without fear of potentially significant economic loss if we want people to engage in the very discussions that get past the differences.

5. Conclusion

At the beginning of this paper we related the story of Dan Cathy and Chick-fil-A. How should we evaluate Cathy's actions? The various organized boycotts of Chick-fil-A began after Cathy expressed his views on gay marriage, and expressed them publicly on the radio. At no point was it claimed that Chick-fil-A or any of its stores discriminated against its employees or customers on the basis of sexual orientation. So while one may not like the views held by Dan Cathy, it seems that he was engaging in expressive acts in the marketplace of ideas.

Given that Cathy's acts were expressive, our account would hold that the proper response would be to engage with him in the marketplace of ideas. An organized boycott would be unjustified, as it would constitute an attempt to coerce Cathy's silence on gay marriage. Of course, having made his view known, our account would still support those who chose to refrain from patronizing Chick-fil-A. In our everyday interactions with others, we may not know (or not care to know) their moral or political convictions. Once those convictions have been made known to us, we may find it hard to maintain our own integrity without disassociating with others. Nothing in our account prohibits these types of individual acts.

References

Asad, Talal (2008). "Reflections on Blasphemy and Secular Criticism." *Religion: Beyond a Concept*, edited by Hent de Vries. Fordham University Press, New York, 580–609.

Cuomo, Chris (2007). "Dignity and the Right to Be Lesbian or Gay." *Philosophical Studies: An International Journal for Philosophy in the Analytic Tradition*, vol. 132, no. 1, 75–85.

Friedman, Monroe (1999). *Consumer Boycotts: Effecting Change through the Marketplace and Media*. Routledge, New York.

Mill, John Stuart (1859). *On Liberty*. Retrieved from Project Gutenberg: http://www.gutenberg.
    org/files/34901/34901-h/34901-h.htm
Mills, Claudia (1996). "Should We Boycott Boycotts?" *Journal of Social Philosophy*, vol. 27,
    issue 3, 136–48.
Rawls, John (1990). *The Law of Peoples*. Harvard University Press, Cambridge, Massachusetts.
Rothbard, Murray N. (1998). *The Ethics of Liberty*. New York University Press, New York and
    London.
Ryan, C.C. (1980). "The Normative Concept of Coercion." *Mind*, vol. 89, no. 356, 481–98.
Stoll, M.L. (2009). "Boycott Basics: Moral Guidelines for Corporate Decision Making." *Journal
    of Business Ethics*, vol. 84, 3–10.

Questions

1. Is coercion a morally neutral concept?

2. In what ways is the argument for or against boycotts utilitarian? In what ways is it
    deontological?

3. What is the difference between an organized boycott and a personal boycott?

4. According to Tomhave and Vopat, when are boycotts not morally permissible?

5. Can some types of speech be harmful? If they can, does this pose a problem for
    Tomhave and Vopat's view of the moral permissibility of boycotts?

Further Reading

Borman, David A. "Protect, Parasitism, and Community: Reflections on the Boycott." In *Social
    Philosophy Today: Power, Protest, and the Future of Democracy*, vol. 31. Charlottesville:
    Philosophy Documentation Center, 2015, pp. 7–22.
Friedman, Monroe. "Ethical Dilemmas Associated with Consumer Boycotts." *Journal of
    Social Philosophy*, vol. 32, no. 2, 1 June 2001, pp. 232–40.
Mills, Claudia. "Should We Boycott Boycotts?" *Journal of Social Philosophy*, vol. 27, no. 3,
    1 Dec. 1996, pp. 136–48.
Stoll, Mary Lyn. "Boycott Basics: Moral Guidelines for Corporate Decision Making." *Journal
    of Business Ethics*, vol. 84, no. 1, 1 Jan. 2009, pp. 3–10.
Zwolinski, Matt. "Sweatshops, Choice, and Exploitation." *Business Ethics Quarterly*, vol. 17,
    no. 4, 1 Oct. 2007, pp. 689–727.

V.

CASE STUDIES

THE TROLLEY PROBLEM

The Trolley Problem is a thought experiment that is analogous to many real-world cases. It originates with Philippa Foot in 1967, though it has been analyzed a great deal since, including in a large number of variations. Despite the many variations, however, the basic ones are consistent with the following story:

> Suppose that you happen along some abandoned railroad tracks. They are abandoned because they used to go across a deep ravine via a bridge that is now collapsed. Thus, any train coming along the tracks would fall into the ravine, killing anyone on board the train. Suppose further that you are standing near a switch that would allow you to shift the path of any train that would come along to another track that would avoid the ravine and collapsed bridge. As you start to move on in your stroll, you look up to see a runaway train car coming down the tracks. There are five people trapped on the train car, with no way to escape in time. If you do nothing, the five people will plummet to the bottom of the ravine and will die. What do you do at this point? The obvious answer is to flip the switch on the tracks, setting the train car to travel down the other path. However, when you go to change the path of the train car, you see that on the other path is a worker who would be unable to avoid the train car. If you divert the train, this person will certainly die, though you will have saved the five people trapped on the train car. What is the right thing to do in this situation?

For other variations, see the references in the note below.[1] Additionally, there are numerous real-world cases that either exactly follow the trolley problem (consider self-driving cars needing to decide between killing the passengers in the car or hitting a pedestrian) or approximate it. Many cases where the details approximate the Trolley Problem invite a much closer examination of the details (how did the situation

---

1   Philippa Foot, "The Problem of Abortion and the Doctrine of Double Effect," *Oxford Review*, vol. 5, 1967, pp. 5–15. For other analyses and variations, see Judith Jarvis Thomson, "Killing, Letting Die, and the Trolley Problem," *The Monist*, vol. 59, no. 2, 1976, pp. 204–17, and F.M. Kamm, "Harming Some to Save Others," *Philosophical Studies: An International Journal for Philosophy in the Analytic Tradition*, vol. 57, no. 3, 1989, pp. 227–60. These sources should by no means be taken as exhaustive, as numerous other articles discuss the Trolley Problem and its variations.

come about in the first place?). Additionally, in a business context there are often decisions that involve weighing outcomes and possible deontological constraints.

THE FORD PINTO

Sold from 1971 to 1980, the Ford Pinto was Ford's first subcompact car. It was designed to compete with subcompacts from Japanese and German auto manufacturers. The car was rushed to production in approximately two years, when the typical design-to-production timeframe is forty-three months. There was a problem with the gas tank on the car. In rear-end collisions, the gas tank would separate from the car and gas would spill out. Additionally, the gas tank could come into contact with other parts of the car that would rupture it further, causing more gas to spill. One spark could cause the gas to ignite and the car would be engulfed in flames. This is alarming enough, but even worse when car doors become jammed at impact. In engineering, mistakes are made that cause injury or death. It would be understandable if Ford did nothing about this design problem provided it did not know about it. However, the problem became apparent to the designers at Ford following numerous internal tests. Only in three tests did the car not have this problem. In all three cases there was a change to the car that affected the gas tank.[2] Thus, Ford knew about the problem before they began selling the car. However, the cost-benefit analysis run by Ford showed that it would be cheaper to pay out on lawsuits for deaths and injuries than to fix the cars or change their production. The cost to fix the cars would have been approximately $11 per car, though a later option was found that would have cost approximately $5 per car. Additionally, Ford used alternative gas tank designs in other cars that would have avoided the problem. The number of deaths due to the problem is difficult to calculate but has been estimated at anywhere from 27 to 180.

It should be noted that the Ford Pinto is not the only example of this kind of approach to decision-making. It is arguable that the much more recent Volkswagen diesel scandal was decided in the same way. This is a standard way to make decisions in business, to determine if the benefits of an option outweigh the costs. This is an example where the financial benefits to the company come into potential conflict with the rights of customers.

---

2   Details of the production and testing of the Ford Pinto can be found in Mark Dowie, "Pinto Madness," *Mother Jones* (Sept. 1977), though it should be noted that the number of people killed by the Pinto is exaggerated in this article.

ENRON

In 2001 it was revealed that Enron had been defrauding investors to the tune of $11 billion. Prior to this discovery, Kenneth Lay, the founder and CEO of Enron, had given repeated, public assurances to stockholders that the company was in good health. This action could be interpreted as an act of strategic bluffing. If enough people believed Enron's stock was healthy, then they would hold onto the stock, which in turn would help maintain its value and stabilize its price. After all, stock price is as much a matter of perception as it is of actual corporate value. Stocks often rise and fall on rumor as much as on corporate quarterly reports. Assuming Enron had bluffed well enough to alleviate the concerns of investors, and had fixed their internal financial problems, would their actions have been morally permissible?

CRAIGSLIST

Are corporations legally required to maximize shareholder value? Can companies choose not to engage in legal business practices that will increase the corporate bottom line in favor of some non-economic ideal? In 2010 the Court of Chancery of the State of Delaware ruled that corporations did in fact have such an obligation. Although Craigslist founders Jim Buckmaster and Craig Newmark wished to maintain the community culture of Craigslist, the courts ruled that their primary obligation was to their shareholders:

> Jim and Craig did prove that they personally believe Craigslist should not be about the business of stockholder wealth maximization, now or in the future. As an abstract matter, there is nothing inappropriate about an organization seeking to aid local, national, and global communities by providing a website for online classifieds that is largely devoid of monetized elements. Indeed, I personally appreciate and admire Jim's and Craig's desire to be of service to communities. The corporate form in which Craigslist operates, however, is not an appropriate vehicle for purely philanthropic ends, at least not when there are other stockholders interested in realizing a return on their investment. Jim and Craig opted to form Craigslist, Inc. as a for-profit Delaware corporation and voluntarily accepted millions of dollars from eBay as part of a transaction whereby eBay became a stockholder. Having chosen a for-profit corporate form, the Craigslist directors are bound by the fiduciary duties and standards that accompany that form. Those standards include acting to promote the value of the corporation for the benefit of its stockholders. The

"Inc." after the company name has to mean at least that. Thus, I cannot accept as valid for the purposes of implementing the Rights Plan a corporate policy that specifically, clearly, and admittedly seeks not to maximize the economic value of a for-profit Delaware corporation for the benefit of its stockholders— no matter whether those stockholders are individuals of modest means or a corporate titan of online commerce.

—William B. Chandler,
Chancellor, Court of Chancery of Delaware

While the court ruled that there is a primary duty to maximize profits, should this be the case? Are there situations that might warrant a corporation not maximizing its bottom line?

TRANSAM TRUCKING V. DEPARTMENT OF LABOR

In January of 2009, Alphonse Maddin was driving a tractor-trailer truck down I-88 in Illinois for the TransAm Trucking Co. Due to the subzero temperatures, the brakes on the trailer froze, making the vehicle unsafe to drive. Maddin reported the problem to TransAm, who told him to wait for a repair truck to arrive.

While waiting for the truck, Maddin discovered that the heater in his cab was not working. After falling asleep for nearly two hours, he awoke to find his torso numb and that he could not feel his feet. He again called TransAm to tell them about the heater and his condition. He was told by the dispatcher to "hang in there." He also called his cousin, who testified that Maddin sounded confused and seemed to be slurring his words.

After waiting another half-hour, Maddin called TransAm and told them he was going to detach the trailer from his truck and seek help. He was instructed by his supervisor to remain with the trailer, or drag it with its frozen breaks. Maddin, did neither, detached the trailer, and drove away. A week later, Maddin was fired from his job for violating company policy "by abandoning his load while under dispatch."

Maddin filed a complaint against TransAm with the Department of Labor claiming that he had been dismissed for essentially "blowing the whistle" by reporting the unsafe vehicle. The DOL agreed and awarded Maddin damages. TransAm later appealed the decision of the 10th Circuit Court. The Court ruled 2-to-1 in Maddin's favor.

In his dissent, now-Supreme Court Justice Neil Gorsuch argued that Maddin was not entitled to compensation. As he writes:

> It might be fair to ask whether TransAm's decision was a wise or kind one. But it's not our job to answer questions like that. Our only task is to decide whether the decision was an illegal one. The Department of Labor says that TransAm violated federal law, in particular 49 U.S.C. § 31105(a)(1)(B). But that statute only forbids employers from firing employees who "refuse to operate a vehicle" out of safety concerns. And, of course, nothing like that happened here. The trucker in this case wasn't fired for refusing to operate his vehicle. Indeed, his employer gave him the very option the statute says it must: once he voiced safety concerns, TransAm expressly—and by everyone's admission— permitted him to sit and remain where he was and wait for help. (*TransAm Trucking v. Administrative Review Board, United State Department of Labor*)

Do you think TransAm's actions were legal? Do you think they were moral? To what extent should a company allow moral considerations to influence its business practices? What other moral issues does this case raise about the relationship between employers and employees?

FURTHER CASES

There are many examples of books that provide further cases for use in business ethics discussions. However, there is a resource that is worth using as a first stop. Since 1997 there has been a national Intercollegiate Ethics Bowl (IEB) competition held in conjunction with the Association for Practical and Professional Ethics (APPE). The organizers for the IEB create 30 cases a year. These cases range over numerous areas of applied and professional ethics. Thus, these cases are a great starting point for more cases. Cases are approximately one page long and deal with both real and hypothetical situations. They are also designed so that reasonable disagreement exists about the cases. Ethics Bowl was created at the Illinois Institute of Technology (IIT), and the Center for the Study of Ethics in the Professions at IIT maintains an archive of all the cases. Please see the websites below both for more information about the IEB and for cases that would be of use.

- Association for Practical and Professional Ethics: www.appe-ethics.org

- Center for the Study of Ethics in the Professions, IIT, Archive: http://ethics.iit.edu/teaching/ethics-case-archive

PERMISSIONS
ACKNOWLEDGMENTS

Ariely, Dan. "Beer and Free Lunches: What Is Behavioral Economics, and Where Are the Free Lunches?" Excerpts from pp. 309–22 of *Predictably Irrational*, Revised and Expanded Edition. Copyright © 2009 by Dan Ariely. Reprinted with the permission of HarperCollins Publishers.

Aristotle. Excerpts from *Nicomachean Ethics*, 2nd edition, translated by Terence Irwin. Hackett, 1999. Reprinted with the permission of Hackett Publishing Company, Inc. All rights reserved.

Arrow, Kenneth J. "Social Responsibility and Economic Efficiency," from *Readings in Public Sector Economics*, edited by Samuel Baker and Catherine Elliott. DC Heath & Co., 1990. This is a revised version of the Carl Snyder Memorial Lecture delivered at the University of California, Santa Barbara, April 1972. Originally published in *Public Policy* 21 (Summer 1973): 303–17. Reprinted with the permission of David Arrow.

Borgerson, Janet. "On the Harmony of Feminist Ethics and Business Ethics," from *Business and Society Review* 112.4 (Nov. 2007): 477–509. Copyright © 2007 Center for Business Ethics at Bentley College. Published by Blackwell Publishing. Reprinted with permission.

Carr, Albert Z. "Is Business Bluffing Ethical?" from *Harvard Business Review*, January-February 1968. All rights reserved. Used by permission of Harvard Business Publishing.

Cascio, Wayne F. "Decency Means More than 'Always Low Prices': A Comparison of Costco to Wal-Mart's Sam's Club," from *Academy of Management Perspectives* 20.3 (Aug. 2006): 26–37. Republished with permission of the Academy of Management via Copyright Clearance Center, Inc.

Kant, Immanuel. Excerpts from *Fundamental Principles of the Metaphysics of Ethics*, translated by Thomas Kingsmill Abbot. London, New York: Longmans, Green and Co., 1895.

Marx, Karl, and Frederick Engels. *The Communist Manifesto*, translated by Samuel Moore, in cooperation with Frederick Engels, 1888.

Mill, John Stuart. Excerpts from *Utilitarianism*, fourth edition. London: Longmans, Green, Reader, and Dyer, 1871.

Orlando, John. "The Fourth Wave: The Ethics of Corporate Downsizing," from *Business Ethics Quarterly* 9.2 (Apr. 1999): 295–314. Copyright © Society for Business Ethics 1999. Reprinted with permission.

Satz, Deborah. "Noxious Markets," from *Why Some Things Should Not Be for Sale: The Moral Limits of Markets*. Copyright © 2010, Oxford University Press, Ltd. Reprinted with the permission of Oxford University Press, USA.

Schrag, Brian. "The Moral Significance of Employee Loyalty," from *Business Ethics Quarterly* 11.1 (Jan. 2001): 41–66. Copyright © Society for Business Ethics 2001. Reproduced with permission.

Smith, Adam. Excerpts from *An Inquiry into the Nature and Causes of the Wealth of Nations*. London: W. Strahan and T. Cadell, 1776.

FROM
THE PUBLISHER

A name never says it all, but the word "Broadview" expresses a good deal of the philosophy behind our company. We are open to a broad range of academic approaches and political viewpoints. We pay attention to the broad impact book publishing and book printing has in the wider world; for some years now we have used 100% recycled paper for most titles. Our publishing program is internationally oriented and broad-ranging. Our individual titles often appeal to a broad readership too; many are of interest as much to general readers as to academics and students.

Founded in 1985, Broadview remains a fully independent company owned by its shareholders—not an imprint or subsidiary of a larger multinational.

For the most accurate information on our books (including information on pricing, editions, and formats) please visit our website at www.broadviewpress.com. Our print books and ebooks are also available for sale on our site.

broadview press
www.broadviewpress.com